THE AWAKENING
OF AMERICAN
NATIONALISM

The

New American Nation Series

EDITED BY

HENRY STEELE COMMAGER

AND

RICHARD B. MORRIS

THE AWAKENING
OF AMERICAN
NATIONALISM

1815 ★ 1828

By GEORGE DANGERFIELD

ILLUSTRATED

1817

HARPER & ROW, PUBLISHERS
New York, Hagerstown, San Francisco, London

LIBRARY OF CONGRESS CATALOG CARD NUMBER: 64–25112

78 79 80 81 10 9 8 7 6 5 4

To my father-in-law and mother-in-law,
MAX SCHOTT *and* ALICE F. SCHOTT,
with love and gratitude

Contents

Illustrations

MAPS

Editors' Introduction

$\mathbf{B}$Y ANY criteria the years following the Peace of Ghent, a period inaugurated by what has been superficially called "the era of good feelings," must be considered a time of exceptional growth and development in the United States. It was a time when the Northeast was making the transition from commercial to industrial capitalism, when the Old South was almost precipitously being transformed into a cotton kingdom and the expanding West was being knit by ever closer ties to the seaboard through the "transportation revolution," still in its infancy. It was a time, too, when the sections were becoming more sharply divided by the issue of freedom and slavery; and although the gathering storm was temporarily abated by the Compromise of 1820, sober statesmen like Thomas Jefferson considered that measure as "a reprieve only."

Above all, perhaps, it may be considered a time of the evolution and ripening of American nationalism. It is the special virtue of Mr. Dangerfield's brilliant synthesis of the period that he manages to keep the focus on this central theme—the contest between the economic nationalism expounded by Henry Clay and John Quincy Adams and the democratic nationalism exemplified by the partisans of Andrew Jackson. That he does so without neglecting America's role in world affairs and particularly her growing economic rivalry with Great Britain, nor without minimizing the parts played by the leading actors on the national stage, attests the balanced judgment and sense of proportion which are evident throughout the volume.

Although America emerged from the War of 1812 as a nation, with a status among the family of nations, the reactionary rulers of Europe, as

xi

Mr. Dangerfield reminds us, regarded the United States as "little more than a grimy republican thumbprint upon the far margin of that page of history which, at Vienna, they were so ingeniously writing backward." Nonetheless, the Great Powers had a momentous confrontation with that young republic in 1823, when the Monroe Doctrine was proclaimed. That classic rule of American foreign policy, as the author perceptively points out, proved a far more severe challenge to industrial England, whose fleet sustained it, than to the Holy Alliance and legitimist France, against whom it was ostensibly directed. Great Britain found it necessary to reshape its rules of trade because of America's insistent demands for a share in international markets.

It is the particular confrontation of American economic nationalism with the Liberal Toryism of Lord Liverpool and William Huskisson which this book delineates with exceptional vigor and depth. The tariff of 1824 served as a warning to the British that American industry proposed to secure a substantial degree of protection from foreign competition, a trend which culminated in the "Tariff of Abominations" of 1828. As on so many other subjects in this volume, Mr. Dangerfield brings us abreast of the most recent scholarship on those interests pushing for tariffs and on the sectional and regional rivalries involved.

Mr. Dangerfield sees a democratic urgency in the 1820's behind the liberalized land laws, and a sectional urgency behind the demand for internal improvements. The nationalism of Clay's American system essentially subserved the interests of industrial capitalism, but failed to satisfy those who wished to curb privilege and eliminate elites. It was the tragedy of John Quincy Adams, visionary, dogmatic, and at times overbearing, but ever the Puritan in his self-mortification, that although he would have superimposed upon Clay's system severe ideas of federal control and national self-restraint, he was talking a language that the people, and certainly the politicians, could not understand. He was in many respects a century ahead of his time. Mr. Adams' career in the White House, his "agonizing doubts," his impractical idealism, down to the strange Presidential campaign of 1828, "when to betray an idea was almost to commit a felony," constitute some of the most absorbing portions of an absorbing book.

All these different threads are skillfully woven by a master craftsman into one magnificent tapestry. This felicitous and fresh retelling of the story of the emergence of American nationalism constitutes a volume in *The New American Nation Series,* a comprehensive and cooperative survey of the history of the area now embraced in the United States from the days of discovery to our own time. Necessarily, certain constitutional issues, such as Marshall's nationalist decision in *McCulloch* v. *Maryland,* are considered in this volume, but a separate volume in this series will be devoted to an account of constitutional developments in this period. Russel B. Nye has already surveyed trends in thought and culture and Francis Philbrick will examine in detail the rise of the West in the years under review.

HENRY STEELE COMMAGER
RICHARD B. MORRIS

THE AWAKENING
OF AMERICAN
NATIONALISM

CHAPTER 1

Madison and Monroe

PEACE with Great Britain·was proclaimed in Washington on February 18, 1815; and with the passing of the War of 1812, the shadow of political Europe withdrew from the scene which it had darkened and confused for many years, and a new light seemed to fall upon the map of the United States. As Henry Adams put it, with pardonable hyperbole: "The continent lay before [the American people] like an uncovered ore-bed."[1] The continent, it is true, or all that part of it which lay west of the Mississippi and east of the Perdido, was still claimed by the King of Spain, and much of this was then believed to be a waterless desert. But "ore-bed" admirably describes the objective of a forward-looking state of mind. The American people, in 1815, endeavored to turn their backs upon Europe, insofar as Europe represented the kind of world history they most detested. For if the Napoleonic Wars constituted (as surely they did) a world war, then the War of 1812, their penultimate phase, could not be entirely freed from this character. It was now over for the Americans, and they naturally preferred to see it as nothing more than a quarrel between themselves and Great Britain. Whether this quarrel was or was not (as to its American origins) an expansionist adventure is still debated; but if there was an element of expansionism in it, then the Peace of Ghent was an ample fulfillment of this healthy impulse.[2] Superficially, to be

[1] Henry Adams, *A History of the United States of America During The Administration of Jefferson and Madison* (9 vols., New York, 1889–91), IX, 173.

[2] For an analysis of different explanations, in terms of frontier expansion, or

sure, the peace treaty which the Senate ratified on February 14 left everything much as it had been before the war began: time alone was to be the arbiter of Anglo-American relations, and the expression "not one inch ceded or lost" would be a more than adequate summary of the treaty's achievements. To the modern student of the negotiations which preceded the treaty, however, a very different idea presents itself; the treaty has become an eloquent register of historical process, because one can observe, in the negotiations themselves, the decay of British mercantilist concepts.[3] If the treaty meant anything at all, beyond a mere end of hostilities, or (as some Anglophobes thought)[4] at best an armistice, it meant that in the future Britain would cease to regard the United States as a colony which paid its own expenses, and that she would look upon American expansion with a favorable eye, so long as it provided an enlargement of British industrial opportunity. In this sense, a whole new world had come into being, and for the Americans the first task was to describe the terms upon which, in America, it was to be organized.

The bonfires, the cannon, the church bells which celebrated the Peace of Ghent constituted less a shout of triumph than a sigh of relief. The American character had not so far been of a militarist nature: no militarists could have endured the mismanagement, the lukewarmness, the disaffection which marred almost every feature of the late war. As a nonmilitarist nation in 1812–15, the Americans put forth just enough energy to get the work done,[5] and when all was over they showed no disposition to make themselves more formidable in a military sense. Efficiency and, soon enough, economy became their goals.[6]

Moreover, the United States was, for a brief while, genuinely at

---

maritime rights, or the alleviation of commercial distress, see Bradford Perkins, *Prologue to War: England and the United States, 1805–1812* (Berkeley and Los Angeles, 1961), Chap. XII. (Napoleon, though his escape from Elba at the end of February deeply alarmed American statesmen when they heard of it, was and remained a mere bad memory to the public at large.)

[3] George Dangerfield, *The Era of Good Feelings* (New York, 1952), p. 89.

[4] A good example would be John Caldwell Calhoun's speech in *Annals of Congress,* 14 Cong., 1 Sess., pp. 829–840.

[5] In economic terms this is well expressed in Chester W. Wright, *Economic History of the United States* (New York, 1941), p. 279. See also *American State Papers, Finance,* III, 21–23.

[6] Leonard D. White, *The Jeffersonians* (New York, 1951), pp. 11, 118, 238 ff., 251 ff., 276 ff. *American State Papers, Military Affairs,* I, 779, 810–13. For reductions in 1820–1821, see 3 U.S. Statutes at Large, 615, 633, 642.

peace with itself. As for the Old World, on the other hand, one has only to contemplate the Final Act of the Congress of Vienna to see that, although it had all the finality of a completed jigsaw puzzle, it was actually an instrument full of chinks and crannies, through every one of which there glared and squinted the Argus eyes of revolution. The effort to avert this dire inspection by filling these gaps with repressive laws varied widely from state to state in Europe, but it served to show that there was no longer a common tradition between the rulers and the ruled. In a community like the United States, now ready and anxious to make new experiments in self-government, it was precisely the emergence of a common tradition that counted most. The very Congress which, in 1815, took up the task of postwar readjustment was composed, as to more than one-third of its membership in both houses, of Federalists;[7] and some of these were not a little tainted with wartime disloyalty. They sat down with their Republican opposites to discuss and to organize the peace; and since their opposition was neither very mischievous nor very resolute, they presumably acquiesced in what was done.

The Federalists, of course, remained a suspect group throughout the period of one-party rule which now began; and although their diminishing numbers and influence, and their accommodating behavior on the federal level, scarcely justified their reputation for persistent conspiracy, their efforts to inflame Republican faction in the several states did something to keep it alive. But they were not very skilled at party warfare; and even in those States where they had a real chance of survival, they were manifestly on the defensive and betrayed every anxious symptom of decline. It might be said that in the brief "Era of Good Feelings," which really ended with the Panic of 1819, the United States was free from those political and social fears which, in one form or another, haunted the Old World. The fact that the only suspect groups in America were those connected with wealthy men merely serves to emphasize the difference.

In short, as Albert Gallatin put it in 1816, "the War," and one ventures to presume that he also meant the peace, "has renewed and reinstated the national feelings which the Revolution had given and which were daily lessened. The people have now more general objects

[7] Shaw Livermore, Jr., *The Twilight of Federalism, 1815–1830* (Princeton, 1962), p. 11.

of attachment with which their pride and political opinions are connected. They are more American; they feel and act more like a nation; and I hope that the permanency of the Union is thereby better secured."[8] In the Old World the concept of nationalism was either imperialistic or subversive of the counterrevolution, or could be accepted only in the terms—even truer for 1815 than for 1845—of Disraeli's "Two Nations."[9]

Albert Gallatin was a most acute observer of the American scene, and he may have confined his ideas on American nationality to his own recollection: he did not arrive on these shores until 1780. Or he may have taken it for granted that national feelings and character were not actually "given" until 1776 or 1775. Like many historical axioms, this is open to technical reproach; but what Gallatin does suggest, and very forcibly, is that the postwar American had a renewed sense of a common national experience, real or imagined, with which he could face the future.

The Peace of Ghent undoubtedly bestowed upon the American nation a status among the family of nations which it had not hitherto enjoyed, but it was a status with a difference. "The mere existence of such a nation," it has been well said, "was a threat to the continuance of class government and special privilege in other countries."[10] To the conservative and reactionary rulers of Europe the United States was little more than a grimy republican thumbprint upon the far margin of that page of history which, at Vienna, they were so ingeniously writing backward. The Tsar of Russia was possibly a friend; the British Tories were soon obliged to regulate their political behavior in terms of an American market they could not afford to antagonize; the others had simply come to accept the fact that if the thumbprint was grimy, it was also ineffaceable. That was the point in 1815.

The problem of readjustment to peace did not, at first, present the

[8] Gallatin to Matthew Lyon, May 7, 1816; *Writings*, Henry Adams, ed. (3 vols., Philadelphia, 1879), I, 700. In other words, they were approaching that nationalistic sentiment which Boyd C. Shafer has described as "unifying a group of people who have a real or imagined common historical experience and a common aspiration to live together in the future." *Nationalism: Myth and Reality* (New York, 1955), p. 10.

[9] Benjamin Disraeli, *Sybil: Or the Two Nations* (London, 1845).

[10] Charles M. Wiltse, *John C. Calhoun: Nationalist 1782–1828* (Indianapolis, 1944), p. 106.

Americans with many difficulties: the Jeffersonian establishment, which had been so shaken by the Embargo of 1807 and had almost dissolved by the end of 1814, was now, all of a sudden, both strong enough and flexible enough to restate its old positions and to adopt a new one. The era of the "new Republicans" had begun. One need look no further for this than the Seventh Annual Message of President Madison, submitted to the Fourteenth Congress on December 5, 1815.

Some fourteen months before, in circumstances of great indignity, Madison had left his capital and fled like a partridge into the Virginia hills, pursued by a British army whose leaders jested that they proposed to catch him and take him back to London "for a curiosity."[11] His prestige, already dim, had thereupon become totally invisible to all but the most friendly eyes. He was now addressing the Congress, in the language of a victor, and in terms which must have occasioned some surprise to the more doctrinaire members of his party.

Throughout his long career, from the early days when he had been a delegate to the Second Continental Congress, Madison had displayed a certain predilection—one might use a stronger term—for nationalist expedients. Had he not told Thomas Jefferson in 1787 that the Constitution "will neither effectually answer its *national object,* nor prevent the local mischiefs which everywhere excite disgust against the State Governments"?[12] It is true that he had never gone so far along the road to centralization as Robert Yates suggested in his *Secret Proceedings and Debates,* or as he himself seems to have proposed in his Number 44 of *The Federalist;*[13] and in his subsequent battles with Hamilton and with Adams he had often discarded his nationalist weapons for the outrageous slings and arrows of particularist dispute. Between the co-

---

[11] Admiral Cockburn, riding through Washington, told some ladies: "You may thank old Madison for this, it is he who has got you into this scrape. . . . We want to catch him and carry him to England for a curiosity." John W. Taylor to Mrs. Taylor, October 8, 1814, John W. Taylor Papers, NYHS.

[12] Madison to Jefferson, September 6, 1787; *Letters and Other Writings of James Madison* (4 vols., New York, 1884), I, 338.

[13] Arnold A. Rogow, "The Federal Convention: Madison and Yates," *American Historical Review,* LX (1955), 323–335; Max Farrand, *The Records of the Federalist Convention* (3 vols., New Haven, 1911), III, 410–416; Adrienne Koch, *Jefferson and Madison: The Great Collaboration* (New York, 1950), pp. 43–44; Irving Brant, "Madison, the 'North American,' on Federal Power," *American Historical Review,* LX (1954), 45–54.

author of *The Federalist* and the writer of the Virginia Resolutions there certainly exists a wide gulf, yet during his later years of executive power he was able to straddle it without too much discomfort. His was a subtle and athletic mind, which only became baffling in his later years. In 1815, much as he may have suffered in reputation from his handling of the War of 1812, he was a victorious statesman; and his Seventh Annual Message is remarkable, not merely for being statesmanlike, but for its candid acceptance of the likelihood that it would sooner or later be called something else.

The Message, in its three more significant passages, is not exactly a ringing document: under the circumstances, it could hardly have been that. But it is an admirable mixture of constitutional prudence and enlightened common sense.

It is [he wrote] essential to every modification of the finances that the benefits of an uniform national currency should be restored to the community. . . . If the operation of the State banks can not produce this result, the probable operation of a national bank will merit consideration; and if neither of these expedients be deemed effectual it may become necessary to ascertain the terms upon which the notes of the Government (no longer required as an instrument of credit) shall be issued upon motives of general policy as a common medium of circulation.[14]

[And again:] In adjusting the duties on imports to the object of revenue the influence of the tariff on manufacturers will necessarily present itself for consideration. However wise the theory may be which leaves to the sagacity of individuals the application of their industry and resources, there are in this as in other cases exceptions to the general rule. . . . Under circumstances giving a powerful impulse to manufacturing industry it has made among us a progress and exhibited an efficiency which justify the belief that with a protection not more than is due to the enterprising citizens whose interests are now at stake it will become at an early day not only safe against occasional competitions from abroad, but a source of domestic wealth and even of external commerce.[15]

[And finally:] Among the means of advancing the public interest the occasion is a proper one for recalling the attention of Congress to the great importance of establishing throughout our country the roads and canals which can best be executed under national authority . . . requiring national

[14] James D. Richardson (ed.), *A Compilation of the Messages and Papers of the Presidents, 1789–1897* (10 vols., Washington, 1896–99), I, 565–566.
[15] *Ibid.*, p. 567.

jurisdiction and national means . . . and it is a happy reflection that any defect of constitutional authority which may be encountered can be supplied in a mode which the Constitution itself has providently pointed out.[16]

It has often been said that this tripartite scheme was more Hamiltonian than anything else, or, at best, that it endeavored to employ Hamiltonian means for Jeffersonian ends. But, in truth, the national bank was the only Hamiltonian feature in it—a feature, to be sure, of a startling prominence; and even here it should be remembered that the rechartering of the First Bank of the United States in 1811 had not met with Madison's disapproval or that of Gallatin, and that it failed for other reasons.[17] Aside from the national bank, which (together with its alternative solution of a national currency in terms of treasury notes) required no little boldness in its advocate, there was nothing especially Hamiltonian in the rest of Madison's program. Did not the great *Report on Manufactures* show that Hamilton really preferred bounties to tariffs; but did not Jefferson, in his Second Inaugural, propose a scheme of internal improvements to be financed by tariff receipts?[18] Would Gallatin's superb *Report* on internal improvements have been relegated to a dusty shelf if the government and the nation had not been bemused and divided by the war fever of 1807 and its aftermath?[19] And in his suggestion that no national system of internal improvements would be valid without a constitutional amendment Madison—like his great predecessor—sounded a note of caution: his nationalism retained a distinctly Jeffersonian bias.

[16] *Ibid.,* pp. 567–568.

[17] Bray Hammond, *Banks and Politics in America: From the Revolution to the Civil War* (Princeton, 1957), pp. 209–226.

[18] The ambiguity in the *Report,* as between bounties and tariffs, can be studied by comparing William A. Williams, *The Contours of American History* (Cleveland and New York, 1961), p. 166, with John C. Miller, *The Federalist Era* (New York, 1960), p. 65. See also Joseph Dorfman, *The Economic Mind in American Civilization* (2 vols., New York, 1946), I, 290. Jefferson's very temperate suggestion is that tariff revenues "by a just repartition" among the states and "a corresponding amendment of the Constitution" be applied (after extinguishing the public debt) in time of peace to rivers, canals, roads, arts, manufactures, education "within each State." Richardson, *Messages and Papers,* I, 379.

[19] Gallatin's *Report, American State Papers, Miscellaneous,* I, 724–741, April 8, 1808, however, dismissed Jefferson's "just repartition" as impracticable, and preferred to finance a system of internal improvements through federal bond issues, guaranteed by the sale of public lands.

A vast and varied experience, needless to say, had interposed itself between Jefferson's Second Inaugural and Madison's Seventh Annual Message. The Message was a document which had been created by the Napoleonic Wars: it was what an unmilitary nation required if it was to profit from all that it had so recently and so painfully learned. For example, the Treasury had become bankrupt in 1814 because the national currency had fallen into such disorder that revenues could not be moved from one place to another. This immobility had been repeated, in another realm, by a difficulty in moving and subsisting the nation's troops: bad currency, with only a local circulation, had found its counterpart in bad roads, with only a local usefulness. As for manufacturers, they had been nourished by embargo and war into an infancy so vigorous that to expose them to free trade might well have seemed a cruelly Spartan measure. Thus a national bank and a system of internal improvements might be seen as an effort to remedy those weaknesses which the War of 1812 had revealed, and a plan for protective tariffs as an effort to preserve what the war had fostered.[20]

The Fourteenth Congress, having been elected in the final autumn of the war, and in the shadow of disaster, was fortunately well qualified to act upon this program: the people had submitted their affairs to their ablest men, of whatever persuasion. The best of the war party were back in the House: Henry Clay, William Lowndes, John Forsyth, Peter B. Porter, Richard M. Johnson, Samuel Ingham, John Caldwell Calhoun. Only Felix Grundy and Langdon Cheves were missing; neither had cared to stand for re-election. The stalwarts of the peace party were also present: Timothy Pickering, Daniel Webster, Thomas P. Grosvenor, John Randolph. In the Senate the old obstructionists, Michael Leib, Samuel Smith, David Stone, Joseph Anderson had all vanished; the President would hardly recognize it for the same body which, since 1808, had practiced so successfully upon his peace of mind.

Once it had swallowed the hard morsel of a continuance of the direct tax, Congress turned its attention to the question of a central bank. The President's carefully qualified proposals in the Annual Message had been implemented by a more direct plea from his Secretary

---

[20] Edward Stanwood, *American Tariff Controversies* (2 vols., Boston, 1903), I, Chap. 5. Richard K. Crallé (ed.), *Works of John C. Calhoun* (6 vols., New York, 1854–57), II, 169. For wartime protective legislation, see 2 and 3 U.S. Statutes at Large, 768; 35, 49.

of the Treasury, A. J. Dallas. In a letter to John Caldwell Calhoun, of South Carolina, chairman of the House Committee on National Currency, Dallas outlined a plan for a national bank and, like the President, refrained from discussing the constitutionality of such a measure.[21]

Certainly, if the government were to regain some control of the national currency—which not everyone thought a necessity—it would have been quixotic indeed if it had set constitutional traps for itself in its own messages. Nor was Dallas the man to have thought them necessary. Born in Jamaica of Scots parentage, a graduate of Edinburgh University, married to the daughter of a British general, he had reached British-occupied New York, by way of the West Indies, in June, 1783. He had then found his way to Philadelphia, and in Pennsylvania, after some preliminary difficulties, he had founded a legal career of mingled brilliance and unpopularity. He was an odd kind of Jeffersonian. A tall and courtly personage, with powdered hair and exquisitely old-fashioned clothes, he never overindulged his courtliness: he never concealed his belief that he was in every respect superior to the usual run of politicians. As a member of the Republican party, he was for ordinary purposes a liability. It was only in a season of despair, when Secretary Campbell had resigned from the Treasury after confessing his own incompetence, that the Thirteenth Congress—then meeting at the Patent Office, the solitary public building which the British had spared— could bring itself to accept the Pennsylvanian as Campbell's successor. In a mordant report upon the difficulties of the Treasury's situation, which was one of virtual bankruptcy, Dallas could only suggest the creation of a national bank; but as Daniel Webster put it all too truly, he founded his bank upon the discredit of the government and then hoped to enrich the government out of the insolvency of the bank.[22] Dallas' best support, in this preposterous dilemma, was the fact that behind him there loomed the figures of John Jacob Astor, Stephen Girard, and David Parish. In April, 1813, Parish and Girard had taken $7,055,800 of Government 6 per cent stock at 88, and Astor had taken $2,056,000 at the same figure. Jacob Barker had also contracted for a huge sum, $5 million, but could find no one to join him: in the March 16, 1814, issue of the *National Intelligencer* he had called for a national bank. One need not impugn the patriotism of these capitalists,

[21] *American State Papers, Finance,* III, 57.
[22] *Ibid.,* II, 866, 872. November 27, 1814; Henry Adams, *History,* VIII, 258.

who were, after all, willing to venture large sums to maintain the nation's credit; but it would be flouting the long annals of financial behavior to suppose that they would not endeavor to protect themselves against the consequences of patriotism, should these prove to be unfortunate. They proposed, in short, to appreciate the price of government bonds by making them exchangeable for stock in a national bank; their plans had been maturing since early 1814; and it is reasonably certain that the influence of Astor and Girard upon the President, and upon certain members of Congress, had been in some measure responsible for Dallas' appointment.[23]

The energetic Calhoun had of course been privy to their plans, and although he had not seen eye to eye with Dallas in matters of detail, in principle they were agreed. When the war came to an end, Dallas was still Secretary of the Treasury and Calhoun was one of the most prominent nationalists in the House of Representatives. Thus, in support of Madison's modest proposal, there existed an alliance between the Treasury, on the one hand, and the Committee on National Currency, on the other. In a very real sense, this was the surviving monument to the efforts of Astor, Girard, and Parish; for while these three were still influential among capitalists, the initiative now lay with Madison, Dallas, and Calhoun, and with a phenomenon which defies exact analysis—the political climate itself.

It was a warm, beneficent climate, eminently suited to the shedding of inconvenient creeds. Now that the war had been, somehow or other, won, now that the Republican party was, somehow or other, still in the saddle and likely to stay there—it was useless to insist upon constitutional quibbles. The Republicans were now administering a state of affairs in which, Albert Gallatin wrote in December, 1815, "we are guilty of a continued breach of faith towards our creditors, our soldiers, our seamen, our civil officers. Public credit, heretofore supported simply by common honesty, declines at home and abroad; private capital placed on a still more uncertain basis; the value of property and the nature of every person's engagements equally uncertain; a baseless cur-

[23] Cf. Kenneth L. Brown, "Stephen Girard, Promoter of the Second Bank of the United States," *Journal of Economic History,* II (1942), 125 ff.; Raymond Walters, Jr., "Origins of the Second Bank of the United States," *Journal of Political Economy,* LIII (1945), 115 ff.

rency varying every fifty miles and fluctuating everywhere."[24]

The obvious remedy for this, if the banks could not be persuaded to resume specie payments, was a national institution with regulatory powers; and James Madison, who had fought the chartering of the First Bank of the United States on constitutional principles in 1791, was now ready, on expedient ones, to consent to the chartering of a second.

Very few men possessed Albert Gallatin's sensitive financial conscience, but Madison's broadmindedness was quite in keeping with the new mood of the times.[25] On January 8, 1816, Calhoun introduced a bill to incorporate the subscribers of a Bank of the United States;[26] and Henry Clay, descending from the Speaker's chair, reminded the House that in 1811 he had sternly opposed the rechartering of the First Bank on the grounds that Congress had no right to incorporate such an institution. "The force of circumstance and the lights of experience," he now said, had convinced him that Congress actually did have this "constructive power."[27] A penitential garb of some kind the Speaker had to wear on such a painful occasion; one cannot say that loose construction was ill-chosen or unbecoming.

The Federalist opposition, at any rate, was purely formal; and that of the unreconstructed Jeffersonians was led by John Randolph of Roanoke, who happened to be more suspicious of the state banks than he was of the projected national one, and who contented himself with insinuations.[28] The bill passed the House, 80 to 71, on March 14 and, after certain Senate amendments had been concurred in, received the President's signature on April 10, 1816.[29]

When the First Bank was incorporated in 1791, it was the North which had supported it and the South which had opposed it. Now their positions were reversed. Combining the votes of both houses, the New England and middle states gave 44 votes for the Bank and 53 against

[24] Gallatin to Jefferson, November 27, 1815; Gallatin Papers, NYHS.

[25] Dallas, for example, may have had to swallow his doubts as to the indispensability of convertible paper money. Raymond Walters, Jr., *Albert Gallatin* (New York, 1957), p. 296; *American State Papers, Finance,* III, 11, 12.

[26] *Annals of Congress,* 14 Cong., 1 sess., pp. 494–515. *American State Papers, Finance,* III, 57–61; Wiltse, *Calhoun: Nationalist,* p. 108.

[27] *Annals of Congress,* 14 Cong., 1 sess., p. 1189.

[28] *Ibid.,* pp. 1112–1113.

[29] 3 U.S. Statutes at Large, 266.

it; the southern and western states gave 58 for it and 30 against. In other words, "Jeffersonian policy had got itself into a position where a national bank was as essential to it as it had been to the Federalists twenty-five years before."[30] To judge from the temper of the debates in House and Senate, and from the regional distribution of the votes, nobody was really eager to call this position into strict account.

As for the Bank which now emerged, it had a capital of $35,000,000, of which the government owned $7,500,000, and the government was to receive a bonus of $1,500,000 payable in three installments during the first years of operation. The head office was to be in Philadelphia; its directors were authorized to establish branches where they saw fit; and its charter was to run for twenty years. It was to be the principal depositary of the United States Treasury, was to report to the Treasury, and was to be subject to Treasury inspection. There were to be twenty-five directors, of whom five were to be appointed by the President, with the approval of the Senate.[31] Finally, in order to fix a day for the resumption of specie payments, a resolution was adopted requiring payment of all government revenues in legal tender after February 20, 1817.[32] Here one may leave the Bank, for the moment a symbol of financial chastity and nationalist order; its relapses will be examined later on.

Having agreed to this substantial and statesmanlike reform, the Fourteenth Congress was not likely to make heavy weather out of protective tariffs. A demand for protection had been more or less coeval with constitutional government itself, and never did it appear more justified than after the Peace of Ghent. The metaphor of a peaceful nation which now turned its face toward the West is historically sound, but only if one concedes that this nation was constantly looking over its shoulder. In fact, the United States was now exposed to the mercies of a world market, as Americans began to contemplate the strange phenomenon of a Europe at peace, "a Europe that had the whole world in which to buy supplies, a Europe that was able to do much of

[30] Hammond, *Banks and Politics*, p. 240.
[31] D. R. Dewey, *The Second United States Bank* (Washington, 1910), pp. 163 ff. Bray Hammond, "Jackson, Biddle, and the Second Bank of the United States," *Journal of Economic History*, VII (1947), 1–4.
[32] *Annals of Congress*, 14 Cong., 1 sess., pp. 1440–1451.

its own ocean carrying, and an England that had new and well-developed manufactures."[33]

To the planters, the farmers, and the land speculators of America this change in world relations had, for the time being, a hopeful aspect. Europe, already blighted by the marching and countermarching of its locust armies, was now subjected to the calamity of poor harvests, and the demand thus created for American staples was further enhanced by a European propensity to gamble in tobacco and cotton. The American manufacturer, on the other hand, the latest child of the Industrial Revolution, was now in danger, through British dumping, of being smothered by his own parent.[34] Madison's call for protective tariffs was statesmanlike, since it recognized the difficulties of adjusting from a state of war to a state of peace, but he did not expect the adjustment to be a lengthy one; he assumed that some equilibrium would soon be established between the forces of American and of British industry. Dallas' report, less mechanistic, was more forthright. He proposed, for example, a duty of $33\frac{1}{3}$ per cent on cotton products and 28 per cent on woolens; the Committee of Ways and Means, which had not blenched at adopting a duty of 56 per cent on sugar, reduced both cotton and woolen duties to 20 per cent; and it was only after some striking scenes in the committee that the 20 per cent was raised to 25 per cent.[35]

The debates in the House were acrimonious, as is the nature of tariff debates, but they were not divisive. There was an underlying agreement which could be expressed in three ways. In the first place, a tariff *did* answer the needs of a wide variety of interests.

War industries, suffering from the dumping of British manufacturers, were crying for protection, from which almost every section of the country expected to benefit. In New England few cotton manufacturers managed to survive the fall in prices unless they adopted improved spinning machinery and the power loom. The few experimental mills in the Carolinas were staggering. Pittsburgh, already a flourishing smelter for iron deposits of the

[33] Walter B. Smith and Arthur H. Cole, *Fluctuations in American Business Enterprise* (Cambridge, 1935), p. 20.

[34] Henry Brougham hoped that a glut would "stifle in the cradle" the manufactures of the United States, which he considered unnatural. Hansard, 1 Ser., XXXIII, 1098, Commons Speech of April 9, 1816.

[35] *Niles' Register*, IX, 437; *Annals of Congress*, 14 Cong., 1 sess., p. 1245.

northern Appalachians, was eager to push its iron pigs and bars into the coastal region, in place of British and Swedish iron. In Kentucky there was a new industry of weaving local hemp into cotton bagging, which was menaced by the Scottish bagging industry. . . . The shepherds of Vermont and Ohio needed protection against English wool; the granaries of central New York, shut out of England by the corn laws, were attracted by the home market argument. Even Jefferson, outgrowing his old prejudice against factories, wrote, "We must now place the manufacturer by the side of the agriculturalist."[36]

In the second place, the tariff as enacted on April 27, 1816, was a very temperate piece of legislation. The duty of 25 per cent on cottons and woolens was to continue until June 30, 1819, after which, it was assumed, a duty of 20 per cent would be sufficient to repel the competition of British manufactures. A duty of 30 per cent was imposed upon rolled bar, leather, hats, writing paper, and cabinetware, and a specific duty of 3 cents a pound on sugar. But the only protective feature in the whole act was the principle of minimum valuation on coarse cottons: all cotton goods whose value was less than 25 cents a square yard should be considered as having cost that sum.[37] (Its object was to exclude all low-grade prints and East Indian fabrics; and, since the price of these imported cottons tended to fall with the price of raw cotton and the use of the power loom, their importation gradually ceased.)

In the third place, the voting in the House was not exactly partisan: 63 Republicans voted for the tariff and 31 against; 25 Federalists were for it, 23 against; and the state divisions themselves were more perplexing than factious.[38] It might seem ironical that maritime New England voted against a principle from which, in due time, it would be the first to benefit, and that congressmen from states that would later

---

[36] Samuel Eliot Morison and Henry Steele Commager, *The Growth of the American Republic* (2 vols., New York, 3rd ed., 1942), I, 439. Whether Jefferson referred to anything more than household manufactures is, of course, debatable.

[37] 3 U.S. Statutes at Large 310; Stanwood, *Tariff Controversies,* pp. 140–141.

[38] K. C. Babcock, *Rise of American Nationality* (New York, 1906), pp. 236–237. For the Federalist postwar attitude, see Livermore, *Twilight of Federalism,* pp. 16–17. For the "mildness" of the Tariff of 1816, see *American State Papers, Finance,* III, 15, 140, 141.

prefer secession to protection were disposed to support the protection of 1816. But here the real meaning of Madison's nationalistic program begins to reveal itself. The South considered that it alone had given the War of 1812 a substantial and decisive support; it identified itself in spirit with the successful outcome of the war; and it observed the nation's readjustment to peace with a benevolent eye. If the Tariff of 1816 had, as its chief beneficiary, the northern manufacturer, did he not deserve to be protected against the dumping practices of the late enemy? It could only have been on patriotic considerations such as these that representatives from southern districts which had no interest whatsoever in manufacturers gave, as many of them did, their votes for protection.[39] Moreover, the southern leaders still believed that they controlled the triumphant Republican party, and with it the machinery of the central government: their nationalism rose and fell with this sense of control, so that one could say, without risking a paradox, that in the last two years of James Madison's Presidency the congressional South was most nationalistic when it was most sectional.

A Utopian element in the mild Tariff of 1816 can be detected, not only in the peculiar character of southern nationalism at this point, but more specifically in a speech which John Caldwell Calhoun delivered on April 4. He believed that the South would soon participate in New England's industrial development, and he argued that in the event of another war with England—which he did not consider unlikely—the interests of the army and navy imperatively required a balanced domestic economy. Should there be no war, however, into what channels could the vast accumulations of capital, themselves derived from a state of war, be peacefully directed? Obviously into manufactures. At this point any doctrinaire Jeffersonian might have protested that a system of manufactures would return America precisely to that kind of history from which, since the beginning of her national existence, his party had sought to divorce her. But Calhoun maintained that despotism and pauperism in England were due, not to England's industrial system, but to bad laws and excessive taxes. He foresaw a national state, in which commerce, navigation, agriculture, and manufacturing would be mutually, indeed serenely, dependent.[40] The most trenchant

[39] Thomas P. Abernethy, *The South in the New Nation, 1789–1819* (Baton Rouge, 1961), pp. 426–433.

[40] *Annals of Congress,* 14 Cong., 1 sess., pp. 1329–1336.

criticism of Calhoun's quasi-corporate state was uttered by a man who was preternaturally quick to detect, though not to correct, an error. "On whom bears the duty on coarse woolens and linens, and blankets, upon salt and all the necessaries of life?" said John Randolph. "On poor men and on slaveholders."[41] From this question and its answer there was never to be an escape, but Randolph was a kind of male Cassandra, more feared than honored; and in spite of his predictions or maledictions, the Tariff of 1816 was the symbol of consensus not conflict.

Into this happy state of affairs there intruded itself one incongruous but most significant event. Since the First Congress itself, surely no body had been more able or more energetic than the Fourteenth. It seems to have decided that its labors should be rewarded in some fitting way. It therefore proposed and passed a Compensation Bill, which changed the emolument of Congressmen from $6 per diem to $1,500 per annum. There were sound reasons for this change; but the open nerve in the bill was soon touched by Calhoun, a statesman to whom intelligence and tact were not granted in equal measure, and who said that its real purpose was "to attract and secure ability and integrity to the public service . . . and any people, as they use or neglect them, flourish or decay."[42]

The people, strange to say, did not agree. What they perceived in the Compensation Bill was an effort on the part of Congress to turn itself into an elite. The result was that in the fall elections, two-thirds of the representatives were replaced. "That this remarkable body of men should have incurred almost instantly the severest popular rebuke ever visited on a House of Representatives, could not have been mere accident."[43] Nor was it. The people evidently wished their House of Representatives to represent them as they were, not as they ought to be; a strain of democratic or egalitarian nationalism was beginning to show itself, and legislators who distinguished themselves even with such modest laurels as a stipend of $1,500 simply did not conform to this.

The second session of the Fourteenth Congress, therefore, was largely

---

41 *Ibid.,* p. 842.
42 *Ibid.,* pp. 1183–1184.
43 *Ibid.,* 2 sess., pp. 517, 535; Adams, *History,* IX, 137, 138.

composed of men who had been repudiated at the polls. They continued, none the less, to act with their former vigor.[44] There was one piece of legislation needed to complete the foundations for Calhoun's Utopia, which was soon to be transformed into Henry Clay's more terrestrial American System: that piece of legislation was a bill providing for internal improvements at the federal expense. Quite apart from the problem, or conundrum, of Congress' power to make any such provision, what a storm it was sure to provoke among a quarrelsome aggregation of "local interests in commerce, taxation, land values, and even manufactures, within and between states and regions!"[45]

Nobody denied that the nation's system of roads and canals was to the last degree unsystematic. By 1816 only 100 miles of canal had been constructed, and these had proved neither profitable nor useful. The greater part of the roads were country roads, little better than paths through the forest, winding from outlying farms to the nearest village or navigable stream, often impassable, but somehow linked together so that a traveler of great determination could move on some kind of continuous highway from Maine to Georgia. He would do so at a pace which would have provoked unfavorable comment in the world of Augustus Caesar. Farther west even this barbarous network vanished into a few trails, struggling over the divide toward the headwaters of the tributaries of the Ohio or to the streams which flowed into the St. Lawrence, the Great Lakes, and the Gulf of Mexico. The turnpikes in eastern Pennsylvania, New York, New Jersey, and southern New England were usually in far better condition, but they were difficult to finance and not economically feasible for the transportation of goods. The National Road, which *was* conceived on Augustan lines, although many doubted whether Congress should have conceived it in the first place, had not yet reached Wheeling. The American economy still moved in a cumbrous counterclockwise fashion, down the Ohio and the Mississippi, up the Atlantic coast, and across the Alleghenies; and the steamboat had not yet begun to reverse this movement, if it ever did.[46]

[44] Congress repealed the Compensation Bill, but in an unrepentant spirit, retaining the $1,500 for the remainder of its existence. See especially *Annals of Congress*, 14 Con., 2 sess., pp. 574–582, 601.

[45] Dorfman, *Economic Mind*, I, 373.

[46] George R. Taylor, *The Transportation Revolution* (New York, 1951), pp.

Calhoun had moved for the appointment of a select committee to consider the possibility of setting apart, as a fund for internal improvements, the $1,500,000 bonus and the net annual dividends to be paid by the Bank of the United States, and the committee duly reported a bill to this effect. It was not until February 4, 1817, with only a month of the session to go, that it was called up before the Committee of the Whole, and Calhoun was able to sponsor it in an extraordinary speech. Beginning with military arguments, he soon moved into more spacious and more dramatic fields:

> Let it not be forgotten, let it be forever kept in mind, that the extent of the republic exposes us to the greatest of calamities—*disunion*. We are great, and rapidly—I was about to say fearfully—growing. This is our pride and danger, our weakness and our strength. . . . We are under the most imperious obligations to counteract every tendency to disunion. . . . Whatever impedes the intercourse of the extremes with this, the centre of the republic, weakens the union. . . . Let us, then, bind the republic together wtih a perfect system of roads and canals. Let us conquer space.

Behind Calhoun at this, his most visionary moment in the House of Representatives, there stood Gallatin's great *Report* of 1808. But the *Report* was only a report; it had long been gathering dust; and in any case, President Jefferson had been determined to implement it with an amendment to the Constitution. Calhoun made a much franker and more radical appeal to the dreaded principles of consolidation and centralization. He announced his indifference to constitutional niceties. "If we are restricted," he said, "in the use of our money to the enumerated powers, on what principles can the purchase of Louisiana be justified?"[47]

When the bill came to a vote, the House did not reveal nearly as much scruple as it did self-interest. New England was opposed because her roads were relatively good, because she feared a western migration of her people, and because she considered that the measure would promote the commerce of New York, Philadelphia, and Baltimore. The South was largely opposed—although the Carolinas were divided—

15–71, gives, with appropriate citations, a brilliant description and explanation of this.

[47] *Annals of Congress,* 14 Cong., 2 sess., pp. 853 ff. For Henry Clay's less Utopian and more Madisonian support of this bill, see Clay, *Works,* Calvin Colton, ed. (10 vols., Philadelphia, 1904), I, 454–455.

presumably because she thought that other sections would benefit more than herself. The West was oddly and inexplicably uncertain. Only from New York and Pennsylvania came almost unanimous support: from New York because she still hoped for federal aid in building an Erie Canal, from Pennsylvania because she believed that Philadelphia could reach the South by way of a Chesapeake and Delaware Canal and that Pittsburgh would profit immeasurably in the West by opening the falls of the Ohio to navigation.[48] The Bonus Bill struggled through the House by 86 to 84; was passed in the Senate, with minor amendments, by 20 to 15; and was accepted by Congress on March 1.[49] On March 2, when Calhoun paid his respects to the Madisons at Octagon House, the President drew him aside as he was leaving and explained that he could not approve the bill on constitutional grounds. Calhoun was bewildered and mortified: nothing now remained to him from his great battle but a taste for radical expedients.

In his Veto Message of March 3, 1817,[50] Madison pointed out that the power proposed to be exercised by Congress did not appear to be among the enumerated powers in the eighth section of the first article, nor could it by any just interpretation be made to fall within the power to make "necessary and proper" laws, nor yet within the power to regulate commerce or the clause "to provide for the common defense and general welfare." Had he not interposed his veto, he would have been guilty of an "inadmissible latitude of construction and a reliance on insufficient precedents," and he would have controverted his dearest belief that "the permanent success of the Constitution depends on a definite partition of powers between the General and State Governments." If there had been *sufficient* precedents, would he then have jettisoned his belief in a definite partition of powers? Only two things seem fairly certain. One is that his veto restored to him and his Seventh Annual Message a distinctly Jeffersonian look.[51] The other is that the

---

[48] Adams, *History*, IX, 150; Taylor, *Transportation Revolution*, p. 21.

[49] For tabulated state and sectional voting, see Wiltse, *Calhoun: Nationalist*, p. 403, Appendix B.

[50] Richardson, *Messages and Papers*, I, 584–585.

[51] E.g., "It was the object of the veto to deny to Congress as well the appropriating power as the executing and jurisdictional branches of it." Madison to Martin Van Buren, June 30, 1830: *Works* (Congressional edition, 4 vols., New York, 1884), IV, 88. Whether an amendment would have restored or revitalized his early idea of a "feudal system of republics," as in Madison to Jefferson, October 24, 1787, *ibid.*, I, 348, is doubtful.

Bonus Bill—unlike the Bank or Tariff Bills—had revealed a profound disagreement, not least within his own party; and this the Veto may be said to have quieted for the time being. When Mr. Madison went into honorable retirement on March 4, 1817, he had done his best, in the face of inevitable change, to construct the peace on Jeffersonian terms,[52] without denying either his nationalist instincts or his deep suspicion of laissez faire.[53]

He therefore urged his successor to include an internal improvements amendment among his recommendations to Congress: "There has never been a moment," he wrote in November, 1817, "when such a proposition to the States was so likely to be approved."[54] Yet this merely emphasizes, to our mind, the peculiar atmosphere of the early postwar nationalism: its mood of *acquiescence* in centralizing measures, a mood which was derived from optimism and from prosperity, and to which Madison's word "moment" is ironically very apt. What *is* the duration of a moment?

Mr. Madison's successor, James Monroe, was by no means a subtle man: he was the third of the Virginia Dynasty, in the order of intelligence no less than in that of succession. His rather solemn mind, though toughened by hard experience and deepened by hard thinking, had none of the brilliance, the flexibility, the profundity of those of his two predecessors; and has suffered no doubt unduly, from the inevitable comparison with theirs. But Monroe was a proud and self-confident man, sometimes impulsive, often courageous, and a career which had been curiously uneven, as full of disappointments as of triumphs, had not robbed him of a belief in his own destiny. But what sort of destiny was it to be?

Thomas Jefferson once said of him—it was in 1786, when Monroe was twenty-eight years old—"he is a man whose soul might be turned wrong side outwards without discovering a blemish to the world."[55]

[52] Adrienne Koch, *Jefferson and Madison: The Great Collaboration* (New York, 1950), p. 258: "The fundamental reasons for changes in the Republican party were changed times and circumstances, largely outside the control of the American Presidents."

[53] He called the "let alone policy" mere theory. Cf. Madison to Charles J. Ingersoll, December 30, 1835, *Works* (Cong. ed.), IV, 388.

[54] Madison to Monroe, November 29, 1817, *Works* (Cong. ed.), III, 50.

[55] Jefferson to William Temple Franklin, May 7, 1786, *The Papers of Thomas Jefferson,* Julian P. Boyd, ed. (Princeton, 1950-), IX, 466. Jefferson to Madison, January 30, 1787, *ibid.,* XI, 97, uses much the same language of

Turned right side outwards, the only side which is presumably available for inspection, his "soul" did display some conspicuous blemishes upon which historians have not failed to comment, and Jefferson's high-flown words suggest little more than a blank—as if Monroe's unblemished soul were a *tabula rasa* upon which his political mentor might inscribe what message he pleased. And, in fact, Monroe, who had once studied law under Jefferson, and had earned his teacher's lifelong respect and affection, was always thereafter somewhat of a pupil—a condition against which he had been known to rebel but never exactly to revolt. He was not, to be sure, as he grew older, seriously tempted by those dreams of an agrarian Utopia which were at once the despair and the inspiration of his great teacher: a more and more moderate agrarian, Monroe's temptations were of quite another kind.

In 1803, Jefferson sent him on a special mission to France. Although Monroe's past scarcely indicated a gift for diplomacy—he had been sent to Paris by George Washington and recalled under circumstances which were faintly discreditable—Jefferson seems to have believed that his friend's known democratic tendencies might not be out of place in a Consular court which was notably undemocratic and which needed a warning that America intended at all hazards to preserve her rights on the Mississippi. What is more to the point here, however, is the language which Jefferson used in order to persuade Monroe to undertake the mission: "All eyes," he wrote, "all hopes are fixed on you; and were you to decline, the chagrin would be universal. . . . I am sensible of the measures you have taken for getting into a different line of business, that it will be a great sacrifice on your part, and presents from the season and other circumstances serious difficulties. But some men are born for the public. Nature by fitting them for the service on a broad scale, has stamped them with the evidence of her destination and their duty."[56]

William Stephens Smith, which of course weakens a charge of particularity to Monroe.

[56] Jefferson to Monroe, January 13, 1803; *Writings* (Ford, ed.), IX, 419–420. For Monroe's mission to France under George Washington, see Samuel Flagg Bemis, "Washington's Farewell Address; A Foreign Policy of Independence," *American Historical Review*, XXXIX (1934), 250–268; also John C. Miller, *The Federalist Era* (New York, 1960), pp. 193–195, and James Monroe, *A View of the Conduct of The Executive* . . . (Philadelphia, 1797).

Some men are born for the public. Any student of Monroe's later career will recognize that this chord was precisely the one which would have to be struck. More plangent than delicate, its reverberations lingered in his mind; he might almost be said to have spent the rest of his life listening to them. But there is much danger in such music.

It insisted that the Presidency itself was an office in which one exercised stewardship not leadership. The public will, which Monroe was to interpret and to obey, resided in the Congress and the state legislatures; only in the realm of foreign affairs did he conceive himself to have a clear constitutional mandate to act on his own. And it is for his action in the realm of foreign affairs that Monroe is chiefly known to-day—for that and for the rather empty phrase "era of good feelings," of which he has become the avatar.

In appearance, he was a living reminder of some past sufficiently distant for everyone to be proud of it. On certain special occasions, his tall, rawboned, venerable figure would appear in the faded uniform of a Revolutionary officer; otherwise he wore the plain dark coat, the knee-length pantaloons, the white-topped boots of an earlier day; his hair was powdered and tied in a cue at the back; his manners were mild, but constrained, awkward, formal, and old-fashioned.

The circumstances surrounding his election were also, but less reassuringly, a little out of date. The choice of a candidate was made by a caucus of Republican congressmen some time before the spring adjournment. The caucus system was already suspect—leading men like William Lowndes and Henry Clay doubted the propriety, still less the expediency, of making nominations at all—and when the caucus first met in the Hall of Representatives on March 10, only 58 out of some 141 Republican members bothered to attend. This was clearly insufficient; a second call was posted for the evening of March 26; and on this occasion 119 members put in an appearance. Over the protests of Henry Clay, an election was held. Monroe received 65 votes, William H. Crawford of Georgia received 54, and the third candidate, Daniel D. Tompkins of New York, had to content himself with 85 votes for the Vice-Presidency. In the fall election, Monroe obtained 183 electoral votes as against 34 for the Federalist Rufus King of New York, and Tompkins 183 against a scattering of votes for four other contestants.[57]

[57] A good picture of the prevailing suspicion of the caucus system will be

The question of whether or not there was an effort in the New York Legislature to steal the caucus nomination from Monroe is now academic: at the caucus meeting all but three of the New York delegation cast their votes for Crawford, without affecting the result.[58] Crawford himself seems to have withdrawn from the contest, on the understanding (at least in his own mind) that he was to be Monroe's successor:[59] what is more significant is that, in spite of his withdrawal, he still received 54 votes. And the significance of these votes, which clearly indicate a partisan objection to the Virginia Dynasty, pales in the queer but vivid light of the electoral vote itself. "In 1816 . . . there was so little opposition to Monroe that the voter interest was negligible."[60] Even if we had the popular figures, which in the mixed system then prevailing were not ascertainable, we are bound to focus our attention on

found in John W. Taylor to John Taylor, Washington, February 28, 1816, John W. Taylor Papers, NYHS; Washington, *National Intelligencer*, March 14, 18, 19, 1816; J. B. McMaster, *A History of the People of the United States from the Revolution to the Civil War* (8 vols., New York, 1883–1913), IV, 363–365; Wiltse, *Calhoun*, pp. 114–115. For table of electoral votes, see McMaster, *History*, IV, 368.

[58] Jabez D. Hammond, *History of Political Parties in New York* (2 vols., New York, 1842), I, 409 ff., says that Martin Van Buren persuaded the state legislature to endorse Tompkins in order to get enough votes away from Crawford to secure the nomination of Monroe. If this was the case Tompkins did not know of it, since on March 13, 1816, V. Birdseye reported to John W. Taylor, the future Speaker, that Tompkins had told him that he thought "the President ought no longer for the present to come from Virginia . . . that if the Republicans of this state [New York] and our delegation in Congress thought proper to make an effort to effect what they conceived a necessary change of dynasty—he was willing to be at their service." John W. Taylor Papers, NYHS. Hammond shows that the New York delegation in any event supported Crawford, with only three dissenting votes. De Witt Clinton, who was of course suspect among New York Republicans at that time, endeavored, he said, to persuade both the state legislature and the congressional delegation to support Monroe. Clinton to N. J. Ingraham, April 10, 1817, MS. letter, NYHS.

[59] J. E. D. Shipp, *Giant Days; or the Life and Times of William H. Crawford* (Americus, Ga., 1909), p. 142, declares, rather disingenuously, that Crawford said he could not run against so venerable a figure as Monroe. The story of Crawford's abnegation, printed with embellishments, appeared in the Savannah *Daily Republican*, January 10, 1824. Crawford's own words are more revealing. On May 6, 1816, he wrote to Gallatin, urging the latter to become Secretary of the Treasury, and adding, "I do not know your feelings towards his [Madison's] successor—nor do I know his feelings towards me; nor is it a matter of any consequence so far as I am concerned." Gallatin Papers, NYHS.

[60] Richard P. McCormick, "New Perspectives on Jacksonian Politics," *American Historical Review*, LXV (1960), 294.

the fact that only Massachusetts, Connecticut, and Delaware had supported the Federalist candidate in the electoral college. From a *national* point of view the Federalist party was dead. It had expired from the effects of a strong self-administered poison, chiefly if not wholly composed of fear and faction: the Hartford Convention was its historical tombstone, with those mild but subversive resolutions as a funerary inscription, drowsily attesting the vices rather than the virtues of the deceased.

The effect of all this, again on the national level, was to subject the nation to what was virtually a one-party system, since almost every coming man outside New England had begun to call himself a Jeffersonian Republican, and since the Federalists had been effectively excluded from all participation in national government. If there were dangers in this one-sided state of affairs, Madison was not called upon to face them, and Monroe, in the spirit of the Founding Fathers, rather hopefully brushed them aside. "The existence of parties," he observed in 1816, "is not necessary to free government."[61]

Benjamin Latrobe's biographer has told us of a misunderstanding which arose between that much-tried architect and President Monroe. It was Latrobe's task to complete the new Capitol Building, which the British had so thoroughly gutted in 1814 as to make its completion almost a matter of rebuilding. Monroe had supposed that the Capitol would be completed by the fall of 1817; and, oblivious to what Latrobe had accomplished in design and construction, had fallen into a "towering rage" when he discovered that this could not be done. "To Monroe," writes Talbot Hamlin, with some exaggeration, but more acuteness, "order, system and expedition were aims in themselves, almost irrespective of their purpose and even of their results."[62]

The cheerful spirit of 1817 Monroe, of course, shared to the full. He seems to have decided that, his own ambition having been satisfied by his election to the Presidency, he could find other men who would be

---

[61] Monroe to Andrew Jackson, December 16, 1816. "The second [object] is, to prevent the reorganization and revival of the federal party, which, if my hypothesis is true, that the existence of parties is not necessary to free government, and the other opinion which I have advanced is well founded, that the great body of the federal party are republican, will not be found impracticable." *Works* (Hamilton, ed.), V, 346.

[62] Talbot Hamlin, *Benjamin Henry Latrobe* (New York, 1955), pp. 447–450.

equally happy with lesser posts in the government. He expected, he said, in his rather tortuous language, "to give effect to the government of the people, through me, for the term of my appointment, not for the aggrandizement of anyone."[63] His administration, in other words, was to be composed of comfortable, capable men who would do their duty and would content themselves with those inner satisfactions which come from the knowledge of duty well done. In his passion for symmetry as well as for peace, he even supposed that he could box the political compass by bestowing the four chief Cabinet posts upon gentlemen from the North, East, South, and West,[64] but here he was faced, at the start, with an unsurmountable difficulty. The Virginia Dynasty, with its instinct for self-perpetuation, had hitherto arranged that the succession to the Presidency should devolve upon the Secretary of State, and even those whose reverence for the Virginia Dynasty was not very pronounced still believed that the Secretary of State was little less than an heir apparent. When Monroe offered the War Department to Henry Clay, the West's most brilliant and ambitious son, he was coldly turned down.[65] Nothing less than the State Department, however, would have satisfied Mr. Clay, who thereafter arranged every detail of his political behavior with reference to his own "aggrandizement" and the discomfiture of the President. As for the West, it was not represented in the Cabinet of James Monroe.

After long deliberation, on March 6, 1817, Monroe offered the State Department to John Quincy Adams of Massachusetts, then Minister to Great Britain. Mr. Adams, never reluctant to examine other men's failings or (to do him justice) his own, had once professed to see a likeness between himself and Henry Clay. "There is," he wrote, "the same dogmatical, overbearing manner, the same harshness of look and expression, the same forgetfulness of the courtesies of society in both." This was written in the critical days of the peace negotiations at Ghent, where both men were commissioners, and where Adams was the champion of the New England fisheries and Clay of the Mississippi. At first sight no comparison could seem more preposterous: surely no two

---

[63] James Monroe to Andrew Jackson, March 1, 1817, *Works,* VI, 6.
[64] W. P. Cresson, *James Monroe* (Chapel Hill, 1946), p. 290.
[65] McMaster, *History,* IV, 377: "That Clay was deeply offended was shown by his conduct, for of all the distinguished men in Washington on that day, he alone did not attend the inauguration."

social *personae* could have been less alike. Clay was a man born to please, high-spirited, mettlesome, convivial, sunny, the airy master of men and events. Yet it would not be unfair to say that he had engrafted upon the geniality of his native Virginia some of the hardness and swagger of his adopted Kentucky; and it is undeniably true that, when his interests were at stake, he could be aggressive, overbearing, the prey to moments of ugly, irrepressible wrath. No man was more quick or more generous in his apologies for such outbursts, but his friends were perplexed.[66]

They need not have been. Every particle of Clay's attractive composition was impregnated with political elements: as Albert Gallatin put it, he was "devoured by ambition"; as Henry Adams has written, he was "transparent."[67] It was quite impossible that James Monroe, who longed for peace in his official family, and who aspired to keep politicians at an arm's length, would have given the State Department to such a man, and distinctly probable (for lack of evidence, one can say no more) that when he offered him the War Department he did so more to gratify the West than to ally himself with Mr. Clay. To a man like Monroe, Clay would have been less awkward and distracting as an opponent than as a colleague.

Mr. Adams, on the other hand, at this point in his immense and eminent career, was not a political figure. In 1808, he had been forced to resign from the United States Senate, of which he was a Federalist member, because he had opposed the Anglophile tendencies of his own party. But he resigned as a patriot, not as a would-be Republican; and when President Madison suddenly and unexpectedly offered him the post of Minister to Russia in 1809, the reception of this news by the orthodox Republicans was not encouraging. "That both Adams' are monarchists," said John Taylor of Caroline, in one of the most felicitous and least accurate of his obiter dicta, "I never doubted. Whether monarchists, like pagans, can be converted by benefices, is a problem the solution of which I always feared Mr. Madison would attempt."[68]

---

[66] John Quincy Adams to Louisa Catherine Adams, December 16, 1814; Adams, *Writings*, V, 239; George Dangerfield, *Era of Good Feelings*, p. 11.

[67] Gallatin to James Gallatin, Henry Adams, *The Life of Albert Gallatin* (New York, 1879), p. 623. Henry Adams, *History*, IX, 51, 52: "transparent beyond need of description or criticism."

[68] W. C. Ford, "The Recall of John Quincy Adams in 1808," *Massachusetts Historical Society Proceedings*, XLV, 354–375. It was not exactly, although it

Of course, neither the second President nor his son had ever been monarchist: they were grim and unbending republicans, and in any case what John Taylor of Caroline thought in 1809 could have meant little to Monroe in 1817. In 1817, Monroe (in the eyes of the faithful) was no more orthodox than John Quincy Adams. The point was that Adams, during his long absence from the United States, had been altogether out of touch with the personal rivalries of the Republican party, nor had he ever sought office. His views on *domestic* policies, insofar as they could be ascertained from his distant record in the Senate, would seem to be in line with the mild nationalism of Monroe; and if Monroe could have looked over Adams' shoulder, as that gentleman wrote to his mother on May 16, he would have been gratified to learn that Adams intended "to enter upon the functions of my office . . . with a suitable impression that my place is subordinate." But Adams added that no Cabinet except Jefferson's had ever been harmonious, and that he did not expect Monroe to be as fortunate as Jefferson.[69]

Adams' experience in diplomatic business had been wide and various. As a youth, he had been secretary to Francis Dana in St. Petersburg, where that valiant gentleman attempted in vain to impress the Empress Catharine with both his own existence and that of the Revolutionary United States. He had been Minister to the Netherlands, to Prussia, to Russia; he had been one of the five peace commissioners at Ghent; and the post of Minister to England, from which Monroe had summoned him, was of the first importance to an education in statecraft.

There was a marked disparity between the diplomatic experience of Mr. Adams, which was ripe, and his manners, which were not. He was no more than correct in saying that he was harsh, dogmatical, overbearing, and forgetful of the courtesies of society.[70] He took a dis-

---

was effectually, a "recall." The General Court first elected a successor to J. Q. A. six months before the normal time for such a choice, and then sent instructions to its senators to insist upon repeal of the embargo. J. Q. A. at once resigned. Bemis, *John Quincy Adams and the Foundations of American Foreign Policy,* (New York, 1949), hereafter designated as *Adams and Foreign Policy,* p. 149. John Taylor of Caroline to James Monroe, November 8, 1809, *John P. Branch Historical Papers,* II, 346.

[69] John Quincy Adams to Abigail Adams, May 16, 1817; *Writings,* VI, 187. For the very mixed reaction to his appointment, see *ibid.,* VI, 133 n.

[70] For a (prejudiced) description of his diplomatic manners, see Hon. W. H. Lyttleton to Sir Charles Bagot, January 22, 1827: "Of all the men whom it

tinct pleasure in reciting these "defects," which he confessed he had not the pliability to reform: it was as if his odd puritanical alchemy were endeavoring to transmute them into virtues. Of course, one hesitates to apply the term "puritan" to such a bundle of complexities as Mr. Adams, yet there are certain more obvious aspects of his character to which no other term seems to be appropriate. He was a puritan in his self-mortification, a puritan in his belief—nowhere expressed but everywhere apparent—that this was evidence of an innate superiority, a puritan in his anxious welcome of personal disaster and in his conviction that every great success must be followed by some compensating failure, a puritan in his virulence, and a puritan in his morality.

For he was, above all, a moral man. It is one of the clues to his greatness, which, if one follows it carefully, will lead one faithfully through all the thorns and briars and nettles to the very heart of the labyrinth. But it was the morality of a man who was not only possessed of a lofty intelligence, imagination, and courage but who was also corroded by meanness, suspicion, and fear. It was a tortuous, not to say a tortured morality, which for years did his reputation great disservice. Every reader of his Diary recognizes, respects, and recoils from it.

The Diary,[71] he thought, might have been, "next to the Holy Scriptures, the most precious book ever written by human hands."[72] His intellectual gifts, he modestly admitted, were insufficient for this high purpose; but no historian has ever denied the value of these immense and angry reminiscences. Mr. Adams had, after all, a passion for the truth; his facts are strictly and accurately reported; and his interpretation of the facts, while less reliable, displays the brilliance of his insights. But when it comes to the interpretation of motive, then the passion turns into a mania: Mr. Adams' unhappy ego peers out

---

was ever my lot to accost and to waste civilities upon [he] was the most doggedly and systematically repulsive. With cotton in his leathern ears, and hatred to England in his heart, he sat in the frivolous assemblies of Petersburg like a bull-dog among spaniels; and many were the times that I drew monosyllables and grim smiles from him and tried in vain to mitigate his venom." *George Canning and His Friends,* Capt. Josceline Bagot, ed. (London, 2 vols., 1909), II, 362.

[71] John Quincy Adams, *Memoirs of John Quincy Adams,* Charles Francis Adams ed. (12 vols., Philadelphia, 1874–77).

[72] Brooks Adams, "The Heritage of Henry Adams," in Henry Adams, *The Degradation of the Democratic Dogma* (New York, 1919), p. 35.

across the world in an agony of suspicion; everything seems to be transformed into a conspiracy against Mr. Adams. It might be said of him that, at one time or another, he successfully misinterpreted almost every character but his own.

The Diary is immensely readable. Like his father, Adams was a born writer; his trenchant gift, like ore in a mountain, veins the huge mass of his papers—the Diary (it was intended for publication), the *Report on Weights and Measures,* the private correspondence, the laborious, learned, and powerful notes to American diplomats and foreign ministers.[73] It is no doubt true that his prose is at its best when he writes as a public man, and even truer that he is happier in attack than in defense, that he has "the instinct for the jugular."[74] And it is really not surprising that a man so endowed should be more at home in the formulation of measures than in the management of men. As for his appearance, it was all of a piece with the rest of him: the short, stout body in its careless and shabby dress, the rheumy eyes, the bald, belligerent forehead, the grim mouth with its thin compressed lips. Such was the man whom James Monroe chose for his Secretary of State, who repaid the choice with a stern loyalty and a surprising appreciation of the President's good qualities, and who looms to this day like a giant in the annals of the State Department.

One cannot say that William H. Crawford of Georgia and John Caldwell Calhoun of South Carolina, the Secretary of the Treasury and the Secretary for War, obtained their portfolios through the most deliberate choice on the part of Monroe. Crawford, a holdover from the previous administration, was left in the Treasury because he was simply too powerful a man, with too many claims on Monroe's gratitude, to be returned to private life against his wish. The War Department reached Calhoun through a process of elimination which, whatever else it might be, was not selective.[75]

[73] John Adams' fragmentary *Autobiography* in *The Adams Papers,* L. H. Butterfield, ed., Vols. III and IV (Cambridge, 1961), is full of extraordinarily vivid passages. John Quincy Adams, *Report of the Secretary of State upon Weights and Measures* (Washington, 1821).

[74] *Holmes-Pollock Letters . . . 1874–1932,* M. D. Howe, ed. (Cambridge, 2 vols., 1941), I, 95. J. Q. A.'s *The Duplicate Letters, the Fisheries, and the Mississippi* (Washington, 1822) was an assault upon Jonathan Russell so deadly as to have hastened Russell's death, and to have increased though not enriched American vocabulary with the transitive verb, "to Jonathan-Russell."

[75] The War Department was offered to Governor Isaac Shelby of Kentucky,

A curious ambiguity still hangs about William H. Crawford. His private papers are unfortunately lost to us, a loss which has deprived him of the services of a good biographer and left him somewhat at the mercy of his enemies. While Gallatin praised his inflexible integrity and Jefferson almost extravagantly lamented his failure to succeed Monroe, Calhoun called him corrupt to a degree and Adams dismissed him as a mere political conjurer.[76] Since Gallatin and Jefferson were his friends, and Calhoun and Adams were his rivals, it is not too difficult to reconcile these praises and denunciations; but the ambiguity does not rest there. Crawford was the standard bearer of the Old Republicans, who detested the program of economic self-sufficiency which Madison and Monroe appeared to support, and whose rigid minds rejected even the process of constitutional amendment; but Crawford was not fanatically opposed to federal control of internal improvements,[77] he was in favor of a mild protective tariff, and he was an earnest friend of the Second Bank of the United States, which (as every orthodox Republican knew) bore upon its forehead the mark of Cain. All he had to offer was a professed belief in state rights and in their corollaries—economy, simplicity, retrenchment, conservatism. It is odd that this should have proved sufficient, and it suggests that Crawford had a consummate control of the somewhat indelicate art of sitting on the fence. But like everything else about him, this is and can be suggestion only.

---

who refused the appointment; then to William Lowndes of South Carolina, who also refused. Andrew Jackson had urged William Drayton of South Carolina, a Federalist, and was himself thought of, as (perhaps) was David R. Williams of South Carolina, before Monroe finally offered the appointment to Calhoun on October 10, 1817. Jackson to Monroe, October 23, November 12, 1816, January 6, 1817, in J. S. Bassett (ed.), *Correspondence of Andrew Jackson* (Washington, 7 vols., 1926–35), II 261, 264, 272. Monroe to Shelby, February 20, 1817, *Writings*, VI, 1; Monroe to Jackson, March 1, 1817, *ibid.*, VI, 4–5; Wiltse, *Calhoun*, p. 139.

[76] Walters, *Gallatin*, pp. 319–320; Jefferson to Crawford, February 15, 1815, in Shipp, *Giant Days*, p. 192; Adams, *Memoirs*, V, 497; Leonard D. White, *The Jeffersonians* (New York, 1951), p. 66 n.

[77] W. H. Crawford to James Tallmadge, Jr., Private (A Copy), July 12, 1819: "Indeed, it is difficult I think even now for the President to avoid giving his approbation to any law appropriating money for a road or canal. It may be even more difficult to induce him to sign an act embracing a system. But a few years in the age of nations is nothing. A system will be introduced gradually, if not directly at once." John W. Taylor Papers, NYHS.

Born in Virginia, but bred to the law in Georgia, he became prominent in his adopted state as a spokesman for the upland planting
interests, and the champions of the democratic small farmers carried
their resentment of him—it was not unusual in that state—so far as
to call him out on two occasions. Crawford killed Peter Van Alen,
Solicitor General of the Western Circuit, and had his wrist shattered
by General John Clark, the Indian fighter. Although Clark expressed a
willingness to meet him again and again until one of them died, Crawford modestly declined this invitation, and soon afterward ascended
to the United States Senate, the Ministry to France, and the Secretary-
ships of War and then of the Treasury in the Cabinet of James Madison. But the enmity of the more democratic elements within his own
state troubled him for the rest of his career.[78]

A man of immense physique, a handsome and magnanimous appearance, a coarse but genuine affability, Crawford was very popular in
Washington:[79] with this popularity, with his reasonable claim to be
Monroe's successor, his orthodox backing, his skill in the use of
patronage and the management of congressmen, was it likely that he
would be a happy influence in Monroe's Cabinet? The one-party
system may have had virtues in Monroe's eyes which are quite invisible
to us; but it had a fatal tendency to encourage personal rivalries to the
point where they became almost irrelevant to the real history of their
times. Mr. Calhoun, if we may believe his most scholarly biographer,
and there is no reason why we should not, was the chief victim of some
of Crawford's more ingenious and deplorable intrigues, and Calhoun
and his supporters replied in kind; but one cannot say that administrative history was much affected by these irritants.[80] Both the Treasury
and the War Departments were consistently well handled.[81] The
political historian, of course, cannot ignore the battles which developed
within Monroe's Cabinet, or the obsessive urge (inevitable under a
one-party system) to build parties around personalities and not issues.

[78] Shipp, *Giant Days,* pp. 46, 50, 71–72.

[79] Margaret Bayard Smith, *The First Forty Years of Washington Society,*
Gaillard Hunt, ed. (London, 1906), *passim; The Life and Times of William
Harris Crawford, An Address Delivered by Charles N. West, A.M., before the
Georgia Historical Society . . . May 2, 1892* (Savannah, 1892).

[80] Wiltse, *Calhoun,* pp. 179, 200–208, 227–228, 241, 262–263.

[81] White, *Jeffersonians,* makes this abundantly clear.

But political history only *appears* to be constellated around these matters, which were at best a kind of rash upon the body politic—the irritable symptoms of an itch to be Monroe's successor.

The central drama of his period, as has been indicated, was thematically one of nationalism—its emergence from the shimmering illusion of 1815–19, the illusion of "a nation unified and free, strong to defend itself but yielding special privilege to no class or group,"[82] into the harsher and more testing realm of interest, prejudice, and appetite. Here the chief members of the Cabinet and their chief rivals in the nonofficial world are conventionally held to be the dramatis personae; but as regards their presidential ambitions one hardly dares think of them as more than creatures in a puppet show, interacting in queer complications and hurrying toward some predestined conclusion. The ultimate, crude, and controlling test, as sufficiently appeared in 1828, was between economic and democratic nationalism: this was a test which Crawford, even if he had not been stricken by paralysis in 1823, could hardly have survived; it transformed John Quincy Adams from one of the greatest of Secretaries of State to one of the more helpless of Presidents; it eclipsed the sunlight of Henry Clay; and its most obviously tragic victim was John Caldwell Calhoun.

Calhoun in 1817 as in 1828 was an economic nationalist, but there was a sinister difference between the innocent and ideal mercantilism of the first year—his schematic faith in central regulation *and* sectional self-restraint as the prime components of a balanced but expanding economy—and the fact that by 1828 he was obliged to found his nationalism upon the imperatives of cotton and the permanence of slavery. In the end, although he became more and more reactionary and more and more particularist, he still endeavored to preserve his franchise as a nationalist with a scheme which would have reduced the nation to immobility within a year.[83] His stern, conventual, metaphysical mind, more happy with theories than with actualities, but perhaps the most original mind of its time, was never really at home with practical politics: compared to a Crawford or a Clay, he was as innocent as a monk. But in 1817, when Monroe somewhat reluctantly offered him the War Department, how could any of this conceivably have been

    [82] Wiltse, *Calhoun: Nationalist,* p. 272.
    [83] Theory of Concurrent Majorities: Calhoun, *Works,* Richard K. Crallé, ed. (6 vols., New York, 1854–57), I, 107, 392 ff.

guessed or foreseen? Calhoun, an upcountry South Carolinian of Scotch-Irish ancestry, a Calvinist who had embraced Unitarianism, a graduate of Yale College and of the Litchfield Law School in Connecticut, was not exactly parochial; and although it would have required a certain stretching of the imagination to call him a man of the world, the imagination was easily stretched in those days, when the public stage was small and the characters appeared larger than life-size. His was still relatively young, ardent, attractive, hopeful: far away from that "cast-iron man who looks as if he had never been born" whom Harriet Martineau observed in the 1830's.[84]

The remainder of Monroe's Cabinet—the Attorney General and the Secretary of the Navy—was more suited to the President's notions of what was necessary to a happy family. The Attorney General was William Wirt of Virginia, one of the most charming men and, what was more to the point, that rarest of early American phenomena—a lawyer who was actually satisfied with the practice of the law. His eloquence was famous, but he reserved it for his pleadings, and his loyalty to Monroe—"that good old man . . . all kindness and amiability"—never wavered for an instant. The Secretary of the Navy, Benjamin Crowninshield of Massachusetts, another survivor from the Madison administration, was a vacillating, unambitious, kindly gentleman who soon retired out of inanition and perhaps nostalgia.[85]

This may serve to emphasize the fact that the heart of Monroe's Cabinet was composed of gifted men, who brought him the sound administrative qualities he needed, but whose personal differences and presidential rivalries, exacerbated rather than soothed by the absence of clear-cut issues, gave to his second administration a note of somewhat aimless rancor.

In the meantime, in the year 1817, the nation appeared to be more

[84] Harriet Martineau, *A Retrospect of Western Travel* (New York, 2 vols., 1838), I, 149.

[85] William Wirt to Judge Carr, January 18, 1818: "My single motive for accepting the office was the calculation of being able to pursue my profession on a more advantageous ground—i.e., more money for less work." So also Wirt to Mrs. Wirt, November 13, 1817. John P. Kennedy (ed.), *Memoirs of the Life of William Wirt* (Philadelphia, 2 vols., 1849), II, 67, 29; for Wirt on Monroe, *ibid.*, II, 96. The best description of Wirt's appearance, eloquence, etc., is in Charles Warren, *The Supreme Court in U.S. History* (Boston, 2 vols., 1926), I, 598 ff., in Warren's discussion of Gibbons *v.* Ogden. For Crowninshield's nostalgia, see Cresson, *Monroe,* pp. 284–285.

optimistic than at any other moment in its history, and in this respect the new President was not behindhand. "I indulge a strong hope," he said, responding to an address from the Republican minority of the Massachusetts legislature, "that our principal dangers and difficulties have passed, and that the character of our deliberations and the course of the government itself, will become more harmonious and happy than it has heretofore been." Nothing is more apt to befuddle a statesman than an indulgence in strong hopes, but Monroe was in the city of Boston, the capital of Federalism, and his reception from the Federalist majority there had been friendliness itself. Indeed, he had considered it necessary to drop a hint to "our old, and honest [Republican] friends" that, in presenting an address on their own, they had done their party no service. In his opinion, they should seek for a union of the two parties, since this union would be "founded exclusively on their own principles." And he told them, "frankly," that his conduct would be invariably directed toward promoting the union of the whole community.[86] However, though not by choice a party man, he never gratified the Federalists with anything more substantial than friendly professions.[87]

Monroe's appearance in Boston—he spent six days there—was part of a tour which he had designed for the inspection of outposts and fortifications from Baltimore to Portland and then westward by way of the lower lakes to Detroit, the expenses of which he had defrayed by borrowing from the Furniture Fund on a pledge of his plate and furniture. From the moment he entered New England until he left it, the tour had been a triumphal progress. Newspapers commented on the way in which the "demon of party" had been exorcised by the mere appearance of the President, with his air of republican simplicity, his plain blue coat and buff waistcoat, his hat and cockade "of the revolutionary fashion." People who could scarcely bring themselves to use the same street now, under the spell of his beneficent presence, actually met in the same room! The student of these scriptures will not fail to notice that, while the exorcism was described as potent, no-

[86] Monroe, *Writings*, VI, 28 n.

[87] For the Boston Federalists' belief that Monroe was prepared to relax the proscription against them, see William Tudor to Monroe, February 22, 1817, and George Sullivan to Monroe, July 10, 1817, Monroe Papers, LC. Monroe's distrust of such advances is sufficiently indicated in a note written on the latter document.

body ventured to predict that it would be lasting.[88] Boston's *Columbian Centinel,* when it "recurred with pleasure" to what it called an "Era of Good Feelings," somehow managed to hint that the Era was confined to Boston, and that it had departed with the President:[89] in short, that it endured for exactly six days.

But so happy a phrase, blown from so harsh a Federalist trumpet, quite naturally continued to echo, until at last it became almost synonymous with the two administrations of James Monroe. It only remains to add that the blight of its origin was upon it, and that, while there was no lack of feelings during the Presidency of Monroe, they were usually anything but good. The President himself, to be sure, as Jefferson's fine instinct had registered many years before, was essentially a good man; and by 1817, with his wishes fulfilled, his goodness had grown ripe. His subsequent quietism, in times of domestic crisis, merely leads us to inquire whether ripeness is all.

[88] For newspaper comments, see *Niles' Register,* XII, 238, 272, 280, 314, 315. There is a comprehensive account of this tour, though a quite uncritical one, in Samuel Putnam Waldo, *A Narrative of a Tour of Observation, made during the summer of 1817* . . . (Hartford, 1817). For financing of the tour, see Lucius Wilmerding, Jr., *James Monroe, Public Claimant* (New Brunswick, 1960), Chap. 2.

[89] Boston, *Columbian Centinel,* July 12, 1817.

CHAPTER 2

Secretary Adams, General Jackson, and the Transcontinental Treaty

WHEN the Louisiana Purchase agreement came under the scrutiny of Thomas Jefferson in 1803, that great man saw in this arrangement the birth of nothing less than an "Empire for Liberty."[1] As to the character of the new Empire, Jefferson was a little uncertain: he supposed that it would at first be useful as an asylum for Indians, and that later on—in some indefinite future—"the world will see here such an extent of country under a free and moderate government as it has never yet seen." No doubt his earliest feelings were those of simple but statesmanlike relief: the United States was now in possession of the heartland of the continent,[2] and had gained a position of *potential* independence from European powers.

The Purchase, none the less, was connected with other and more enticing visions. One cannot discover anywhere in Jefferson's writings a specific mention of the Asian trade; on the other hand, as one commentator has suggested, his instructions to Meriwether Lewis "probably took for granted the importance of the trade with the Orient."[3] His vision, one of the most delectable in American history but not the easiest to decipher, is indistinct on this point; he was, after all, primarily concerned with an agrarian Utopia, and until the existence of an American "desert" was announced in 1810 by Zebulon Pike, he may have been involved in dreams of a fee-simple empire stretching out to the Rockies. After 1810, he began to think of a North-

---

[1] Jefferson to Andrew Jackson, September 19, 1803; Adrienne Koch, *Jefferson and Madison* (New York, 1950), p. 244.

[2] R. W. Van Alstyne, *The Rising American Empire* (New York, 1960), p. 91.

[3] Henry Nash Smith, *Virgin Land* (Cambridge, 1950), p. 22.

West Republic, beyond the Rockies, to be colonized by Americans, but to have a separate political existence.[4]

Thus the agrarian *nationalism* of Thomas Jefferson appears to have stopped at the so-called desert, an impassable barrier, which only his agrarian colonialism is able to overleap, and the connection between Louisiana and the Northwest in terms of territorial expansion and of the Asian trade begins to emerge more clearly in the neomercantilist mind of John Quincy Adams. In either case, it depended upon the acquisition of the Floridas from Spain, the first problem with which President Monroe and Secretary Adams had to deal, and one which deployed, a little irregularly, the nationalist energies of postwar America.

This problem was itself a holdover from the administration of James Madison, indeed from much farther back than that: the Louisiana Purchase itself had left the status of the Floridas unclear, a situation which neither the Mobile Act of 1804 nor the "Two Million Act" of 1806 had done much to clarify. Only one thing was certain. The Floridas, as the map itself all too graphically showed, resembled a pistol aimed at the vitals of the United States, East Florida representing the butt of the pistol and West Florida the barrel. In 1810, after a somewhat dubious experiment with the revolutionary sentiments of West Florida, President Madison had felt himself obliged to occupy that province as far as the Pearl River. In 1812 this portion of West Florida was added to the State of Louisiana, and a further slice, extending to the Perdido River, was bestowed upon the Territory of Mississippi; all this was justified by the famous No-Transfer Resolution of January 15, 1811. The pistol had now acquired a somewhat snub-nosed look, but it was not the less deadly for that.[5]

---

[4] Jefferson to Madison, April 27, 1809, says: "I am persuaded that no constitution was ever before so well calculated as ours for extensive empire and self-government." Koch, *Jefferson and Madison*, p. 245, citing W. C. Rives Papers, LC. Whereas Jefferson to John Jacob Astor, November 9, 1813, speaks of Astoria as "the germ of a great, free, and independent empire on that side of our continent." Van Alstyne *Rising American Empire*, p. 93. Both Smith (pp. 16–17) and Van Alstyne (p. 80) mention his fantastic instructions to John Ledyard in 1783—to go by land to Kamchatka, cross to Nootka Sound, "fall down into the latitude of the Missouri," and penetrate to the United States—as evidence of his early and passionate interest in the Northwest; but whether this, or the great expedition of Lewis and Clark, had any explicit connection with the Asian trade cannot be asserted with confidence.

[5] It had not escaped the attenion of Robert R. Livingston and James Monroe,

It was, by the end of the War of 1812, obvious to everyone that this geographical weapon would sooner or later have to pass into the hands of the United States: obvious even to Spain, whose government, although almost hawklike in its view of the irretrievable past, rarely perceived what was in front of its nose. The only question was, upon what terms and how soon would the Floridas pass from Spanish to American hands? The Americans, on their side, were able to urge certain gross violations of Pinckney's Treaty of 1795. Had Spain prevented the Indians under her control from depredating north of the Florida boundary? Had she settled American claims for damages arising from her suspension of the right of deposit at the mouth of the Mississippi? Or claims for spoliations committed during the Napoleonic Wars in violation of the freedom of the seas?[6] These were certainly formidable levers with which to pry the Floridas loose from Spain. But, considering the massive counterclaims of Spain, would even these prove sufficient? For Spain had already informed James Monroe, when he was Secretary of State under Madison, not only that America must first hand back what she had taken of the Floridas before the Floridas could in turn be formally ceded to her but also that she must consent to the Mississippi River as her western boundary! In other words, America was expected to confess that there had been no Louisiana Purchase at all. Such was the state of affairs when John Quincy Adams became Secretary of State.

Needless to say, no sensible man supposed that Spain could hope to undo such a *fait accompli* as the Louisiana Purchase. The question raised by her extravagant demands, a question to which the cession of

the American plenipotentiaries, that they had been instructed to purchase the east bank of the Mississippi and had purchased the west bank instead. For their subsequent endeavors to prove that France had also sold them the Floridas, see George Dangerfield, *Chancellor Robert R. Livingston of New York: 1746–1813* (New York, 1960), p. 374. 2 *United States Statutes at Large* (Boston, 17 vols., 1850–73), 251, 285, 708, 734, gives the enactments mentioned. For Madison's proclamation, Richardson, *Messages and Papers,* I, 480–81; this maintains R. R. L.'s and Monroe's position that the territory occupied was part of the original purchase. The No-Transfer Resolution—"The United States . . . cannot without serious inquietude see any part of the said territory pass into the hands of any foreign power"—is in *Annals of Congress,* 11 Cong., 3 sess., pp. 374–376.

[6] For the original text of Pinckney's treaty, see Samuel Flagg Bemis, *Pinckney's Treaty* (Baltimore, 1926), App. V. Indian depredations violated Article V; suspension violated Article XXII; spoliations, Articles XV and XVI.

the Floridas had become central, was this: what exactly *was* the Louisiana Purchase? When Livingston and Monroe had attempted to discover the precise nature of their bargain west of the Mississippi, they could get no more from Talleyrand than the cryptic remark that the bargain was a noble one and that he supposed they would make the most of it; and the language of the Treaty of San Ildefonso, which had ceded Louisiana to France in 1800, was certainly of such a kind as to baffle explicit definition from that day to this. The standard American argument was that the Purchase extended at least as far to the southwestward as the Rio Grande; but Monroe (with Madison's connivance) had been prepared to retreat in 1815 to the Colorado of Texas or even to the Sabine as the southwestern boundary. No American statesman could have gone further in that postwar world.[7]

There were many reasons why he need not have gone as far as that, and the first of these was the lamentable situation of the Spanish Empire. It was now in an acute stage of disintegration. When Napoleon placed his brother Joseph upon the imperial throne of Spain, while Ferdinand VII was consigned to a prison at Valençay, he provoked a rebellion in the Spanish colonies, first in favor of Ferdinand VII, but then in favor of independence. In April, 1810, Simon Bolívar obtained control of Caracas, and from that moment onward the vast Spanish Empire began visibly to crumble. At the Congress of Vienna, Pedro Gomez Labrador found himself completely isolated; it seems that Europe had, for the time being, little interest in transatlantic affairs, and Labrador—a man of excessive vanity and limited judgment—was not equipped to revive such an interest, even if it had existed. As for the Court of Ferdinand VII, who had been restored to his throne in 1814, it was a distasteful combination of grandees, priests, and parvenu favorites, and seemed peculiarly well adapted to preside over his immense imperial dissolution.

As the war in South America turned more and more in favor of the insurgents, the United States naturally began to occupy a menac-

---

[7] *American State Papers, Foreign Relations,* IV, 424–426. Henry Adams, *History,* II, 72. Bonaparte himself is supposed to have said that if an uncertainty had not already existed as to the extent of the purchase, it would have been a good idea to put one there. François de Barbé-Marbois, *Histoire de la Louisiane* (Paris, 1829), p. 312; Philip Coolidge Brooks, *Diplomacy and the Borderlands: The Adams-Onís Treaty of 1819* (Berkeley, 1939), 66; Bemis, *Adams and Foreign Policy,* p. 305.

ing position in the thoughts of Spanish statesmen. On the one hand, she might take it into her head to recognize the independence of the rebellious Spanish provinces; on the other, the borderlands of the Spanish Empire were contiguous with hers, and they were not defensible. A cession of the Floridas, therefore, implied as *quid pro quo* both a neutral attitude toward the rebels and a definition of the borderline, but here another set of difficulties presented themselves.

Henry Clay, for example, not unwilling to mingle republican principle with political advantage, was already calling for South American independence.[8] On the Alabama River, a group of Bonapartist exiles was known to be dreaming of an incursion into Texas, in order to place the crown of Mexico upon the head of ex-King Joseph; and this fantastic plan, which foreshadowed if anything the occasional affinity between later Bonapartism and *opéra bouffe*, was taken quite seriously in 1817. Above all, in response to a call from revolutionary agents in North America, both Amelia Island in the St. Mary's River and Galveston in Texas had become the bases for privateers against Spanish shipping; the privateers soon failed to see much difference between the Spanish and the American flags, and the United States had at length (December 23, 1817) been obliged to seize Amelia Island. If Governor Coppinger's inability to control the Seminole Indians should provoke an American punitive expedition across the Florida border, it seemed not improbable that, before the cession of the Floridas was properly discussed, there would be no Floridas to cede. And then what would happen to the Spanish borderlands?[9]

It was the duty of the Spanish Minister, Don Luiz de Onís y Gonzales, to postpone the cession of the Floridas until the Americans had agreed to accept a borderline east of Texas to New Mexico, and the farther east the better; for Spain was particularly anxious to keep the bacillus of American democracy from finding its way into Mexico. Onís, a native of Cantalapiedra in the province of Salamanca, had

---

[8] Calvin Colton (ed.), *The Works of Henry Clay* (New York, 10 vols., 1904), I, 234.

[9] Brooks, *Borderlands,* 87. Monroe, First Annual Message to Congress, Richardson, *Messages and Papers,* II, 13, 14, and Special Message of January 13, 1818, *ibid.,* II 23–24. The Special Message promised that the suppression of "the establishment . . . at Galveztown . . . will soon follow," but this did not actually take place until May 1820. Bemis, *Adams and Foreign Policy,* p. 308 n.

studied law at the University of Salamanca, diplomacy at the Court of Saxony, statesmanship as an active participant in the negotiations leading to the Peace of Amiens (1802), and heroism under the Junta Central in 1808. It was an impressive record, and the character which had been forged by it might be said to have displayed only two conspicuous flaws, both Spanish and both fatal. One was a certain inflexibility of the mind, which sometimes amounted to feebleness and sometimes approached petrifaction; the other was a frequent inability to recognize what century he was in. These failings were not likely to become less conspicuous after an exposure, which began in December, 1817, to the merciless intelligence of John Quincy Adams. Moreover, having arrived in the United States in 1809 as the envoy of the Junta Central, Onís had not been recognized until December 9, 1815; in the interval he had cooled his. heels in Pennsylvania, where he had occupied his time—such time as he could spare from the composition of voluminous dispatches—in industrious but futile intrigues and in courting the Federalists. This cannot have improved either his temper or his standing in Republican circles.[10]

At any rate, his first encounter with Adams gave him little comfort. It must be admitted that to the task of postponing the inevitable he brought a well-developed command of all the arts of officially sticking in the mud. In this respect he was by no means a contemptible opponent. As for the borderlands he, or his superiors in Madrid, relied upon an immense treatise, composed by two priests between the years 1805 and 1812, from which it was possible to claim (1) that the United States had no right to any territory east or west of the Mississippi delta, or (2) that she could in no case go farther west than the Sabine River.[11] Onís' instructions from his chief, José García de Leon y Pizarro, permitted him, at the very most, to offer the United States

---

[10] Brooks, *Borderlands*, 17; J. Fred Rippy, *Rivalry of the United States and Great Britain over Latin America, 1808–1830* (Baltimore, 1929), pp. 252–253; Richardson, *Messages and Papers*, I, 488–489, for Madison's Special Message of January 10, 1811, which is highly critical of Onís.

[11] *A Treatise on the Limits of Louisiana and Texas*, ed. and trans. Charles W. Hackford (Austin, 4 vols., 1931–47), esp. I, ix–xx. This had been written by Father Melchior de Talamantes (until his arrest for complicity in a revolutionary plot) and after him by Father José Antonio Pichardo. It had attained a peculiar sanctity in Spanish eyes, less perhaps from its priestly origin than from the fact that it amounted to nearly a million words. Brooks, *Borderlands*, pp. 81–85.

a border at the Red (or Colorado) River of Natchitoches. After many discussions, he had found himself able to offer Mr. Adams a southwest border between the Mermentau and Calcasieu Rivers in the middle of the State of Louisiana! When Mr. Adams countered this with the quite modest proposal of the Colorado River of Texas, Onís answered in his most lapidary manner that "truth is of all times, and reason and justice are founded upon immutable principles. It is on these principles that the rights of the Crown of Spain are founded to the territories eastward and westward of Louisiana." And he added that by the Colorado River of Texas he assumed Mr. Adams to mean the Colorado River of Natchitoches. The reply was crushing. Adams said that by the Colorado River of Texas he meant, strange to say, the Colorado River of Texas. "The observation," he continued, "that truth is of all times and that reason and justice are founded upon immutable principles has never been contested by the United States, but neither truth, reason, nor justice consists in stubbornness of assertion, nor in the multiplied repetition of error." As far as prose could do it, Onís had been annihilated; and yet he still stood like a rock—or was it a fossil?—firmly implanted between the Mermentau and Calcasieu Rivers in the middle of the State of Louisiana.[12]

Measures for dislodging him had already been taken. On December 26, 1817, General Andrew Jackson, then commanding the Southern Division, was requested to proceed to Fort Scott and assume command of an expedition which involved the chastisement of certain Seminole Indians, who lived across the border in Spanish Florida. Now it was well known to everyone that General Jackson was filled with nationalism of the frontier, with its fierce hatred of Indians and of Spaniards. And Jackson himself was, at the time, in very good relations with the new administration: Ever since 1815, he had been on confidential

[12] Adams to Onís, January 16, 1818, *American State Papers, Foreign Relations,* IV, 450. Adams' offer was the Colorado of Texas to its source, and thence to the northern limits of Louisiana, which, though unfixed, were then considered to be the watershed of the Mississippi-Missouri system west of the Lake of the Woods; the reader will readily see that Adams at this juncture was not thinking transcontinentally. Such a line, while preserving Louisiana intact, would have kept the United States forever on the eastern side of the Rockies. If Onís perceived this, and he was presumably sensitive to Spanish claims on the Pacific, he failed to take advantage of it. A strict regard for his instructions, of course, would not have permitted him to do so. Onís to Adams, January 24, 1818, *ibid.,* IV, 464–467; Adams to Onís, March 12, 1818; *ibid.,* p. 480.

terms with James Monroe. It is true that this relationship had been threatened when Jackson, in an agitated correspondence with the Assistant Secretary of War, President Monroe, and Mr. Secretary Calhoun, had insisted that he was the sole channel through which the commands of the War Department might be transmitted to his subordinates. But the difficulty had been smoothed over, and, although the administration must have realized that the military virtues of the Southern general did not include a nice respect for authority, Jackson was restored to favor. But was it because of his nationalism, or in spite of it, that he had been intrusted with the delicate task of a Seminole campaign in Spanish territory?

At this moment in his extraordinary career, General Jackson was the Military Hero, still poised in the minds of his countrymen above the mud rampart of the Rodrigues Canal: behind that victory of New Orleans, which had shown him at his soldierly best, as a man of dauntless courage and fierce intractable spirit, there lay a military experience of remarkable brevity and no overwhelming importance. He was an activist, a nationalist, a leader of men—so much could be said of him in his public capacity; but what of his private one? Here, it must be admitted, few people outside the State of Tennessee knew much about the details of his civilian life. He had been a horse coper, a lawyer, a politician, a judge, an enterpriser—by these rungs he had climbed to the position of slaveholder and country gentleman. It was the typical progression of the frontier *arriviste;* and Jackson had been saved from a rather stultifying predicament—the predicament of an *arriviste* who has arrived—by the fact that he had military ambitions. It was as a major general of militia that he had been plunged into the vortex of history, transformed into a major general of regulars, and given a national status as the victor of New Orleans. For the rest, one would have not gone far wrong in calling him one of the more conservative figures in middle Tennessee, at least in his politics. Personally he was a man of passionate loyalties and hatreds, the kindest of husbands, the most merciless of duelists—all tenderness on the one hand, all savagery on the other, imaginative, impulsive, convinced that he was always right: in short, if he was a political and economic conservative, he wore his conservatism with a difference.[13]

---

[13] T. P. Abernethy's article on Jackson in *Dictionary of American Biography,* IX, 526 ff., exposing Jackson's conservatism, has been disputed by Arthur M.

In 1818, Jackson had already begun to resemble the Jackson of presidential history: the long narrow face, scored by pain and passion; the crown of stiff gray hair; the small fierce blue eyes; the arrogant bony nose, firm chin, and generous mouth; the emaciated body. Although his manners, when he chose to use them, were those of a high, fine gentleman, his physical appearance was distinctly alarming and seemed to match his character, or what was known of his character. Was it likely that such a man, let loose upon the Seminoles and the Spaniards, would allow himself to be bridled by the abstractions of international law?

The Seminoles were members of a tribe called the Oconee, affiliated with the Creeks, but always on the outer edge of the Creek confederacy: the word "Seminole" is equivalent to "frontiersman." They may have come to Florida in 1750. They were increased, from time to time, by runaways from the Creek nation, and after the Creek War of 1813–14, with its invasion of the sacred grounds at the Battle of Horseshoe Bend, and its crowning affront of the Treaty of Fort Jackson, more Creeks went across the border and transformed themselves into Seminoles. They lived in villages of log and palmetto huts, surrounded by cleared fields of from two to twenty acres of land; and from their custom (which was distinctly Creek) of circulating red war clubs among these villages as a preliminary to going to war, were sometimes known as "Red Sticks."[14]

Schlesinger, Jr., in *The Age of Jackson* (Boston, 1945), p. 43 n., chiefly on the grounds that "no amount of inference based on what Jackson was like before 1828 can be a substitute for the facts after 1828." This does not, of course, invalidate what Abernethy has to say about Jackson *before 1828*. Richard Hofstadter, *The American Political Tradition* (New York, 1948), p. 48, qualifies Abernethy's position moderately and judiciously when he says: "A man like Jackson who had been on the conservative side of economic issues in Tennessee could become the leader of a national democratic movement without feeling guilty of any inconsistency. . . . He became the favorite of the people and might easily come to believe that the people chose well." Charles G. Sellers, Jr., "Banking and Politics in Jackson's Tennessee, 1817–1827," *Mississippi Valley Historical Review*, XLI (1954), 61–84, argues that Jackson's opposition to bank reform was motivated by a distrust of *all* banks, which makes him a conservative in orthodox Jeffersonian terms, and not an opponent of popular reform *per se*. Jackson's military experience previous to the battle of New Orleans had been crowded into a space of only fourteen months: for its relative insignificance in terms of military success, see especially R. S. Cotterill, *The Southern Indians* (Norman, 1954), pp. 186 ff.

[14] John R. Swanton, "Early History of the Creek Indians and Their Neigh-

The Red Sticks were naturally on bad terms with the inhabitants of lower Georgia, as was the Spanish Empire in that region, since it offered a convenient asylum for escaped slaves. Nor had the War of 1812, in which Spain was a tacit ally of Great Britain, exactly soothed the ill-tempered nationalism of the frontier. When trouble broke out early in 1817, it would be hard to say who was responsible, for the American frontiersman was adept in all the arts of savage intercourse, such as lifting scalps and cattle; and when the Seminoles, in September 1817, observed that the Americans had slain ten warriors and owed them three—in other words, that they themselves had committed seven murders—their accounting may have been correct.[15]

In November, Brevet Major General Edmund P. Gaines, commanding in Georgia, made an effort to bring the Seminole chiefs and warriors into Fort Scott for a conference; this invitation was, understandably, declined; the Seminole border village of Fowltown was burned in retaliation; and the Seminoles thereupon ambushed an American hospital ship as it crawled the Apalachicola, killing thirty-four soldiers, seven women, and four children, and (it was generally believed) torturing the commander to death.[16] This horrid transaction, which took place on November 30, could be used to show what little control Spain exercised over the Seminoles within her borders; but already, on December 16, before the news could have reached Washington, Gaines had been sent orders to cross the Spanish line if necessary and hunt the Seminoles down *"unless they should shelter under Spanish post."* A copy of these orders was, of course, sent to General Jackson for his information: by way of acknowledgment he wrote an extraordinary letter, in confidence, to President Monroe in which he urged that the

bors," Bureau of American Ethnology, *Bulletin 73* (Washington, 1922), pp. 398 ff.; Jedediah Morse, *A Report to The Secretary of War, on Indian Affairs, Comprising A Narrative of a Tour Performed in the Summer of 1822* (New Haven, 1822), p. 311; *American State Papers, Indian Affairs,* I, 837 ff.; Charles J. Kappler, *Indian Affairs, Laws and Treaties* (Washington, 3 vols., 1892–1913), II, 108–109; Cotterill, *Southern Indians,* pp. 188–189.

[15] General D. Mitchell, governor of Georgia in 1817, said that the first outrage committed after the Treaty of Fort Jackson was by white banditti--"a set of lawless and abandoned characters." James Parton, *Life of Andrew Jackson* (3 vols., Boston, 1859–85), II, 409. He repeats this in a letter to the Secretary of War, February 24, 1817, *American State Papers, Indian Affairs,* I, 156. For the Seminoles' claim of seven murders against ten, see Major General E. P. Gaines to the Secretary of War, October 1, 1817, *ibid.,* I, 159.

[16] *American State Papers, Military Affairs,* I, 687.

"whole of East Florida be seized and held as indemnity for the outrages of Spain upon the property of our Citizens. . . . Let it be signified to me through any channel (say Mr. J. Rhea [a member of Congress from Tennessee]) that the possession of the Floridas would be desirable to the United States, and in sixty days it will be accomplished." Whether Monroe did read this letter or whether (being then on his sickbed) he merely handed it to Calhoun to read is a question which did not arise until some years later. It is at any rate certain that the letter was read by Calhoun, and that nothing in the way of admonishment was sent in reply.

While this letter of January 6 was traveling north, it was crossed by another set of orders, dated December 26 and traveling south, in which the Florida expedition was transferred from Gaines to Jackson. On December 26, therefore, the boldness of Jackson's views (though it could have been surmised) was not actually known in Washington: it was assumed that he would be bound by Gaines's instructions regarding the Spanish posts; and, on this assumption, Calhoun permitted himself some rather broad language. "Adopt the necessary measures," he wrote, "to terminate . . . the conflicts." By the same post there came a note from Monroe: "The movement against the Seminoles . . . will bring you on a theatre where you may possibly have other services to perform. . . . Great interests are at issue." This was written on December 28; and although the language was vague, it was nothing if not inflammatory.[17]

As for Jackson, his motives might be described as a simple application of frontier logic to nationalist premises. On the one hand, Spanish Florida was a threat to the Mississippi Valley. On the other hand, there were the speculations of Jackson's friends and relatives in Florida

[17] Calhoun to Gaines, December 16, 1817, *American State Papers, Military Affairs*, I, 689. In his letter of January 6, Jackson also said that the order to Gaines, requiring him to halt if the Seminoles took refuge in a Spanish fort, might result in "defeat and massacre," Jackson to Monroe, January 6, 1818; *Correspondence*, II, 345; Calhoun to Jackson, December 26, 1817; *American State Papers, Military Affairs*, I, 690; Monroe to Jackson, December 28, 1817, cited in James, *Jackson*, p. 307. In his letter to Calhoun of January 12, 1818, *Correspondence*, II, 347, Jackson makes no mention of his scheme to reduce East Florida: that was reserved for the eye of the President, and Monroe's note of December 28 can hardly have quieted Jackson's hope for some special understanding between the Commander in Chief and himself. Wiltse, *Calhoun: Nationalist*, p. 156.

lands;[18] the fact that the Seminoles had never agreed to that gigantic land grab, the Treaty of Fort Jackson; a sympathy with the slave-holders of Georgia; and a suspicion that Spaniards and British were encouraging the Seminoles in their resistance. The logic was mixed, but to a mind like Jackson's it was unanswerable. The General seemed to regard himself as an extragovernmental force, a special spirit, un-accountable to anyone or anything but the nation and the frontier. All he needed was a letter from Mr. Rhea, a member of Congress from Tennessee; and a letter, indeed, he did receive; it seemed to convey some kind of approval, on some undefined topic, from President Monroe; but since it was written on January 12, it could not conceiv-ably have been an answer to his missive of January 6.[19]

In the meantime, Mr. Adams stood firmly upon the Colorado River of Texas, Mr. Onís was no less firmly planted between the rivers Mer-mentau and Calcasieu; only Andrew Jackson, it seems, could move them from their respective positions.

What faced Jackson, when he received his orders to undertake the Seminole campaign, was something which demanded neither strategic imagination nor tactical skill: all, indeed rather more than all, that was required was relentless pursuit, unmitigated self-confidence, in-flexible purpose—and of these Jackson was supremely capable. General Gaines, who remained to assist in the action, having advanced too far to contemplate a withdrawal to Amelia Island, could certainly have chastised the Seminoles: dispirited and outnumbered, they never put up a fight. But General Gaines, although a brave and vigorous man, was also the kind of officer who believed in a literal obedience to his orders; he had none of Jackson's disposition to read between the lines. Left to himself, Gaines would never have come to the conclusion that the Spaniard and not the Seminole was his real objective.

The details of Jackson's irruption into Spanish Florida are too famous to need more than a summary relation. When he reached Fort Scott (on the Florida border) on March 6, he was in command of some two thousand troops, and his most intractable opposition con-sisted no longer of Seminoles or Spaniards but of starvation, sickness, swamps, and foul weather. Plunging across the border, he at length got in touch with Captain McKeever of the Navy with his gunboats and

---

[18] James, *Jackson*, pp. 300–301.
[19] Rhea to Jackson, January 12, 1818; Jackson, *Correspondence*, II, 348.

provisions. He was now assured of protection on his right flank as he advanced toward St. Marks, and around St. Marks his mind, as it revolved the immediate future in that steamy wilderness, was already spinning a somewhat coarse imperialist web. "The Spanish government," he informed the Secretary of War, "is bound by treaty to keep the Indians at peace with us. They have acknowledged their incompetency to do this and are consequently bound, by the laws of nations, to yield us the facilities to reduce them. Under this consideration, should I be able, I shall take possession of the garrison as a depot for my supplies, should it be found in the hands of the Spaniards, they having supplied the Indians; but if in the hands of the Indians, I will possess it, for the benefit of the United States, as a necessary position for me to hold, to give peace and security to this frontier." With these words the Seminole campaign became inextricably interwoven with a plan to seize the Floridas.[20]

On April 6 Jackson came within sight of the Spanish fort of St. Marks: he had now been reinforced by a party of friendly Creeks and a detachment of Tennessee volunteers. The helpless Spanish commandant and his garrison were furnished with transport to Pensacola; the Spanish flag was lowered; the Stars and Stripes floated in its place. "My love," wrote General Jackson to his wife, "I entered the Town of St. Marks on yesterday. . . . I found in St. Marks the noted Scotch villain Arbuthnot. . . . I hold him for trial."[21] Arbuthnot was a kindly old gentleman from the Bahamas, who had earned the enmity of the dominant firm of Forbes & Co. by trading fairly with the Indians in Florida. Forbes & Co., who never dreamed of tempering their injustice with mercy, and who regarded fair dealing as a form of criminal negligence, had already noised it abroad that Arbuthnot was a paid agitator; and Arbuthnot had given some faint color to this accusation by writing, at the Indians' request, a series of letters to British, Spanish, and American officials, in which he argued that the Treaty of Fort Jackson was not in accord with the Treaty of Ghent.[22]

While Jackson thus secured this "noted villain," Captain McKeever,

[20] Jackson to Calhoun, February 26, March 25, 1818, *American State Papers, Military Affairs*, I, 698; Parton, *Jackson*, II, 443.

[21] James, *Jackson*, p. 311; *American State Papers, Military Affairs*, I, 700.

[22] The gist of this correspondence will be found in *American State Papers, Military Affairs*, I, 682, 723–726, 729.

by the ingenious but rather shady device of flying a British flag, had tempted aboard his ship the Seminole prophet Francis, who entertained an innocent faith in the ubiquity of the British Empire. With him was another Seminole dignitary, "a savage-looking man . . . taciturn and morose," whose name was Chief Homollimico.[23]

Jackson hanged the prophet and his companion on April 8, presumably on general principles, and then, on April 9, plunged with his army into a gloomy uncharted, indefinite forest, dismally rooted in swamps and quagmires. His objective was the village of a famous chief named Boleck, some 109 miles to the southwest, on the banks of the mysterious Suwannee. At sunset on April 18, the hungry, desperate soldiers rushed upon the village, but it was almost empty; warned in advance, Chief Boleck, his warriors, his women, and the ex-slaves who had entered his service had slipped across the river. That night, as the army lay encamped, there stumbled into the arms of one of its pickets a certain Lieutenant Robert C. Ambrister, late of the British Royal Colonial Marines, with two Negro attendants, upon one of whom was discovered certain documentary evidence, presumably connecting Arbuthnot with the escape of Boleck. Jackson made the return march to St. Marks in five days. He was now of the opinion that "the Indians are divided and scattered, and cut off from all communication with those unprincipled agents of foreign nations who have deluded them to their ruin."[24]

The further discovery of suspicious documents on Arbuthnot's schooner, when it was seized at the mouth of the Suwannee, convinced Jackson that he had captured the foreign agents who were (he was sure) at the bottom of the Seminole disturbances.[25] There was no doubt that Arbuthnot had sent a letter warning Chief Boleck of the approach of Jackson's army, and begging him not to resist but to fly. A special court was convened at St. Marks, composed of fourteen officers, on April 26; and before this court Arbuthnot and Ambrister were tried for their lives. Arbuthnot, who pleaded not guilty, was condemned to be hanged for inciting the Indians to war, and for acting as a spy;

[23] Parton, *Jackson*, II, 458.
[24] *American State Papers, Military Affairs*, I, 700–701; Parton, *Jackson*, II, 462, quoting from the MS. Journal of J. B. Rodgers of the Tennessee Volunteers.
[25] *American State Papers, Military Affairs*, I, 702.

while upon Ambrister, who pleaded "guilty with justification" to the charges of aiding and comforting the enemy and of levying war against the United States, was passed the verdict of death by shooting. After reconsideration, this was changed to a penalty of fifty lashes and one year's imprisonment. The trial ended on April 28; and on April 29, Jackson approved the sentence of Arbuthnot, and the finding and first sentence on Ambrister, but disapproved the reconsideration. The sentences were carried out that same morning.[26]

Jackson's sense of justice was, to say the least, draconic, but, according to his lights, he had behaved correctly. On the other hand, the fact that two British subjects had been condemned to death by an American military court in a Spanish town presents the historian with some difficulties, which may perhaps be dismissed as insoluble. Jackson himself, quite innocent of any knowledge of international law, proceeded with an unperturbed conscience in the direction of Fort Gadsden. Having arrived there he was, for once, undecided. Should he go home, or should he not? Across the border, in the exiguous Spanish province of West Florida, lay the shabby little town of Pensacola; and in Pensacola, which served him as a capital, was Governor Don José Masot. Jackson was coming to the conclusion that Masot had been responsible for certain Indian atrocities in the Territory of Alabama; but here he was unjust to the Governor, whose commerce had been entirely with pirates and slave traders. In any case, Jackson had carried Pensacola by assault in the War of 1812, and the temptation to do so again was altogether too much for him.[27] On May 5 he wrote to Calhoun to say that such a measure—"adopted in pursuance of your instructions"— would be certain to meet with the President's approbation.[28]

The result was that, on May 24, Jackson had occupied St. Michael's

[26] Arbuthnot to J. Arbuthnot, April 2, 1818, *American State Papers, Military Affairs*, I, 722; James, *Jackson*, 313. For the belief that Ambrister was plotting with Gregor McGregor, the Venezuelan patriot, to make an invasion of Tampa Bay, see Brooks, *Borderlands*, p. 94, and Davis T. Fredrick, "McGregor's Invasion of Florida," Florida Historical Society *Quarterly*, VII, 4–5. For the trial, see *American State Papers, Military Affairs*, I, 721–734.

[27] On April 20, 1818, Jackson wrote to his wife to the effect that he would merely disperse "a few red sticks" west of the Apalachicola, and then return home. On the same day, he wrote to the same effect to Calhoun, but added rather ominously that Governor Masot was feeding and supplying these Indians. *Correspondence*, II, 360, 362.

[28] Jackson to Calhoun, May 5, 1818; *American State Papers, Military Affairs*, I, 702.

Fort, overlooking Pensacola, while Masot had fled to the fortress of Barancas, commanding the harbor, some six miles away. He was prepared, he said, to defend himself "to the last extremity." On May 28, Jackson was outside Barancas with one nine-pound piece and eight howitzers; and, after a sharp exchange of fire Masot, his honor satisfied, hoisted the white flag. On May 29, Jackson seized the royal archives, appointed Colonel King of the Fourth Infantry to the post of civil and military governor of Pensacola, and announced that the revenue laws of the United States were now in force in West Florida.[29] After this there was nothing more to do but return home, and at home—he had, after all, conducted his campaign with great speed and *élan*—he was received at first with the utmost enthusiasm.

The news of the storming of Pensacola reached Washington with unusual speed and was known to the President as early as June 18. On June 24, Onís was writing to the Secretary of State—who, being quite in the dark, could make no answer—to demand an explicit account of Jackson's proceedings. On June 26, Monroe discreetly vanished in the direction of his Virginia home. On July 8, both Onís and the French Minister, the Baron Hyde de Neuville, had had an interview with Adams, who told them that Jackson's dispatches had just arrived, but that nothing could be done until the President had read them. But Adams, who by now was quite aware of the advantages to be derived from Jackson's invasion, warned de Neuville that the President would probably support his general.[30]

[29] Jackson and Masot had already corresponded regarding the American navigation of the Apalachicola and Escambia Rivers. Jackson to Masot, March 25, 1818; *American State Papers, Foreign Relations*, IV, 562; Masot to Jackson, April 16, 1818; *American State Papers, Military Affairs*, I, 706 (also in *American State Papers, Foreign Relations*, IV, 506, with some verbal alterations and dated April 15). Masot to Jackson, May 23, 1818, demands that he retire from West Florida; and Jackson to Masot, April 27, 1818, attempts to implicate Masot in the massacre on the Apalachicola of November 30, 1817. *American State Papers, Military Affairs*, I, 709, 712; Masot to Jackson, May 24, 1818; Jackson to Masot, May 25, 1818; *ibid.*, I, 712–13; *Correspondence*, II, 374, for Jackson's proclamation of May 29. The army with which he assaulted Pensacola numbered 1,092 officers and men; *American State Papers, Military Affairs*, I, 718. Jackson told Monroe on June 18 that his men were "literanny [*sic*] barefoot" from continued wading in the water; *Correspondence*, II, 738. Parton, *Jackson*, II, 503, says that Captain McKeever had also landed two guns.

[30] Adams, *Memoirs*, IV, 102. Onís to Adams, June 24, 1818; *American State Papers, Foreign Relations*, IV, 495–496. Adams, *Memoirs*, IV, 104, says of Monroe's departure that "though the moment is critical and a storm is rapidly

Here he spoke only for himself. When the Cabinet met on July 15, and for four meetings thereafter, it appeared that everyone but Mr. Adams was in favor of disavowing General Jackson. Such were the preliminaries to one of the greatest diplomatic feats in American history. They were, if not exactly ungrateful, certainly cautious and formal.[31]

As an ardent nationalist, Calhoun, in particular, could hardly in private have disapproved of Jackson's deeds. As Secretary for War, however, he permitted himself to be astounded by the capture of Pensacola because it defied his orders not to pursue the Indians "should they take refuge under a Spanish fort." This thinking enabled him, on the one hand, to demand a court-martial for Jackson and even to suggest that his real motive had been a speculation in Florida lands, and, on the other, to inform a man as close to Jackson as Captain Gadsden that he detested his colleagues' willingness to sacrifice their "best friend" to their own interests.[32] The hint to Gadsden was, no doubt, aimed at William H. Crawford.

Crawford wished to disgrace Jackson because he believed that such a move would discredit Monroe: his reasoning was political, his eye was always on the succession, and the press most fierce in its denunciations was the Crawford press.[33] His ostensible reasons, however, were

---

thickening, he had not read many of the papers I left with him, and he puts off everything to a future time." This seems a trifle disingenuous, since the storm was in Adams' favor. Monroe, more sensible, remarked that he was waiting until he could avail himself "of the aid of the heads of departments"; Monroe to James Madison, July 10, 1818, *Writings,* VI, 55. For the interviews with Onís and de Neuville, see Adams, *Memoirs,* IV, 105.

[31] It should be remembered that a constitutional authority for seizing the Floridas could, by stretching the point a little, be found in the No-Transfer Resolution of January 15, 1811: it read, in part, "that a due regard for their own safety compels them [the United States] to provide under certain contingencies for the temporary occupation of the said territory; they, at the same time, declare that the said territory shall, *in their hands,* remain subject to a future negotiation." Only a very strong Executive, very sure of its hold on Congress and the people, would, however, have ventured to take such a step.

[32] Adams, *Memoirs,* IV, 109; Bemis, *John Quincy Adams,* p. 315; *American Historical Association, Annual Report* (1899), pp. 285–287; Calhoun to Charles Tait, July 20, 1818, in Wiltse, *Calhoun: Nationalist,* p. 417, n. 13; Gadsden to Jackson, September 18, 1818, in James, *Jackson,* 319, n. 18.

[33] John W. Ward, *Andrew Jackson: Symbol for an Age* (New York, 1955), pp. 60–63, gives a succinct account of these newspaper maneuvers. Crawford

that he feared a war with Spain, and the consequent destruction of trade and depletion of revenue.[34] Nobody answered that Spain was in no position to make a war: the only reply—it came from Adams—was that if a war broke out "in this, as in all other cases, the event must rest with the Disposer of Events."[35]

Monroe was always slow to make decisions, but could always be counted upon to accept the most forcible argument. At first, he took the view that there might be justifying circumstances but that Jackson had not made out his case; or, as Adams put it, "the fear of charges of usurpation, of duplicity, and of war, operated [in him] to such a degree that there is no vigor to bear out the bold energy of Jackson."[36] So far the picture is one of a weak and disunited Executive, uncertain of its constitutional powers, its popular support, or its own internal loyalties; and although the picture is largely the work of John Quincy Adams, there is no evidence to dispute it.

Adams himself was in a fortunate position. As he afterward told his father: "There was no other member of the Administration who had less or even so little concern with General Jackson's acts, or agency over them, until long after they were past and irretrievable. The orders by which he was authorized to enter Spanish Florida had issued from the War Department, without my being consulted, and without my knowledge. His correspondence was entirely with that department."[37] From the very beginning he proposed that Jackson should be justified on the grounds that he had acted defensively, not against the Spanish government, but against its officers. On July 21, he won the President over. It was agreed that the Attorney General should write a letter to the *National Intelligencer,* designed to satisfy all shades of opinion, and that Adams should tell Onís that the forts would be given up, but that Jackson, though acting on his own responsibility, would not be censured for having captured them.[38]

also let it be known in Jacksonian circles that Calhoun had been in favor of an investigation of Jackson, as appears in John Williams to Van Buren, March 22, 1831; Van Buren Papers, LC.

[34] Adams, *Memoirs,* IV, 110.

[35] *Idem.*

[36] *Ibid.,* p. 109.

[37] J. Q. A. to John Adams, February 14, 1819; Adams, *Writings,* VI, 530.

[38] Adams, *Memoirs,* IV, 111, 115, where Adams describes this as, at best, a

Monroe had now returned to the position which he had held in 1817: he was prepared to put pressure on Spain, and would relax it only if he encountered great opposition from European powers.[39] The extremely delicate question of Arbuthnot and Ambrister had not been discussed in the Cabinet, but nobody knew what position Great Britain would take on it. As for popular opinion, would it have upheld the administration if, by retaining the forts (as Adams had first suggested), it had virtually committed an act of war upon Spain? The strongest newspaper support for Jackson only supported him because he had inflicted vengeance upon lawless Indians and Englishmen.[40] In the eyes of America, the General was always a martial rather than a militarist figure: that distinction, and it is a very great one, should always be borne in mind.

The President, however, once he had come over to Adams' side, gave his Secretary of State a very respectable and quite essential measure of support. Once he had made a decision, it was not Monroe's

---

partial disavowal; Adams to Onís, July 23, 1818; *American State Papers, Foreign Relations*, IV, 497. Adams was in much the same position as he had been at Ghent during the treaty negotiations, when he had pressed for a thorough airing of American actions in Florida. He was not then, or thereafter, privy to the Florida intrigues in Madison's Cabinet; and, in 1818, he knew nothing about Monroe's and Calhoun's correspondence with Jackson.

[39] Monroe to J. Q. A., September, 1817, cited in Bemis, *John Quincy Adams*, 306. In the end, one finds Monroe telling James Madison, February 17, 1819: "On the receipt of Genl. Jackson's report of his proceedings there we had three great objects in view, first to secure the constitution from any breach, second to deprive Spain and the allies of any just cause of war, and third to turn it to the best account of the country"; Monroe, *Writings*, VI, 87–88. This whole letter describes his position before it. At one time, in his distress, Monroe had even suggested to Jackson, July 19, 1818, that his dispatches should be rewritten. *Ibid.*, VI, 54–61.

[40] The Nashville *Whig and Tennessee Advertiser*, May 30, 1818, for example, said: "Let our eastern friends look to the situation of the frontier in the western country. . . . In such a situation what would be his feelings; would he go to some learned treatise on national law and enquire what was right to propose to be done; or would he complain of a general who would afterwards inflict the heaviest vengeance upon such lawless offenders?" Another pertinent comment comes from an old gentleman of Poughkeepsie, New York—James Tallmadge, Sr., to James Tallmadge, Jr., January 7, 1819—"As to polecy, I think it is on the generals side as it will strike a terrow on the Indians and Negros and all the unprincipled scampering traders that harbour about in them regons," Tallmadge Papers, NYHS. Here again the General is seen as acting defensively.

habit to retreat from it. In the events that followed, the two marched together, with Adams just a little in the lead.

The invasion of Florida became a new and most important *impulse* in the negotiations which were now resumed between Onís and Adams. Onís was in a truly dangerous predicament. He could and he did ask for a suitable indemnity for the "outrage," and for "lawful" punishment of General Jackson: that was an empty but indispensable formality.[41] He could not have foreseen that the Spanish Foreign Minister, Pizarro, on receiving the news of Pensacola, would instruct him to offer very large concessions.[42] If he had done so, it would have given him little comfort. Concessions no doubt he would have to make; it would be no more than his duty, if he were to draw an adequate boundary on the southwest; yet he served a monarch who was apt to reward the performance of duty, not with thanks, not with honors, but with exile to some forbidding monastery or bleak and isolated town. Ferdinand VII was in every respect a monstrous personage. His first wife, on being presented to him, said that she truly believed she had lost her senses.[43] A short, thick body, a traplike mouth, an immense, jutting chin: these were the most prominent physical features of Ferdinand the Well-Beloved. In imprisonment, he had cultivated all the more futile and terrifying resources of a feeble mind: superstition, vengeance, fear. On his return to the throne, he had been greeted with immense enthusiasm, as if he had been some hideous but beneficent idol; he responded to this greeting by depriving his subjects of such constitutional liberties as they had been granted in his absence. He surrounded himself with "ignorant and stupid *nigauds* [boobies]"— so Onís admitted in a moment of exasperation: his most influential counselors were a former chocolate seller of Cadiz called Juan Esteban Lozano de Torres, and a horsy patrician named the Duke of Alagon. Of these gentlemen, it has been asserted with some confidence that they did not even know where the Floridas were. A third counselor was the Russian envoy, Dmitri Pavlovich Tatischev, a mischievous

---

[41] Onís to Adams, June 9, 17, July 8, 1818; *American State Papers, Foreign Relations,* IV, 494–97.

[42] Pizarro to Onís, August 30, 1818; Brooks, *Borderlands,* p. 167 n.

[43] William W. Kaufmann, *British Policy and The Independence of Latin America, 1804–1828* (New Haven, 1951), p. 77.

but talented intriguer.[44] Pizarro himself was honest and incorruptible, but his day was almost over. When he received the news of Pensacola, he wrote a long and angry note to George W. Erving, the American Minister, suspending all negotiations with him until the General had been punished, the fort restored, and a suitable indemnity paid. But at the same time, he had been obliged to send instructions to Onís, permitting him to move (if necessary) to the Colorado River of Texas as a western boundary. For this performance of an unpleasant, a painful duty—but a duty nonetheless—he was sent into exile on September 14.[45]

Such was the uncertain background against which Onís was working in July. In his attitude toward the territorial sanctity of the Spanish Empire, he was distinctly out of date; but it is small wonder that he should have regarded any concession, however necessary, as dangerous to his own career. On July 11 and July 16, however, he had two momentous discussions with Adams, at the end of which he was obliged to report to Pizarro that he could see no alternative except to make the best settlement possible. On July 11, Adams told him that he still insisted upon the Colorado River of Texas as his western boundary, but was prepared to draw a line from the source of the Colorado to the source of the Missouri, and thence west to the Pacific. On July 13, Monroe returned to Washington. On July 16, Adams told Onís that he was prepared to move eastward to the Trinity River, take a line north from the Trinity to the Red River, follow the Red River to its source, cross to the Rio Grande, follow its course or the summit of a chain of mountains running parallel to it, and either stop there or take a line to the Pacific.[46]

It was this suggestion of a line to the Pacific, coming so hard upon the news of Jackson's invasion, which shook the resolve of Onís. To

[44] Adams, *Memoirs*, IV, 219. C. C. Griffin, *The United States and the Disruption of the Spanish Empire* (New York, 1937), p. 191. Brooks, *Borderlands*, p. 180, citing Henry Wellesley to Lord Castlereagh, F. O., 72/224.

[45] Griffin, *Disruption of the Spanish Empire*, pp. 171–175.

[46] Adams, *Memoirs*, IV, 106–107, 110. In his diary, Adams says of the meeting of July 11 only that he insisted upon the Colorado from source to mouth—i.e., that he was merely defining a southwestern boundary. Onís in his dispatch to Pizarro, No. 134, of July 18, says that it was on July 11 that Adams suggested the line to the source of the Missouri and so west; Bemis, *Adams and Foreign Policy*, pp. 318–319, adding—"We must, I think, accept the accuracy of these details from Onís's dispatch."

him, the whole Pacific coast as far as 56° north belonged by right to the King of Spain. If Adams made so extraordinary a demand as a line across the Rockies, then it was evident (so he told Pizarro) that the Americans were prepared to go to all lengths, including a recognition of the independence of Spain's revolting colonies. He was unable as yet to see that the American proposals contained at least as much hesitation as they did heroism. On July 11, Mr. Adams was still as far west as the Colorado River, but was willing to bring the Spanish American frontier as high as 45° 20' north, which was where he believed the source of the Missouri to be. On July 16, after Monroe's return, he was ready to retreat as far east as the Trinity, but was demanding a far more favorable line to the Pacific.

On July 16, Monroe was still prepared to disavow Jackson, and in the same mood he seemed ready to take the ominous step of abandoning Texas. He never had been and he never would be very interested in that region.[47] It is now known that as early as February he had instructed Adams to go, if necessary, as far east as the Trinity River for his western boundary, while at the same time, though at first favoring a joint commission to settle the matter, he had yielded to Adams' insistence that America should demand a line to the Pacific. Hitherto, Adams had been determined to cling to the Colorado, and we must assume that his eastward move to the Trinity was due to the anxious pressure of Monroe. But Monroe, at the same time, was ready to give up his preference for a joint commission, and to support his Secretary in going all the way to the Pacific. Such were the oscillations of the President's mind before the *fait accompli* of General Jackson; such were the linear consequences of the storming of Pensacola.

The line to the Pacific was something more than a superb generalization. It is true that all to the north of it, between the Rocky Mountains

[47] The following letter, Monroe to Albert Gallatin, May 26, 1820, should, in my opinion, be taken as the President's considered judgment: "So strong is the inclination, in some, to seize on Texas, particularly, that I should not be surprised, if we should be compelled to act, on that principle, & without a treaty, if that province, at least as well as Florida, should be taken possession of. Internal considerations . . . *are favorable to moderate pretensions on our part. With me they have much weight,* as I am persuaded they do with many others, but still so seducing is the passion for extending our territory that . . . it is quite uncertain within what limit it will be confined." Gallatin Papers, NYHS. The italics are mine. See also Monroe to Jefferson, May 1820, in Monroe, *Writings,* VI, 119–123.

and the coast, was presumably subject to negotiations with Great Britain, and that all to the south of it was Spanish. It is true that Adams, though he drew his lines with assurance, had no very exact idea of the territory over which they passed.[48] The map which he and Onís used, in those discussions of July 11 to July 16, was the latest (January 1, 1818) edition of John Melish's "Map of the United States and the Contiguous British and Spanish Possessions." This was a great piece of cartography, but one has to admit that it conveyed no true idea of where the mountains ended and the plains began, or of the sources of the principal rivers. All was uncertainty. And yet, when he drew his July 16 line to the Pacific, Adams was not indulging simply in some exhilarating abstraction. What he had in mind, surely, was the control of the Columbia River basin.

Unlike Jefferson, John Quincy Adams did not think of the Pacific Northwest as the seat of some future and separate American republic: he was nothing if not a continentalist. He was not dismayed by the common misconception (which of course he shared) that a waterless desert heaved itself between the Mississippi Valley and the Rocky Mountains. His object was first to deprive Spain of all claims to the Pacific Northwest; then to unseat the Russians and the British. The whole northwest coast was to come under the dominion of the United States, which would "form establishments there with views of absolute territorial right, and inland communication. . . ."[49]

As for the inland communication, would not the Columbia and the

---

[48] He called it "a wilderness, with unknown geography." *Memoirs,* IV, 235.

[49] Adams to Rush, July 22, 1823; Manning, *Diplomatic Correspondence,* II, 5. This represented his thinking all along. See *Memoirs,* IV, 438, 439 (November 16, 1819), where, in reply to Crawford, who said that the United States must be guarded and moderate in its expansionist policy, Adams asserted that the world must be familiarized with the idea "of considering our proper domain to be *the continent of North America. . . .* Spain had possession upon our southern and Great Britain upon our northern border. It was impossible that centuries should elapse *without finding them annexed to the United States. . . . The United States and North America are identical"* (italics inserted). Even Thomas Hart Benton, more an expansionist at this time than an agent for the fur trade, told the Senate in 1825 that Pacific coast, from the westward slope of the Rockies to the sea, would become in due time a separate American republic. The continental thinking of Adams was, if not unique, certainly nearly so. For Benton see Frederick Merk, *Albert Gallatin and the Oregon Problem* (Cambridge, 1950), p. 13; also *Register of Debates,* 18 Cong., 2 sess., pp. 713–717 (March 1, 1825).

Missouri Rivers form a channel between the Pacific and the Mississippi?[50] Thus, regardless of the difficulties of populating the so-called desert, Asiatic-American exchanges would flow between the mouth of the Columbia and the city of St. Louis.

It is clear, of course, that Spain herself could offer no opposition to this enticing dream, except in the limited sense of denying a line to the Pacific: she had never exercised any control over the mouth of the Columbia.[51] The British, who had equal access to the Oregon country, were the great opponents. But if the United States could draw a Spanish boundary line south of the Columbia River, it would come so much closer to its objective of urging the British out of the Columbia basin. Whether Monroe thought colonially (as Jefferson and Benton did, for example) or continentally (as Adams did) is not known; and it is irrelevant in the sense that in either case he would wish for a transcontinental line once the idea had been forcibly presented to him.

The negotiation between Adams and Onís was now conducted through an intermediary, Hyde de Neuville, the French Minister, for Onís, quite correctly, felt obliged to retire to Bristol until such time as the forts should be restored to Spain. De Neuville, according to Adams, was an odd mixture of "ultra royalism and republican liberality"—a walking compendium of the predicament in which his country found itself after the Restoration. He was a nobleman of moderate attainments and considerable vanity, flighty but not inconstant, honest, honorable, and on the whole conciliatory. His instructions and his predilections both warned him that England would profit from any breach between America and Spain.[52] All that summer, Onís clung obstinately to his line between the Calcasieu and the Mermentau Rivers. It was in

[50] Merk, *Gallatin and the Oregon Problem,* pp. 15–16.

[51] The idea of fortifying the mouth of the Columbia did occur to Onís in the spring of 1818; in July the Spanish War Office told the Viceroy of Mexico to put the place in a state of defense, "without giving the slightest motive of complaint to the United States"; and the Viceroy protested in December that he had exactly one brigantine, and that in a state of disrepair, with which to perform such a task! Brooks, *Borderlands,* p. 154.

[52] Duc de Richelieu to Count Fernan Nuñez, September 11, 1817, and Richelieu to de Neuville, September 1, 1818, in Brooks, *Borderlands,* pp. 125, 127, both say that de Neuville is to be a "conciliator"; and Bemis, *John Quincy Adams,* p. 320, shows that de Neuville feared a British intrusion into the Caribbean. Adams, *Memoirs,* IV, 303, remarks on de Neuville's detestation of the English, and gives an amusing but on the whole favorable character sketch.

vain that Monroe found himself able, on the one hand, to bring the boundary all the way to the Sabine while, on the other, he threatened the seizure of the Floridas, a claim to all of Texas, and war itself, if Onís did not move.[53] Onís was unshaken. On October 24, the forts having been restored to Spain, he reopened the direct negotiation with an offer which merely repeated all that was unacceptable in his previous demands. At this Monroe told his Secretary of State that the time had come either to bring Onís to the point or else to break with him, and Adams prepared and dispatched what he himself called an "ultimatum." His line began at the mouth of the Sabine and ended on the Pacific Ocean at 41° north.[54]

Left to himself, Adams might not have abandoned Texas in this way; and Onís, who had now received those instructions from Pizarro which permitted him to go west of the Sabine if necessary, was only too happy to accept what Adams offered. But the stubbornness of Onís' character, and the delicacy of his circumstances, did not permit him to give way easily; and he indulged in his usual procrastination until Adams said that he withdrew all offers, reserved all claims to the Rio Grande as the southwestern limit of Louisiana, and yet would be glad to discuss a treaty which fixed no western boundary.[55] A boundary in

[53] Monroe to Adams, August 10, 1818; Monroe Papers, LC.

[54] Onís to Adams, October 24, 1818; *American State Papers, Foreign Relations,* IV, 526–530. Onís offered a line between the Calcasieu and Mermentau Rivers, up to Arroyo Hondo, across the Red River at 32° north, thence north to the Missouri and up that river to its source. This offer, he told Madrid, was intended only to delay matters. Onís to Pizarro, October 31, 1818; Griffin, *Disruption of the Spanish Empire,* p. 181; Adams, *Memoirs,* IV, 144; Adams to Onís, October 31, 1818, *American State Papers, Foreign Relations,* IV, 530–531. Adams' line was as follows—the Sabine from its mouth to 32° north; then due north to the Red River, and up the Red River to its source. According to Melish's map, the source of the Red River was just beneath the Sangre de Cristo Mountains at 37° 25′ north and 106° 15′ due west. He then proposed to follow the Sangre de Cristo Mountains (or Snow Mountains, as he called them) as far north as 41° and "follow the parallel of the latitude to the South Sea." This offer, as Bemis points out, would have obtained for the United States the entire Columbia River—at any rate, it would have done so according to Melish's map; Bemis, *John Quincy Adams,* p. 324. Adams, *Memoirs,* IV, 275, says that this was the first time the offer to the Pacific was made in a written form.

[55] Onís to Adams, November 16, 1818, offering settlement by a commission; *American State Papers, Foreign Relations,* IV, 531–553. On November 17, Monroe's Second Annual Message, taking a strong line in defense of Jackson and

the southwest, however, as far east of the Rio Grande as possible, was precisely what Onís had to fix. The initiative had now passed to the United States, and at much the same time Pizarro's angry letter to Erving had reached the Secretary in Washington and had been discussed and answered.

Adams' famous instruction to Erving, in which he annihilated Pizarro's argument that Jackson should be dismissed and punished, was written between November 7 and November 28, and, although somewhat softened in Cabinet discussions, bears upon every line the imprint of the Secretary's genius. From beginning to end it adhered to the principle, if principle it be, that when one's position is morally a little doubtful it is better to attack than to defend. And so, while it cleared General Jackson of all blame, the chief targets for its skill and eloquence were the feebleness of the commandant of St. Marks, the futility of the governor of Pensacola, and the villainy of Mr. Arbuthnot and Lieutenant Ambrister. It proclaimed—one would scarcely say it proved—that Arbuthnot and Ambrister had been engaged "in a creeping and insidious war, both against Spain and the United States . . . to plunder Spain of her province, and to spread massacre and devastation along the borders of the United States." General Jackson, after all, had merely pursued "a defeated savage enemy beyond the Spanish Florida line." How innocent was this "necessary" pursuit when compared to Colonel Nicholls' "shameful invasion" of Florida during the War of 1812! And yet against this shameful invasion of Colonel Nicholls, "if a whisper of expostulation was ever wafted from Madrid to London it was not . . . energetic enough to transpire beyond the walls of the palaces from which it issued, and to which it was borne."[56]

This remarkable document, with its resounding eloquence, its reiterated and formidable invective, its feral arguments, was to be communicated in full to the Spanish government. One may assert, with perfect confidence, that it was by no means the sort of diplomatic correspondence to which they were accustomed. It is a classic among

distinctly hostile to the Spanish lack of control in Florida, was delivered to Congress; Richardson, *Messages and Papers,* II, 39–43. Adams replied to Onís, November 30, 1818; *American State Papers, Foreign Relations,* IV, 545.

[56] Adams to George W. Erving, November 28, 1818; *American State Papers, Foreign Relations,* IV, 539 ff. See also Adams, *Writings,* VI, 474 ff., esp. 502 n., for the comments of Christopher Gore and Jeremiah Mason.

American state papers; and if state papers were generally considered to be within the pale of literature, it would have been given a wider recognition long before this. And yet, after all, its powerful cudgeling of the Spanish government is not the most remarkable thing about it. The most remarkable, indeed the most obvious, thing about it is that its central challenge is a challenge to the British Empire.

The British Empire, however, or at any rate the London government, was singularly quiescent. The news of Pensacola had created a "sensation" in Paris and London, and the Spanish may have reached the conclusion that Great Britain would intervene in their favor.[57] But when the executions of Arbuthnot and Ambrister were known in London, and the "public anger," said Richard Rush, was "exceedingly strong against us . . . I have never known anything like it since I have been here"; when, as Lord Castlereagh afterward admitted, "such was the temper of parliament and such the feeling of the country, he believed WAR MIGHT HAVE BEEN PRODUCED BY HOLDING UP A FINGER"—nothing was done, the finger was not held up, and Rush was able to inform his colleague in Paris that "we shall have with [Lord Castlereagh] no difficulty: you may confide in what I say."[58] Indeed, as early as January 2, 1819, Castlereagh was writing to the British Minister in Paris that Arbuthnot and Ambrister had been "engaged in unauthorized practises of such a description as to have deprived them of any claim on their own Government."[59] And on February 12, he told Minister Rush that Great Britain did not feel bound to offer protection to such men as the two "who intermeddled with the Indians along your borders."[60]

For Lord Castlereagh, while distinctly European in his thinking,

[57] Albert Gallatin to Richard Rush, July 30, 1818. Gallatin had been convinced in March that Great Britain would try to prevent our acquisition of East Florida; Gallatin to Rush, March 13, 1818. Both in Rush Papers, NYHS.

[58] Richard Rush, *Memoranda of a Residence at the Court of London* (Philadelphia, 1845 ed.), p. 153. Of the words which he printed in capitals, he confessed, "I thought them memorable at the time. I think them so still." *Idem.* Rush to Gallatin, January 20, 1819; Gallatin Papers, NYHS.

[59] Castlereagh to Charles Bagot, January 2, 1819: P.R.O./F.O., 115/34, cited in Brooks, *Borderlands,* p. 117.

[60] John Adams Smith to J. Q. A., Private, No. 38, London, January 24, 1819; Alexander Everett to J. Q. A., Private, No. 2, Brussels, April 11, 1819, remarks on the quiescence of the British government under the rage of the London press. Adams MSS., cited in Bemis, *Adams and Foreign Policy,* p. 328; Rush, *Memoranda,* p. 159.

was not blind to the importance of the South American market, and had already hinted to Richard Rush that his views on South American affairs were near to the ideas of the United States rather than to those of Spain.[61] And there was another and more potent influence, which had been revealed by the War of 1812, during the curious involutions of the peace negotiations at Ghent: that influence was the economic dependence of England upon an untrammeled North American market. It was unlikely that the British Government, asked to antagonize this market by threatening war for the sake of Arbuthnot and Ambrister, would take so very altruistic a step. The two victims of Jackson were simply written off, a mere item, a necessary loss, in the balance sheet of Anglo-American exchanges. When Parliament opened in November 1819, and the Speech from the Throne remarked upon the depressed state of British manufactures, there followed many allusions to the connection between this state of affairs and the very similar one then existing in America. Mr. Rush noted that the Prince Regent's speech attributed British distress to the embarrassed situation in other countries, whereas the American newspapers blamed their country's depression "chiefly [upon] distress in England. Both [he concluded] were, to a certain extent, true: and what more can show the dependence of countries upon one another!"[62] It would be too much to say that Mr. Rush had, at this important moment, realized that Great Britain, with its backward and insensitive Tory government, was actually turning toward the doctrines of Adam Smith and the principles of free trade. Yet this was in truth the case; it had been gently announced by the quietism of the British government when confronted with the deeds of General Jackson and the denunciations of John Quincy Adams. A profound and fruitful change in Anglo-American relations was to be one of its consequences.

Two months before the Erving note was so much as written, the Marquis de Yrujo (Pizarro's successor) had already dispatched an instruction to Onís which showed how deep, how paralyzing an impression had been made by General Jackson. Yrujo was afraid that too great an obstinacy on the boundary question would produce, perhaps a recognition of the revolted Spanish colonies, perhaps an invasion of Mexico; and he told Onís that, if he could not obtain the Sabine, he

---

61 Rush to Gallatin, London, April 22, 1818; Gallatin Papers, NYHS.
62 Rush, *Memoranda*, p. 231.

was to make such arrangements as he could, and that a boundary along the Missouri to its source and thence to the Pacific as far north as possible would be preferable to any other. Thus the Spanish government had, for the first time, officially accepted a transcontinental line. These instructions reached Washington on January 4, 1819. On January 11, Onís informed Adams that he was ready to renew negotiations, and hinted—it was perhaps a little unnecessary—that he was now in a compromising mood.[63]

The hint, at any rate, came at an auspicious moment, for the United States was on the verge of ratifying the Anglo-American Convention of October 20, 1818. This Convention arose from the necessity of renewing, and the hope of improving, the commercial agreement which had been negotiated with Great Britain in July 1815—an agreement so very disagreeable that the American government had already retorted it upon the British with the Navigation Acts of 1817 and 1818.[64] Any retort of this kind was apt to make an impression upon British mercantilism, which was growing infirm; and if the British were as yet unprepared to make substantial changes in the agreement of 1815, they were singularly affable on certain other questions, which had been left undecided by the Treaty of Ghent. Among these was the problem of the Northwest Boundary, which was still hovering undecidedly upon the northwestern margins of the Lake of the Woods. It was now agreed that the boundary line should proceed along the line of 49° north all the way to the Rocky Mountains; and that, beyond that barrier, the whole North West Coast of America should be open, for a term of ten years, to the vessels, citizens, and subjects of both nations, without prejudice to the claims of either, or to those of any other state or power. Vague as this agreement seems to be, it preserved the Columbia River for the time being; and, merely as an agreement, it uttered a distinct warning to the Spaniards that the time had come for them to give way.[65]

---

[63] Brooks, *Borderlands,* p. 155.

[64] For the agreement of 1815, and the Navigation Acts of 1817 and 1818, see Chapter 5, pp. 148–150.

[65] For the administration's attitude toward the boundary question, see Adams' instructions to Albert Gallatin and Richard Rush, July 28, 1818, in Adams, *Writings,* VI, 399 ff. See also *American State Papers, Foreign Relations,* IV, 378–406; Rush, *Narrative of a Residence at the Court of London,* (London, 1833), pp. 306 ff.; Rush, "Notes on the Joint Negociation at London in 1818, from the Unofficial Journal of one of the Plenipotentiaries," Monroe Papers, LC.

In the meantime, on January 12, a somewhat loud but rather hollow debate had begun in the House of Representatives, where the combined forces of Mr. Speaker Clay and Mr. Secretary Crawford attempted to ruin General Jackson and weaken the administration. But it was all in vain: on February 8, four resolutions, designed to disgrace the General, were voted down by substantial majorities.[66] On January 30, 1819, the Anglo-American Convention was ratified; from that moment onward Onís' chief hope was to keep the boundary at a safe distance from Taos and Santa Fe. He had lost his fingerhold upon the Columbia River itself and, although the "ultimatum" of October 31, 1818, gave him Texas, he would (it appears) have yielded that province to a little extra pressure. But the spirit of Monroe's Cabinet was a compromising one, and Adams himself was more interested in keeping Spain out of the Columbia River basin than in forcing the Texas issue. Indeed, under pressure from his colleagues, he yielded to Onís so far as to withdraw from the 41st to the 42nd degree of north latitude for his line to the Pacific and from the 102nd to the 100th degree of west longitude for his line between the Red and the Arkansas. On February 16, nothing remained to be settled but Onís' demand that the boundary line should run up the middle of the rivers concerned. Monroe was all compliance; but Adams, weary of retreating, grimly insisted that Spain must content herself with the southern and western banks of the Arkansas, the Red, and the Sabine. Onís had diplomatic custom on his side, but then he had Texas as well; and on February 20, he consented. On February 22, the great Transcontinental Treaty was signed and sealed. On February 24, the Senate unanimously agreed to its ratification.[67]

Gallatin and Rush asked (in vain) for the line of 49° north all the way to the Pacific; the final agreement was more in accordance with Adams' instructions, since Adams believed that the British hoped to go south of 49°, west of the Rockies, while he himself wished to go north of it. The problem of sovereignty in this undetermined region, said Adams, "will certainly come upon us again, for which I ought to be prepared." *Memoirs,* V, 260.

[66] James F. Hopkins and Mary W. M. Hargreaves (eds.), *The Papers of Henry Clay* (Lexington, 1959–), II, 636–660; Clay, *Works,* Colton, ed., VI, 181 ff.; McMaster, *History,* IV, 451–456; Bassett, *Jackson,* I, 283; Parton, *Jackson,* II, 536. Jackson believed that Crawford and Clay were plotting to overthrow Monroe in 1820; Jackson to Gadsden, August 1, 1819. *Correspondence,* II, 241; Gadsden to Jackson, February 6, 1820, Jackson Papers, LC; James, *Jackson,* p. 322.

[67] These final stages in the negotiation may be traced in *American State*

The Transcontinental Treaty, even without Texas, was a triumph for the continentalism of John Quincy Adams. For months he and Onís had been disputing about rivers whose wanderings were erratically plotted and whose sources, indeed whose very existence, were sometimes a matter of sheer guesswork. They had argued about mountains which few men had ever seen and which stumbled across the map, like giants or legends, and in all the wrong places. The prairies which Onís sought to wrest from the United States were, to Adams, who protected them, nothing more than waterless and irreclaimable deserts. It was a battle where precision counted for little: a battle between two kinds of imagination and two orders of intellect. Onís was defending, as if it were very much alive, a moribund, revolted, and helpless empire; Adams, drawing his lines with less exactness than assurance, was thinking and dreaming of an America of the future whose westward movement, in those days before the railroad, was hardly calculable. If, as seems probable, he had been the first to suggest a boundary to the Pacific,[68] he had made the suggestion before anything had been heard from Jackson. His had been the plan; the General had activated it; for if the General thought only of the Floridas and the southwestern boundary, his seizure of the forts and his execution of the two Englishmen were events which reverberated all the way to the Pacific. Adams' defense of Jackson was the defense of an idea, at last in motion.

Monroe should be credited with supporting Adams in his line to the Pacific, but as a former Secretary of State in James Madison's prewar administration, he was naturally and excusably Florida-minded. A

Papers, Foreign Relations, IV, 616–621. See also Adams, Memoirs, IV, 237, 244, 246, 248–256, 261, 264–269; and Brooks, Borderlands, pp. 155, 157–158. Bemis, Adams and Foreign Policy, 331, n. 44, shows that Texas could have been obtained with a little extra pressure; and, pp. 329–332, gives a close and able correlation of Melish's map with modern geography.

[68] Monroe's memorandum of February 1818, in his handwriting, was bound between two documents, dated February 5 and February 23, in a volume of his correspondence with Adams, in the Adams MSS.; see Bemis, John Quincy Adams, p. 310, n. 27. This appears to be a summation of a discussion or of discussions between the President and his Secretary after Onís' note of January 24. Monroe suggests a boundary from the Trinity to the Arkansas at its nearest point, along the Arkansas to its source, and thence due west to the Pacific. As an alternative, he proposes that the western limit should be settled by commissioners. Since Adams never thereafter would accept anything but a line to the Pacific, and always solemnly maintained that the line was his suggestion, we may assume that the alternative represents Monroe's indecision: there is no evidence to the contrary.

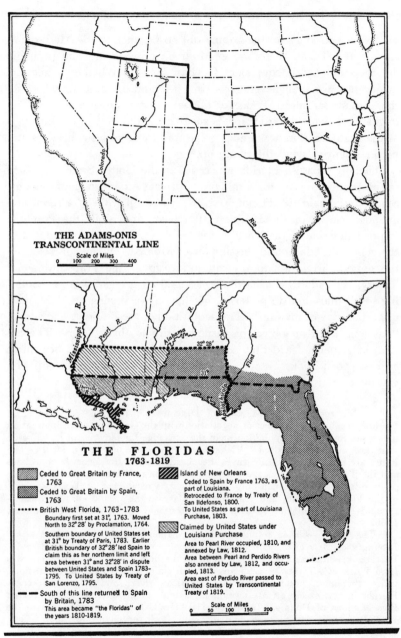

THE ADAMS-ONIS
TRANSCONTINENTAL LINE

Scale of Miles
0   100   200   300   400

THE FLORIDAS
1763-1819

Ceded to Great Britain by France, 1763

Ceded to Great Britain by Spain, 1763

•••••• British West Florida, 1763-1783
Boundary first set at 31°, 1763. Moved North to 32°28' by Proclamation, 1764.

Southern boundary of United States set at 31° by Treaty of Paris, 1783. Earlier British boundary of 32°28' led Spain to claim this as her northern limit and left area between 31° and 32°28' in dispute between United States and Spain 1783-1795. To United States by Treaty of San Lorenzo, 1795.

—— South of this line returned to Spain by Britain, 1783
This area became "the Floridas" of the years 1810-1819.

Island of New Orleans
Ceded to Spain by France 1763, as part of Louisiana.
Retroceded to France by Treaty of San Ildefonso, 1800.
To United States as part of Louisiana Purchase, 1803.

Claimed by United States under Louisiana Purchase
Area to Pearl River occupied, 1810, and annexed by Law, 1812.
Area between Pearl and Perdido Rivers also annexed by Law, 1812, and occupied, 1813.
Area east of Perdido River passed to United States by Transcontinental Treaty of 1819.

Scale of Miles
0   50   100   150   200

From *A Short History of American Diplomacy* by Lewis Ethan Ellis

southwest boundary on the Sabine did no violence to the Madisonian canon; and Texas, therefore, in Monroe's mind, could and probably did represent a fair equivalent for East Florida. Whether it actually did or not, we shall never know, but it would be most unfair to say that Adams sacrificed Texas for the sake of the Oregon country. He might have worked harder for Texas than he did, but in the last days of the negotiation he was under great pressure from his colleagues and his President to wind the treaty up.[69]

Officially, Spanish Florida was ceded to the United States in return for an assumption, up to $5 million, of private American claims against Spain, but Spain would not have treated at all without a discussion and delineation of the Louisiana Purchase; and, since the Purchase stopped this side of the Rockies, the line beyond must be attributed to the genius of Adams and the support of Monroe. The loss of Texas, in this sense, is irrelevant to any candid scrutiny of the Transcontinental Treaty, and Adams can hardly be accused of exaggeration for confiding to his diary and to posterity that the day of signing was "the most important day of my life." "The acquisition of the Floridas," he added, "has long been an object of earnest desire to this country. The acknowledgement of a definite line of boundary to the South Sea forms a great epoch in our history. The first proposal of it in this negotiation was my own. . . ."[70]

[69] In Monroe's Annual Message of December 3, 1817, he said that East Florida "has been the subject of negotiation with the Government of Spain as an indemnity for losses by spoliation *or* in the exchange for territory of equal value westward of the Mississippi." Richardson, *Messages and Papers*, II, 14. The italics are inserted. The "or" leaves the question uncertain. Years later, Adams told the Twenty-ninth Congress flatly that "That negotiation was for the purpose of Florida . . ." which can only be construed as meaning that Texas was part of the Florida bargain, and that the boundary to the Pacific—a superb afterthought—had nothing to do with it. *Congressional Globe*, 29th Cong., 1 sess., I, 663.

[70] The treaty will be found in Hunter Miller (ed.), *Treaties and Other International Acts of the United States* (8 vols., Washington, 1931), III, 3–18. Its three essential articles are III, defining the boundary; XII, which removes from Pinckney's Treaty of 1795 any Spanish claim to navigate the Mississippi, which thereupon becomes a purely American river; and XI, which cedes Florida in return for an assumption of claims "to an amount not exceeding Five Millions of Dollars." In Article II: "His Catholic Majesty cedes to the United States in full property and sovereignty, all the territories which belong to him . . . known by the name of East and West Florida," the absence of a

And yet—it was entirely in character—he found it hard to believe that so great a triumph would not be followed by some compensating disaster.[71] He waited anxiously, almost eagerly, and not long. On March 8, Mr. Speaker Clay called on the President and told him that he had just heard, on sound authority, that King Ferdinand's huge grants of Florida land to the Duke of Alagon, the Count of Punonrostro, and Señor Pedro de Vargas had been dated January 23, 1818.

According to Article VIII of the treaty all land grants in Florida, if made before January 24, 1818, were valid grants. The horrid news was not the less distressing because of the character of the messenger— Henry Clay, an active enemy to the administration, a man whom Adams had distrusted ever since they had clashed so angrily at Ghent! Adams searched the correspondence of Minister George W. Erving, and there he discovered that Erving had faithfully transmitted a copy of an order of the Captain General of Cuba, requiring him to put the agents of the Count of Punonrostro in possession of his Florida lands. The order was dated February 18, 1818, but it stated that the grant had been made known to the Council of the Indies as early as December 17, 1817. Adams had been inexcusably careless: he had mistaken the date of the order for the date of the grant. He was afterward able to prove that the Vargas grant had been made after January 24; but the Alagon and Punonrostro grants were apparently valid; they were now the owners of the better part of East Florida, and the United States had been presented with an empty sovereignty.[72]

Adams did not, of course, remain inactive. The new Minister to Spain, John Forsyth of Georgia, was instructed, upon exchanging ratifications of the treaty, to insist that the grants should be declared null and void. Mr. Forsyth, who shared the prevailing American belief that the grants were nothing more than a piece of royal jobbery, did not exactly veil these sentiments in diplomatic language;[73] the Council of

comma between "territories" and "which" would appear to support the claim that West Florida was not the property of the King of Spain but part of the original Louisiana Purchase! The Adams entry will be found in *Memoirs*, IV, 274.

[71] Adams, *Memoirs*, IV, 289.

[72] *Ibid.*, p. 290, where he calls this a judgment on his "vanity." Whether Onís had or had not consciously deceived Adams is still doubtful. Brooks, *Borderlands*, p. 176; Griffin, *Disruption of the Spanish Empire*, p. 195.

[73] Forsyth to Gonzales Salmon, June 13, 1819; *American State Papers,*

State thereupon advised His Catholic Majesty that the treaty ceded too much land and contained no promise not to recognize the revolutionary government of Buenos Aires; and at a midnight council, on June 31, 1819, Ferdinand announced that he would not ratify the treaty.[74]

There was nothing to do but to wait. The Spanish monarch, like some deciduous tree, sullenly preparing for a political winter, was beginning to shed his ministers and cronies. In June the Marquis de Casa Yrujo, Pizarro's successor, was banished to the monastery of Valverde at Ávila; in October the Russian Ambassador, no longer *persona grata*, saw fit to take a permanent leave of absence. In October, too, the former chocolate seller of Cadiz, Lozano de Torres, ceased to dispense Grace and Justice. Onís, who had been recalled from America (perhaps to succeed Yrujo, perhaps to share his fate) lingered in England, while the new American Minister, Don Francisco Vives, seemed in no hurry to get to Washington. When at length Onís ventured to appear in Spain, he was told to prepare a detailed report on the American navy; but if the King was contemplating a war against the United States, or an expedition against his revolted colonists, a military mutiny in Cadiz soon put an end to such schemes. Beginning in January 1820, the mutiny spread to Madrid, and Ferdinand the Well-Beloved was forced to accept another hateful constitution.[75]

Already, in London, Vives had been bluntly told by Castlereagh that his government had better come to terms with the United States; and, according to the American Minister in St. Petersburg, Count Nesselrode had been using much the same language.[76] The emergence of a quasi-liberal Cortes from the mutinies at Cadiz and Madrid was hardly

---

Foreign Relations, IV, 654–655. A handsome and agreeable personage, he admitted that he was no diplomat. Forsyth to Gallatin, June 13, 1819, Gallatin Papers, NYHS.

[74] Brooks, *Borderlands,* p. 179. Rush in London and Forsyth in Madrid both suspected that the British were against the treaty. Two conversations with Lord Castlereagh convinced Rush that this was not the case; Rush to Gallatin, July 24, 1819. It was not until September that Forsyth confessed that his suspicions of Sir Henry Wellesley, British Ambassador to Spain, were totally unfounded. Forsyth to Gallatin, September 11, 1819. Both in Gallatin Papers, NYHS.

[75] Brooks, *Borderlands,* pp. 178, 183. Forsyth to Gallatin, October 31, 1819, Rush to Gallatin, June 30, 1819 (on a rumor in London that Onís was to be Yrujo's successor) ; Gallatin Papers, NYHS.

[76] Griffin, *Disruption of the Spanish Empire,* p. 224. G. H. Campbell to Gallatin, October 26–November 7, 1819; Gallatin Papers, NYHS.

calculated to change these opinions. In the end, the Spanish Council of State, recognizing at last that no help was coming from Europe, recommended that the treaty be signed; the helpless king did so, after one last effort to retrieve something for the grantees, on October 24, 1820; and on February 13, 1821, the treaty was resubmitted to the Senate by President Monroe. On February 19, the Senate approved it, with four dissenting votes; on February 22, ratifications were exchanged with Vives, and the great treaty was at last proclaimed in Washington.[77]

[77] Brooks, *Borderlands,* p. 189; *American State Papers, Foreign Relations,* IV, 696–701; Richardson, *Messages and Papers,* II, 83–84; *Senate Journal of Executive Proceedings,* III, 242–244; Adams, *Memoirs,* V, 283, 289.

CHAPTER 3

The Panic of 1819

THE Transcontinental Treaty, actually though not officially con-
summated on February 24, 1819, is one of the outstanding achievements of early postwar nationalism. It received substantial support on
March 6, 1819, from Chief Justice John Marshall, who, in his decision
in the case of *McCulloch* v. *Maryland,* pronounced the following
words: "Throughout this vast republic, from the St. Croix to the Gulf
of Mexico, *from the Atlantic to the Pacific,* revenue is to be collected
and expended, armies are to be marched and supported."[1] Thus in
February the Secretary of State had called a new continent into being
by drawing lines upon a map, and in March the Chief Justice began
to conjure a coextensive government out of the eighth section of the
first article of the Constitution. These were great achievements; but by
March 1819 certain events had already occurred, and were still oc-
curring, which made the Chief Justice's decision one of the most
unpopular that even he had ever made.

These events, which profoundly modified American nationalism,
had their origin in European postwar adjustment. The ending of the
War of 1812 had unsealed the bulging warehouses of Liverpool. From
these and from various depots in Canada, Halifax, and Bermuda a
mass of manufactures descended upon the Atlantic ports of the United

[1] 4 Wheaton 408. Italics inserted. For McCulloch *v.* Maryland, see *infra,*
pp. 89–96.

States. The first year's importation was readily absorbed; the second was more ominous. No doubt the Tariff of 1816 did something to correct this situation; but the Tariff was extremely cautious, and it was easily circumvented.[2]

If one listened to the complaints of the manufacturers, one could only conclude that the immediate postwar years in America were years of hard times; but the manufacturers represented a very small percentage of the population, and their distress was swallowed up in the shimmering optimism of the land and planting interests. Here, too, the problems of Europe exercised an unhealthy influence. Crop failures on the other side of the Atlantic enhanced the demand for American corn, flour, beef, and pork; and nobody stopped to consider that Europe had, after all, an agriculture of its own and that it might be resilient. With the help of a government land policy which encouraged the purchase of the public domain on credit, an immense speculation in land began; and nobody could be blamed in those days for not perceiving that heavy speculation in land always preceded an economic crisis. The speculation reached, in 1818, a height which it was not to attain again for many years, and this speculation was given a new impetus by the Liverpool market, which was fatally conjuring with American cotton. In 1818, the price of cotton at one moment was quoted at the staggering figure of 32½ cents a pound. The British re-export market could not absorb such a price, nor could the British manufacturer. The latter, searching for a remedy, hit upon East Indian cotton; and although in the end it proved to be unsuited to British machinery, the proof came too late. Substantial importations from the East Indies in 1817 and 1818 were too much for American cotton. In 1818, its price in the Liverpool market began to waver, and at the end of the year it fell to 24 cents, with every sign of going lower. When the

[2] For circumvention via the auction rooms, particularly, see McMaster, *History*, IV, 341, and Robert Cheseborough to John W. Taylor, December 8, 1820; John W. Taylor Papers, NYHS. In the John W. Taylor Papers will be found a digest of the dealings of leading New York auctioneers: the nine leading firms—there were many lesser ones—in 1818–19 made sales of nearly $8,500,000. The auctioneers were influential in the state legislatures and (in New York) were a fruitful source of patronage; hence it was not easy to correct a system which defied both the tariff and the honest importer. A cogent analysis of the system will be found in Aaron Leggett, *An Address to the Honorable The Legislature of the State of New York* (Albany, 1829), p. 5.

news reached America in 1819, cotton dropped in one day to 26 cents, and continued to drop until it averaged only 14.3 cents at New Orleans.[3]

The "fantastic" side of the American boom in land and cotton can most easily be understood now in the light of the fact, not clearly perceptible then, that the whole western world was suffering from a fall in prices. This was partly due to a shortage of specie. The mines of Mexico and Peru, the chief sources of supply, had been seriously disorganized by war and revolution; and, at the same time, there was a formidable competition for the world's stock of precious metals because of the payment of French indemnities, the effort of Great Britain and of middle and eastern Europe to return to convertibility, and the disappearance of large amounts of specie into the undisgorging treasuries of the East. In the United States, there were signs of a break in wholesale commodity prices at least as early as 1816.[4] Thus a depression in prices ranged from the Bosphorus to the Mississippi at the very time when speculators and brokers were giving a different and delusive interpretation to the American scene.

A fall in prices of this kind would not in itself, of course, have accounted for the disaster which struck the United States in 1819; it merely provided an ominous background against which the disaster worked itself out. "The crisis that overtook American business at the close of 1818 was largely due to a shift in the world's demand for American staples."[5] In other words, the demand had been a stimulus to the nationalist optimism of postwar America; and when it shifted,

[3] The price of 32½ cents was reached at Savannah in October, 1818. An *average* annual price of 30 cents was maintained at New Orleans in 1817–18; L. C. Gray, *History of Agriculture in the Southern United States* (2 vols., Washington, 1933), II, 697. British importations of East India cotton have been estimated at 117,955 bales in 1817 and 227,300 bales in 1818; J. Marshall, *A Digest of All the Accounts* (London, 1833), p. 112. For tobacco prices, which began falling earlier, and declined to one-fifth of the peak attained in 1815–16, see J. C. Robert, *The Tobacco Kingdom: 1800–1860* (Durham, 1938), pp. 137–140.

[4] A. H. Cole, *Wholesale Commodity Prices in the United States, 1700–1861* (Cambridge, 1838), p. 85; Walter Buckingham Smith, *Economic Aspects of the Second Bank of the United States* (Cambridge, 1953), p. 100; Walter Buckingham Smith and Arthur Harrison Cole, *Fluctuations in American Business* (Cambridge, 1935), p. 29.

[5] Smith and Cole, *Fluctuations in Business*, p. 20.

there was nothing immediately to take its place. On October 19, 1818, the prescient *Aurora* of Philadelphia told its readers that "a great crisis approaches . . . compounded of foreign contagion acting upon internal predisposition."[6]

The word "contagion" insufficiently covered a variety of conflicting circumstances—the need of British industry for American cotton, the irresponsibility of the Liverpool cotton market, the British Corn Laws, the resilience of European agriculture, weather, convertibility, readjustment. "Contagion" had, in fact, a distinctly isolationist overtone, implying that Europe was corrupt and sick; but the *Aurora* had none the less recognized that American history and world history could not very well be separated. Such recognitions always dealt a blow to early American nationalism in its most innocent—that is to say, its most political—form. As for the "internal predisposition"—how natural it was for American optimists to respond to this "foreign contagion" with an inflation of mercantile and banking credit! The westward movement itself, the very symbol of a vigorous postwar nationalism, was being financed by one of the strangest emissions of doubtful paper money in the history of the modern world.

The inflationary bubble had grown and grown between 1815 and 1818—glamorous, shimmering, fraudulent, opaque: in the middle of 1818 it began to heave and tremble, and with the collapse of cotton in Liverpool it burst. Land values plunged downward by 50 to 75 per cent; the price of staples fell accordingly; businessman, speculator, merchant, farmer—all were involved.[7] Searching for an immediate scapegoat, the public fell upon the most outstanding of America's nationalist expedients—the Second Bank of the United States.

The Bank, incorporated in April, 1816, was ready to begin business in January, 1817. Its first object was to reform the currency, and its first effort, therefore, was to secure the resumption of specie payments. A joint resolution of Congress, in April, 1816, required that payments to the United States on and after February 20, 1817, should be either in specie, or Treasury notes, or Bank notes, or in state bank notes redeemable on demand. The government's receipts were chiefly from

---

[6] *Ibid.*, p. 21.
[7] Frederick Jackson Turner, *The Rise of the New West* (New York, 1906), p. 137.

taxes upon importers, who usually paid them in state bank notes, so that, if the state banks found themselves unable to comply with the joint resolution, if they had not resumed specie payments on February 20, the government would be unable to collect its revenues. The Bank was forced by its charter to go into business by the first Monday in April; and if the state banks still hung fire on that date, it stood to lose large sums of specie, since its notes would be redeemable and theirs would not. In January, 1817, the state banks were still stubbornly refusing to resume specie payments until July, and the situation was becoming exceedingly critical.[8]

The reluctance of the state banks may be ascribed less to their inability to undertake a nominal resumption than to the fact that they were making large profits out of unredeemable paper, on the one hand, and, on the other, to the situation in which they would stand when they did resume. The Bank was then to become their regulator. As statutory keeper of the public deposits and transferer of the public funds, it would receive state bank notes from the customs collectors and would become, in effect, the creditor of the state banks. By maintaining a constant pressure upon the banks, it could therefore restrict their issue of notes and curb their tendency to lend too much and so depreciate their circulation. It is not to be supposed that the private banking interests were exactly happy with this state of affairs—this servitude to an institution with headquarters in Philadelphia, with four-fifths of its directors elected by the stockholders of that city, and with all the prestige of the national government behind it.[9]

It was not until February 1, 1817, that their resistance was ended, and they agreed to resume on February 20; but they did so upon distinctly odd, not to say, ominous terms. On that day a convention of associated banks of New York, Philadelphia, Baltimore, and Richmond accepted or exacted an offer from the representatives of the Bank, in

[8] Ralph C. Catterall, *The Second Bank of the United States* (Chicago, 1903), p. 23; Smith, *Second Bank*, pp. 102–104; Bray Hammond, *Banks and Politics in America* (Princeton, 1957), pp. 246 ff.; J. T. Holdsworth and D. R. Dewey, *First and Second Banks of the United States* (Washington, 1910), p. 300. For the joint resolution of April 30, 1816, see *American State Papers, Finance*, IV, 764.

[9] Bray Hammond, "Jackson, Biddle, and the Second Bank of the United States," *Journal of Economic History*, VII (1947), 1.

which the Treasury concurred. By this offer, the Bank became responsible to the government for the public deposits held by the state banks, but agreed to withhold their transfer until July 1; at the same time, it promised not to call for other balances accumulating against the state banks until it had itself discounted for individuals ("other than those with duties to pay") the very uncomfortable sum of $6 million.[10] Thus the Bank extended its credit dealings while the state banks, in preparation for the day of reckoning, contracted theirs. This, of course, prevented the Bank from drawing specie from the state banks, while the state banks—since a large amount of notes would be put in circulation in order to discount $6 million—would be free to draw specie from the Bank.[11] Most of the public money was with the banks of the middle states (who were therefore spokesmen for all the others), and the more responsible of these banks may well have been in favor of resuming specie payments: the ominous character of the agreement—ominous as regards the more distant future—lay in the fact that, from the beginning, they begrudged their assistance to the federal institution.[12]

The Bank had, however, now provided a stable currency for taxes, something which the Treasury had been unable to do; and for a brief while all was sunshine.

At 10 O'Clock on the 20 Feby [wrote John Jacob Astor] bills on Baltimore were 2½ pct Premium for our Bank Notes. We oppend here our office and agreed to take Bills on Baltimore Virginia & Phila in half an hour all was at par . . . . The New York branch has plenty money of Government tho not much of our own . . . We have no preasure for money all good paper is Readily Discounted at the bank . . . the U.S. Bank thus far may be called a national blessing. [A year later, however, he was writing in a very different strain.] There has been too much speculation [he complained] and too much assumption of power on the part of the Bank Directors which has caused the Institution to become unpopular & I may say generally so. . . . [Money is so cheap owing to too free discounting in order to raise the price of the stock] that

[10] *American State Papers, Finance,* IV, 769. The discounts were to be $2 million in New York, $2 million in Philadelphia, $1,500,000 in Baltimore, $500,000 in Virginia.

[11] William M. Gouge, *A Short History of Paper Money and Banking in the United States* (2 vols., Philadelphia, 1833), I, 90; Catterall, *Second Bank,* p. 26.

[12] *American State Papers, Finance,* IV, 813, shows that there were slight misunderstandings even with eastern banks, as with the State Bank of Boston and the Kennebec Bank of Maine.

everything else has becom Dear & the Result is that our Merchants instead of shiping Produse ship Specie, so much so that I tell you in confidence that it is not without difficulty that specie payments are maintained the Defferent States are still going on making more Banks & I shall not be surprized if by & by there be not a general Blow up among them—I think Mr. Jones is losing ground as president of the Bank.[13]

Mr. Astor's thinking on such matters was a good deal less irregular than his English, and the appearance of Mr. William Jones, as a final item in his bill of complaints, was perfectly appropriate. The organization of the Bank had been such that, even before it went into business, it was in serious trouble. Mr. William Jones, a Philadelphia merchant who had recently gone through bankruptcy, had been elected its president on October 29, 1816, much to the satisfaction of James Madison and James Monroe, and much against the will of Stephen Girard, that astute, conservative, and powerful banker. Girard thought that Jones was "not a man of solid means," and that a majority of the directors elected with him were neither honest nor independent. Jones himself had a good record as Secretary of the Navy and a rather poor one as Assistant Secretary of the Treasury during the War of 1812, and it would be no more than reasonable to assert that he owed his Presidency to his knowledge of men and not of banking. His political adroitness has never been questioned.[14]

At any rate, under the leadership of Mr. Jones and his directors, the Bank soon became a kind of choragus in the dance of speculation. One notices, first of all, how—even before it had opened its doors—it had tended to strain its own credit. According to its charter, private subscribers were to pay for their stock in three installments: the first consisting of $5 in specie and $25 in government stock; the second, coming six months later, of $10 in specie and $25 in government stock; and the third, due twelve months after the second, also of $10 in specie and $25 in government stock. But specie was then at an 8 per cent premium and government stock was at par, so that it began to look as if the purchase of stock would be rather expensive. At this interesting junc-

[13] J. J. Astor to Albert Gallatin, March 7 (?), 1817, March 14, 1818; Gallatin Papers, NYHS.

[14] Smith, *Second Bank,* p. 99; Hammond, *Banks and Politics,* p. 252; Leonard D. White, *The Jeffersonians,* pp. 271–272; Madison, *Writings* (Cong. ed.), III, 563; *Dictionary of American Biography,* X, 205.

ture, the stockholders sought for relief from the Bank directors, and those obliging gentlemen agreed that they could pay for their second installment on the security of the stock itself, while on August 27, 1817, they went even further and gave them the privilege of discounting on their stock at an advance of 25 per cent! Specie payments were avoided simply by forfeiting the first dividend. Under these circumstances, it seems not improbable that those who made large purchases were able to retain their stock without paying for it, and it is certain that the stock itself became a prey to speculators. Powerful as he was, Stephen Girard uttered his protests into a void; and in Congress itself, the voice of criticism was raised in vain. As Hezekiah Niles put it, congressmen could be made into stockholders too.[15]

If the provisions of the charter had been obeyed, the Bank should have received $7 million in specie from its private stockholders and $21 million in government stock. What it really did receive is beyond exact calculation: the statement that it collected $2 million in coin, $14 million in government securities, and $12 million in personal notes may be taken only as a rough picture of its situation.[16] It was, at any rate, obliged to send John Sergeant to London to look for more specie at a time when the competition for precious metals was almost fierce, and from the summer of 1817 to the end of 1818 it suceeded in importing $7,300,000 at a cost to itself of some $500,000.[17]

President Jones himself seems to have believed that there was plenty of specie in the country, and to his mind the attempt to obtain a sizable amount abroad was simply a form of restoring confidence to those who

[15] Holdsworth and Dewey, *First and Second Banks,* pp. 176, 177; Catterall, *Second Bank,* pp. 1, 32 n.; *American State Papers, Finance,* III, 341–2; Gouge, *Paper Money,* II, 87–88; *Niles' Register,* XVI, 104; *Annals of Congress,* 15 Cong., 2 sess., p. 1282 (for Lowndes' attack on discounts on a pledge of stock), and Charles R. King (ed.), *The Life and Correspondence of Rufus King* (6 vols., New York, 1894–1900), VI, 38–39 (for King's protest); Hammond, *Banks and Politics,* p. 254; Smith, *Second Bank,* p. 100; *House Doc.* 92, 15 Cong., 2 sess., p. 7.

[16] Hammond, *Banks and Politics,* p. 154, says of this statement by D. R. Dewey that it is "uncertain . . . because the capital was not paid in all in one operation or before the Bank opened. . . . Since the Bank's specie and government portfolio began to turn over in the course of operations, and since much 'specie' was fictitious (i. e., the Bank 'lent' its notes to stockholders and these were 'accepted' as specie) I do not see how the exact amounts received from stockholders could be distinguished even nominally."

[17] Gouge, *Paper Money,* II, 94–95; Hammond, *Banks and Politics,* p. 255; Smith, *Second Bank,* p. 100.

had cautiously hoarded it at home. Actually, circumstances were such that specie—especially in 1816—was flowing from the country because of an apparent excess of imports over exports, and because the carrying trade was not at that time in a position to fill the gap. As Jones himself was soon to find, his predictions had been incorrect: there was little specie in hiding anywhere.[18] The useful fiction of a general convertibility was never more of a fiction and never less useful than it was under the Presidency of Jones—not because most of the banks were weak, which they demonstrably were, but because he was the last man to insist upon giving convertibility some appearance of fact.[19]

It is in the matter of the branch offices of the Bank that Jones's amiable laxness becomes most visible to the inquirer of today. By the end of 1817 there were eighteen of them, and it seems that no effort was ever made to fix their capitals. Moreover, their directors were spectacularly ignorant of the principles of sound banking. These gentlemen were the happy captives of local conditions: they loaned on mortgages, they renewed their notes over and over again, they issued notes and drafts without giving any thought to redemption. Indeed, the central purpose of the Bank at that time, the maintenance of a uniform currency, was flagrantly and consistently flouted by their generosity. It had been agreed that the notes of any one branch should be payable on presentation at any of the others; and since the course of exchange was usually in favor of the East and the North, it became the usual procedure for the notes of the South and West to be presented in the East and the North with demands for redemption. The branch offices in the South and the West, in response, overissued their bank notes—in July, 1818, the Cincinnati branch discounted $1,800,000 and the Lexington, Kentucky, branch $1,619,000—so that specie was siphoned away from the branches in the East and North. At the end of a year and a half of business, the discounts of the Bank as a whole amounted to $41,500,000; and because these extensive operations were concentrated in areas of unsound money, there was very little pressure on the state banks to contract their loans and retire their issues.[20]

[18] Smith, *Second Bank,* p. 102.

[19] *House Doc.* 460, 22 Cong., 1 sess., p. 352; Smith, *Second Bank,* p. 113.

[20] Catterall, *Second Bank,* pp. 32, 34, 160 n.; Gouge, *Paper Money,* II, 94, 95; *American State Papers, Finance,* IV, 351–359; *House Doc.* 121, 22 Cong., 2 sess., p. 140.

Since overtrading was one of the most prominent features of early postwar nationalism, one might charitably ascribe the mismanagement at Philadelphia to nationalist exuberance: it has been noticed that the Treasury itself did not exactly frown upon the extravagance of Mr. Jones and his branch directors.[21] But there were places where mismanagement became indistinguishable from fraud. The president of the branch office at Baltimore was James A. Buchanan, a partner in the great commercial firm of Smith & Buchanan, which for twenty-five years (said John Quincy Adams) had "formed, controlled, and modified almost entirely" the moral, political, and commercial character of the city. Buchanan now proceeded to "modify" the city's character, not to mention his own, in a manner which has, from that day to this, never failed to astound the imagination. Together with G. R. Williams, a fellow director, and James McCulloch, the branch cashier, he made purchases of bank stock which, by December 1817, amounted to $4,-451,376. These purchases were financed partly by the firm of Smith & Buchanan, partly by loans from the bank on a pledge of stock, and partly by advances made by the conspirators to themselves on no security at all. When the board of directors questioned these extraordinary transactions, the three speculators answered that they had authority from Philadelphia to make stock loans; when outsiders became inquisitive, they blandly replied that they had permission from their own board. If Buchanan's name had not been above suspicion, and if it had not been well known that he stood very high with the mother Bank at Philadelphia, these frauds would probably have been detected and exposed, even in the permissive climate of 1817 and 1818. At it was, McCulloch was actually able to lend himself $85,000 without Buchanan's knowledge: when the end came, in March, 1819, it was discovered that his total unsecured indebtedness was $429,049.80. Williams was indebted and unsecured for the sum of $628,423.09, and the firm of Smith & Buchanan for $344,212.43.[22]

[21] W. B. Smith, *Second Bank,* p. 105.

[22] Adams, *Memoirs,* IV, 282; Catterall, *Second Bank,* pp. 44–50. According to Catterall, they bought an additional 15,490 shares in March, 1819, which brought their total purchases to $6,397,626. The first teller, J. S. LaRenitrie, also dipped his hand into the till to the extent of $50,000. According to the existing laws, such malpractices were breaches of trust, not punishable by the criminal law, except under the vague term of "conspiracy"; for how, it was

In the meantime, while this huge defalcation was going on under his very nose, Mr. Jones was beginning to ask himself whether his inflationary measures were altogether sound. Even his dim and kindly vision had begun to perceive that the branches in the West and South were doing more business than was necessary, while those in the East and North were doing hardly any business at all. Even he began to be alarmed by the cheerful manner in which bankers, speculators, and traders extracted coin from his vaults by the simple method of buying Bank notes with state bank paper, presenting these notes for redemption in specie, selling the specie at an advance, and buying more notes. In July, 1818, the Bank's demand liabilities were $22,372,000 and its specie fund was $2,357,000—a ratio of ten to one, or about double the statutory limit. A contraction was clearly indicated, and a contraction did take place under Mr. Jones's orders; but it fell, strange to say, on good business paper and scarcely touched the large sums of money loaned on stock pledges. In August, it was decreed that no branch office could receive any notes but its own, except in payments to the United States; but the western offices responded to this sensible if belated measure by increasing their loans, usually by the purchase of bills of exchange as a species of renewal of notes or bills drawn on them—in other words, by transforming an interest-bearing debt into a non-interest-bearing one. In short, everything was done at Philadelphia except to call the southern and western branches to strict account; the curtailment fell upon the East, where it was not wanted; and the southern and western branches continued to expand their business, tying up the Bank's capital in notes and bills constantly renewed.[23]

In this way, a curtailment of some $7 million had successfully pros-

---

argued, could one steal what was already in one's possession? Even here, however, there was a discrepancy; as Nicholas Biddle pointed out, there was "a dangerous inequality in the punishments inflicted by our legislation. If, for instance, any person employed in the General Post Office embezzles or secretes the smallest amount of property confided to him he may be publicly whipped and imprisoned for ten years—whilst the officer of a Bank in which the revenue of the U.S. is deposited and in the profits of which the U.S. are so largely interested, may defraud the institution of millions and escape the criminal law of the United States." Biddle to Monroe, July 5, 1819, Monroe Papers, LC.

[23] Catterall, *Second Bank,* pp. 47, 51, 54; *American State Papers, Finance,* III, 325–326; Gouge, *Paper Money,* II, 96, 104; *Niles' Register,* XXIII, 90. Hammond, *Banks and Politics,* p. 260, succinctly describes the Bank's original principle—that each part must honor the obligations of every other part—as "operating on a basis of inter-regional parity that did not exist."

trated the branches in the East and North, and had shifted the Bank's capital to the South and West: it had manifestly defeated its own purpose, and the end was not far off. In October 1818, specie was at 6½ to 7 per cent advance in Boston, and 7 per cent in New York. The fiction of convertibility was ended, but the fiction of prosperity was maintained for a little while longer by the great land boom in the West and South.[24] In October, the government demanded $2 million of its deposits in specie in order to redeem a part of its Louisiana purchase stock. Making one last effort, Mr. Jones managed to furnish bills on London in lieu of specie, but he could do no more. A desperate effort to bring the banks of Ohio into some kind of specie relation with the branch bank at Cincinnati—since there had been extensive sales of the public domain in Ohio, these banks were very vulnerable—only produced a suspension of specie payments in Cincinnati and a business recession which heralded the panic to come. In January, 1819, cotton broke, and in January Mr. Jones discreetly resigned.[25]

By this time the Bank itself was becoming an object of popular suspicion, and if the Baltimore frauds had come to light in January it is doubtful if even the House of Representatives—where the Bank was still supported by a large majority—could so easily have resisted proposals for repeal. In the opinion of many responsible men, the stockholders would have been better off if their charter had been surrendered.[26] What followed the resignation of Jones completed the Bank's disgrace in the public mind; for his successor, Mr. Langdon Cheves of South Carolina, a man of humble birth and stern disposition, merely carried to its logical conclusion the curtailment begun by William Jones. He cut his own salary from $7,000 to $6,000 a year; he

[24] J. J. Astor to Albert Gallatin, September 5, 1818. "Although trade is not Brisk the country at large seems to be doing well. Speculations in lands to the westward and South are running very high here property appears not to fall." Gallatin Papers, NYHS. The public-land sales ran: 1815, 1,306,400 acres; 1816, 1,742,500 acres; 1817, 1,886,200; 1818, 3,491,000. The 1818 figure not only exceeded by far any previous figure but it was not reached again until 1833: *Historical Statistics of the United States, Colonial Times to 1957* (Washington, 1960), p. 239.

[25] Catterall, *Second Bank*, p. 57; Smith, *Second Bank*, p. 112; Harry R. Stevens, *The Early Jackson Party in Ohio* (Durham, 1957), pp. 17–19; *American State Papers, Finance*, IV, 864.

[26] Hammond, *Banks and Politics*, p. 259; Adams *Memoirs*, V, 38–39; Henry Clay to Martin D. Hardin, February 21, 1819, in Hopkins and Hargreaves (eds.), *The Papers of Henry Clay*, II, 673.

instituted similar cuts for his subordinates; he probed, he dismissed, he prosecuted. He engineered a loan of $2 million, largely in specie, from Baring Brothers and Hope and Company. He commanded the branches in the South and West to issue no more notes so long as the exchanges were against them, and he refused to purchase and collect drafts on the South and West. When he took over the presidency at Philadelphia, the Bank was (he said years later) "a ship without a rudder or sails or masts, on short allowance of provisions and water, on a stormy sea and far from land." Within seventy days the storm had been weathered and the vessel was shipshape or at any rate seaworthy: the only trouble was that, rightly or wrongly, it had come to resemble a pirate ship. As William Gouge put it: "The Bank was saved and the people were ruined."[27]

We may question the validity of the term "ruined" as applied to a nation with a predominantly farming population: "ruined" has an urban sound. And it may well be that journalists were "unduly impressed by the plight of the cities," of manufacturing centers, of commercial and business enterprises.[28] On the other hand, this emphasis upon the woes of the business community shows how deeply the whole economy was involved in the collapse of the land boóm and the panic of 1819. The contraction instituted by Jones and rigorously pursued by Cheves was rather an effect than a cause, but it appeared to be causal; and after it had taken place, the delirium of speculation seemed to many to have been succeeded by a trance of death. Trade languished; prices sank precipitously; real property depreciated and its rents and profits vanished; and unemployment spread like a plague. The value of real and personal property in New York State, as recorded in the Comptroller's office, dropped from $315 million in 1818 to $256 million in 1819; in Baltimore rents declined from 40 to 50 per cent; in Virginia, wrote Thomas Jefferson, "lands cannot now be sold for a year's rent"; in Philadelphia unemployment was reckoned rather wildly at anywhere from 5,000 to 20,000; in Pennsylvania a committee of the state senate reported 14,537 actions for debt; in Massachusetts commercial capital was reported to have taken a loss of 25 per cent, while the volume of revenue bonds for which the government had entered suit against the

[27] Smith, *Second Bank,* p. 119. *Niles' Register,* LIII, 8, quoting Cheves in answer to Thomas Cooper, August 18, 1837; Gouge, *Paper Money,* II, 109.
[28] Smith, *Second Bank,* p. 124.

debtor merchants increased from less than $2 million to more than $3 million. And so it went.[29]

But it was along the urban frontier that the depression was most noticeable or most dramatic. In Pittsburgh, the panic drove 30 per cent of the population out of the city, and as early as February, 1819, the *Gazette* declared mournfully that "the mechanical and manufacturing community is languishing into annihilation." In Kentucky, where, it was said, "a deeper gloom hangs over us than was ever witnessed by the oldest man," the manufacturing center of Lexington never recovered from this final blow. In Cincinnati, the depression passed downward from the local bankers and merchants to "draymen, carters, boatmen, coopers . . . mechanics, especially those dependent on the export trade"; it "afflicted all levels of society"; and in Cincinnati, as it happened, the Bank found itself the owner of hotels, coffeehouses, warehouses, stores, stables, iron foundries, and vacant lots. Years later, the somewhat rhetorical memory of Thomas Hart Benton recalled the Bank as "the engrossing proprietor of whole towns." Throughout the land it was familiarly known as the Monster.[30]

The Bank's role, however, had been misinterpreted by its popular critics. It had not acted piratically or monstrously because it was strong: the Jones-Cheves curtailment had been a confession of weakness. It was by no means the protagonist in the Panic of 1819 or the Panic's aftermath; it was one of the supporting players in that melancholy drama, and if its histrionics had not been so woefully exaggerated and clumsy, it might have eluded all but the most general criticism. There is no doubt that it was mismanaged from the start, that it had failed to put pressure on the state banks, and that—by extending credit

---

[29] Samuel Rezneck, "The Depression of 1819–1820," *American Historical Review,* XXXIX (1933), 31 ff.; Charles S. Sydnor, *The Development of Southern Sectionalism* (Baton Rouge, 1948), pp. 111–112; Thomas Jefferson to John Adams, November 7, 1819, *Writings,* Ford ed., XII, 144–145; William A. Sullivan, *The Industrial Worker in Pennsylvania, 1800 to 1840* (Harrisburg, 1955), p. 51.

[30] James A. Kehl, *Ill Feeling in the Era of Good Feeling* (Pittsburgh, 1956), p. 27; Richard C. Wade, *The Urban Frontier* (Cambridge, 1959), pp. 167–169; Catterall, *Second Bank,* pp. 65 ff.; Stevens, *Early Jackson Party,* p. 20; Thomas Hart Benton, *A Thirty Years View* (2 vols., New York, 1854–56), I, 198. It must be noticed that Lexington's hemp manufacturers had been in trouble since 1816, as had Pittsburgh's manufacturers of cotton, woolens, glass, and iron.

at the wrong time and withdrawing it at the wrong time—it had acted, not like a central bank, but like the very personification of the usurious instinct. But it could hardly be held responsible for the world's readjustment to the ending of the Napoleonic Wars, which, after all, lay at the bottom of the whole business. It had not been taken into the government's confidence when the Treasury decided to use the land-boom revenues, derived from the West, for the purpose of debt retirement in the East. If it had been foolishly indulgent to the state banks, the Treasury had encouraged this indulgence.[31]

Moreover its *direct* control was limited to those banks whose paper was used extensively in payments to the government; and these banks were only part of a system the abuses of which (wrote Condy Raguet, a relatively judicious and keen-sighted critic) lay "*first* in the excessive number of banks, and secondly in their universal bad administration." "If we had mines as rich as Potosi," said William Gouge, "and paper should be issued in excess, we should not be able to retain in the country even that small amount of silver which is necessary to keep Bank notes convertible."[32] As Jefferson put it, "the paper bubble is then burst. This is what you and I, and every reasoning man, seduced by no obliquity of mind or interest, have long foreseen."[33] In the end, it was "obliquity of mind and interest" that counted with Jefferson; and Benton's rather superficial judgment that the country had stockjobbed and overtraded itself into a depression remained, paradoxically enough, as deep an accounting of the situation as any study of debt retirements or specie movements.

The debt to the government for public lands stood at $3 million in 1815, at $17 million in 1818, and at $22 million in 1819.[34] This was less a measure of growth than a fever chart, and these startling figures were surrounded and to some extent interpenetrated by a less manageable debt—a debt from individuals to their neighbors, to merchants, to

[31] Smith, *Second Bank*, p. 105. For arguments for and against the Bank, see Joseph Dorfman, *The Economic Mind in American Civilization* (2 vols., New York, 1946), I, 368 ff.

[32] Condy Raguet, a Pennsylvania lawyer, whose investments in coal lands and city lots were destroyed in the Panic, headed a state senate committee to enquire into the causes of the distress; Pennsylvania, *Senate Journal*, 1819–20, p. 223. Gouge, *Paper Money*, II, 95.

[33] To John Adams, see n. 29, *supra*.

[34] *American State Papers, Public Lands*, III, 460.

banks, a debt among banks innocent of any rational credit system, a debt which had a way of expressing itself in a circulating medium approaching, if it did not pass, the borders of insanity. The Bank itself may even be considered, charitably, as the victim of a private banking "system" which was relatively sound in the New England states, less sound in the middle Atlantic states, shaky in the south Atlantic states, and often simply weird in the West and the Southwest. In 1815 the state banks were numbered at 204, in 1816 at 246, in 1819 at nearly 400.[35] The number of unchartered banks and of towns, villages, business houses, and individuals issuing paper money is beyond estimation. All that was necessary to start a bank, said Hezekiah Niles, was plates, presses, and paper; "a church, a tavern, a blacksmith's shop" would be considered a suitable site.[36] Nor were the chartered banks always in much better shape, for charters were easy to acquire, their flimsy regulations encouraged evasion, and even the soundest of them scorned to furnish information about their assets or methods. Bankers, after all, were persistent lobbyists and state legislators, strange to relate, were not incorruptible.[37]

In August, 1819, when the panic was at its worst in Baltimore, the notes of the District of Columbia were often at a 60 per cent discount, the notes of Maryland at anywhere from 1 to 40 per cent, of Virginia from 1½ to 25 per cent, of the Ohio banks from 10 to 50 per cent, and of Indiana, Illinois, and Missouri from 15 to 60 per cent.[38] Thus business between district and district, and state and state, was rendered even more desperate by ruinous fluctuations in the rate of exchange.

The state banks, always jealous of the national Bank, now endeavored to conceal their own shortcomings by vilifying that unhappy institution—which, indeed, never could regain the confidence of the people. When state banking recovered, the enemies of the Bank tended to concentrate in the East; but the Panic had been most dramatic in the West, and when the Bank succumbed at last, it was a western President who brought about its downfall. It cannot very well be doubted that the whole American community was grievously shaken

[35] *Historical Statistics*, p. 623. Chart XI-5; Davis R. Dewey, *Financial History of the United States* (New York, 1939), p. 144. *Niles' Register*, XV, 162.
[36] *Niles' Register*, XIV, 2.
[37] Dewey, *Financial History*, pp. 144, 153–154.
[38] Gouge, *Paper Money*, II, 167–168.

by the Panic of 1819; but the greatest loser, the man at the bottom of the chain of debt, was presumably the farmer who believed and expected that his loans would be renewed over and over again. This custom was, after all, adapted to "the needs of a large population, with the knowledge, the intelligence and the habits which belong to civilized life, amply supplied with the means of subsistence, but without any other active capital, but agricultural produce."[39] Caught between falling prices and rising charges, with the emphasis moving away from subsistence farming and toward improvement in equipment and livestock, his mind was naturally inflationist: he did not condemn the local banker for practices which appeared to create capital, however shifty these practices may have been; but he did condemn the national Bank for attempting to put an end to them.[40] And so it came about that in the West and Southwest the Bank was hated because it tried to restrain the local banks from issuing excessive paper money; whereas in the East, the mechanic (who was so often paid in depreciated notes) suspected it because it was after all itself a bank of issue. To the hard-money theorists, it was the graven image of the demon of paper money, and the private banking interests deplored its tendency to control their issues and decrease their power. In a sense, and no doubt deservedly, it had become the scapegoat for a national dilemma.

The Panic of 1819 was really a focus for this dilemma. To be sure, one cannot describe its superficial symptoms without giving the impression—as John Marshall's biographer put it—that the nation had somehow or other fallen into a condition of "moral chaos."[41] This does not appear to be an adequate description. One might come nearer to the truth by observing how very difficult it was for an agricultural community to accept, in its innocent midst, what could best be de-

[39] Albert Gallatin, *Considerations on the Currency and Banking System of the United States* (New York, 1831), p. 68.

[40] Joseph A. Schumpeter, *Business Cycles* (2 vols., New York, 1939), I, 294 n: "It makes a great difference whether a given pattern of behavior is condemned by the conscience of the community or supported by a large and vociferous sector of public opinion—the American banker who resorted to all kinds of shifts to make it impossible for the holders of his notes to present them successfully, did something which, for this reason, *differed* from an analogous behavior of a European banker. . . ."

[41] Albert J. Beveridge, *The Life of John Marshall* (4 vols., Boston, 1916–19), IV, 169.

scribed as historical process. The Industrial Revolution, a barely recognizable concept in those days, had stolen upon it unawares. Its economic life, between the War of Independence and the War of 1812, had been in many respects a continuation or fulfillment of the colonial relations between the New World and the Old. Then the wars passed, and the spirit of enterprise was released like a djinn from a bottle, ready to obey with gleeful and appalling promptitude the commands of men who were mostly unprepared for their responsibilities. "Enterprise," it has been wisely written, "had placed such subtle instrumentalities as a credit, accounting, and the corporate forms of organization at the disposal of people unaccustomed to such things. . . . An economy in which barter had been important and financial transactions had been wholly subordinate to the exchange of goods was giving way to an economy concerned more and more with obligations, contracts, negotiable instruments, equities, and such invisible abstractions."[42] The visible and audible nationalism of the immediate postwar years, the nationalism which had made men "think and act more like Americans," was to some extent a response to this delusive but exhilarating process. Meanwhile the readjustments of postwar Europe, the "foreign contagion," infected the economy with recession, inflation, and collapse; and the nation, as it recovered from the Panic, did indeed resemble a convalescent from some malady rather youthful than dangerous, some economic measles or chickenpox. It was fearfully spotted with the marks of fraud and corruption, and deeply sunk in debt. In this condition, it began to formulate what was soon to be the grand Jacksonian question of *cui bono?* Who was to profit by the expansion of business and of enterprise? Jacksonian nationalism was born in the Panic of 1819.

The decision of the Supreme Court in the case of *McCulloch* v. *Maryland,* coming at an early stage of the Panic, remains to this day—if it is stripped of Marshall's great nationalist generalizations—a most ironical comment upon this emerging distinction between privilege and opportunity. The decision rescued the Bank at a moment when that institution was tottering upon the verge of collapse; when it was already connected in the public mind with the shadier kinds of business enterprise; when William Jones had just resigned in despair if not

[42] Hammond, *Banks and Politics,* p. 274.

disgrace; and when the larcenies of McCulloch, Buchanan, and Williams were within a few weeks of being known to all the world.

Of course, a contest between the idea of nationalism and the doctrine of state rights is present in the case and even central to it; but it seems that in the public mind, at a time when every debtor conceived the Bank to be his enemy, what was really involved was the nature of democratic opportunity itself.[43] Otherwise, why should Marshall's decision have been, even for him, so very unpopular? But let us first look briefly at the case and its actors.

On February 11, 1818, a law of Maryland announced that all banks established "without authority from the state" were required to issue notes only upon stamped paper purchased from the state, and only in certain denominations, at a forfeit of $500 for each offense; or else such banks could compound with the state by paying an annual tax of $15,000.[44] The Baltimore branch of the national Bank, however, continued to issue its notes upon unstamped paper, and declined to pay the required tax; whereupon John James, Treasurer of the Western Shore, sued James McCulloch, as cashier of the branch bank, for recovery of the penalties prescribed by law. This was on May 8, 1818, and with all the speed which can accompany an "arranged" case *McCulloch* v. *Maryland* reached the Supreme Court on a writ of error, by way of adverse decisions in the Baltimore County Court and the Maryland Court of Appeals.[45]

The political atmosphere in which the case was to be decided had been thickened to the point of murkiness by the growing Panic of 1819; it remained to be seen whether or not the light of judicial logic, shed by that master of deductive exposition, Chief Justice John Mar-

---

[43] This has been well stated as follows: "A constant criticism of the second Bank of the United States was that throughout its history it had operated for the few rather than the many. This opinion had considerable basis in fact for the period extending from its conception in 1816 to the publication of a critical report by a congressional committee in 1819 and the subsequent resignation of Jones from the presidency." Harold J. Plous and Gordon Baker, "McCullough versus Maryland, Right Principle, Wrong Case," 9 *Stanford Law Review* (1957), p. 712.

[44] *Laws of the State of Maryland* (Annapolis, 1818), p. 174.

[45] Max Lerner, "John Marshall and the Campaign of History," 39 *Columbia Law Review* (1939), 423.

shall, would be strong enough to penetrate it, or would be permitted to do so.

John Marshall is one of the central figures in the annals of postwar nationalism.[46] Having escaped the nerve-racking vengeance of Thomas Jefferson,[47] the traps laid for him by his own speculating past,[48] his Federalist attitude toward the War of 1812, and the temptation to indulge too strongly in English conservative thought,[49] Marshall was now one of the few prominent Federalists in government who was beyond the reach of Republican proscription. His position was serene and appeared to be almost Olympian: the Supreme Court was said to be "Marshall's Court." This, to be sure, was by no means the case. As Felix Frankfurter has suggested, Marshall himself would have been much amused by such a claim. It is true that the Court, under Marshall's direction, had ceased to deliver its decisions *seriatim,* and that in most cases, especially when they involved constitutional issues, he wrote and delivered them himself. He also made it a point—there were exceptions to this rule, but not many—not to dissent when he found himself at odds with his brethren. But the infusion of Republican justices had made this Court, while unanimous on questions of national power, both restless and divided when it came to the relation between

[46] For his alliance with the moderate wing of the Federalists under John Adams, see Beveridge, *Marshall,* II, 577; Charles Fairman, "American Judicial Tradition," in W. Melville Jones (ed.), *Chief Justice John Marshall* (Ithaca, 1956), p. 91; and John Marshall, *The Life of George Washington* (2 vols., Philadelphia, 1835), II, 232. It is still uncertain whether he regarded the Alien and Sedition Acts as an invasion of rights, or as a display of weakness unbecoming in a central government.

[47] Beveridge, *Marshall,* III, 196. Fred Rodell, *Nine Men* (New York, 1955), pp. 91–92, shows that in the trial of Justice Chase, Marshall so far lost his nerve as to suggest that Congress be empowered to overrule the Supreme Court! Henry Adams, *History* III, 441–471, makes the Burr trial the scene of Marshall's triumph over Jefferson.

[48] In 1793, Marshall was one of a syndicate formed to purchase 160,000 acres from the heirs of Lord Fairfax in defiance of two acts of Virginia; the ensuing litigation, both state and national, pursued him to the Supreme Bench: 7 Cranch 603 (1813), 1 Wheaton 304 (1816), where he disqualified himself, and 6 Cranch 87 (1810)—or Fletcher *v.* Peck—where, declaring that a land grant became a contract, and that a contract was sacred regardless of its ethics, he seemed to cast the protection of federal law over much that was dubious in the land business.

[49] Lerner, "Marshall," p. 398; Beveridge, *Marshall,* I, 56.

national power and state power.[50] No one, therefore, could have predicted with complete confidence what the nationalist Chief Justice's decision would be in the case of *McCulloch* v. *Maryland*.

Polite Washington, ladies as well as gentlemen, elbowed its way into the modest little room beneath the Capitol where the case was heard in February, 1819. A most distinguished cast had been assembled for its entertainment: for the Bank, William Pinkney, Daniel Webster, Attorney General Wirt; for Maryland, Luther Martin, Joseph Hopkinson, Walter Jones. Among these the most popular were Pinkney, a corseted, flowery old rip, but a master of nationalist exposition, and Daniel Webster, fresh from his triumph in *Dartmouth College* v. *Woodward,* where, in the first of his famous perorations, he had tearfully imposed the image of a small, charitable, persecuted institution upon the huge and businesslike pretension that property contracts should be expanded to apply to corporate charters.[51] His arguments in *McCulloch* v. *Maryland* may be allowed to speak for all three of the Bank's attorneys. These revolved, with a rather simple motion, around two queries. The first was: Has Congress the power to charter a bank? The second, which logically followed, was: Can the states tax federal property?[52]

Such questions would be easy to answer in favor of the Bank, but

---

[50] Warren, *Supreme Court,* II, 129; Felix Frankfurter, *The Commerce Clause* (Chapel Hill, 1937), pp. 4, 43; W. W. Crosskey, "Mr. Chief Justice Marshall," in Allison Dunham and Philip B. Kurland (eds.), *Mr. Justice* (Chicago, 1956), pp. 19–20. According to Donald G. Morgan, "Marshall, the Marshall Court and the Constitution," in Jones (ed.), *Chief Justice John Marshall,* pp. 168 ff., Bushrod Washington (an Adams appointee) and Joseph Story (a Madison appointee) favored exclusive national powers—i.e., the automatic withdrawal from the states of any power granted to the national government; Marshall tended to favor such powers, but approached them empirically; and William Johnson, Brockholst Livingston, Thomas Todd (all Jefferson appointees), and Gabriel Duvall (a Madison appointee) "shifted with the issue," forming a loyal opposition, which never coalesced.

[51] 4 Wheaton 518 (1819); S. G. Brown (ed.), Rufus Choate, *Works . . . With a Memoir of His Life* (2 vols., Boston, 1862), I, 516; Lerner, "Marshall," p. 417.

[52] Webster capped these with the famous words "a power to tax involves, necessarily, a power to destroy." 4 Wheaton 327. Of Pinkney's speech—*ibid.,* pp. 377–400—Justice Story wrote: "He spoke like a great statesman and great patriot. All the cobwebs of sophistry and metaphysics about State rights and State sovereignty he swept away with a mighty besom." Beveridge, *Marshall,* IV, 287 n.

only if one avoided a more thorny problem: To what extent was the Bank a governmental institution?

It has been said that the counsel for Maryland did not present their most forceful argument, since they paid relatively little attention to the conflict between state and federal powers. By this neglect, although they could not have known it at the time, they lost their best opportunity of dividing the Court. On the other hand, there can hardly be any doubt that they discovered and pierced the real chink in the Bank's armor. Mr. Hopkinson asserted that the Bank's branches had been established "with a single view to trading, and the profit of stockholders, and not for the convenience or use of the government." This assertion could not have been maintained alone; but he qualified it in masterly fashion by admitting that, under the charter, government could request the establishment of a branch wherever it pleased. This being so, he said, all he required was, first, that the power to establish a branch should have been exercised by the government alone and not (as he contended) by the directors without any control from the government; and second, that the Bank should have been divested from the beginning of its private and profit-taking character.[53] This had never been the case. All the United States had done was, in effect, to hold stock in the Bank. They had not controlled its directors; they had not influenced its management. Although Hopkinson was unaware of the inflationary pressure which the Treasury had put upon President Jones,[54] his argument was well founded. As he put it, the usefulness of the Bank as a collector and distributor of the public revenues would have to be balanced against the fact that it had been operated in the interests of its private stockholders and had been openly engaged in private trade for private profit. Mr. Walter Jones pursued the same argument, but to an even more forthright conclusion. If the United States, he said, "will mix their funds with those of bankers, their sovereign character and dignity are lost in the mercantile character which they have assumed; and their property thus employed becomes subject to local taxation, like other capital employed in trade."[55]

---

[53] Plous and Baker, "McCullough versus Maryland," p. 721.

[54] See n. 31, *supra*.

[55] 4 Wheaton 335, 340–341, 372. Under Nicholas Biddle, who succeeded Cheves as president, and whose management during the decade was wise, one

Counsel for Maryland did not, of course, rest solely upon this argument, which would have left them in the awkward position of calling for a more centralized Bank than any Congress would have dared create. They also maintained—in formal, almost ritualistic language—that the Constitution gave the several states a right to tax everything but imports and exports, and that this right was "absolute and unqualifiable."[56] They declared that a national Bank, immune from state taxation, wielded a kind of power which even the original supporters of the Constitution had disclaimed, "and which, if [it] had been fairly avowed at the time, would have prevented . . . adoption."[57] Nonetheless, the problem they raised seems, to the modern observer, to be precisely this—that the Bank suffered, not from too much, but from too little government control.

Marshall could have met this problem by ruling (1) that Congress had the power to create a Bank for the purpose of collecting the revenue, controlling the currency, paying the government's debts, and so forth; (2) that the states had no constitutional right to levy discriminatory taxes against an arm of the federal government; but (3) that the second Bank of the United States, as then constituted, was not such an arm.[58] This would have been within the theoretical confines of *McCulloch* v. *Maryland;* but it would have left the Bank naked to its enemies, and would have crippled the legal nationalism of which he conceived himself to be the champion.

In his decision, therefore, which he read to an almost empty room on March 6, Marshall avoided *all* discussion of the private character of the Bank, and resorted instead to general principle and deductive exposition. Thus he was able to deduce from the "necessary and proper" clause the power of Congress to incorporate a bank, since this power was clearly "incidental" to the great enumerated powers "to lay and collect taxes; to borrow money; to regulate commerce; to declare and

---

finds the "private" nature of the Bank upheld. See Biddle to Monroe, May 28, 1824; Monroe Papers.

[56] Here Hopkinson quoted directly from *The Federalist,* No. 32 (p. 194 in the Modern Library ed. [New York, 1937]).

[57] See both Luther Martin and Walter Jones, 4 Wheaton 316, 373.

[58] Plous and Baker, "McCullough versus Maryland," pp. 727–728. To this article I am much indebted.

conduct a war; and to raise and support armies and navies."[59] It was, therefore, the "unanimous and decided" opinion of the Court that the Bank Act of February 10, 1816, was constitutional. The establishment of a branch bank at Baltimore was also constitutional, and the Maryland taxing Act was, *per contra,* repugnant. All this was perhaps to be expected, but what followed was more audacious. Marshall readily admitted that the power of taxation was retained by the states and not abridged by the grant of a similar power to the general government; but he went on to announce, in his most Olympian manner, that the Constitution was of so paramount a character that "its capacity to withdraw any subject from the action of even this power is admitted." In effect, the national government might withdraw from state taxation *any* taxable subject, and not merely those which the Constitution specifically withdrew! Since there was nothing in the Constitution to sustain this argument, and much that appeared to refute it, he rested his case upon the "great principle that the constitution and the laws thereof are supreme; that they control the constitution and laws of the respective states, and cannot be controlled by them."[60] Could legal nationalism go any further?[61]

As a matter of fact, it could. Audacious Marshall may have been, but he was also delphic, in the sense that he imported into his most sweeping conclusions a saving—one might add a statesmanlike—ambiguity. At the heart of this "unanimous and decided" opinion there lurked, unanswered, a very uncomfortable question: Did the grant of a power to the national government automatically withdraw that power from the states, or could the states exercise a concurrent power unless or until congressional legislation said that they could not? Since he failed to recognize this question, one senses in Marshall's opinion the admonishing presence of the Republican justices. Marshall, in fact, admitted the states' concurrent power. This being so, why did he

[59] 4 Wheaton 407.

[60] *Ibid.,* pp. 424–426.

[61] Possibly, in a politico-legal sense, Marshall went further in his statement: "Throughout this vast republic, from the St. Croix to the Gulf of Mexico, *from the Atlantic to the Pacific,* revenues are to be collected and expended, armies are to be marched and supported." 4 Wheaton 408 (italics inserted). At this moment the United States owned nothing much more beyond the Rockies than a line to the Pacific.

then make use of Webster's "a power to tax involves a power to destroy," if he did not assume that the phrase was double-edged?[62] All in all, this great opinion, establishing the national character of the United States, was also a mediating opinion: it showed that economic nationalism could not be expressed without a certain caution.

[62] "In America the powers of sovereignty are divided between the government of the Union and those of the States. They are each sovereign with respect to the objects committed to it, and neither sovereign with respect to the objects committed to the other." 4 Wheaton 410. His use of Webster's words is still a great comfort to holders of municipal and state bonds. On the other hand, in Weston v. Charleston, 9 Wheaton 738 (1824), he declared in one of his rare dissenting opinions that interest on federal bank securities was immune from state taxation.

CHAPTER 4

The Missouri Compromises

$\mathbf{A}$MONG the many attacks upon Marshall's decision,[1] the most suggestive appeared in 1820, in the form of a little book entitled *Construction Construed and Constitutions Vindicated.* Its author was John Taylor of Hazlewood, in Caroline County, Virginia, a wealthy planter,[2] agricultural reformer, and political philosopher, better known and deeply respected as John Taylor of Caroline. Several chapters of this book were devoted (without naming him) to Chief Justice Marshall and his decision in favor of the Bank. Here Taylor displayed his rather baffling gift for construing the Constitution loosely in terms of its basic philosophy and strictly in terms of its actual Federalist

---

[1] *Niles' Register,* XVI, 41 ff., called upon those who hated monopoly and privilege to rise and "purge our political temple of the money-changers." (Of Marshall's two famous decisions in February, 1819—Dartmouth College *v.* Woodward, 4 Wheaton 518, so kind to holders of corporate securities, and Sturges *v.* Crowninshield, 4 Wheaton 192—so unpopular among debtors everywhere—it must be remarked that Niles ignored the first and, XVI, 2, approved the second.) The formidable Judge Spencer Roane, president of the Virginia Court of Appeals, then took up the cudgels under the *noms de guerre* of "Amphicyton" and "Hampden"—"Amphicyton" threatening, in language more appropriate to a Hampden, an appeal to force, and "Hampden" declaring, in amphictyonic terms, that the general government "is as much a 'league' as was the former confederation"; Richmond *Enquirer,* March 30, April 2, June 11, June 15, June 22, 1819. For attacks in the legislatures of Pennsylvania, Tennessee, Ohio, Indiana, and Illinois see H. V. Ames (ed.), *State Documents on Federal Relations* (Philadelphia, 1900–1906), III, 3 ff.

[2] He owned two other plantations—Hayfield and Mill Hill.

origin.[3] The "people" became synonymous with "the states," and could be defined only as "the people of each state"—a very useful definition for an agrarian who believed that national banks, protective tariffs, and internal improvements were little better than organized theft to be defeated in the state legislatures; to whom the United States was an association of discrete "nations"; and who was truly horrified by Marshall's words that the general government "is the government of all; its powers are delegated by all; it represents all, and acts for all."[4] Thus, in his direct attack upon the Chief Justice, Taylor addressed himself to Marshall's argument that the Bank could not be taxed because it was the fiscal agent of the general government, and did so in the simplest terms. Since Congress and the states had a concurrent right of taxation, with the single exception of taxation upon imports and exports, then "congress in virtue of this concurrent right, can inflict no tax, to which the same right in the states does not extend."[5] This was unanswerable except in Marshall's terms—namely, that the same "paramount character" that expressly restrains the states from taxing imports and exports may also forbid them, if necessary, to tax anything else.[6] Did not this consist (said Marshall) "with the letter and spirit of the Constitution?"[7] In other words, Taylor was contending that the Constitution had been "given" once and for all; Marshall was proclaiming that it was organic, susceptible to change, capable of growth. In such a contest, Taylor could only succeed at the cost of proving that the letter gives life, but the spirit kills.

This he was perfectly willing to do. Even his great *Inquiry,* one of the most searching indictments of the Hamiltonian system ever written, somehow failed to touch the realities of American life because Taylor

[3] *Construction Construed and Constitutions Vindicated* (Richmond, 1820), p. 109: "The words of the Constitution are literally *imperious* in reserving to the states, for the *publick good* also, a right of taxation subject only to a positive limitation. The means by which the states may provide for raising a revenue, being expressly bestowed by the people, are surely as sacred, and as constitutional, and as likely to advance the *publick* good, as any conflicting conjectural means, which can be imagined by congress." See also E. T. Mudge's brilliant *The Social Philosophy of John Taylor of Caroline* (New York, 1939), pp. 2 ff.

[4] 4 Wheaton 405.

[5] *Construction Construed,* 96.

[6] 4 Wheaton 424–425.

[7] *Ibid.,* p. 421.

was too literally agrarian.[8] He refused to accept the proposition (which Adam Smith and Turgot had already accepted) that feudalism was becoming capitalism, from which it followed that nothing could resist the advance of capitalism into the empty lands of America. The *Inquiry* has been described as the "definitive statement of the agrarian-physiocratic doctrine in American history";[9] and this is true in the sense that the Physiocrats had constructed a philosophy for landlords and scientific farmers, just as Adam Smith may be said to have constructed one for merchants. Even the Physiocratic belief in benevolent despotism is not annulled by hyphenating Taylor's philosophy into "agrarian-Physiocratic."[10] Taylor, although somewhat cryptically, as a great landlord and slaveholder, believed in despotism too.[11]

This is where *Construction Construed* becomes very suggestive as an answer to the nationalism of *McCulloch* v. *Maryland*. *Construction Construed* ended with a defense of slavery, then under attack in the Missouri debates in Congress: it had obviously occurred to Taylor that if Congress could incorporate a bank, it might also in the end emancipate a slave. Unlike the French Physiocrats, who were endowed with the noble optimism of the eighteenth century, Taylor had in truth a despairing mind. He was not a Utopian, since the Utopian is interested in the steps by which one may get *into* Utopia: he seems rather to have conceived of America as an Eden, where one already and always *is,* and from which it becomes necessary to remove—as ideally it should be impossible to conceive—anything that might lead to expulsion. He had already perceived that an *unrestricted* capitalism must reduce the

---

[8] *Inquiry into the Principles and Policy of the Government of the United States* (Fredericksburg, 1814). For an enchanting discussion of its section on "Aristocracy," see Adams to Jefferson, September 15, 1813, and Jefferson to Adams, January 24, 1814; Lester J. Cappon (ed.), *The Adams-Jefferson Letters* (2 vols., Chapel Hill, 1959), II, 376, 421.

[9] William Appleton Williams, *The Contours of American History* (Cleveland and New York, 1961), p. 151.

[10] Except that, since there was an abundance of surplus land in America, the American "agrarian-physiocrat" could claim that agriculture *distributed* wealth, whereas a financial aristocracy *appropriated* it. *Inquiry,* pp. 550, 552 ff.

[11] It would not be an exaggeration to say that with the Physiocrats sovereignty and private property in land become identical; thus, when Marshall declared that "the power of creating a corporation is one appertaining to sovereignty," Taylor replied that "sovereignty" nowhere appears in the Constitution and that corporation is an "innately despotick" word; 4 Wheaton 408; *Construction Construed,* p. 87.

mechanic to wage slavery.[12] His answer was, in effect, abolish the whole business. Get rid of the mechanic along with the capitalist. Cancel the nineteenth century.

What then would be left? Taylor, whose private character was one of the noblest of his times, and who was a benevolent master to his many slaves, had once admitted that slaveholding was a crime.[13] He now declared that slaves were private property not subject to governmental control, and that if this property was threatened both states and individuals had a natural right of self-defense which was anterior to all political power.[14] Hitherto, private property had been something which he opposed to the "artificial" property created by the "legal faction of capitalists,"[15] as being natural; that is to say, as the effect of mixing free labor with the soil. But if slavery was private property, then was he not implying that slavery was also "natural"? Only upon these horrifying terms could the slave be kept in Eden.

Taylor was one of the great agricultural reformers of his day,[16] and his book *Arator* was one of the early bibles of soil conservation. "There is a spice of fanaticism in my nature," he said, "upon two subjects— agriculture and republicanism."[17] Of agriculture he could say that it was the source of the highest human happiness, "a constant rotation of hope and fruition."[18] This was the language of the Enlightenment, and Thomas Jefferson; but it reminds us also of Virgil's poignant *O fortunatos:* for Taylor, like Virgil, was fighting in a lost cause. The economy of the southern planter was such that it almost forced him to exhaust his soil. When it came to republicanism, however, Taylor's cause, which

---

[12] *Arator* (Georgetown, 1814), p. 36.

[13] Comparing "stock-slavery," or slavery to bankers, with chattel slavery, he had written that the former was "a slavery in which the sufferer is ignorant of his tyrant, and the tyrant is remorseless, because he is unconscious of his crime"; *Inquiry*, p. 354. This implies that the slaveholder also committed a crime, but was conscious of it.

[14] *Construction Construed*, pp. 29 ff. Compare this with Marshall's statement that contract was "anterior to and independent of society"; Ogden *v.* Saunders (1827), 12 Wheaton 334 ff.

[15] *Arator*, 35.

[16] Avery O. Craven, "The Agricultural Reformers of the Ante-bellum South," *AHR*, XXXIII (1928) 308; L. C. Gray, *History of Agriculture in the Southern United States* (2 vols., Washington, 1933), II, 801.

[17] Taylor to Jefferson, March 5, 1795, cited in Craven, "Agricultural Reformers," p. 305.

[18] *Arator*, p. 188.

he was defending against the nationalist doctrine of John Marshall and the nationalizing tendencies of the Tallmadge Amendment,[19] seems to the observer of today to be even more lost.

Behind that slave-ridden aristocracy of which Taylor was so conspicuous and so exceptional an ornament, there can be discerned a very old and formidable scheme of political coherence. This scheme was neither Jeffersonian nor Taylorian, but entirely *sui generis*. In what might be called its prelapsarian state—as it conceived itself to be, for example, in 1776—Jeffersonian Republicanism implied a faith in an America which should be composed of very small self-governing communities. Jefferson himself, at the first session of the Virginia legislature after the Declaration of Independence, introduced a bill for the more general diffusion of learning, the object of which was to divide each county into wards of five or six square miles for the establishment of free schools. "My proposition," he told John Adams,

had for a further object . . . to have made them little republics, with a Warden at the head of each, for all those concerns which, being under their eye, they could better manage than the larger republics of the country or state. A general call of ward-meetings by their Wardens on the same day thro' the state would at any time produce the genuine sense of the people on any required point, and would enable the state to act in mass, as your people have so often done, and with so much effect, by their town meetings.[20]

Such a scheme, he considered, ought to have been "the key-stone of the arch of our government." But, try as he would, he could never persuade Virginia to have anything to do with it. He was in no doubt as to the reason for his state's resistance to this nominalistic plan. It arose, he said, from "the vicious constitution of our county courts (to whom justice, the executive administration, the taxation, police, the military appointments of the county, and nearly all our daily lives are confided) self-appointed, self-continued, holding their authorities for life."[21]

[19] See p. 107, *infra*.

[20] Jefferson to John Adams, October 28, 1813; *Writings*, Ford (ed.), **X**, 346–347. "A Bill for the More General Diffusion of Knowledge," No. 79 in "Catalogue of Bills Prepared by the Committee of Revisions"; Julian P. Boyd (ed.), *The Papers of Thomas Jefferson* (Princeton, 1950), II, 526, 535.

[21] Jefferson to John Taylor of Caroline, May 28, 1816; *Writings*, Ford (ed.), **XI**, 530–531.

This system, or its equivalent, extended far beyond the borders of Virginia. In Kentucky, justices of the peace held legislative, judicial, and executive sway over local affairs, and they, too, were self-perpetuating. In North Carolina and Tennessee, county court justices held offices for life, but vacancies were filled by the legislatures. Since the justices controlled the legislatures, their peace of mind was not disturbed by this arrangement. In Maryland, county government was in the hands of four bodies—the levy court, the county court, the orphans' court, and the commissioners of the peace—whose members were appointed, sometimes for life, sometimes for limited terms, by a Governor and Council who were themselves chosen by the state legislature. But in Maryland the apportionment of seats in the lower house—four for each county—favored the more sparsely populated and more aristocratic east, while the Senate was heavily weighted toward the Eastern Shore. The Maryland legislature may have controlled the county governments, but the control was not democratic. In short, these states were still dominated, in large measure, by country squires—men who clung to their commissions as justices even when elected to the state legislatures, who made up a large proportion of the militia officers, and who were the most significant factor in party organization. In South Carolina, on the other hand, local affairs were in the hands of boards, the members of which—except for the sheriffs and the commissioners of the poor—were chosen by the legislature and usually for short terms of office. This slight concession to democracy was modified by the fact that the legislature—owing to an ingenious apportionment of seats between the number of white inhabitants and the amount of taxes paid the state—was firmly controlled by wealthy men. As the cotton kingdom moved south and southwest, still seeking an empire, it had its border satrapies in Georgia, Alabama, and Mississippi, where local affairs had a tendency to adapt themselves to frontier conditions and to remain in the hands of the people; although here (as in Louisiana) there were significant exceptions.[22]

On the whole, therefore, the oligarchic character of local govern-

---

[22] Charles R. Sydnor, *The Development of Southern Sectionalism* (Baton Rouge, 1948), Chap. 2; Chilton Williamson, *American Suffrage from Property to Democracy* (Princeton, 1960), p. 235, for reforming emphasis on representation rather than suffrage; Clement Eaton, *The Growth of Southern Civilization, 1790–1860* (New York, 1961), p. 173.

ments or the unfair apportionment of seats in the legislatures gave the old-fashioned southern squirearchy, in the days of the Tallmadge Amendment, something of the appearance of Sir Lewis Namier's "political nation." Its congressional delegations did not speak for poor men. This does not mean that they necessarily voted against the wishes of a powerless majority. If the movement toward a more equitable representation had been pronounced and passionate in the slave states in 1820—so pronounced and so passionate as to succeed in modifying the structure of local and State governments—would it then have produced a congressional South that was less unanimous in defense of slavery? So little is known of the attitude of the nonslaveholding majority in those days that one can only suggest an answer. It is not reassuring. Virginia's Staunton Convention of 1816, for example, was undoubtedly a very powerful effort on the part of a predominantly nonslaveholding section to remedy the defects in an aristocratic state constitution; but slavery itself did not enter into this particular controversy. In 1829, one observes the first public dawning of the idea that white manhood suffrage might safely be promoted as a proslavery instrument; and when the great debate in Virginia's House of Delegates in 1832 revealed a surprising determination to explore and settle the problem of slavery, it seems that this had been inspired by the Nat Turner rebellion of 1830—by fear, that is to say, and not by a troubled conscience. It is true that, as late as 1827, there were more antislavery societies in the South than in the North; but all of these were in the upper South, and mostly in eastern Tennessee or the Quaker counties of North Carolina. Elsewhere the opponents of slavery had either emigrated or been intimidated or had begun to listen to the hollow music of that respectable siren, the American Colonization Society.[23] If the congressional southern delegation represented an oligarchy in 1819, 1820, and 1821, one cannot with confidence assert that the majority whom they did not represent would have disagreed with them. What one *can* say with confidence is that this southern congressional bloc was still bound to the Republican Ascendancy, through which it hoped to maintain its accustomed control over the machinery of the federal

[23] T. P. Abernethy, *The South in the New Nation* (Baton Rouge, 1961), pp. 435–436; Williamson, *Suffrage*, pp. 231–232; Sydnor, *Southern Sectionalism*, pp. 95–96, 227; Louis Filler, *The Crusade Against Slavery* (New York, 1960), pp. 18–19; Dwight L. Dumond, *Anti-Slavery* (Ann Arbor, 1961), p. 95.

government. An accommodation was in the air, from the very beginning.

The need for a political accommodation did not, of course, alter the fact that the Republican Ascendancy—as a workable but loose liaison between old-line political leaders of the North and South—was already passing beyond the point where any real accommodation could be made. The only real accommodation would have been prohibition of slavery in Missouri, on the one hand, and a low tariff on the other. The Panic of 1819 made it unlikely that the manufacturing and free-soil-farming interests would continue to conceive of a home market in terms of the Tariff of 1816; and the phenomenal growth of upland cotton was an eloquent, if unrealistic, plea for the extension of slavery. The cotton gin alone could never have solemnized the dismal marriage between American slavery and the British textile industry if upland cotton had not superseded sea-island cotton as the great cash crop of the South. Upland (or short staple) cotton was not too expensive to cultivate, it was hardy, it could grow over large and ever larger areas: two hundred frostless days, twenty-four annual inches of rainfall—these were its requirements. Its western boundary, to be sure, was held to be the 94th meridian of longitude; its northern march stopped at the southern border of Virginia and excluded all but the western tip of Kentucky; its typical movement was southwest. But it was a natural, as the gin had been a logical, response to the appeal of Lancashire, and wherever it went it carried slavery with it: although it could be cultivated by a farmer with few slaves or none, it encouraged the gang system. Before 1815, it had been confined to the upper region of South Carolina and the eastern portion of central Georgia; but after the Peace of Ghent it moved into Alabama, Mississippi, and Louisiana, doubled itself within five years, and was to double itself again within another five.[24] Once this development had begun, a corresponding change took place within the slaveholding conscience, and the foundations of the Republican world began to sag.

Virginia was then the chief keeper of the Southern conscience, and the situation of tobacco in Virginia was such that she could not afford (even had she wished to do so) to take a moral attitude toward the claims of cotton. By 1817, the lower areas of the state had begun to

[24] Gray, *Agriculture,* II, 691. Eaton, *Southern Civilization,* p. 29.

turn a desolate face to the sky—dilapidated mansions, sedgy fields, tumbledown churches, deserted log cabins. As Jefferson was to put it: "We must either attend to recruiting our lands or abandon them & run away to Alibama [sic] as so many of our countrymen are doing."[25] The tobacco towns and ports—Georgetown, Alexandria, Tappahannock, Yorktown, Norfolk, Williamsburg—were half in ruins. Yet Virginia, then and throughout the decade, had the largest slave population in the South. If restriction in Missouri were to lead in time to emancipation by congressional fiat—as Jefferson feared it would—what could emancipation offer to the slaves in this fainting economy but "freedom & a dagger"?[26]

By the end of the decade, Virginia was beginning to set her agricultural house in order, and the agony of the unreformed tobacco kingdom was over; but it was over too late. By then the defense of slavery had become inextricably interwoven with the doctrine of state rights. The resulting texture was dreadfully coarse, and the coarseness could be observed more readily in the cotton kingdom as it moved Southwest than anywhere else. The new slaveowning cotton planter had a way of life that could hardly have recommended itself to the earlier Virginian aristocrat: it was not easygoing, it was not well-bred. Nor could it hope to mimic the serious but cosmopolitan standards of the South Carolina magnate, the master of rice and of sea-island cotton. As he pushed his way into the expanding realm of "upland" cotton, the new planter had little time for gracious living, and it is more than probable that he had less aptitude than time; that he was a product of the eighteenth century backwoods, not the eighteenth century tidewater; a creature of the continuously evolving frontier; a

[25] Edwin M. Bells (ed.), *Thomas Jefferson's Farm Book* (Philadelphia, 1953), p. 43; Eaton, *Southern Civilization*, p. 4. There was a third solution, which would not have appealed to Jefferson. During the cotton boom before the Panic, the price of a prime field hand in Virginia was $700, whereas in New Orleans it was $1,100. Gray, *Agriculture*, II, 666. Virginia might have decided to become a slave-selling state.

[26] J. B. De Bow, *Statistical View of the United States* (Washington, 1854), p. 85; Jefferson to John Adams, January 22, 1821, *Writings*, Ford (ed.), XII, 198. The fear of the slave is ironically but aptly illustrated by Justice Mills of the Kentucky Court of Appeals in Rankin *v.* Lydia, 2 A. K. Marsh 467, October 1820—"A slave by our code is not treated as a person, but [as] *negotium*, a thing . . ." cited in Helen T. Catterall (ed.), *Judicial Cases Concerning American Negro Slavery* (5 vols., Washington, 1926–37), I, 294. Justice Mills had forgotten that *"negotium"* could also mean "some undefinable terror."

symbol of that social fluidity which had, in fact though if not in legend, given its motion to the older South. His "mansion" was usually a box composed of four rooms divided by a passageway, upon which in time he might superimpose another box of similar design. It was wind-swept in winter and verminous in summer. Its front and back porches would be strewn with guns and saddles, whips and farm implements; and somewhere among this litter would be found the humble wash-basin and the dirty towel. It was the home of a busy man, who was engaged in wresting a living from a speculative crop, and who, like the volatile market which he served, was commonly on the move. In time, if bankruptcy or mobility did not supervene, his house might acquire a coat of white paint, a portico, a garden, and the usual retinue of stables, ginhouse, smokehouse, and slave "street." But rarely did he, his wife, his children, or his slaves represent a complex which had in it any trace of "Cavalier" past. If it survived its competitive and uncertain conditions, this complex was moving toward the consolidation of the 1850's, where large holdings in land and slaves had passed or were passing into fewer and fewer hands, where the ordinary slaveholder was hardly a planter, and where three-quarters of the South's white population owned no slaves at all. Even in the 1820's the concept of a South composed of planters, slaves, and poor whites was quite unreal. The typical Southerner was a yeoman farmer; and the "peculiar institution," though still a woeful burden to those who spoke for the Jeffersonian past, was already holding out delusive promises of social status and economic profits which could be realized only by a small parvenu slaveholding minority, but were not the less alluring for that. Mingled with the fear of servile revolt, these promises were easily dis-tilled into the social nostrum of White Supremacy; it is one of the tragedies of the Missouri controversy that it should have served as an alembic for this disastrous process.[27]

The debates on the admission of Missouri as a slave state, and on

---

[27] Wilbur J. Cash, *The Mind of the South* (New York, 1941), pp. 151–152; Francis B. Simkins, *The South, Old and New* (New York, 1949), p. 43; Eaton, *Southern Civilization,* p. 121; Ralph E. Morrow, "The Proslavery Argument Revisited," *Mississippi Valley Historical Review* XLVIII (1961), 81–82; Kenneth M. Stampp, *The Peculiar Institution* (New York, 1956), p. 30. Cal-houn in 1820, in a conversation with Adams, maintained that southern equality was based on the fact that no domestic servants were ever white. Adams, *Memoirs,* V, 10.

her constitution, had been preceded by certain arguments or warnings concerning congressional powers in a Territory; none the less, the famous Tallmadge amendment to the Missouri enabling bill, offered on February 13, 1819, seems to have caught the House off its guard. The amendment resolution was worded as follows:

Provided, That the further introductory of slavery or involuntary servitude be prohibited, except for the punishment of crimes whereof the party shall have been duly convicted: and that all children born within the said State [of Missouri] after the admission thereof into the Union shall be free, but may be held to service until the age of twenty-five years.[28]

James Tallmadge, Jr., a representative from the Poughkeepsie district of New York, was a somewhat solitary and puzzling figure. He had obviously consulted with John W. Taylor of the New York delegation, and possibly with others; but the maneuvers which preceded his amendment, if any, were secret enough to have left no trace behind them. Tallmadge was then supposed to be a member of the Clintonian faction in New York politics; and, since he was not a candidate to succeed himself in Congress, the Clintonians had already nominated him for state senator in 1819. According to Tallmadge, however, they had done little to support him, the inference being that he was out of favor with De Witt Clinton.[29] In spite of his legal abilities, his fine presence,

[28] *Journal of the House of Representatives*, 15 Cong., 2 sess., p. 272; *Annals of Congress*, 15 Cong., 2 sess., I, 1170, has "Shall be free at the age of 25"; see James D. Woodburn, "The Historical Significance of the Missouri Compromise," *American Historical Association, Annual Report* (1893), p. 255. John W. Taylor's attempt to insert, into a bill establishing a Territory in Arkansas, an antislavery clause similar to that of Tallmadge was defeated in the House 89–87, and the Senate 19–14. *Annals of Congress*, 15 Cong., 2 sess., pp. 1273–1274, 274. The right of Congress to prohibit slavery *in a Territory* was less likely to be disputed by a majority of Southerners in those days; hence the potential importance of the Taylor amendment, if it had passed. It was in this debate that Felix Walker of N.C. distinctly avowed what was afterward to be known as a doctrine of "Squatter Sovereignty"; *ibid.*, p. 1227.

[29] His great exertions in the Florida debate, where he made an eloquent speech for Jackson, *may* have offended Clinton more than anything else. For these exertions, see Laura Tallmadge to Mrs. M. B. Tallmadge, January 22, 1819; Tallmadge Papers, NYHS. Tallmadge wrote, "I am denounced for my support of the Administration at Washington—The Federalists are offended at my defence of Jackson—Clinton that I aided to prevent embarrassment to Monroe. . . . Before I came home I was nominated a candidate for Senator—opposed by Tammanies as a Clintonian—opposed by Federalists as a friend of Monroe—suspected and squinted at by Clinton." Tallmadge to Taylor, April

his agreeable manners, he never could make his way in New York. Jabez D. Hammond, who believed that Tallmadge wished to form his own party, called him "politically eccentric and wrongheaded." "I can safely say," wrote one of his Poughkeepsie neighbors in 1828, "that he has contrived to make himself more odious to all parties than any man who had not committed a capital crime. . . . The truth is [that] in regard to political operations, Tallmadge is one of nature's *bad bargains*."[30] Political invective in New York should not be taken too seriously: Tallmadge's faults seem to have been little more than independence, ambition, and too small a sense of the incongruous.[31] Unlike his colleague John W. Taylor, who was a politician through and through, and who believed that a stand on slavery would increase his political influence, Tallmadge may have offered his amendment because his conscience was affronted, and for no other reason. He never contemplated any interferences with slavery where it had already taken root east of the Mississippi or in Louisiana; and if he believed that Congress should exercise its national powers to the extent of legislating slavery forever out of the remainder of the Louisiana Purchase, or supposed (as he seems to have done) that the slaveholding South could be persuaded to assent to such a transaction, then his conscience was merely voicing a nationalist optimism. This optimism, in turn, was not ill-tuned to the more practical views of the North and the East. They had never been happy with the federal ratio, which turned the slave into three-fifths of a man for the purpose of apportioning representa-

---

4, 1819; John W. Taylor Papers. His senatorial district included New York City, where the free Negro vote was important (as well as the Manumission Society and Quaker vote). So Theodorus Bailey to M. B. Tallmadge, April 27, 1819; Tallmadge Papers, and New York *Columbian*, April 26, 1819. (There seems to be no ground for asserting that this was the reason behind the amendment resolution.) Clinton was not personally fond of the Tallmadges, although Judge M. B. Tallmadge was his connection by marriage. See Clinton MS. Diary, NYHS Vol., for March 13, 1822—September 12, 1823. The Diary, incidentally, gives no sign that Clinton ever consulted with Tallmadge or Taylor before or during the Missouri debates.

[30] Thiron Rudd to John W. Taylor, February 27, 1828; John W. Taylor Papers, NYHS.

[31] Tallmadge actually had some notion that he would receive a post from Monroe, in spite of his Missouri amendment! So Tallmadge to Taylor, April 4, 1819 ("Will Mr. Monroe see [me] thus sacrificed?"), and July 17, 1819 (where he suggests a commissionership under the Spanish Treaty). It was not until January 1820 that he saw the light—Tallmadge to Taylor, January 11, 1820; John W. Taylor Papers, NYHS.

tives; and it hardly agreed with their various interests for this apportionment to move across the Mississippi. Tallmadge himself, as a matter of fact, was quite frank on this subject. The trans-Mississippi region, he said, "had no claim to such an unequal representation, unjust in its results upon the other States."[32] The federal ratio, however, had hitherto been an object of Federalist-Clintonian concern; whether the Republicans of the North and East would have gone to battle over Missouri if their hands had not been forced by the Tallmadge amendment is quite another question. Only one thing is fairly certain: Tallmadge and Taylor had not been prompted by Clinton; they had not consulted with the Federalists of New York; it was on their own that they threatened to upset the Republican Ascendency and with it the peace of the Jeffersonian world.

Missouri was unlikely ever to become a great slaveholding state. Its southern soils were not favorable to cotton as a major crop, while hemp, to which its western soils were well suited, was already in need of protection. But hemp culture was so disagreeable that it was held to be fit only for slave labor: with this attraction (or excuse) to lead them on, the most characteristic immigrants since the War of 1812 had been slaveowners.[33] In 1810, Missouri contained 3,000 slaves; by 1820 this number had increased to more than 10,000; and this increase, in a total population of 66,000, and with the Northwest Territory closed to slavery because of the Ordinance of 1787, held out a promise to slaveowners at least as compelling as it was specious.[34] Missouri was a strange land, of course, for such a migration—strange and rather sinister. It was meant for diversified farming, where slavery was useless or nearly so, and its manners often displayed all the mindless ferocity of an early pioneering region. When one crossed the Mississippi, it was said, one traveled beyond the Sabbath. Probably Missouri's closest connection was with the fur trade; and where it thrust itself toward the northwest, so little was known of what lay beyond that people still owlishly declared that there was an active volcano near the sources of the Missouri River.[35] With its borders adjacent to free-soil

[32] Glover Moore, *The Missouri Controversy* (Lexington, 1953), p. 51.

[33] H. A. Trexler, *Slavery in Missouri* (Baltimore, 1914), p. 102.

[34] *Seventh Census,* 1850, p. 665; *Historical Statistics,* p. 9; Moore, *Missouri Controversy,* p. 32; De Bow, *Statistical View,* p. 65.

[35] Timothy Flint, *Recollections of the Last Ten Years* (Boston, 1826), p. 173;

Illinois and slave-soil Kentucky and Tennessee, the would-be state was a challenge both to the concept of a democratic new West and to the program, already formulated, of a diffused and beneficent slavery. With the exception of Louisiana, Missouri would be the first state to be formed out of the Louisiana Purchase. It was therefore quite possible to believe that, if slavery were excluded from Missouri, then future trans-Mississippi states would be obliged to come in upon the same terms.

Moreover, the slave-holding States, in terms of population, were already in a minority; and, with the admission of Maine and Alabama being taken for granted, it became a matter of deep concern that Missouri should enter the Union as one of the slaveholding sisterhood. In that case, her legislature would elect proslavery Senators, and the free-soil-slave soil equilibrium in the Senate could be maintained.

When Illinois was admitted in 1818, however, there had been signs of much preliminary intrigue between her antislavery and proslavery leaders. The former were able to write a constitution which, nominally at least, made her a free-soil state; the latter received, along with two proslavery senators, permission to enact a savage Black Code. How sanguine one must have been to call Illinois, at that interesting moment in her history, a member of the "northern" bloc! Yet when Tallmadge, in 1818, attacked the indentured service and limited slavery provisions in the Illinois constitution, only thirty-four representatives voted with him against admission.[36] The Tallmadge amendment of 1819, therefore, must also be considered the first serious challenge to the extension of slavery.

The debate which followed was relatively brief. However distasteful the subject might be to Republicans, there was no possible excuse for treating Missouri as if she were another Illinois. On February 16, 1819, the Committee of the Whole, by a vote of 79 to 67, included the Tallmadge amendment in the enabling bill. When the bill was reported to the House, however, and John Scott, the territorial delegate from Missouri, attacked it in terms which seemed to threaten disunion, "I hope," wrote Salma Hale of New Hampshire, "that a similar discussion

Caleb Atwater, *Remarks Made on a Journey to Prairie du Chien, Thence to Washington City in 1829* (Columbus, 1831), p. 232.

[36] Theodore Calvin Pease, *The Frontier State, 1818–1848* (Springfield, Ill., 1918), p. 47; *Annals of Congress,* 15 Cong., 2 sess., pp. 305–311.

will never again take place within our walls."[37] He was at once disappointed. After some fiery and even bloodthirsty exchanges, the House passed the amendment: by a vote of 87–76 (on its first part, prohibiting the further introduction of slavery), by a vote of 82–78 (on its second part, freeing all children born after the state's admission). In the Senate, the first part was stricken out by a vote of 22 to 16, and the second by a vote of 31 to 7. The Fifteenth Congress had only two more days to live; the House refused to concur in the Senate's action; the Senate remained obdurate.[38] Thus on March 4, 1819, the Missouri question was temporarily put to rest.

The most prominent feature of the voting at this stage was its apparently sectional character. In the House of Representatives no gentleman from a slaveholding state—except one from Delaware who had been born in Massachusetts, and one from Maryland who had been born in Pennsylvania—supported the amendment; in the Senate there was no slave-state support for either clause. In the House, only ten free-state Representatives voted against the first clause of the amendment and only fourteen against the second. If the second clause was lost by a wide margin in the Senate, this may have been due to constitutional scruples; the first clause (banning forever the further introduction of slaves) would have been passed but for the action of five free-state senators, two of them from Illinois.[39] Small as these free-state defections were, however, they were extremely suggestive. Since history is allowed to predict the past, they might today be called predictive.

In its simplest and perhaps its most deceptive form, the question raised by the Tallmadge amendment was one of the control of the Mississippi Valley. Would the amendment, if successful, dissolve the old alliance between the free-soil Northwest and the slaveholding

[37] Salma Hale to William Plumer, February 21, 1819, cited in Moore, *Missouri Controversy*, p. 49.

[38] *Annals of Congress*, 15 Cong., 2 sess., pp. 279, 1203–1205, 1214, 1215–1217.

[39] Willard Hall, representative from Delaware, born in Massachusetts, voted for both clauses; Samuel Smith of Maryland, born in Pennsylvania, voted for the second. The five free-state senators were William Palmer of Vermont, Harrison Gray Otis of Massachusetts, Abner Lacock of Pennsylvania, and Jesse B. Thomas and Ninian Edwards of Illinois. Moore, *Missouri Controversy*, p. 52; Margaret C. Norton (ed.), *Illinois Census Returns* (Springfield, 1934), p. 153; *Annals of Congress*, 15 Cong., 2 sess., pp. 272–274.

South? In the Fifteenth Congress, six representatives from the Northwest had voted for and two against the Tallmadge amendment as to its first clause, and they had divided four against four on the second. In the Senate, Indiana and Ohio had voted to retain the first clause and had been divided on the second, and Illinois had been consistently proslavery. In the Sixteenth Congress, however, the Northwest representatives were all antislavery when the choice was fairly put up to them, and in the Senate only the two senators from Illinois retained their proslavery position. It would seem, therefore, that the northwestern states, in spite of their strong infusion of southern immigrants, inclined toward the North and East as the Missouri debates continued, and that a political "north" was beginning to emerge. Would it be proof, in the Sixteenth Congress, against the kind of defection which had been revealed, or glimpsed, in the Fifteenth?

The Missouri situation was complicated from the start for the Sixteenth Congress by the fact that the District of Maine was also applying for admission to statehood, so that the enemies of slavery restriction in Congress were able to assert that the admission of Missouri would be no more than a fair equivalent for the admission of Maine. "Equality is equality," said Henry Clay, when the Maine Enabling Bill came before the Committee of the Whole on December 30, 1819, "and if it is right to make the restriction of slavery the condition of the admission of Missouri, it is equally just to make the admission of Missouri the condition of that of Maine."[40] Mr. Clay had just been elected Speaker of the House in this new, or Sixteenth, Congress; and his definition of "equality" carried with it all his authority in the matter of selecting committees. Otherwise, since no one doubted that the admission of Maine satisfied every moral and constitutional condition, he could only have been understood to mean that unless members of the House did what many of them presumably believed to be wrong, he himself had no intention of doing what he acknowledged to be right.

The Enabling Bill was passed after a stiff debate, and sent up to the Senate on January 3, 1820. It emerged from the Senate Judiciary Committee with a bill tacked on to it by a wafer, and this bill admitted Missouri without restriction. Senator Roberts of Pennsylvania at once moved to recommit; his motion was lost (January 14) by a vote of 25 to 18; a further motion of his, adding an antislavery proviso to the

40 *Annals of Congress,* 16 Cong., 1 sess., I, 832.

PEACE.

Office of the Political and Commercial Register,
Sunday, Feb. 12th, 1815—2 o'clock, P. M.

We have the heartfelt satisfaction of announcing to our Fellow Citizens, that an express passed through Philadelphia this morning for Washington, bearing the most welcome intelligence that a Treaty of PEACE had been signed by the American and British Commissioners on the 24th of December.

Mr. Carrol, who brings the Treaty, arrived at New York in the British Sloop of War Favorite, Capt. J. Maxwell.

When the Express left New York last night at 11 o'clock, the City was brilliantly Illuminated in honor of this most grateful event.

Our Church Bells are now saluting the great occasion with a joyful peal.

The Southern Mail of this day brings nothing new.

---

1. A broadside gives news of the signing of the Treaty of Ghent

(Courtesy of the New-York Historical Society, New York City)

2. JAMES MONROE by Asher B. and after Gilbert Stuart

(Courtesy of the New-York Histo Society, New York City)

3. A section of the Monroe Doctrine in Monroe's handwriting, from the message to Congress, December 2, 1823. Original in the Library of Congress

(Culver Service)

4. ANDREW JACKSON by Thomas Sully

(In the Collection of the Corcoran Gallery of Art)

5. JOHN QUINCY ADAMS by Thomas Sully

(Mellon Collection, National Gallery of Art, Washington, D.C.)

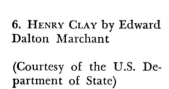

6. HENRY CLAY by Edward Dalton Marchant

(Courtesy of the U.S. Department of State)

UNITED STATES BANK,

7. Second Bank of the United States, c. 1824

(Historical Society of Pennsylvania)

DETROIT IN 1820,

WITH VIEW OF WALK-IN-THE-WATER.

8. Detroit in 1820

(The I. N. Phelps Stokes Collection, the New York Public Library)

9. GEORGE CANNING
by Sir Thomas Lawrence

10. MARTIN VAN BUREN

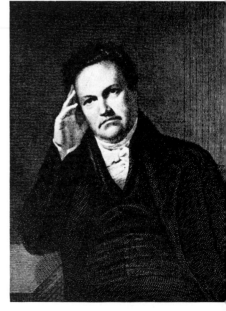

11. ROBERT BANKS JENKINSON,
Earl of Liverpool

12. DE WITT CLINTON

13. THOMAS H. BENTON

(Bettmann Archive)

14. CHIEF JUSTICE JOHN MARSHALL
by John B. Martin

15. WILLIAM HARRIS CRAWFORD
by John Wesley Jarvis

Pennsylvania Academy of the Fine Arts)

16. JOHN C. CALHOUN
by John Wesley Jarvis

(Yale University Art Gallery, gift of John
Hill Morgan)

17. Election scene c.1815 by John L. Krimmel

18. The Old House of Representatives by Samuel F. B. Morse

(In the Collection of the Corcoran Gallery of Art)

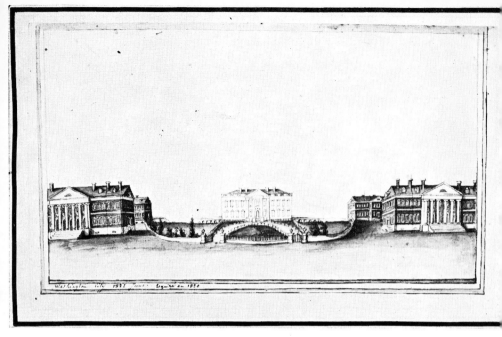

19. City of Washington in 1821

(The I. N. Phelps Stokes Collection, the New York Public Library)

20. Capitol of the United States, Washington

(The I. N. Phelps Stokes Collection, the New York Public Library)

21. JOHN RANDOLPH
by John Wesley Jarvis

ourtesy of the New-York Historical So-
ty, New York City)

22. DANIEL WEBSTER
by G. P. A. Healy

(Courtesy of the New-York Historical Society, New York City)

23. JAMES MADISON
by Asher B. Durand

ourtesy of the New-York Historical So-
ty, New York City)

24. ALBERT GALLATIN
by William H. Powell

(Courtesy of the New-York Historical Society, New York City)

"*Jackson is to be President, and you will be HANGED.*"

25. Campaign cartoon against Andrew Jackson, 1828

(Bettmann Archive)

Some Account of some of the Bloody Deeds of
GEN. JACKSON.

26. A broadside against Jackson, 1828

(Courtesy of the New-York Historical Society, New York City)

27. An 1824 caricature engraving

(Courtesy of the New-York Historical Society, New York City)

28. New York's Broadway, water color by Baron Axel Leonhard Klinckowström, 1818-1*

(Courtesy of the New-York Historical Society, New York City)

29. The plain of West Point, drawing by J. Milbert, 1818

(Courtesy of the New-York Historical Society, New York City)

30. Governor De Witt Clinton opening the Erie Canal in October, 1825

(New York Public Library)

31. A Mississippi steamer, 1823
(Culver Pictures)

32. The Mississippi at New Orleans, drawing by Basil Hall
(Courtesy of the New-York Historical Society, New York City)

33. Interior of the Park Theatre, New York City, November, 1822. Water color by John Searle

(Courtesy of the New-York Historical Society, New York City)

amendment admitting Missouri, was lost (February 1) by a vote of 27 to 16.[41] On February 16, the Senate concurred in the report of its Judiciary Committee, uniting the Maine and Missouri bills by a vote of 23 to 21. Whereupon Senator Jesse B. Thomas of Illinois proposed an amendment to the combined bills, prohibiting slavery in the organized Louisiana Purchase north of 36°30'. This amendment, in effect, admitted Maine as a free state and Missouri as a slave state, left Oklahoma and Arkansas open to slaveholders, and freed the soil of the remainder of the Louisiana Purchase north of 36°30'. On February 17, this amendment was passed by a vote of 34 to 10; and the Maine-Missouri bill, with the Thomas amendment, was then ordered to be engrossed and read a third time by a vote of 24 to 20.[42]

The Thomas amendment and the Maine-Missouri bill with the amendment were both acceptable to senators from slaveholding states: they were 14–8 for the former and 20–2 for the latter. On the other hand, if Ninian Edwards and Jesse B. Thomas of Illinois, William Hunter of Rhode Island, and John F. Parrott of New Hampshire had not voted for engrossing the Maine-Missouri bill, this measure would have been lost by 24 to 20.[43] The sectional nature of this vote must be examined in due time; at the moment it is necessary to point out that, among the legal and constitutional arguments which the slaveholding senators employed, and in which they excelled, there were two expositions of quite another character. On January 26, Senator William Smith of South Carolina, a strict Jeffersonian (of whom, however, one could not say "like master, like man"), uttered an impassioned justification of slavery, in which he begged the assembled senators, as a final argument, to consult Leviticus xxv, 44–46. "Mr. President," was his memorable conclusion, "the Scriptures teach us that slavery was universally indulged among the holy fathers. The chosen people of God were slaves."[44] Mr. Smith seems to have forgotten the book of Exodus; his arguments, in any case, were not pleasing to his fellow South Carolinians; and he is notable only for having anticipated the

---

[41] *Ibid.*, pp. 8, 41, 85, 118, 359.

[42] *Ibid.*, pp. 424, 427, 428–430.

[43] Edwards and Thomas were consistently proslavery in these debates; both were Southerners by birth. Parrott voted against the Roberts motion to recommit the Senate's Missouri bill, *ibid.*, p. 118; and Hunter and Parrott against the Roberts proviso to strike slavery out of the Bill, *ibid.*, p. 359.

[44] *Ibid.*, pp. 269–270.

day when they, too, would justify slavery by an appeal to the laws of God. A more significant speech was made by Senator Nathaniel Macon of North Carolina, one of the most venerated figures in that body, as he was one of the simplest and most honest, who looked and behaved like the survivor from some pure and almost imaginary past, and whose long record of negative votes attested his reluctance to accept the future. Now he stepped out of the past, of which he was so conspicuous an ornament, and began to adjust himself to a future in which the South would assert that slavery was not a necessary evil but a positive good. But this was not all. "A clause in the Declaration of Independence has been read," he said, "declaring that 'all men are created equal'; follow that sentiment and does it not lead to universal emancipation?" The Declaration of Independence, he declared, "is no part of the Constitution or of any other book. . . . *There is no place for free blacks in the United States.*"[45]

This last sentence brought the Missouri question into premature focus with an aim which, it has justly been written, was far more revolutionary than freedom. "The attainment of equality," C. Vann Woodward has reminded us, "involved many more relationships than

[45] *Ibid.,* pp. 227–228. In the course of the same speech Mr. Macon said: "I wish that [Senator James Burrill of Rhode Island and Senator Jonathan Roberts of Pennsylvania] would go home with me, or with some other southern member, and see the glad faces and the hearty shaking of hands." This idealized picture was echoed in the House, far more deplorably, by Charles Pinckney of South Carolina on February 14, 1820. "Every slave has a comfortable house, is well fed, clothed, and taken care of; *he has his family about him,* and in sickness has the same medical aid as his master, and has a sure and comfortable retreat in old age. . . . During his whole life he is *free from care,* that canker of the human heart." *Ibid.,* II, 1325. It was then well known that the kindest of masters could not prevent a slave family from being broken up, after his death, to satisfy the debts of his estate. See Negro George *v.* Corse, 2 Harris and Gill, June 1827, Court of Appeals of Maryland, and Cannon *v.* Jenkins, 1 Devereux Eq. 422, June 1830, where a North Carolina judge said that slave families *must* be dispersed whenever the executor discovers that the interest of the estate requires it; under these circumstances the marriage contract was held to be "dormant" during servitude, as appears in Good *v.* Lewis, 10 Martin La. 558, May 1819. Or again, the slave could hardly be carefree when he was exposed to what Justice Ruffin of the Supreme Court of North Carolina called "the harsh but necessary discipline [which is] a curse of slavery," in State *v.* Mann, 2 Devereux 263, December 1829; or when subjected to the brutality which Justice Abraham Nott of South Carolina, in 2 Nott and McCord 460, January 1819, held to be its own reward since it "damaged the most valuable species of personal property held in this country." Catterall, *Judicial Cases,* IV, 69; II, 59; III, 461; II, 57, 336.

those between master and slave. It was a revolution that was not confined to the defeated and discredited [post-bellum] South, as emancipation largely was. It was a revolution for the North as well."[46] Before the weary debates of 1820–21 were over, the principle of equality had been brought home to the North and had become—to the observer of today—the issue which defeated and discredited everyone.

It was, to be sure, an issue which, in those days when the lights of anthropology had scarcely been lit, was so wrapped in obscurity as almost, but not quite, to defy inspection. Jefferson himself, who held as a cardinal belief that mankind was a single species, descended from an original two parents, spent many an agonized hour over his own Declaration. Had God, he sometimes asked himself, made a special creation of Negroes? As a humane and enlightened man, no less than as a strict Linnaean, he shuddered away from an affirmative answer; and even as a slaveholder, to whom an affirmative answer would have been final and consoling, he felt obliged to admit that the Negro, subjected to a favorable environment, would one day "become" the white man's equal. This did violence to his natural philosophy, which held that environment produced nothing more than variety; but it did worse damage to his republican faith, since it forced him to admit that the United States, with all its superb and exemplary promises, could never provide such an environment.[47] In 1820 and 1821, northern legislators, less subtle, less enlightened, but with no slaveholdings to darken their thinking, reached the same conclusion with hardly any thought at all.

Thus the political and sectional problem originally raised by the Tallmadge amendment, the problem of the control of the Mississippi Valley, quite failed to conceal this profound renunciation of human rights. To put it another way, the control of the trans-Mississippi West was still somewhat abstract and compelled the imagination (with which the Sixteenth Congress was not notably endowed) more powerfully than it affected the interest of those involved. Until the Thomas amendment line of 36°30' appeared in 1820, the West was a huge expanse of territory stretching from the Lakes to the Gulf. Mr. Adams'

---

[46] C. Vann Woodward, *The Burden of Southern History* (Baton Rouge, 1960), p. 79.

[47] Daniel Boorstin, *The Lost World of Thomas Jefferson* (New York, 1948), Chap. 3.

treaty with Spain had drawn its trans-Mississippi confines as far as the Rockies, after which (according to the treaty) it became a line—laden with promise, but still a line—all the way to the Pacific. With the Thomas amendment a trans-Mississippi Southwest took shape. It consisted of the Territory of Arkansas, unorganized Oklahoma, and the State of Louisiana. In Arkansas there were a little over 14,000 persons, 11 per cent of whom were slaves.[48] Of Oklahoma nothing was known until 1820, when it was reported unfit for agriculture.[49] No great leap into expansionism was required in order to perceive in Texas a future American province, or to look for more remote advantages as the Spanish Empire crumbled; but the question of when or how or why this should occur was still very much up in the air. Cotton was believed to be incapable of passing the meridian of 94, which gave it at best an interest in the nearer river-bottom lands of Texas; while the mountains and valleys of New Mexico and Arizona were of concern only to trappers until the first Santa Fe expedition was organized in 1821. Over the whole area there still brooded an immense surmise. It was all very well for Senator Rufus King, who incidentally voted for it, privately to condemn the Thomas amendment because it gave the North "a prairie, without wood or water, excepting the great River and its branches," whereas south of the line there was room for "at least five slave states." He did not explain, and hardly could have explained in 1820, how or when these slave states were to come into being. In the new Northwest, above the Thomas line, the existence of an American desert was, it is true, so taken for granted that it was not even mentioned in Congress;[50] but the South's apparent willingness to accept the

[48] *A Century of Population Growth*, p. 57.
[49] Report of Major Stephen H. Long, in Edwin James (ed.), *Account of an Expedition from Pittsburg to the Rocky Mountains, 1819, 1820* (Glendale, 1905); W. Eugene Hollon, *The Southwest Old and New* (New York, 1961), pp. 92, 469.
[50] Rufus King to J. A. King, March 4, 1820; *Life and Correspondence*, VI, 289. Moore, *Missouri Controversy*, pp. 115 ff., argues that the existence of a "great American desert" north of 36° 30′ was not mentioned in Congress because this particular myth arose from Long's exploration, which was not concluded until after the amendment had been adopted. However the existence of such a "desert" had been announced by Zebulon Pike in 1810. Henry Nash Smith, *Virgin Land* (Cambridge, 1950); Elliott Coues (ed.), *The Expeditions of Zebulon Montgomery Pike* (3 vols., New York, 1895), II. Henry M. Brackenridge, *Views of Louisiana* (Baltimore, 1814), p. 72, attacked the "prevailing idea [prevailing in 1811, when he made his journey] of these western regions

doctrine that slavery could be forbidden in unorganized territory shows, also, how uncertain it was concerning the remoter aspects of the new Southwest.[51]

The Missouri debates are a witness to the great postwar shift in economy from a colonial to an internal and national orientation; but as regards large portions of the trans-Mississippi West, the shift was scarcely discernible. The Transportation Revolution was still in its infancy. The steamboat was already on the western waters, but it was waiting for its great release in *Gibbons* v. *Ogden*. The railroad did not exist. The Erie Canal, that artery from west to east, was incomplete. The frontier itself had barely struggled out of the forest.[52] The whole United States waited for some impulse which would hurl it across the Mississippi. In the meantime, the internal northwestern market was still organizing itself to some extent toward southern and southwestern slavery, which was beginning to consolidate around a one-crop system and was no longer willing to subsist its slaves from the produce of its own plantations.[53] At the same time, the price and

---

being . . . susceptible to cultivation." By 1817 leading Missourians spoke of the region west of their proposed state as "naked and sterile plains on the way to the Rockies." Floyd C. Shoemaker, *Missouri's Struggle for Statehood* (Jefferson City, 1916), p. 323. The fact that *no* free state opposing the Thomas amendment mentioned the Pike or Brackenridge reports is more in favor of their having been accepted by, than of their being unknown to, a large group of presumably literate men.

[51] The principle of popular sovereignty is to be discerned in the South's constitutional position, i.e., that Missouri might frame a constitution permitting slavery if a majority chose to do so. Had the South, in 1820, expected to expand in the near future beyond the limits of the Louisiana Purchase, the Compromise might have been more bitterly contested, since popular sovereignty and congressional prohibition of slavery *anywhere* are incompatible. Of course, many Southerners held the Ordinance of 1787 could not be made to apply to the condition of *statehood;* i.e., it was not binding in Ohio, Indiana, and Illinois. Therefore, if the lands were acquired, by purchase or conquest, beyond the Louisiana Purchase line, no new congressional restrictionist ordinance could apply to the eventual condition of statehood there. Cf. James Madison to James Monroe, February 10, 1820, *Works,* Cong. ed., III, 165. A majority of southern congressmen were at least willing to concede, in 1820, that Congress could always prohibit slavery in a Territory; this indicates a lack of interest in the future of unorganized Oklahoma. A minority refused to make even this concession, of course. Moore, *Missouri Controversy,* p. 63; cf. *Annals of Congress,* 16 Cong., 1 sess., pp. 164, 293, 322, 1001–1002, 1222, 1282–1287.

[52] Bidwell and Falconer, *History of Agriculture,* p. 531.

[53] The flow of western produce from the Ohio Valley toward the South and Southwest shows, in the increase in the exported surplus of pork and pickled

acreage of cotton, although cotton and slavery had become insepa-rable,[54] could not have justified that separation from the Union which southern legislators threatened if they did not get their way, and which would have thrown them upon the dubious mercies of the Liverpool market. All talk of secession or of civil war in 1821 seems mere gas-conade in the light of an economy and a geography which *at the time* rather conspicuously demanded a composition of differences. Only a real concern for Negro rights, for equality as well as freedom, could have inspired the northern majority to hold the line; and of this there was little trace.

The debates in House and Senate alike ranged endlessly over the validity or otherwise of the three-fifths clause; over the meaning of the Constitution when it referred to "migration"; over the proper in-terpretation of the Louisiana Purchase Treaty of 1803, and the condi-tional or unconditional admission of the State of Louisiana. Time and time again one side advanced and the other repelled the idea that if slavery were diffused over the Union its evils would be diminished without an increase in its numbers. Nothing was proved beyond the fact that slavery was all too easy to attack, impossible to justify with-out impugning the revolutionary past, and readily defended by the interminable chopping of constitutional logic.[55] In the end, legislators

---

beef, that the subsistence of slavery was a strong feature. 1822–24 average re-ceipts of produce at New Orleans: pork, 3,062,000; pickled beef, 495,467. 1825–1828 average receipts: pork, 7,828,000; pickled beef, 1,026,420 (all in lbs.). Some of this increase is of course due to increased acreage and popula-tion. Bidwell and Falconer, *ibid.*, p. 173; U.S. Bureau of Statistics (Treasury Department), *Report on the Internal Commerce of the United States* (Wash-ington, 1887), pp. 195, 196, 200–202. The completion of the Erie Canal in 1825 was followed in time by the great migration of wheat to the western plains and a flow of western produce into the East. In 1820 and 1821, there was no such movement to counteract the produce alliance between the old Northwest and the slaveholder of the South and Southwest. For freight rates between West and East in the early 1820's, see W. Faux in R. G. Thwaite (ed.), *Early Western Travels*, XI, 291; *Early Western Travels*, X, 142; Turner, *Rise of the New West*, p. 100; *Annals of Congress*, 18 Cong., 1 sess., I, 991.

[54] Douglass C. North, *The Economic Growth of the United States* (Engle-wood Cliffs, 1961), p. 123, says that only once in the years 1815–60, i.e., "for a brief period in the 1840's," was the price of cotton so low as to suggest a profit-able shift of capital and labor to other employment.

[55] On the meaning and scope of "migration," for example, Charles Pinckney of South Carolina said that, as a member of the Constitutional Convention, he could swear that it referred solely to *free whites!* *Annals of Congress*, 16 Cong., 1 sess., II, 1325. See also James Madison to Robert Walsh, November 27, 1819,

grew weary of their own language. "The words civil war and disunion," said Henry Clay, "are uttered almost without emotion."[56]
These words were a threat not so much to the Union as to the Republican Ascendency: it was the latter and less venerable structure
which the free-state and slave-state delegations were about to pull down,
if language could do it, upon their own heads; and from this act they
recoiled, at last, in dismay. Their speeches had become more sectional
than their spirit.

An insinuation made very early in the House debate pointed the
way. Mr. Holmes, who lived in the District of Maine, had apostasized
to the proslavery ranks because he wished to disentangle the admission
of Maine from that of Missouri, and he was the first to suggest openly
that the purpose behind the movement to restrict Missouri was a new
alignment of parties. New York, he hinted, was the center of this
conspiracy; and he barely concealed his belief that Rufus King and
De Witt Clinton—a Federalist and (as many believed) a crypto-
Federalist—were its leaders.[57]

It was Clinton's fate, and in some measure his deserts, to be suspected of everything; but King was a man upon whom the character
of conspirator sat very oddly indeed. His long career spoke only of
respectability, dignity, patriotism: no one had ever seriously questioned
his public or his private virtue. In 1819, however, he spoke with what
seemed to many too great a warmth in favor of the Tallmadge amendment, and in January, 1820, he was re-elected to the Senate by a
legislature composed almost entirely of his political opponents. The
reason for this was that both New York factions believed that his
influence would be important in the coming campaign for governor
between De Witt Clinton and Vice-President Daniel D. Tompkins.[58]
But from then onward the notion that a Federalist-Clintonian alliance
was "plotting" to build a new northern party out of the ruins of the
Republican Ascendency was never absent from the Missouri debates.

Works (Cong. ed.), III, 150–151, where it is argued that "migration" refers
to migration from overseas.

[56] Clay to Adam Beatty, January 22, 1820; Parton, *Works,* IV, 60.

[57] *Annals of Congress,* 16 Cong., 1 sess., I, 225.

[58] Hammond, *Political Parties in New York,* I, 480. Van Buren, before throwing his support to King, said that the Missouri question "conceals *as far as he is
concerned* no plot," Van Buren to M. M. Noah, December 17, 1819, Van
Buren Papers, LC.

When King heard of these rumors, he was most unhappy. First he tried to transfer the odium to Clinton; then, when he himself was accused of presidential ambitions, he disclaimed them as "views and motives which I am by no means influenced by—my sole and only object being to oppose the extension of slavery."[59] And yet, when he was asked by Van Buren to throw his support to Tompkins, he replied in confidence that Tompkins was unsound on slavery restriction—a question which, he continued, "w[ith] respect to opinion in the northern states will swallow up all other divisions."[60] Van Buren's support for restriction in Missouri (as he later confessed in his autobiography) was purely nominal because he suspected that it would foster just such thoughts as King's. But he was, as usual, careful to keep all this to himself and King continued to believe that Van Buren's "views and principles, as far as I have understood them, deserve my hearty approbation"; whereas Clinton had succeeded in "breaking up and degrading the federal party in 1812," to such an extent that "in the State it is in my view dissolved."[61] When it came to throwing his influence to Tompkins, however, King still confessed he could not do so: Tompkins was unsound on slavery extension.

It is impossible not to read this cautious and somewhat muddled correspondence without perceiving that the idea of a new antislavery party was faintly dawning upon King's respectable mind.[62] It all comes out in a letter from a Maryland Federalist, Senator Robert H. Goldsborough, and in King's answer to it. Senator Goldsborough, who had voted *against* restriction, declared that the Federalist party could never again get a foothold in the general government, that "perhaps our keeping it alive might rather operate against our wishes at a Presidential election after Mr. Monroe's next term expires," but that Mary-

[59] King to J. A. King, February 20, February 25, 1820, Rufus King Papers, NYHS.

[60] Martin Van Buren to Rufus King, March 12, 1820, Rufus King Papers, NYHS. Rufus King's notation on this letter says that he answered it on March 17, 1820.

[61] Martin Van Buren, *Autobiography*, John Fitzpatrick, ed. (in *American Historical Association, Annual Report*, 1918), pp. 99–100. Rufus King to J. A. King, March 18, 1820, Rufus King Papers, NYHS.

[62] Rufus King to C. King, February 20, 1820. Here he places far more emphasis on the breakup of the Republican party east of the Mississippi than he does upon sectional ambitions to the west of it. *Life and Correspondence*, VI, 279.

land must preserve her own Federalist party so as to "give her weight
in the scale of the Presidential election to a gentleman from the
North." The northern and eastern states must then compromise all
political differences; they must unite with Pennsylvania, Ohio, Indiana,
and Illinois; Delaware and Pennsylvania must become their southern
frontier; and so they "would rule the destiny of this country until the
Day of Disunion." Of this quaint if not demented prospectus, Mr. King
said in reply: "You have correctly understood and expressed my
political Principles and opinions."[63]

When he received this letter he had long since made those two
speeches at which (said John Quincy Adams) "the great slaveholders . . . gnawed their lips and clenched their fists," speeches
which afforded the orator such gratification as is derived from the
successful exercise of moral rhetoric, but which were soon followed by
the first Compromise.[64] It was not until after this apparently decisive
event that King—according to the available evidence—ever committed
himself as thoroughly as he did in his reply to Senator Goldsborough.
No doubt the Missouri question did awaken, in some minds, this curious
pale dream of a northern antislavery party, in which Federalists and
Republicans would compose their differences; and King was one of
the dreamers. But he had only a slight interest in the trans-Mississippi
West,[65] and he never could have assumed the character of a free-soil

[63] Robert H. Goldsborough to Rufus King, May 30, 1820; Rufus King to
Robert H. Goldsborough, June 4, 1820; Rufus King Papers, NYHS.

[64] These speeches are merely mentioned in *Annals of Congress*, 16 Cong.,
1 sess., I, 373, 418. They are printed in *Life and Correspondence*, VI, 690–
703. His speeches in the Fifteenth Congress on the Missouri question are
printed as *Substance of Two Speeches . . . By the Honorable Rufus King of
NewYork* (New York, 1819). Adams, *Memoirs*, IV, 522. On February 11, King
excited great wrath by saying that slavery was "contrary to the law of nature,
which is the law of God . . . and . . . paramount to all human control." On
February 16, he was understood to say that he felt "degraded" by having to sit
in the same chamber with men who represented slaves. He explained to the
editors of the *National Intelligencer* [Messrs. Gales and Seaton] that he meant
"politically inferior" because of the 3/5 ratio. King to "Mm Editors," rough
draft, apparently written July 20, 1820, Rufus King Papers, NYHS.

[65] When the Transcontinental Treaty was concluded, he wrote that he would
believe this the greatest treaty ever made, the Treaty of Peace and Independence only excepted, "if I could believe that an extension or increase of Territory
was a blessing or desirable object." King to C. King, February 23, 1819, Rufus
King Papers, NYHS. Years before, when Minister to London, he made much
the same objection to the Louisiana Purchase. King to R. R. Livingston, May
16, 1803, Robert R. Livingston Papers, NYHS.

leader. On the other hand, he may well have been using a genuine moral conviction for the sake of political advantage. If the Federalist party was, as he said, "dissolved" in New York, perhaps the Republican proscription would be relaxed if Federalists in that state admitted the dissolution.

The evidence hardly admits any other conclusion. There is no trace of a Federalist "plot," at least as regards the origins of the Tallmadge amendment; there never was a Federalist-Clintonian "conspiracy," at any rate in the mind of Rufus King, its reputed leader, who abjured Clinton.[66] But the word "conspiracy" was, then as now, unduly persuasive; it was a portmanteau word to which men consigned their irrational fears and suspicions, and the Federalists had long been credited with conspiratorial powers which they did not possess. In this way, the sectional character of the Missouri question—a character which, of course, it never lost—was overlaid, as it were, by considerations of Republican unity, and a battle which might have been very noble began to degenerate by degrees into the last stand of an outdated organization.[67]

The House had been debating its own Missouri bill, with an antislavery amendment by John W. Taylor, who had become the doubtful leader of the restrictionist forces.[68] On February 23, by a vote of 93–72,

[66] As a further argument, Shaw Livermore, Jr., *The Twilight of Federalism, 1815–1830* (Princeton, 1962), pp. 92–93, shows that Representative Henry Baldwin of Pittsburgh, for example, "feared Southern opposition to economic legislation more than he did slavery in Missouri," and that others, such as Senator Harrison Gray Otis, believed that Federalist opposition would merely serve to unite the Republicans. (Otis, of course, still hoped to cajole from the Republicans a payment to Massachusetts on account of her militia expenses in the War of 1812.)

[67] Just how high the desire for party unity should be placed in any hierarchy of causes is naturally debatable. Moore, *Missouri Controversy,* pp. 106–107, 178, gives convincing evidence of the fear of a Federalist renaissance, and says that when sufficient northern Republicans believed that Federalists and Clintonians were out to make political capital, "a compromise with the South was inevitable." Livermore, *Twilight of Federalism,* pp. 88–95, argues that a compromise was not widely acceptable in the North, and that the "plot" was used as an excuse. In either argument, concern for the party structure seems a leading cause. That a small majority of the southern legislators was *openly* willing to accept a favorable compromise suggests an unwillingness to abandon the traditional southern leadership in Republican affairs, and a fear of economic isolation. Adams, *Memoirs,* IV, 518, points out that the South had, both emotionally and factually, more to lose if there had been no Compromise.

[68] The amendment, since it declared all children born of slaves to be free at

it declined to accept the Senate bill, in so far as it had been amended to unite the admission of Maine with that of Missouri; it then decided, 102 to 68, to disagree with the residue of the Senate amendments (the details of the Missouri bill), with the exception of the Thomas amendment; and the Thomas amendment it dismissed by a vote of 159 to 18.[69] On February 25, it succeeded in passing the Taylor amendment by "from 12 to 18 votes."[70] On February 26, the Senate having sent a message insisting upon all the amendments to its own bill, the House declined by a vote of 97 to 76 upon the first eight sections, and of 160 to 14 upon the last.[71] If ever a moral deadlock had been reached, this was it.

But now, as if by prearrangement, resistance began to crumble and dissolve. On February 29, the House agreed to a conference with the Senate; and on March 1, while the conference was still being held, passed its own Missouri bill and sent it upward.[72] On March 2, the Senate returned this bill, after striking out the restrictionist proviso and adding the Thomas amendment, and on that day the joint conference committee recommended compliance.[73] Nothing remained but to vote on the Compromise, not as a whole, but in two portions. On the question of striking out slavery restriction, the House agreed to do so by a vote of 90 to 87. It then accepted the Thomas amendment by 134 to 42.[74]

Such a reversal of opinion, so sudden and so ignominious, has been attributed to parliamentary management: specifically to Mr. Speaker Clay, who chose the right kind of men for the conference committee, and who saw to it that the Compromise was voted upon in two sections. His influence in the committee choice can hardly be denied, but there were parliamentarians upon the antislavery side who could have

---

birth, was somewhat stronger than that of Tallmadge in the Fifteenth Congress, but Moore, *Missouri Controversy*, p. 86, shows that Taylor was already suspected of lukewarmness. The amendment is in *Annals of Congress*, 16 Cong., 1 sess., I, 947. Supporting this amendment on January 27, 1820, Taylor contrived to suggest that Missouri restriction was a lost cause, and then to predict the awful consequences of this preordained loss. *Ibid.*, pp. 965–966.

[69] *Ibid.*, II, 1455–1457.
[70] *Ibid.*, 1540.
[71] *Ibid.*, 1553, 1556.
[72] *Ibid.*, 1572.
[73] *Ibid.*, I, 469; II, 1576–1577.
[74] *Ibid.*, II, 1586–1588.

forced a vote on the Compromise as a whole, had they wished to do so. On the crucial vote, for them, to strike slavery restriction out of the Missouri bill, the free-state representatives voted 87 to 14 against such a measure, with four abstentions. On the acceptance of the Thomas amendment, their end of the bargain, the slave-state representatives voted in its favor, 39 to 37. It can thus be argued, and has been argued, that the Compromise, so far from being a compact between the North and the South, was "merely an agreement between a small majority of Southern members of Congress and a small minority of Northern ones."[75] The argument is succinct, and gives to this dismal compact an air of compactness; but is it well founded? Can a small minority, for example, get its way without at least a tacit consent on the part of the majority?[76] It is more probable that antislavery feeling in the House was simply not strong enough to face the disagreeable results of a prolonged quarrel. If the fourteen voters and the four absentees had not decided for slavery, there were others (said John Randolph, always preternaturally keen to detect a weakness) who would have done as much.[77] Thus the Republican Ascendency was saved for the time being, and the first great free-soil battle was lost.[78]

The Compromise became a focus for prophecy—that is to say, for the frank recognition that compromise and postponement are not quite the same thing. As Thomas Jefferson put it, he considered the controversy itself to be the knell of the Union, hushed by the Compromise but not stilled. He said that a geographical line, coinciding with a

[75] Moore, *Missouri Controversy*, p. 111.

[76] It is well founded only if one assumes that most northern legislators believed with Representative Joseph Hemphill of Pennsylvania that the Compromise was an ordinary act, which could be repealed at any time. *Annals of Congress*, 16 Cong., 1 sess., II, 1134. There is no evidence for this.

[77] Rufus King to John A. and Charles King, March 5, 1820; *Life and Correspondence*, VI, 29. Randolph said he had known "these would give way. They were scared of their own dough faces! We had *them*, and if we wanted *three* more, we could have had them: yes, and if *these* had failed, we could have had three more of these men. . . ." Moore, *Missouri Controversy*, p. 104, citing Pittsburgh *Statesman*, April 26, 1820.

[78] Randolph voted for the majority on March 2, for the sole purpose of moving to reconsider the next day. He was twice ruled out of order by Henry Clay on March 3, while the business of receiving and referring petitions was going on, in the course of which Clay surreptitiously signed the bill and had it smuggled into safety. Randolph never forgave him for what Adams called "an unprincipled artifice." *Annals of Congress*, 16 Cong., 1 sess., II, 1590; Adams, *Memoirs*, V, 4.

marked principle, moral and political, had been held up to the angry passions of men, and that it would never be obliterated. "The cession of that kind of property," he said, "for so it [slavery] is misnamed, is a bagatelle which would not cost me a second thought, if, in that way, a general emancipation and *expatriation* could be effected; and gradually, and with due sacrifices, I think it might be. But as it is, we have the wolf by the ears, and we can neither safely hold him, nor safely let him go."[79] Diffusion was the answer for Jefferson, as it was for Madison. To both these great and good men, the wrong committed by the Compromise was that it prohibited slavery in certain areas instead of permitting it to go where it pleased.[80] President Monroe had originally been of the same mind, and had actually written the draft of a veto message.[81] But as the end approached, he was able to persuade himself that the contest had been, for the northern leaders, a matter of power only.[82] In his final judgment, the Compromise was "auspicious" because in a controversy of this kind a victory for either side would have been dangerous. Was he speaking for intersectional peace? Or intraparty unity? Or had they become synonymous? On March 6, 1820, he signed the Missouri Enabling Bill.[83]

John Quincy Adams publicly approved the Compromise on the grounds that nothing more could be effected under the Constitution; but in private he told himself that it would have been better to persist in the restriction of Missouri, because this would have led to a new

[79] Jefferson to John Holmes, April 22, 1820; *Writings,* Ford (ed.), XII, 158.
[80] Madison to Monroe, February 10, 1820; *Works* (Cong. ed.), III, 368.
[81] *Congressional Globe,* 30 Cong., 2 sess., Appendix, pp. 64–67.
[82] In February a Richmond caucus, about to select presidential electors, let it be known that, if Monroe did not promise to use his veto, it would look elsewhere for a President. Monroe, already hesitant, decided that silence would be best, and the caucus nominated electors friendly to him. This appears in George Hay to Monroe, February 17, 18, 1820, Monroe Papers, LC.
[83] Maine had been admitted by the Act of March 3. *Annals of Congress,* 16 Cong., 1 sess. Appendix, pp. 2554–2559. 3 U.S. Statutes at Large 544–548. On March 3, knowing that if he signed the Missouri Bill he would be deceiving the leaders in his own state, Monroe consulted his Cabinet on two questions. (1) Had Congress the power to prohibit slavery in a Territory? (2) If so, did the word "forever" in the Missouri Bill apply not only to Territories north of 36°30' but also to statehood? Adams, *Memoirs,* V, 5 ff., says that he alone gave an affirmative answer to both. The second question was therefore rephrased to ask: Was the eighth section of the Missouri Bill, interdicting slavery north of 36°30', consistent with the Constitution? Either side could answer this in the affirmative, and thus the Cabinet made its own compromise.

convention to revise and amend the Constitution, and from such a convention there might have arisen a new union of thirteen or fourteen states unpolluted with slavery.[84] This was certainly a more "liberal" prediction than Senator Goldsborough's; although, if he wished to play games with the might-have-beens of history, Mr. Adams could with almost as sound a justification have foretold that a persistence in restriction would have brought the South to heel. The slave interest had much to gain from the admission of an unrestricted Missouri; but did it not, in any future it could then foresee, have more to lose from disunion? And would the "thirteen or fourteen" states unpolluted with slavery have encouraged or would they not rather have forbidden the migration of free Negroes or outworn slaves from below? And in either event what would have been the status of the free Negro in a free Union? This essential question soon came to the forefront and, once there, remained there.

The Constitution of Missouri was promulgated on July 9; the general assembly, the state officers, and the national representative were all elected at the end of August; and on October 2 the legislature voted for David Barton and Thomas Hart Benton as United States senators.[85]

Soon after their election, the two senators-designate began their long journey to Washington, mostly on horseback, often through a vacant and forbidding wilderness. Wherever they touched civilization, however, in every inn or settlement or town, they heard always the same tale. "No employment for industry—no demand for labor—no sale for the produce of the farm—no sound of the hammer, but that of the auctioneer—DISTRESS, the universal cry of the people: RELIEF, the universal demand."[86] A recent and careful study maintains that the nation as a whole was too preoccupied with its economic troubles to pay much attention to the Compromise of 1820.[87] What indignation there was consisted mainly of editorials. In the North and East the Federalist press excoriated, and the Republican newspapers approved

[84] Adams, *Memoirs,* V, 12.

[85] William Nisbet Chambers, *Old Bullion Benton* (Boston, 1956), pp. 96–97, 99–100.

[86] *Ibid.,* p. 101; Benton, *Thirty Years View,* I, 5–6.

[87] Moore, *Missouri Controversy,* pp. 171 ff. Though not invariably in agreement with this scholarly work, I have found it of great value.

or palliated what had been done. Representative Edwards was burned in effigy at Carlisle, Pennsylvania, and the likeness of Senator Lanman was fed up to the flames in Hartford, Connecticut.[88] In the South, the Richmond *Enquirer* gave voice to that intransigence which had already so alarmed Monroe, and there were murmurs of rebellion in Georgia. That was all. The fate of the eighteen northern Representatives who had voted for the Compromise or abstained from voting indicates, it is true, that the Compromise of 1820 was more unpopular in the North than in the South.[89] But its unpopularity was not violent or even pronounced. Would a more prosperous state of affairs have produced a different and more humane response? The congressional debates which must now be touched upon do not, unhappily, give a very reassuring answer.

Everyone had supposed that congressional approval of the Missouri Constitution would be a simple matter: if the recent bargain offered any hope, so much could be expected from it. But this was to reckon without Missouri. In the Territory itself the writing of a constitution had been preceded and attended by a revival of local jealousies, incomprehensible elsewhere; something like an antirestrictionist party had come to grips with something like a restrictionist one; and electioneering in St. Louis had been very bitter.[90]

The restrictionist slate was headed by the eccentric Judge John B. Lucas, and was backed by Joseph Charless, editor of the *Gazette;* the *Enquirer,* under Thomas Hart Benton, was the bombinating organ of the antirestrictionists. Between Benton and Lucas there stood the implacable shade of Lucas' son Edward, whom Benton had killed in a duel in 1817, under circumstances which did him little credit, but

---

[88] McMaster, *History,* IV, 592. Fullerton voted with the South to strike out the antislavery clause, in *Annals of Congress,* 16 Cong., 1 sess., II, 1556–1557. Lanman was friendly to antirestriction in the first Compromise, but distinctly more antisouthern in the second. *Ibid.,* 16 Cong., 2 sess., p. 388. According to Paxton Hibben, *Henry Ward Beecher* (New York, 1927), p. 34, Representative James Stevens of Connecticut was similarly treated, and young Beecher pranced around the flames.

[89] Moore, *Missouri Controversy,* pp. 199–201, 239–241, 245. On the other side, the fate of William Smith, who lost his re-election to the Senate to Robert Y. Hayne, shows that the South Carolina Senate at the time was not uncompromising. *Ibid.,* p. 248.

[90] Chambers, *Benton,* pp. 70, 93; H. A. Trexler, *Slavery in Missouri* (Baltimore, 1914), p. 110.

brought him a certain notoriety, not altogether without value in such an environment.[91] Lawyer, editor, land lobbyist, even a banker of sorts, Benton was still, as it were, composing his public character; and he was doing so, characteristically enough, in full view and at the top of his voice. The performance, in retrospect, seems far too loud, but Missouri was not fastidious; and even in those days, at one of the lowest stages of a memorable and valiant career, Benton's ability was very impressive. It remained to be seen at whose service it would be put; whether that heavy egotistical mind, that incongruously vaulting imagination, would place themselves, as unhappily as they did in 1820, entirely at the disposal of the established interest, or whether in time they would take the larger view.

Having arrived in Missouri by way of North Carolina and Tennessee, Benton had as yet no qualms about the extension of slavery; those were to come later; but it is doubtful if, even in 1820, slavery extension was as important to him as was fur or lead or Spanish land titles. The antirestrictionists of Missouri were not, like the leaders of the established slave states, defending what they conceived to be a way of life; they were promoters, to whom slavery was one means among many. One of their most prominent men, for example, was Edmund Bates, who ended his career as Attorney General in the Cabinet of Abraham Lincoln. Their backing came chiefly from the former "little junto," from men who represented the old-French business leaders and holders of huge *arpentages* under Spanish land grants. It would seem that the antirestrictionist party was the mongrel offspring of an engrossing land policy; while the restrictionists, to judge from the fact that Lucas had been Jefferson's first land commissioner after the Louisiana Purchase, and that he was sternly antijunto, may have been the legatees of a slightly more strict but more egalitarian approach to the acquisition of land. Moreover, somewhere in the background of the contest, there loomed a more recent controversy: those who mourned for the Bank of St. Louis, now defunct, were ranged against the patrons of the still

[91] Joseph Charless (or Charles) to John W. Taylor, April 19, 1819: "It is well known that he called Lucas to the fatal spot armed with patent breech'd pistols. . . . Mr. B. wishes to fill a Senator's chair and will go through thick and thin to obtain it." John W. Taylor Papers, NYHS. This version is too political to be credited; but in Chambers, *Benton,* pp. 72–75, 452 n., the story of the second and fatal duel (there were two) is not favorable to Benton. Benton regretted it deeply in his old age.

surviving and more exclusive Bank of Missouri, to which Benton (for example) stood in the dual relation of director and debtor.[92]

To call the restrictionists democratic would be using language which had very little meaning in Missouri at that time, and certainly, if they were, they were poorly rewarded. They were so badly beaten that only one of their delegates to the constitutional convention—Benjamin Emmons of St. Charles—was actually elected. The triumphant delegates had no time for originality: they loyally limited their studies to the constitution of Kentucky, which they copied almost verbatim. Only in the 26th section of the third article did they presume to speak for themselves; but here they vented their spite, first upon Judge Lucas and his shattered following, and then upon the restrictionist majority in Congress. In the new West vengeance was sweet and imperious. In the first paragraph of that article, therefore, they declared it illegal for the state to emancipate slaves without their owners' consent; in other words, they did not merely permit slavery, they also attempted to make it irrevocable. And then, in the first clause of the fourth paragraph, they enjoined the Missouri legislature to pass such laws as might be necessary "to prevent free Negroes and mulattoes from coming to and settling in this State, under any pretext whatsoever."[93]

In their hour of victory, they seemed to have forgotten or they proposed to ignore the right of Congress to disapprove at any rate the first clause of the fourth paragraph of this 26th article. The *ci-devant* restrictionists in Congress, if they were to retain any self-respect, would have to demand the elimination of this insulting clause before Missouri was admitted to statehood. They would have to argue that it was repugnant to the Federal Constitution, which, in the second section of its

---

[92] *Dictionary of American Biography*, XI, 485–486, shows that Lucas was also an active land speculator. But his land commission had rejected "as many [old Spanish] claims as it had approved" and he represented "ambitious, more recently arrived enterprisers and speculators, determined to clear the way for buying low." Chambers, *Benton*, pp. 64, 65. J. B. C. Lucas to John W. Taylor, January 4, 1822, says that Benton's election was due to the efforts of the Spanish land claimants (and that his fees were contingent on the confirmation of their claims). The directors of the Bank, he adds, "without ceremony divided amongst themselves the capital of the Bank and then stopped payment." John W. Taylor Papers, NYHS. For the Bank's suspension of August, 1821—its chief debt was $152,343 to the U.S. Government for deposits and interest—see Chambers, *Benton*, p. 106.

[93] B. P. Poore (ed.), 2 *Federal and State Constitutions* (2 vols., Washington, rev. ed., 1878), 1108.

fourth article, declared that "the citizens of each State shall be entitled to the privileges and immunities of the citizens of the several States." But such an argument would involve the status of the free Negro in the free states. If he were not, in fact, both free and equal in those states, what then became of the restrictionist philosophy, behind which there had always loomed, like a gigantic question mark, the doctrine of natural rights and equal creation? The answer might have been that the phrase "all men are created equal" was not an historical truth but a value judgment still struggling to transform itself into fact; and at least one "liberal" Southerner in the Senate had been inclined to accept some such point of view.[94] He had accepted it, however, on the understanding that the struggle would be immensely long and the transformation indefinitely postponed, and upon such gradualist terms as these even the preamble to the Declaration of Independence could be read without alarm. It was now to be seen whether the North had anything more to offer, or whether it had even as much.

In New Jersey, in 1821, the Supreme Court declared that "black men are *prima facie* slaves." And again, in 1826, and in even stronger language, it announced "a settled rule . . . that black color is the proof of slavery . . . which must be overcome." In New Jersey, as it happened, the extinction of slavery was proceeding at a slower pace than in any other free state, and this may have had some bearing upon these appalling dicta.[95] As between 1821 and 1826, however, they give evidence of a deterioration in the status of the free Negro—a deterioration which the Missouri Compromises did much to hasten and something to predict.

This became evident as soon as the Sixteenth Congress met again in November 1820. The Missouri Constitution was then submitted to a select committee of the Senate; the committee dutifully reported a resolution admitting Missouri to the Union; and to this resolution Senator Eaton of Tennessee moved the following proviso: "That noth-

---

[94] Senator Richard M. Johnson: "We should contentedly wait that gradual change in the moral world—that slow but certain progress of improvement, which will one day give universal liberty, to the race of Adam," *Annals of Congress,* 16 Cong., 1 sess., I, 357. For Johnson's liberalism, see Schlesinger, *Age of Jackson,* p. 114.

[95] Gibbons *v.* Morse, 2 Halstead 253, November 1821; Fox *v.* Lamston, 3 Halstead 275, May 1826; Catterall, *Judicial Cases,* IV, 335, 337; De Bow, *Statistical View,* p. 65.

ing herein contained shall be so construed as to give the assent of Congress to any provision in the Constitution of Missouri, *if any such there be,* which contravenes that clause in the Constitution of the United States which declares that 'the citizens of each State shall be entitled to the privileges and immunities of the citizens of the several states.' "[96] This proviso, always supposing that any sense could be made of it, was intended to beg the question: Could the State of Missouri prohibit a class of persons who were, for example, citizens of the Commonwealth of Massachusetts and the State of New York? It was indeed true that Kentucky in 1808, to take another example, had passed a law prohibiting the entrance of free Negroes and mulattoes.[97] But Kentucky's constitution had not, like that of Missouri, enjoined upon its legislature the passing of such a law. As Senator Burrill of Rhode Island pointed out, there was nothing in the federal Constitution which recognized color as a bar to citizenship.[98] The obvious, if oblique, reply to this was to cite the discriminating practices of the several states—to construe the Constitution, in other words, in terms of its infractions and not of its silences.

As might have been expected, Senator Smith of South Carolina first committed himself to this form of construction; but he had been doing a little research, and the evidence he produced, while rarely to the point, was extremely suggestive. In Massachusetts there was a law that prohibited the marriage of a white person to an Indian, Negro, or mulatto; and "we must look [said Smith] to the reason for this law, as in all the other states, in the universal assent to the degraded condition of the class of person, and from which none of the States would, perhaps, ever think it expedient to raise them." He forbore to mention—it was no doubt unnecessary—that no other free states except Rhode Island and Indiana prohibited interracial marriage. But he did point out that the constitutions of Ohio and Connecticut limited the franchise to free white males, that Vermont and New Hampshire barred Negroes from their militia, and that Indiana gave them the franchise but would not allow them to appear as witnesses in any suit against a white man.[99] This fragmentary evidence was enough to indicate that

[96] *Annals of Congress,* 16 Cong., 2 sess., pp. 10, 26. Italics inserted.

[97] John C. Hurd, *The Law of Freedom and Bondage* (2 vols., Boston, 1862), II, 16.

[98] *Annals of Congress,* 16 Cong., 2 sess., p. 48.

[99] *Ibid.,* 67 and 55 ff.

there was a general acquiescence in the degradation of the Negro, and that acquiescence was sufficient to bring this degradation within the pale of the Constitution. The same appeal to acquiescence (in the First Bank) had been made in favor of the incorporation of the Second Bank of the United States: that it should now be used against equal rights for the Negro was a dim, weird prevision of the uses to which the Fourteenth Amendment would one day be put.

By the time Senator Smith had finished, the question of Missouri's constitutional right to exclude free Negroes had been totally submerged, nor did it again arise from those depths to which Mr. Smith had consigned it and from which something more sinister and (to do Mr. Smith justice) more pertinent had emerged to take its place. Did not public opinion, North and South, hold the Negro to be congenitally inferior to the white man? Time and time again, in both Houses of Congress, the friends of Missouri stated that this was *and should be* the case; nor did the restrictionists deny it, except in language that was fearfully disingenuous.[100] The most the restrictionists could offer, and very unwillingly at that, was evidence of a troubled and gloomy conscience. A partial answer might have been that the denial of freedom in one part of the Union made it extremely difficult to concede equality in the other; but even this was never made, because the first Compromise had shown that slavery itself was something to be tolerated, if not encouraged. As Senator Otis of Massachusetts put it—and here he spoke for all—"I do not wish to be distinguished as a zealot in the cause of emancipation."[101]

The Senate resolution of November 20, with Eaton's toothless proviso annexed to it, was passed on December 12 without a vote.[102] In the less conservative House, as before, the matter would have to be decided. Here Henry Clay had resigned the Speakership—from the pressure of gambling debts it was somewhat uncharitably rumored—and

[100] Senator David Morril of New Hampshire spoiled the most liberal speech to be heard—"color has no share in characterizing an inhabitant or a citizen"— by refuting Smith's accusation that Negroes were barred from the New Hampshire militia in these words: "This only places them among the exempts, generally the first class in society. . . . They have the privilege of walking about with the other gentlemen and seeing the soldiers train." *Ibid.*, pp. 105 ff.

[101] *Ibid.*, pp. 95 ff.

[102] *Ibid.*, p. 119.

his place had been taken, on the twenty-second ballot, by John W. Taylor of New York.[103] This was hailed as a victory by the former restrictionists, but Taylor was not a very impressive trophy. He was from the beginning immersed in routine, and his committee appointments, strange to relate, displayed a certain "impartiality" toward the South.[104]

On November 23, the select committee to which Missouri's constitution had been referred presented the following resolution: "That the State of Missouri shall be, and is hereby declared, one of the United States of America, and is admitted into the Union on an equal footing with the other states, in all respects whatever."[105] It was presented by William Lowndes of South Carolina, one of the original War Hawks, a nationalist who had supported the Bank and upheld the tariff, and who now demonstrated that the doctrine of state rights and the principle of loose construction were not, after all, particularly incompatible. Coming from one of the most respected members of the House, who had (as everyone knew) not long to live, the demonstration was rather sad; but Mr. Lowndes was endeavoring to placate and not to provoke, and when he returned to strict construction—arguing that discrimination between whites and Negroes, "wherever a case occurs which must necessarily involve the decision of it, should be remitted to judicial cognizance"—he seemed to find favor with both sides.[106] He might well have led the slavery forces to a more seemly triumph than the one they actually enjoyed. His resolution was de-

---

[103] *Ibid.*, pp. 434–435, for Clay's resignation, p. 438 for Taylor's election. Adams, *Memoirs*, V, 59, mentions gambling debts. Clay to Langdon Cheves, March 15, 1820, attributes his resignation to "reduction of rents and a still greater depression of the value of all property." *Papers of Henry Clay*, II, 795.

[104] Taylor to N. G. Spafford, January 20, 1821, demonstrates his immersion in routine. Taylor to Mrs. Taylor, February 20, 1821: "with the utmost care and constant aim at impartiality I have not been able to escape censure." Both in John W. Taylor Papers, NYHS.

[105] *Annals of Congress*, 16 Cong., 2 sess., pp. 454–455.

[106] When Lowndes spoke, his audience crowded around him, for his voice was weak and low, and his condition was "verging to the grave." Benton, *Abridgement*, VII, 12 n. His final speech of November 25, *Annals of Congress*, 17 Cong., 2 sess., p. 455, referred to "judicial cognizance." His second, of December 6, combined particularism with loose construction. *Ibid.*, pp. 508–517. The South could take a chance on the Supreme Court, even under the mistrusted and dominant Marshall, since Marshall was a Virginian and presumably quite "sound" on this question.

feated, however, on December 13 by a vote of 93 to 79, and thereafter he was too ill to carry on the battle.[107] With the New Year came Henry Clay; to his management was committed the task of breaking a deadlock between those who held that Missouri was still a Territory and those who believed that she was already a state or, if not a state, then an independent nation.

The role of peacemaker was not a new one for Clay, but it is ironical that the Peace of Ghent ("a damned bad treaty," as he called it) should have been the only really fruitful compromise in which he was ever to be engaged, and that he should have returned to America a discontented man.[108] As a nationalist Speaker he had been of some service to President Madison; to Monroe he had been a troublemaker, on the whole a Speaker in opposition; and even his efforts to bring about the first Missouri Compromise had been themselves seriously compromised by the trick he had played at the end. He was now to perform the part of *deus ex machina* in the worst sense of that term—in the sense of a mere device for unraveling a hopelessly tangled plot. With his sunny and captivating presence, his marvelous voice, the urgency of his demands, he was wonderfully equipped to perform, as well as it could be performed, this empty part. But the part was too much, or too little, even for him: the machine descended, but without the god.

On January 29, 1821, Clay requested that the Senate resolution, with the Eaton proviso, should be substituted for the House resolution: he did this, he said, in the interests of peace, for he did not believe (it was an odd confession for a nationalist) that any resolution was needed.[109] On the same day, Samuel Foot of Connecticut moved to strike out the Eaton proviso and to substitute a formula which, if unduly polite, would at least have required Missouri to expunge the offending section within two years. It was lost by a large majority.[110] Every subsequent amendment offered in the place of Mr. Foot's in-

[107] *Ibid.*, p. 670.

[108] On his return from Europe, he wrote to Gallatin: "Rumor here represents you as about connecting yourself with Mr. Astor for commercial objects. Getting rather tired of politics, I believe I will come and join you, if you will take in a third party." Clay to Albert Gallatin, 21 December 1815, Gallatin Papers, NYHS.

[109] *Annals of Congress,* 16 Cong., 2 sess., p. 982.

[110] *Ibid.*, p. 986.

variably required that the offending section should never be construed in such a way as to be repugnant to the federal Constitution.[111] How then was it to be construed? Only by following the advice of Charles Pinckney of South Carolina, who now claimed that he was the author of the second section of the fourth article of the Federal Constitution: "I perfectly knew," he said, "that there did not then exist such a thing in the Union as a black or colored citizen, nor could I then have conceived it possible that such a thing could ever have existed in it; nor, notwithstanding all that is said on the subject, do I now believe that one exists in it." Were not Negroes "created with less intellectual powers than the whites and . . . most probably intended to serve them, and be the instruments of their cultivation?" These were the last words to be spoken on the subject.[112] Meanwhile the northern majority had sullenly rejected amendments and resolutions, waiting for Henry Clay to lead the Congress out of its predicament. This he did with a great display of eloquence and in two steps. He moved and won the appointment of a committee to consider the Senate's resolution and to write one of its own; and when (as was expected) this committee's resolution was not granted a third reading, he secured the appointment of a joint committee with the Senate. On February 26, 1821, the resolution of the joint committee was passed by a vote of 87 to 81.[113] This was the wording:

Resolved, by the Senate and the House of Representatives of the United States in Congress assembled, That Missouri shall be admitted into the Union on equal terms with the original States in all respects whatsoever, upon the fundamental condition, that the fourth clause of the twenty-sixth section of the third article of the Constitution submitted on the part of the said State to Congress shall never be construed to authorize the passage of any law, and that no law shall be passed in conformity thereto, by which any citizens of either of the States of this Union shall be excluded from the enjoyment of

[111] Joshua Cushman of Maine, for example, who had previously attacked the first Compromise, and who had written a confidential letter to be circulated among a few friends, apparently calling for a Federalist- (Northern) Republican alliance—the letter somehow appeared in the press in January and February—now made a most appeasing speech. *Ibid.,* p. 1019; cf. Moore *Missouri Controversy,* 161. Cushman was a Republican.

[112] *Annals of Congress,* 16 Cong., 2 sess., pp. 1134–1135.

[113] *Ibid.,* p. 1094; for Clay's influence on the joint committee, see *Congressional Globe,* 31 Cong., 1 sess., p. 125; Moore, *Missouri Controversy,* pp. 148, 155.

any of the privileges and immunities to which such citizen is entitled under the Constitution of the United States: *Provided,* that the Legislature of the said State, by a solemn public act, shall declare the assent of the said State to the said fundamental condition, and shall transmit to the President of the United States, on or before the fourth Monday in November next, an authentic copy of the said act; upon the receipt whereof the President, by proclamation, shall announce the fact: whereupon, and without any further proceeding on the part of Congress, the admission of the State into this Union shall be considered as complete.[114]

Thus it became a "fundamental condition" of the admission of Missouri that her *unamended* Constitution should require the General Assembly to pass laws excluding free Negroes and mulattoes "under any pretext whatsoever," but that no law, so passed, should ever be interpreted as meaning what it did mean. It is not surprising that her legislators should have subscribed to this logical proposition by passing, on July 26, a solemn act that may well be unique in the history of legislative business, in that it solemnly declared itself unnecessary and not binding on the state. It was accepted on August 10, when President Monroe announced by proclamation that the admission of Missouri was now complete.[115]

The future of such an arrangement might have been predicted: it was repudiated by Missouri.[116] For the present, the credit, such as it was, went to Henry Clay, since Clay was the only gentleman in the House whose prestige, effrontery, and parliamentary skill could have sustained so ignoble a retreat from common sense. Otherwise, everyone was involved in it; for, as Clay pointed out, he "could always secure large majorities for any collateral motion which was designed to promote a compromise."[117] He accepted, with some complacency, Benton's accolade of "*Pacificator* of ten millions of Brothers," and certainly such

---

[114] *Ibid.,* p. 1228.

[115] Floyd C. Shoemaker, *Missouri's Struggle for Statehood* (Jefferson City, 1916), pp. 360–362; Frank Heywood Hodder, "Side Lights on the Missouri Controversy," *American Historical Association, Annual Report* (1909), pp. 160–161; Richardson, *Messages and Papers,* II, 96.

[116] An Act of 1825 excluded Negroes and mulattoes, unless they could present naturalization papers. Since the states where they were regarded as citizens had not naturalized them, they were effectually excluded. An Act of 1847 openly nullified the fundamental condition. Hodder, "Side Lights," p. 161, citing R. L., Mo., 1825, 600; and R. S., Mo., 1855, 1101.

[117] Everett S. Brown (ed.), *The Missouri Compromises and Presidential Politics, 1820–1825* (St. Louis, 1926), p. 43.

a word carried with it what Clay most desired, the implication of statesmanship.[118] He was a man who, in the course of a vivid and various
career, had become the pride and emblem of the cis-Mississippi West,
and who seemed in 1821, as men contemplated the conditions of their
internal development, eminently capable of leading his people toward
some Promised Land upon the other side. The path still lay, it would
seem, through the desert; but Clay was a notable exponent of the great
American dream, which subdued all nature in advance: the trouble
was that his exposition, embodied and at length embalmed in his
American System, was already growing too rigid and materialistic.
When he arranged the second Compromise, was he more concerned for
the Union or for his own System, upon the survival of which his career
depended? With all its gifts and fascinations, his was too transparent a
character not to reveal the pertinence of such a question. His System
had been badly hurt by the Panic of 1819, not least because Langdon
Cheves was still president of the Bank of the United States and still
dispensing those hateful policies which his successor would reverse in
1822.[119] And the Bank lay at the very heart of Mr. Clay's economy.
The semblance of intersectional peace and of intraparty unity must
somehow be maintained if the System itself were to last until, in due
time, it received the sanction of Mr. Clay's Presidency.[120] Upon some
such descending scale of values as this, transforming the nationalist
statesman into the archetype of a clever transatlantic politician, one
can understand his passionate endorsement of a verbal and quite un-
worthy Compromise.[121]

[118] St. Louis *Enquirer,* June 23, 1821.
[119] The vital importance of Biddle's policies to a recovery from the great
recession, and a succinct comparison with the methods of Cheves, will be found
in Thomas Payne Govan, *Nicholas Biddle* (Chicago, 1959), pp. 84–87.
[120] The nationalism of Calhoun, at this juncture not dissimilar to Clay's with
not dissimilar though less transparent ambitions, led him to praise the Compromises; he, too, required the maintenance of the Republican Ascendency.
[121] The semblance of intraparty unity had almost vanished before the completion of the second Compromise. James Monroe had been re-elected in November (see Chapter 5 *infra*), and on February 14, 1821, the electoral votes had
to be counted before Congress. At the suggestion of James Barbour a joint committee was appointed, which came up with this formula: The President of the
Senate should first declare what the result would be if the electoral vote of
Missouri were counted, and then what it would be without Missouri's vote. He
was then to announce: "But in either case, James Monroe is elected President
of the United States." Henry Clay reported this dubious formula to the House
and secured its approval by 90–67. On February 14, a prolonged and disgrace-

What place moral judgments have in any philosophy of history is, of course, always debatable. Perhaps they are "outside" history; or, if they are brought "inside" it, as indispensable categories of thought, perhaps they should be applied to institutions and not directed against persons. As a slaveholder from a state whose interest radiated in every direction, Henry Clay is no more to be blamed than anyone else; whereas the two Compromises—even if they saved the Union from dissolving then and there, instead of assuring (which is more probable) its *eventual* dissolution in civil war—had the bad quality of hurting all that they touched. An argument with slavery in the future would be, fundamentally, less concerned with discussion of principles than with demarcation of areas. More closely, it becomes noticeable that from this time onward the literary spokesmen for the slave interest began to define their institution, not as a necessary though lamentable evil, but as something historical, Christian, and humane.[122] At the same time, support for that dubious enterprise, the American Colonization Society, increased throughout the South. The Society's object was to "promote and execute a plan for colonizing (with their consent) the Free People of Colour residing in our country, in Africa, or such other place as Congress shall deem most expedient"; but the number of slaveholders on its list of vice-presidents gave some grounds to the suspicion that the Society's unadmitted purpose was to increase the price of slaves by getting rid of free competition. In spite of the approval of Thomas Jefferson, James Madison, and James Monroe—and it would be blank folly to suppose that such men were interested in the price of slaves— the Society was a visible formulation not only of the prevailing racist myth but also of its dismal corollary: that America, "man's last best

---

ful scene occurred before the President of the Senate could make this announcement. The acceptance of the formula is sometimes called the Second Missouri Compromise. *Annals of Congress,* 16 Cong., 1 sess., pp. 345–347, 1147–1166; McMaster, *History,* IV, 600; Brown (ed.), *Missouri Compromises,* pp. 35–38. Moore, *Missouri Controversy,* p. 153.

[122] Edwin C. Holland and others, *A Refutation of the Colonies Against the Southern and Western States, Respecting the Institution of Slavery Among Them* (Charleston, 1822); Richard Furman, *Exposition of the Views of the Baptists, Relative to the Coloured Population of the United States* (Charleston, 1823). Holland, p. 86, betrays the weakness of his case by saying, "Our Negroes are truly the *Jacobins* of the Country"—i.e., the institution was less benevolent than counterrevolutionary.

hope," was literally incapable of educating the Negro for freedom and equality.[123]

And then, in 1822, as a direct result of the Missouri debates, which he misinterpreted as a sincere attack by the North upon slavery, a free Negro called Denmark Vesey—an itinerant preacher among the neighboring plantations—prepared a terrible massacre for the city of Charleston. The plot was discovered in time, and revenged without too much savagery; but from then onward the position of the Negro in the South, bond or free, became somewhat less tolerable than it had been before. Religious exercises were more closely supervised; education of any kind became more suspect; and the fear of servile rebellion was exploited, with more and more telling effect, by the slaveholder and the nonslaveholding white supremacist.[124]

The Missouri Compromises may be judged as well in this way as in any other. They registered only deterioration and defeat. The whole nation had been shown that it must either accept the undemocratic dogma that the Negro had not been created the equal of the white man or else confess that something was seriously wrong with every part of its democratic structure. The Compromises intimated that the nation preferred the former of these alternatives. In the North, the free Negro—to whom the compromises rendered a grave disservice by calling attention to him—found that his chances of education, equal opportunity, and enfranchisement dwindled with every year and in every state but one. The free states, said one acute observer, "usually do what they can to render their territory disagreeable to the Negroes as a place

[123] Early L. Fox, *The American Colonization Society* (Baltimore, 1919), pp. 47, 66; Jefferson to Jared Sparks, February 4, 1824, *Writings,* Ford (ed.), XII, 334–339; P. J. Staudenraus, *The African Colonization Movement* (New York, 1961), pp. 44, 48, 171, 183; Adams, *Memoirs,* V, 292–293. For Monroe's assistance as President, see *27 Cong., 3 Sess.,* HR Report No. 283, p. 2.

[124] Herbert Aptheker, *Negro Slave Revolts* (New York, 1943), pp. 270–272. In such cases as this, figures are notoriously unreliable: it was rumored that 9,000 were involved, 6,600 being from outside the city. Joseph C. Carroll, *Slave Insurrections in the United States* (Boston, 1938), p. 94, gives details of this plot, and puts the arrests at 131; executions, 37; transported, 43; discharged with a whipping, 48. Denmark was captured on June 22 and hanged on July 2; he had originally planned his attack for July 14, and set it back to the night of June 16, whereupon the authorities struck in the morning of that day. *Dictionary of American Biography,* XIX, 259, puts the arrests at 139. Savannah *Republican,* August 29, 1822; Stampp, *Peculiar Institution,* p. 135.

of residence. . . . A kind of emulation exists between the different states in this respect."[125] No doubt the peace of the past should be allowed to fall upon the individual performers in the Missouri Compromises, but not, surely, upon the performance itself.

[125] Alexis de Tocqueville, *Democracy in America* (2 vols., New York, Phillips Bradley, ed., 1945), I, 368 n. Written after 1830, these words are true for the 1820's. Cf. Leon F. Litwack, *North of Slavery* (Chicago, 1961), Chap. IV. The possible exception, as time went on, was Massachusetts.

CHAPTER 5

Toward the Monroe Doctrine

R E-ELECTED in 1820, with only one adverse vote in the electoral college, James Monroe devoted a part of his Second Inaugural to an explanation of this event. To the modern observer, the presidential election of 1820 represents an act of almost unanimous indifference; but the President, although he modestly disclaimed any personal credit for this singular unanimity, was disposed to think that it represented "union." Union, in one form or another, became the theme of his Inaugural Address, which was delivered to a damp audience in the Hall of Representatives on Monday, March 5, 1821.[1]

Powerful causes, said the President, "indicating the great strength and stability of our Union, have essentially contributed to draw you together." These, it appeared, were two in number. The first was "the extraordinary prosperity of the United States," which had effected the repeal of internal taxes, the extinction of $67 million of public debt, and the beginning of a system of coastal defenses which would soon stretch from the St. Croix to the Sabine. The second was the absence of any serious conflict between the national and state governments, or of any contest between them but "such as are managed by argument and by a fair appeal to the good sense of the people."

With the second Missouri Compromise only a week old, and not yet confirmed by Missouri herself, it was perhaps only natural for a

---

[1] Richardson, *Messages and Papers,* II, 86–94.

cautious President to make no more distinct a reference to it than such as might be subsumed under his second cause. "There is every reason to believe," he said, "that our system will soon attain the highest degree of perfection of which human institutions are capable." A few more such fair appeals to good sense and there would be nothing more to wish for.

The prevailing economic depression could hardly be dismissed in quite so optimistic, if not euphoric, a manner. "Under the present depression of prices," said Monroe,

affecting all the productions of the country and every branch of industry, proceeding from causes explained on a former occasion, the revenue has considerably diminished, the effect of which had been to compel Congress either to abandon these great measures of defense [extinction of debt and coastal fortifications] or to resort to loans or internal taxes to supply the deficiency. On the presumption that this depression and the deficiency in the revenue arising from it would be temporary, loans were authorized for the demands of the last and present year. . . . It will be seen by the next session of Congress whether the revenue shall have been so augmented as to be adequate to all these necessary purposes. Should the deficiency still continue, and especially should it be probable that it would be permanent, the course to be pursued appears to me to be obvious. I am satisfied that under certain circumstances loans may be resorted to with great advantage. I am equally well satisfied, as a general rule, that the demands of the current year, especially in time of peace, should be provided for by the revenue of that year.

I have never dreaded, nor have I ever shunned, in any situation in which I have been placed making appeals to the virtue and patriotism of my fellow-citizens. . . . Independently of the exigency of the case [the present depressions] many considerations of great weight urge a policy having in view provision of revenue to meet to a certain extent the demands of the nation, without relying altogether on the precarious resources of foreign commerce. I am satisfied that internal duties and excises, with corresponding imposts on foreign articles of the same kind, would, without imposing any serious burdens on the people, enhance the price of produce, promote our manufactures, and augment the revenue, at the same time that they made it more secure and permanent.[2]

Two members of the President's immediate audience, the British Minister and the Secretary of State, have agreed that his speech was

[2] *Ibid.,* p. 91.

occasionally interrupted by queer and disorderly noises from gallery.[3] It is not surprising. When the whole nation was desperately seeking relief from a mass of debt, even its virtue and patriotism might have been unequal to the President's suggestion that a renewal of taxation would be the best way out of its troubles.

The Second Inaugural, in fact, had sounded a valedictory and not an inaugural note. Monroe detested party warfare, and it was quite in character for him to describe his late re-election as "surmounting, in favor of my humble pretensions, the difficulties which so often produce division in like occurrences." As he had already demonstrated, however, he would make the friendliest professions, toward the surviving Federalists, but never follow them up with political preferments.[4] To him, at any rate, however humble his pretensions, "union" was one-party rule, and one-party rule was of necessity Republican. The Missouri Compromises themselves, since they had notably not produced "division" in the election of 1820, had presumably patched up the party structure, at least for the duration of Monroe's second term; and he asked no more, and cared to foresee no farther.

Indeed, his Second Inaugural, in spite of its fiscal threats and even because of them, was a notable example of the backward look. Monroe was conjuring, out of a deep but (to him) unrecognized abyss, what might be called the spirit of 1817—the vanished "good feelings" of the postwar boom. Except for the Second Bank of the United States, admittedly a large and by now a somewhat notorious exception, there was nothing in the mild nationalism he had inherited from Madison which was specifically obnoxious to Jeffersonian principle, and what little there was had been expunged by presidential veto. The party still held together, although the conditions of internal development were such that it could not do so much longer. Monroe hoped to prolong its existence, as a mild and beneficent elite, by slowing down the pace of internal development; this he proposed to accomplish through national self-restraint ("internal duties and excises") and a moderate protective

[3] Adams, *Memoirs*, V, 317–318; Canning to Edward Planta, March 8, 1821 in Stanley Lane-Poole, *The Life of the Right Honorable Stratford Canning* (2 vols., London, 1888), I, 318.
[4] Livermore, *Twilight of Federalism*, p. 106, believes that Monroe would have been more generous but for the opposition of Republican leaders. See also Adams, *Memoirs*, VI, 494.

tariff ("corresponding imposts on foreign articles"). A nation which remained, on the surface, predominantly agricultural would thus advance cautiously, paying its way for every step, into the West if not the future.

Monroe was a good man, all of whose ambitions happened to be satisfied. If he proposed, as he seemed to be proposing, a policy of barely controlled drift, it was not from imbecility or incompetence but from lack of incentive. Had he not secured the Floridas, marked out the Louisiana Purchase, advanced to the Pacific, vetoed internal improvements, and otherwise refrained from meddling? It had now become his fate to personify an interim: if the interim was necessary, the personification was not ignoble.

Only in one respect did Monroe indicate that immediate action might be required of him. "No agreement," he said, "has yet been entered into respecting the commerce between the United States and the British dominions in the West Indies and on this continent. The restraints imposed on that commerce by Great Britain, and reciprocated by the United States on a principle of defense, continue in force." The statement was almost *sotto voce;* but with it, at once, a subtle and important change takes place, both in the character of the Address and in that of the President. The former sheds its vapid pieties. The latter ceases to resemble Keats's Joy, his finger ever at his lips, bidding farewell; he is no longer inert and complacent, with the Republican Ascendency collapsing all around him. One could search the whole Address and find nothing of concern, if it had not been for this one statement, this juxtaposition of its most hopeful and its least gratified pronouncements, this suggestion that if the United States were to attain that degree of perfection which Monroe predicted, it could not do so unless it regularized its commercial and political relations with the British Empire.

Mr. Stratford Canning, the British Minister, in his quizzical account of the Inauguration—the cold, the wind, the touch of sleet, the damp crowds sullenly pushing their way into the Hall of Representatives—made only a brief and unflattering reference to the "poor *Prezzy.*" The attitude of Great Britain toward the United States was nowhere better expressed than in its choice of such an envoy. A cousin of George Canning, Stratford Canning was a tall, handsome man, with alarming gray eyes, and such forbidding proconsular manners that Lady Hester

Stanhope said he always put her in mind of some permanent head of a society for the suppression of vice. He was also bad-tempered and honest to the point of simplicity. Like other British diplomats (said John Quincy Adams) he regarded this particular tour of duty as "the real purgatory,"[5] and he barely concealed his distaste for social Washington; but he did not make the mistake, which had proved fatal to more than one of his predecessors, of underestimating the importance or the difficulty of his task. He may have been "an unconscionable bore . . . who thought nothing of idling away three or four hours of a morning, at the Secretary's expense,"[6] but John Quincy Adams knew that there was a purpose behind these idlings and rather enjoyed his encounters with a gentleman whose manners impressed him somewhat against his will, and whose mind he knew to be in every respect inferior to his own.

The government which Stratford Canning represented undoubtedly shared its Minister's contempt for republican institutions in general, and American ones in particular; but it had not sent him to Washington in order to try his patience or school his susceptibilities. It believed him to be a coming man, just the man to represent it at the capital of a nation whose influence upon the industrial British Empire, now emerging with such dingy promise from the matrix of the Napoleonic Wars, it was forced to calculate. At the head of this government stood Robert Banks Jenkinson, second Earl of Liverpool, who had learned something about the United States before and during the War of 1812, and who, to do him justice, did not forget what he had learned.

Lord Liverpool used to be considered a good example of Macaulay's "stern and unbending" Tories—the Tories of the right wing.[7] Indeed, it was once quite customary to accept him as an unimpressionable reactionary, looming like some kind of dolmen in the political landscape of nineteenth-century England, an object which would look all the more disagreeable if one attempted to disguise it with a coat of whitewash.[8] This interpretation tends to ignore the fact that some Tory

[5] John Quincy Adams to John Adams Smith, May 7, 1819, cited in Bemis, *John Quincy Adams and the Foundations of American Foreign Policy*, p. 269.
[6] Brooks Adams in Henry Adams, *The Degradation of the Democratic Dogma*, p. 41.
[7] Macaulay, *Critical and Historical Essays* (6 vols., London, 1900 ed.), IV, 244.
[8] Cf. Arthur Bryant, *The Age of Elegance* (New York, 1950), pp. 369–370,

leaders, however stern, were not always unbending, and that at times a certain discreet pliability might be considered their foremost characteristic.

The Tory party, still in office in 1815 and maintaining its majority until 1830, was composed of three groups: great landed noblemen, who controlled a number of seats in the unreformed Commons; independent country gentlemen; and conservative bankers, shipowners, and merchants. It professed a faith in some symmetrical and even organic relationship between King, Lords, Commons, and people, each in an allotted sphere; acknowledged, when it thought at all, the intellectual pre-eminence of Pitt and Burke, both of whom were relapsed Whigs; and was supposed to commit its destiny to the leaders of the old "pigtail" school—such "ultras" as Wellington, Westmorland, Eldon, and Sidmouth—whose statesmanship chiefly consisted in the iron repression of useful innovations. But there was also a minority, which gained control in the 1820's.[9] This minority is sometimes, with some justice, known as the "Liberal" wing, and the Earl of Liverpool was its leader.

"Liberal," needless to say, must be preserved or pickled in its own context. Lord Liverpool betrayed no sympathy for the plight of industrial workers, though he had been known to express a mild disapproval of child labor. He was an anxious and immovable opponent of Catholic emancipation. He had been as responsible as anyone for the notorious Six Acts with which his government, in 1819, smothered the outcry of a despairing people. A representative system which allowed rotten boroughs to return two members to Parliament, but denied a seat to the new industrial towns, aroused his deepest loyalty: he confessed that he did not think it susceptible to further improvement. As a Frenchman put it, with more wit than insight, had Lord Liverpool been present at the Creation, he would have cried out in panic: *"Mon Dieu, conservons le chaos."*[10] But if his social philosophy was sadly to seek, there was another and most incongruous side to his thinking; for when it came to a sympathetic understanding of the

---

who offers an especially brilliant misunderstanding of Liverpool. E. L. Woodward, *The Age of Reform* (Oxford, 1938), p. 51, is more judicious. W. R. Brock, *Lord Liverpool and Liberal Toryism* (London, 1941), is Liverpool's chief contemporary apologist.

[9] Brock, *Liverpool,* p. 45.
[10] Woodward, *Age of Reform,* p. 51.

needs, the dynamics, and the future of commerce and industry the Earl of Liverpool was a "Liberal" indeed. It was the release of energy which concerned him, not the rights of man.

The Jenkinsons were a respectable family of landed Oxfordshire baronets, neither very wealthy by the standards of those days nor very landed,[11] who had gained their steps in the peerage through professional services to the Tory party; and the second Earl, though careful not to break with the High Tories, not infrequently took counsel with men upon whom (though less particular in this respect than their Whig counterparts) the High Tories turned their backs in alarm and distaste—reformers and parvenus who would not have survived a month without Liverpool's unwavering support. His was a curiously tactful and, at the same time, a very durable character. Other members of his government received more attention than he; but, as Madame de Lieven observed, and here her instinct was infallible, it was the amiable, the awkward, the fidgety Liverpool who really pulled the strings.[12]

In the concluding stages of the War of 1812, when he wrestled by proxy with the American commissioners at Ghent, he had been obliged to calculate and to accept the vital importance to Great Britain of a friendly, untrammeled market in the United States. Thereafter he endeavored to impart this lesson to his countrymen. It was certainly needed in the postwar years; for it was then, as this study has already tried to suggest, that the resurgent nationalism of the United States began to challenge the British Empire over the question of the West Indies carrying trade. This question had worried Americans in the far-off days of the ratifying conventions; and only the recurrent exigencies of European war, which opened the British ports in the West Indies by proclamation, had kept it in abeyance. Since it was a Caribbean question, it touched and irritated an international nervous system not directly connected with the immediate problem it raised; and one should not be surprised to find that British industrialism entered into it. British industrialism now becomes a constant factor in the relations between the Old World and the New.

[11] *Annual Register*, LII, App. 637, says that his estate at his death amounted to about £15,000 per annum, of which £3,000 was from land.

[12] Peter Quennell (ed.), *The Private Letters of Princess Lieven to Prince Metternich* (New York, 1938), *passim*, esp. pp. 37, 160.

The Anglo-American Convention, negotiated by Richard Rush and Albert Gallatin in London and signed on October 20, 1818, clarified the Canadian-American boundary and restored to the Americans substantially the same fishing "liberties" which they had enjoyed before the War of 1812.[13] Here, as in the lesser but vexed case of the slaves deported during the war, the British had shown a conciliatory spirit; and when one considers the Rush-Bagot Agreement of 1817, one might say that it was a spirit which smiled upon American expansion in a very general sense of the term.[14] Some agreement might even have been reached on the question of impressment if the negotiators had not become entangled in certain technicalities concerning naturalization. But at the very heart of the Convention of 1818 lay the renewal of the Commercial Convention of 1815, and here the British had proved more obstinate.

The Commercial Convention of 1815 provided for freedom of com-

---

[13] The American contention regarding the Newfoundland fisheries was that the "liberty" to fish and to cure and dry fish had not been abrogated by the War of 1812 and could not be abrogated by any future war. To secure this, John Quincy Adams was willing to limit the liberty to certain stipulated coasts. *American State Papers, Foreign Relations,* IV, 375–378. The British commissioners—Henry Goulburn and Frederick John Robinson—would not agree, but did accept the words "for ever" without an express provision that the liberty could not be abrogated by a future war. The "liberty" agreed upon was (1) to take fish of every kind on the shores of southern Newfoundland from Cape Ray to Rameau Island; of western and northern Newfoundland, from Cape Ray to Quirpon Islands; of the Magdalen Islands; and of Labrador northward from Mont Joli, without prejudice to the exclusive rights of the Hudson's Bay Company; (2) to dry and cure fish in any of the unsettled coasts of Labrador. *Ibid.,* IV, 378–406; Bemis, *Adams and Foreign Policy,* pp. 289–291. "Unhappily, in Gallatin's haste to be done with the negotiations, the article covering the fisheries was drafted so poorly that there was almost continuous diplomatic controversy over the matter until 1910." Walters, *Gallatin,* p. 311.

[14] The question of slaves deported during the War of 1812, and of compensation, was referred in Article V of the Convention to the arbitration of some friendly sovereign or state. This turned out to be the Tsar of Russia. In the end, Great Britain agreed to pay America $1,204,960. J. B. Moore, *Digest of International Arbitrations,* I, 350–390. The Rush-Bagot Agreement of April 28–29, 1817—Richard Rush, Acting Secretary of State and Charles Bagot, British Minister—limited naval armament on the Great Lakes to stipulated revenue cutters. *American State Papers, Foreign Relations,* IV, 202–207, and Hunter Miller, *Treaties,* II, 644–54. "It was the first instance of reciprocal naval disarmament in the history of international relations. . . ." Bemis, *Adams and Foreign Policy,* p. 231.

merce, in British or American ships, between the United States and British ports *in Europe,* and prohibited discriminatory duties by either nation against the commerce or ships of the other between these termini; but the British had sternly refused to change their colonial system, which decreed that only an enumerated list of American products could be imported into the British West Indies and British North America, and then only in British ships. They seemed, in other words, unwilling to admit that the British Empire, emerging victorious from the Napoleonic Wars, was very much different from the one which had been dismembered by the American Revolution. Sea power, colonial produce, trade monopoly, European coalitions—had not this combination defeated Napoleon? That Waterloo was the bloody but consummate expression of early and competitive British industrialism is a truth which failed to penetrate the British mind in the Convention of 1815. The American commissioners—John Quincy Adams, Henry Clay, and Albert Gallatin—protested, but in vain. The British simply answered that they had been careless about their old policy during the War of 1812, but that they now proposed to reinstate it in all its severity. Thus they began to enjoy a triangular trade from Great Britain to the United States to the West Indies and back, while the Americans were restricted to the direct trade between the United States and Great Britain. The effect of this was ruinous. By 1816 more than half the tonnage of the United States was lying in its docks, rotting and useless.[15]

The British philosophy, if philosophy it could be called, was perspicuous enough: it was constellated around the old mercantilist equation between trade monopoly and national welfare. But if it was perspicuous it was also out of date, not merely because it had little relation to England's future (the British could be forgiven for not seeing that), but because American conditions themselves had changed. They were now such as permitted a direct rejoinder. On March 1, 1817, a Navigation Act restricted the importation of British West Indian produce to vessels of the United States or vessels belonging to West Indian merchants.[16] It did not forbid the exportation in British

---

[15] F. Lee Benns, *The American Struggle for the West Indian Carrying Trade* (Bloomington, 1923), p. 37; *Annals of Congress,* 14 Cong., 2 sess., pp. 781–782.

[16] 3 U.S. Statutes at Large, 351.

vessels of United States produce to West Indies, and was therefore not very strong; but more was to follow. President Monroe's first Annual Message suggested sterner measures; on April 18, 1818, Congress passed another bill, closing the ports of the United States to all British vessels arriving from a colony that was legally closed to the vessels of the United States;[17] and by the end of 1819, British tonnage entering American ports had shrunk from 174,935 in 1817 to 36,333.[18]

With the Navigation Act of 1818, the United States had seriously disturbed the British triangular trade and had succeeded in putting pressure upon the British West Indies themselves. The British had in some measure anticipated this pressure with free ports and entrepôts; but cries of protest from their West Indies planters showed that an indirect trade could never be a happy and still less a permanent solution.[19] There was a natural exchange between American tobacco, rice, grain, beans, and flour and West Indian rum, molasses, and coffee. On May 15, 1820, Monroe approved another act of Congress which tampered with nature in a new and even more agonizing way. In effect, it decreed a total nonintercourse (in British vessels) with all the British-American colonies, and it even stipulated that colonial articles might not be taken to England and thence re-exported to the United States.[20]

Monroe, though he called for strong measures in his Third Annual Message, had done so with reluctance, and he had signed both Navigation Acts with grave misgivings.[21] John Quincy Adams, on the other hand, who had been the President's mentor, declared that it was the first time we had had a chance of trying our strength since the Constitution.[22] He saw the whole affair as a contest between American nationalism and British mercantilism; and this character, though somewhat delusive, it certainly bore from beginning to end. When Richard Rush, the American Minister in London, gave the details of

[17] Richardson, *Messages and Papers,* II, 12, 13; *Annals of Congress,* 15 Cong., 1 sess., pp. 341, 1720.

[18] Benns, *American Struggle,* p. 64. W. W. Bates, *American Navigation* (New York, 1902), p. 182.

[19] Benns, *American Struggle,* pp. 65, 66; Order in Council, May 27, 1818, 58 Geo. III, c. 19, 27; *Niles' Register,* XV, 156.

[20] 3 U.S. Statutes at Large 602.

[21] *American State Papers, Foreign Relations,* IV, 371.

[22] Adams, *Memoirs,* V, 41.

the Act of 1820 to Lord Castlereagh in the Foreign Office, that nobleman indicated that he would rather let the West Indies starve to death
than go to the trouble of upsetting the British Navigation Laws. As
a London newspaper put it: "The American Acts affect only a small
and inconsiderable . . . portion of our general trade."[23]

Behind Lord Castlereagh's back, however, or beneath his scrutiny,
certain events of the greatest significance had already taken place. In
May, 1820, petitions from merchants and manufacturers of London,
Glasgow, Howick, and Manchester had been presented to Parliament,
all of them asking for a free trade.[24] The petitioners did not expect an
immediate transformation, but what they demanded was revolutionary
enough. Realizing that freedom of intercourse must precede a freedom of trade, they concentrated their attack upon the Navigation
Laws—an appalling heap of legislation, some of it medieval, which
had presumably been compressed into the great Navigation Act of
1660. Subsequent modifications had not altered the political gravity
exerted by this massive document. Shipowners, landowners, merchants,
statesmen had for years revolved around it, unable to release themselves from its mighty spell. Originally designed to monopolize colonial intercourse, on the one hand, and to ruin the Dutch carrying
trade, on the other, it had been eminently successful; and, as recent
investigations tend to show, it had not been seriously questioned even
by the American colonists as they moved toward Revolution.[25] As
originally written, it provided that no goods could be transported
from British colonies into England except in British and colonial ships;
that no goods the growth, produce, or manufacture of Africa, Asia,
or America should be imported into England, Ireland, or Wales except in English, Irish, Welsh, or colonial bottoms, with a British master and a crew three-quarters British; that the foreign goods of Asia,
Africa, and America must be brought directly from the place of
growth or manufacture; and that no alien tonnage should be engaged
in the English coastal trade.[26]

---

[23] *American State Papers, Foreign Relations,* V, 84, interview of July 13,
1820; Benns, *American Struggle,* p. 71.

[24] Hansard, 2 Ser., I, 168, 424, 432, 478.

[25] E.g., Oliver M. Dickerson, *The Navigation Acts and the American Revolution* (Philadelphia, 1951), *passim.*

[26] 12 Charles II, c. 18 and 19; Alexander Brady, *William Huskisson and*

With all the legislation that had gathered around it, it became (one might almost say, at the cost of extreme simplification) the axis of the old mercantilist Empire, its poles being the two propositions that colonies were the nurseries of seamen, and that a monopoly of intercourse was essential to any colonial system. In 1820 its prestige was still such that only a counterattraction of great power could detach the English mind from it. The promise of industrial supremacy was, of course, just such a counterattraction, and the petitions of 1820 were among the many signs that this tremendous force was beginning to exert itself.

The debates of 1820 were concerned with the economic distress of Great Britain; and when the question was aired in the House of Lords, on May 26, the Earl of Liverpool made one of his more startling entrances into postwar American history. He told their Lordships on that portentous day that the disastrous falling off in British exports had little to do with the trade to Europe. On the contrary, it should be "principally, *if not exclusively*" attributed to the condition of the United States, where distress, he said, was greater than anywhere else within the orbit of British trade.

And how has she [the United States] felt it? During the whole of the late war, America was the principal neutral power. During a part of that war she was the only neutral power. She enjoyed the most extensive carrying trade. She supplied this country, and she supplied many other countries with many articles, which neither this country nor other countries could obtain elsewhere. What was the natural consequence? That America increased in wealth, in commerce, in arts, in population, in strength more rapidly than any nation ever before increased in the history of the world. . . . The state of America, my Lords, at this moment is not so much the effect of present positive distress, as of extraordinary past prosperity. She must retrograde to a certain point. . . . I am far from saying this invidiously. On former occasions I have sufficiently stated my convictions that there is no country more interested than England is, that the distress of America should cease, and that she should be enabled to continue that rapid progress which has been for the time being interrupted; for, of all the powers on the face of the earth, America is the one whose increasing population and immense territory furnish the best prospect for British produce and manufactures. Everybody, there-

Liberal Reform (London, 1928), pp. 74 ff.; G. N. Clark, *The Later Stuarts* (Oxford, 1934), p. 51.

fore, who wishes prosperity to England, must wish prosperity to America.
. . . My Lords, we are now in a situation in which it is impossible for us,
or any nation, but the United States of America to act unreservedly on the
principle of unrestricted trade. The commercial regulations of the European
world have been long established, and cannot suddenly be departed from.[27]

The dolmen aspect of Lord Liverpool shows itself for a moment,
and perhaps invidiously, in this extraordinary speech. Had he not been
a member of that government whose orders in council had done their
best to Anglicize the American carrying trade? And then again how
could any country, with any taste for independence, "act unreservedly
on the principle of unrestricted trade" while the rest of the world
continued its policy of restriction? Lord Liverpool's meaning, of
course, lay in the words "and cannot *suddenly* be departed from":
he was speaking as the herald of a free trade, however distant. In the
meantime, the gist of his speech is unmistakable: America might attack the Navigation Laws at their most vulnerable point, in the West
Indies, and industrial England would not abate one jot of her good
will so long as the American market was not hampered with a high
protective tariff. Does one quarrel with one's best single customer?
Such a speech, by such a man, must be recognized as a decisive incident in Anglo-American relations—an incident which presents itself
as one of the more important clues in any attempt to unravel and
recompose the events now to be examined.

Two years had to pass, a certain degree of prosperity had to return
to Great Britain, before the attack on the Navigation Laws could be
properly concerted. Then Frederick J. Robinson, president of the
Board of Trade and a "Liberal" Tory, made the astonishing proposal
that British vessels and vessels belonging to countries in America should
be permitted to carry into certain free ports in the West Indies all
articles legally importable into those colonies, and to carry away all
articles the produce of the British dominions and all articles legally
imported. A moderate duty would be imposed upon this trade, "so
justly apportioned as not to deprive the people of the United States
of their fair proportion"; and foreign vessels thus admitted into the
West Indies trade were to be on the same footing, as to other duties

[27] Hansard, 2 Ser., I, 574–575. In *ibid.*, 547–554, the Whig Marquess of
Lansdowne offered an interesting support to this view.

and charges, as British ships. But the law would not apply to vessels of foreign states that did not grant equal and reciprocal advantages to British shipping.[28]

On June 24, 1822, a bill containing all Mr. Robinson's recommendations was enacted, and the Anglo-American world should have caught its breath in astonishment. Never since the days of William Pitt, and never in a positive enactment, had the United States been so openly wooed. The most careless mind could see that the new act was exclusive to the United States, since European shipping was not mentioned and Great Britain had not yet recognized the independence of any Latin American country. As far as the Navigation Laws were concerned, the new act (with its sequel, the Colonial Trade Act) had not effected a total repeal: much still remained to be done. "It did not imply," said William Huskisson, "a sudden or entire departure from our former system, *bad as it might be,* but such a modification as it was hoped would accomplish gradually the desired end."[29] But what was the desired end? Had not the act, for those times, accomplished something like a revolution in the traditional concept of colonial exchanges? It was very nearly the first piece of legislation since the days of Richard II, said the *Edinburgh Review,* which placed navigation or commerce "on a fair principle of reciprocity."[30]

There were many who attributed this revolution to the American Act of 1820 and the pressure of West Indian interests in Parliament. "The controversy," said Joseph Planta, "turned upon the question, whether we should first be starved into compliance, or they first be tired of the loss of a profitable trade. The victory was theirs, we yielded." No event of such magnitude as this can take place without the influence of a number of successive or simultaneous pressures; and Mr. Planta, who as George Canning's secretary had a semiofficial status, must be given the attention due to him.[31] But George Canning,

---

[28] *Ibid.,* VI, 1418, speech of April 1, 1822.

[29] The Act of June 24—"The West Indies and American Trade Act"—is 3 Geo. IV, c. 44; The Colonial Trade Act is 3 Geo. IV, c. 45. For Huskisson's speech, see Hansard, 2 Ser., VI, 1428.

[30] Benns, *American Struggle,* p. 84, citing *Edinburgh Review,* XXXVIII, 487.

[31] A. G. Stapleton, *Political Life of George Canning* (3 vols., London, 1831), III, 14. L. J. Ragatz, *The Fall of the Planter Class in the British Caribbean, 1763–1833* (London, 1928), p. 346 n., shows that, as a result of the United

in after years, said that the best way to challenge the American inter-
diction, and to satisfy the demands of the West Indian planters, would
have been to open to other commercial and maritime nations the
trade refused by the United States. This was never considered. And
it was not considered, one ventures to suggest, because, in the light of
Lord Liverpool's speech of 1820, it was already out of date. England's
industrial system, expanding, coarse, not burdened with historical pieties, did not wish to argue with a lucrative market, and a market protected with nothing more formidable than the Tariff of 1816. It was
this industrial instinct, quite as much as the declining influence of the
West Indian planter, which imparted such reforming vigor to the
British "American Trade Act" of 1822.[32] And then, of course, there
was the simple fact that the needs of the British West Indies could
most naturally be supplied by the United States. Industry and nature,
capitalist and agrarian, for once saw eye to eye.

The burly figure of William Huskisson, as it rose from the Tory
back benches to support the recommendations of Mr. Robinson, de-
serves some particular attention. In the previous year, as the member

---

States Navigation Act of 1820, exports of rum and molasses from the British
West Indies to the U.S.A., already low, fell from 476,139 and 241,187 gal-
lons respectively to 53,941 and 11,959. Since the West Indian planters and
merchants resident in London represented around £70 million in investments,
one must listen to Planta. Again, Ragatz, *idem,* shows that as a result of the
British "American Trade Act" exports of British West Indies rum and molasses
rose to an average between 1822 and 1826 of 650,102 and 1,330,317. For a
similar rise in coffee exports. see *H.R. Doc. 144,* 19 Cong., 2 sess., pp. 315–316.
Huskisson later stated that the British Act of 1822 was passed because supplies
from the U.S.A. were "so necessary" to the British West Indies. Hansard, 2
Ser., XVII, 645.

[32] Canning to Gallatin, September 11, 1826, *American State Papers, Foreign
Relations,* VI, 25. Quantitatively, the influence of the American market—as
against the figures quoted in the preceding footnote—may be expressed in the
following terms: In 1822, 95 per cent of all U.S. imports of woolens and 89
per cent of its imports of cotton goods were of British manufacture, and 47 per
cent of its total imports were of the growth, produce, or manufacture of
Great Britain and her colonies. *American State Papers, Commerce and Navigation,* II, "Annual Report of the Secretary of the Treasury on the State of the
Finances," 1824. *H.R. Misc. Doc. No. 117,* 52 Cong., 2 sess., 1893, x-xi, gives
the total U.S. imports coming from *the United Kingdom only* as 40.39 per
cent. This means, on the British side, that one-sixth of the *total* British export
was consumed by the U.S. in 1822. Pitkin, *Statistical View,* 183; J. Marshall,
A Digest of all the Accounts . . . (London, 1833), p. 124. In 1820, according
to G. R. Porter, *The Progress of the Nation* (London, 1912, rev. ed.), App.
477, this had sunk to one-twelfth.

of a parliamentary committee on agricultural distress, he had dared to assail the Corn Laws, that jerry-built cathedral of landlords and protectionists.[33] Mr. Huskisson was a moderate and erudite free-trader, a man whose knowledge of finance was said to be unequaled, and to whom—although his appearance was "slouching and ignoble" and his diction jarred their ears—the Commons always listened with attention.[34] In 1822, he was no more than the colonial agent of Ceylon, and the moderation of his views must be attributed in part to the modesty of his circumstances. He was a man of decent family, who had been brought up in Paris by Dr. Gem, the worthy friend of Jefferson and Tom Paine; and Dr. Gem, as physician to the British Embassy, had got him his start. It was scarcely an auspicious one. Mr. Huskisson was a nobody; he had not been born, like Liverpool and Robinson, into the inner circle of professional Tory politicians; he was not, like Lord Eldon (the son of a coal merchant), a useful pillar of reactionary law; he was simply a man of keen intelligence, enlarged views, and copious learning. That such a man should be gratified in his dearest wish—to get into government—seemed undesirable, if not absurd.

It becomes, therefore, of some importance to record that Lord Liverpool in 1822 began to call upon an unofficial Cabinet for advice in fiscal affairs; that Huskisson was a member of this shadowy council; and that toward the end of the year he was offered the presidency of the Board of Trade. The post was not to be accompanied by the customary elevation to Cabinet rank. George IV despised Mr. Huskisson and even Lord Liverpool thought that his social standing precluded him from such a promotion. Mr. Huskisson protested, with unusual vigor; and Liverpool was too kind-hearted to snub a lieutenant, especially a lieutenant whose services he so badly needed. In August, 1823, over the King's protests, and after a good deal of shuffling, Mr. Huskisson was edged into the Cabinet.[35] It was Liberal Toryism's most significant *coup d'état:* the high-tide mark of early reform.

The tide had already borne into Washington the British "American Trade Act" of 1822. At first its reception seemed all that could be

[33] Brady, *Huskisson*, p. 56.

[34] *Greville Memoirs, Reigns of George IV and William IV* (3 vols., London, 1875 ed.), II, 49.

[35] Brock, *Liverpool*, pp. 55, 164, 168–169.

wished for: Mr. Monroe's Proclamation—of August 24, 1822—was generosity itself.[36] A closer study of its wording, however, revealed that the President had not removed the tonnage duty of $1 a ton, or the light money, or the 10 per cent upon imports customarily charged against vessels not privileged by treaty stipulations. No doubt it was an oversight, and Mr. Stratford Canning hastened to Secretary Adams to have it corrected.[37] But Mr. Adams, strange to relate, was most evasive. Seven months later a new bill was enacted, and this bill was a direct response to the "American Trade Act" of 1822.[38]

Here, too, the language seemed most conciliatory; and only a careful scrutiny of the second section revealed that it was nothing of the sort. This section announced that British vessels, trading from the enumerated West Indian ports, would be treated in matters of impost and tonnage exactly like American vessels trading from the same ports,

on proof being given to the President of the United States, satisfactory to him, that, upon vessels of the United States, admitted into the above enumerated ports, and upon any goods, wares or merchandise, imported therein, in the said vessels, no other or higher duties of tonnage or impost, and no other charges of any kind, are levied and exacted than upon British vessels, or upon the like goods, wares and merchandise, imported into the said British ports from elsewhere.

One word had changed the whole meaning of the act. For if "elsewhere" meant anything, and it did, it meant that the United States now demanded that its vessels and goods should be admitted into British colonial ports upon the same terms as British vessels and cargoes from every other part of the British Empire. The industrial instinct of Great Britain was strong and coarse, but it was not strong or coarse enough to expect any government, Whig or Tory, to venture upon such extreme concessions; and years were to pass before any government did so. Mr. Huskisson himself described the "elsewhere" clause as a "pretension unheard of in the commercial relations of independent states."[39] He little knew that the emphasis had passed from "commercial" to "independent." The genesis of the "elsewhere"

[36] Richardson, *Messages and Papers*, II, 184–185.
[37] *Niles' Register*, XXIII, 87; *American State Papers, Foreign Relations*, VI, 214–215, 217; Adams, *Memoirs*, VI, 104.
[38] 3 U.S. Statutes at Large 740–742.
[39] Hansard, 2 Ser., XII, 1106.

clause still lacks adequate documentation, but there is good reason to believe that it was conceived in the State Department, drafted in the Senate Foreign Relations Committee, and presented to a Senate whose membership as a whole was either very complacent or not in the secret.[40] Stratford Canning, to do him justice, got wind of it while it was still in committee; but Mr. Adams, to whom he applied at once, blandly informed him that the American government interpreted "elsewhere" as meaning "anywhere else," and that the United States proposed to trade in British colonial ports on equal terms with the mother country and her dominions.[41] The nationalism which followed the Second War of Independence had reached a new climax, in so far as the individual purpose of the Secretary of State could make it do so.

Mr. Adams' concept of commercial reciprocity embraced far more than a simple protection of the American carrying trade, for such a protection would have been amply secured by the conciliatory British Act of 1822. The American Act of 1823 reveals, however dimly, a new intention. Great changes were taking place, just visible among the guarded agrarian platitudes of Monroe's Second Inaugural, not anticipated at all in the hopeful overtures of Liverpool's speech in 1820. The capital of New England, for example, was already being diverted from shipping to industry, although New England conservatism was still silent on this point. American internal development, although somewhat blurred by the Missouri Compromises, might take any shape —even the neomercantilist shape of which Mr. Adams was already speaking, and to which the President mildly inclined his ear. For if Liverpool, Robinson, and Huskisson had been wooing a lucrative and (as they thought) a somewhat helpless agrarian market, it was not Mr. Adams' intention that the market should remain helpless.[42] The British government might be peering, a little uncertainly, into some free-trading future, but Adams had (he hoped) already set a very different arrangement in motion. Isolationism, self-sufficiency, commercial reciprocity, the antinaval freedom of the seas—all these moved forward under his banner with its strange device of "elsewhere."

[40] Adams to Rush, June 23, 1823, *American State Papers, Foreign Relations,* VI, 228; Benton, *Thirty Years View,* I, 125.

[41] *American State Papers, Foreign Relations,* VI, 221, 228.

[42] Adams, *Memoirs,* V, 411.

The year 1823 became one of the climactic years in the history of Anglo-American relations, not least because it found the British still in a conciliatory mood. In this year and in 1824, Lord Liverpool's "economic Cabinet" laid the foundations for Mr. Robinson's free-trade budgets of those years, and made its plan for the famous assault upon the silk-trade monopoly, for the Warehousing Bill, the Reciprocity Duties Bill, the tentative attack upon the Corn Laws. Through Mr. Huskisson there was the closest connection between this inner group and the Foreign Office. The whole government looked with some complacency upon the economic ties between Great Britain and the United States. The American merchant easily availed himself of the banking and credit facilities open to British manufacturers and merchants; the basic Anglo-American exchange was still raw cotton for textiles; and this combination gave the United States a somewhat colonial dependence in British eyes.[43] The tariff of 1824 was the first cloud upon this relatively serene sky, the first sign that American industrialists proposed to do what Lord Liverpool hoped they would never do, and that was to extract from Congress a substantial protection.

In 1823 no Liberal Tory was clairvoyant enough to predict such an event. And so, when the American Navigation Act was received and studied in Whitehall, the answer was an order in council of July 17, imposing a duty of 4s. 3d. per ton and 10 per cent on the cargo of all United States shipping to enter the ports of British colonies in North America and the West Indies.[44] The order was a firm and equivalent retaliation, but it was not hostile, and it is not difficult to perceive the thinking behind it. To get the order repealed, Monroe and Adams had simply to institute conversations in London which would lead to more temperate definition of the word "elsewhere," and this would at once produce a mutual suspension of tonnage and cargo duties. The Americans were now angling for a commercial convention, and, not knowing the intransigent character of Adams' instructions to Minister Richard Rush, the Liverpool government assumed

[43] Norman S. Buck, *The Development of the Organization of Anglo-American Trade* (New Haven, 1925), p. 135. L. H. Jenks, *The Migration of British Capital to 1875* (New York, 1927), p. 67, says that 80 per cent of Lancashire cotton supplies came from the U.S. cotton fields in the period of 1820–30.

[44] Benns, *American Struggle,* p. 99.

that the question would be settled in a preliminary, or at worst in a final, discussion. It was not an unreasonable assumption.

Thus in 1823 the Anglo-American climate was, in an economic sense, both mild and fair when George Canning made those political overtures to Richard Rush which were to produce an unexpected and unwelcome response in the Monroe Doctrine.

CHAPTER 6

The Monroe Doctrine

T HE intrusion of "elsewhere" into the grammar of Anglo-American commercial relations came at a tense and dramatic moment in the history of the Western World. It was in the year 1823 that the conquerors of Napoleon reached a parting of the ways: the industrial and constitutional British moving toward the principle of nationalism (or competition) and the great reactionaries of Russia, Prussia and Austria, making a disorderly retreat toward that of order (or monopoly). France, acting very much on her own, became the leader of the retreat in 1823 by staging a successful invasion of constitutionalist Spain, thus offering the world a lunar glimpse of a revived Bourbon Empire.

British diplomacy was manifestly, if only for the time being, at a loss; and to an American mind, as to an Irish in later years, England's difficulty was America's opportunity. John Quincy Adams, at any rate, whose chief opponent was always the British Empire, was hardly the man to refrain from using the distractions of London to further his own ideas of a truly continental United States.

In order to appreciate the influence of Europe upon the thoughts and actions of the State Department in Washington, it is necessary to recall three arrangements which followed the overthrow of the Napoleonic Empire.

The first of these was the Final Act of the Vienna Congress, an intricate design of dynastic and territorial adjustments, which "reaffirmed the idea of indefeasible monarchical rights—and over wide areas failed to restore the previous rules. Nor were the proprietary and quasi-contractual rights attributed to dynasties or Estates compatible with the new social and economic conditions: for these ideas were connected with the land; they were alien to the intelligentsia . . . and to the modern cities."[1] "In the first decades of the nineteenth century," to put it another way, "power appeared to consist principally of land and human beings. The significance of technology and intensive industrialization had not been fully understood."[2] Such an understanding had, to be sure, begun to dawn upon the government in London, and it had even made some impression upon that government's Foreign Secretary, Lord Castlereagh, a nobleman whose gaze (undoubtedly a searching one) was sometimes concentrated upon a Europe that had vanished with William Pitt. It was ironical, and for Castlereagh tragic, that the passionate and unappeasable unrest, the true "note" of post-Napoleonic Europe, and one which he deplored and feared, should have prefigured a competitive world from which industrial England was most likely to profit. He literally sacrificed his reason and his life in an attempt to solve this painful conundrum.

The second arrangement was known as the Quadruple Alliance, between Great Britain, Prussia, Russia, and Austria. It had its origins in the Treaty of Chaumont (March 1, 1814), and was patched up or renewed on November 20, 1815. Its object was to prevent the Napoleonic dynasty from ever returning to France and also to preserve the dynastic and territorial adjustments of 1814–15, and its operative article was the sixth. According to this Article VI, the four powers were to continue to meet at fixed intervals in order to discuss such measures as should be "most salutary for the repose and prosperity of nations and for the maintenance of the peace of Europe."[3] Thus was originated the conference system, with which we are still familiar.

The third arrangement was, as to its beginnings, manifestly deranged. The Holy Alliance of September 25, 1815, was the brain child

---

[1] Sir Lewis Namier, *Vanished Supremacies* (New York, 1963 ed.), p. 24.

[2] William W. Kaufmann, *British Policy and the Independence of Latin America* (New Haven, 1951), p. 81.

[3] Nicolson, *Congress of Vienna*, pp. 70–71; Charles K. Webster (ed.), *British Diplomacy, 1813–1815* (London, 1921), p. 166.

of the Tsar Alexander, an autocrat whose quasi-Platonic liberalism was already declining into a quasi-mystical pietism, whose indecisions were becoming more and more pronounced, and whose method of composing them through the practice of sortilege was, to say the least, alarmingly unmethodical. It was he who proposed that the sovereigns of Russia, Prussia, and Austria should pledge themselves to base their relations upon "the sublime truths which the Holy Religion of our Savior teaches," and to consider themselves and their subjects as "members of the same Christian nation." This Holy Alliance was to be concluded in the names of the three sovereigns personally; other rulers were invited to append their signatures, and many did so; but neither governments nor peoples were included in it. At first, the comment of Lord Castlereagh (whose sovereign, being a constitutional monarch, could not join the Alliance) that it was all "sublime nonsense," and of Prince Metternich that it was "a loud sounding nothing," probably expressed the general opinion. In the course of time, however, the Austrian statesman realized that the Holy Alliance could be very useful, but only upon the understanding that one could subject the term "Holy" to what an American would have called loose construction.[4]

Neither the Final Act of Vienna nor the Quadruple Alliance can be separated in spirit from that persuasive and unbalancing concept which was then (and until quite recently) honored as "the balance of power."[5] For a while the conference system appeared to work: at the Conference of Aix-la-Chapelle (1818) it was agreed that a mediation between Ferdinand VII and his disaffected colonies was always in order, but that the colonies should not be restored by force of arms or commercial boycott.[6] These were, after all, terms agreeable to commercial and industrial England. In 1820, however, there were revolutionary uprisings in Naples, Piedmont, Spain, and Portugal; and at

[4] H. W. V. Temperley, *The Foreign Policy of Canning* (London, 1925), p. 5; Nicolson, *Congress of Vienna*, p. 250; Webster, *British Diplomacy*, p. 384; Kaufmann, *British Policy*, p. 89.

[5] "Power" has now been changed into "terror," which is even more unbalancing.

[6] Webster, *The Foreign Policy of Castlereagh* (2 vols., London, 1925), II, 413, 419; Wellington, *Supplementary Despatches, Correspondence and Memoranda* (15 vols., London, 1858–72), XII, 805; Dexter Perkins, "Russia and the Spanish Colonies," *American Historical Review*, XVIII, (1913), 667.

the conference of Troppau, Metternich issued a *protocole prélimi-naire,* which proposed that any state subjected to revolution was no longer in good standing with the Holy Alliance, and that the remaining Holy Allies could restore it to membership by force. Under such conditions, the balance of power—British style—would cease to exist. The British government now dissented in a stern circular; whereupon the three original Holy Allies, retiring to Laibach, rephrased the *protocole* in even more sinister language.[7] It was evident that the Quadruple Alliance was becoming somewhat Holy—a fact which became painfully evident when an Austrian army was let loose upon Naples. And then in 1821 the Greek War of Independence broke out, dragging the Eastern Question into the nineteenth century. In the same year the French began to threaten an armed invasion of Spain, in order to rescue Ferdinand VII from his Constitutionalist captors. It was to discuss these questions, so threatening to the repose of Europe and the continued existence of its Concert, that a new Congress was called for the fall of 1822. It was to be held at Verona, and Lord Castlereagh proposed to attend it in person.

John Quincy Adams had never allowed himself to be seriously alarmed by the thought of an armed European intervention in the revolutions of Latin America. "It may be observed," he wrote to Henry Middleton, our Minister to Russia, "that for the repose of Europe, as well as of America, the European and American political systems should be kept as separate and distinct from each other as possible."[8] He did not believe that this would present many difficulties and, until the Florida Treaty had been ratified, he did not propose to emphasize this separation by recognizing the colonists' independence. Monroe was much in favor of the colonists; their exploits had blown upon the embers of his revolutionary past; but he, too, favored a cautious approach. It was not until March 8, 1822, that he wrote a Message to Congress, recommending, in very temperate language, the recognition of the United Provinces of the Rio de la Plata, Colom-

[7] *The Cambridge History of British Foreign Policy* (3 vols., 1922–23), II, 662, cites Castlereagh's memorandum of May 15, 1820, with its hitherto unprecedented distinction between constitutional and autocratic states. Cp. Lieven to Nesselrode, May 16, 1820; Webster, *Foreign Policy,* II, 565.

[8] J. Q. A. to Henry Middleton, July 5, 1820; *Writings,* VII, 49–50. For Monroe's approval of this statement, see Bemis, *Adams and Foreign Policy,* p. 365 n.

bia, Chile, Peru, and Mexico. Congress responded with an appropriation of $100,000 for the expenses of "such missions as the independent nations on the American continent [*sic*] as the President might deem proper." An act to this effect was signed on May 4, 1822.[9]

This was the first recognition accorded to the patriots by any power; but it promised nothing in the way of financial or military assistance, nor can it be construed as a reaction to the difficulties which Great Britain was beginning to experience with the neo-Holy Allies.[10] On May 13, Adams wrote to Minister Rush in London asking him to assure Lord Castlereagh that "it was not understood or intended as a change of policy on the part of the United States nor adopted with any desire of turning it to the account of our own interests."[11] Since Adams was now at the heart of American foreign policy, and since he was not in the habit of addressing the British Foreign Office in quite such deprecating terms, it becomes of some interest to inquire into his reasons for doing so.

In the first place, he did not as yet put much faith in the future of Latin America. He believed that the ruins of the Spanish Empire, now passing into the control of the insurgents, were deeply and perhaps fatally impregnated with the harsh spirit of the soldier and the theocrat.[12] In taking this view, he had been influenced partly by the contradictory findings of the President's fact-finding commission of 1818,[13] and partly by the fact that Henry Clay was making political capital out of the Spanish Americans. As a Westerner, and a very imaginative one, Clay was naturally enchanted by their grand defiance of the Spaniard; but he scarcely concealed his desire to embarrass the

[9] Richardson, *Messages and Papers*, II, 116–118; S. F. Bemis, *Latin American Policy of the United States* (New York, 1943), p. 46. At this time Peru was not liberated (this did not occur until the battles of Junin and Ayacucho had been fought in 1824), and Mexico was merely in a state of truce.

[10] That is, with Russia, Prussia, and Austria after the writing and rephrasing of the *protocole*.

[11] Adams to Rush, May 3, 1822; Webster, *Foreign Policy,* II, 427.

[12] Adams, *Memoirs,* V, 325.

[13] *American State Papers, Foreign Relations,* IV, 217 ff. Its members were John Graham, Caesar A. Rodney, and Theodorick Bland. See also William R. Manning (ed.), *Diplomatic Correspondence of the United States Concerning the Independence of the Latin-American Nations* (3 vols., New York, 1925), I, 382 ff., for the independent observations of Joel R. Poinsett. See also Adams to Anderson (first Minister to Colombia), May 27, 1823; *Writings,* VII, 441 ff., esp. deleted passage on pp. 442–443.

administration by repeated calls for a more republican and positive approach toward their struggle for freedom. In 1818 he had told the Congress: "I am strongly inclined to believe that they will in most, if not in all parts of their country establish free governments. . . . They adopt our principles, copy our institutions, and, in many instances, employ the very language of our revolutionary papers." He even proposed, in terms designedly loose, that they might well be incorporated into his American System.[14]

Adams' reply to this sort of manifesto was usually sour. "As to an American system," he wrote in 1820, "we have it, we constitute the whole of it; there is no community of interests or of principles between North and South America."[15] It might seem that between the views of Mr. Adams, who saw the heroes of the Liberation as the founders of *caudillismo,* and of Mr. Clay, who gave them an almost Anglo-Saxon character, there was a difference so abysmal that only gross prejudice, on the one hand, or blind enthusiasm, on the other, could possibly account for their respective positions. To some extent, however, their differences—as has been suggested—were such as naturally exist between a state of opposition and one of incumbency. When Clay became Secretary of State, his opinions grew less fervent; while Adams, once he had accepted the need for Latin American friendship, at least endeavored to "warm himself more and more into the spirit of Monroe."[16]

In the second place, Adams was a continentalist, and between 1820 and 1823 he was not concerned with hemispheric unity, if indeed he ever was. As he watched the gradual dissolution of the Concert of Europe, the rise of the Holy Alliance, and the increasing embarrassment of Great Britain, he began to calculate the advantages which the continental United States might extract from this situation. Toward the advance of the British Empire into the Far West, as toward British overtures in the matter of a freer trade, he was apt to be belligerent and exacting. In January 1821, in the course of a wonderful two-day quarrel with Stratford Canning, he asserted that Great Britain had no claim to the Columbia River or its mouth, and indeed no

[14] *Works,* Colton (ed.), VI, 145–146; *Annals of Congress,* 15 Cong., 1 sess., II, 1482.
[15] *Memoirs,* V, 176, 325.
[16] Bemis, *Adams and Foreign Policy,* p. 361.

claim to the shores of the Pacific. " 'And in this,' said he, 'you include our northern provinces on this continent?' 'No,' said I, 'there the boundary is marked, and we have no disposition to encroach upon it. Keep what is yours, *but leave the rest of the continent to us.* '"[17]

By the third article of the Convention of 1818, the Oregon country west of the Rockies was open to the vessels, citizens, and subjects of both countries, so that Adams' assertion was either meaningless or else it resounded with the doctrine of noncolonization, which he was to make peculiarly his own.[18] Six months later, he gave a July 4 address before a packed and startled audience in the Hall of Representatives; it turned out to be tremendous anti-British tirade; and although Adams had taken the precaution of draping himself in a professor's gown, the manner (if not the matter) of his oration was severely criticized.[19] Mr. Adams described his critics as "malevolent and vulgar," among other things;[20] but even a critic not malevolent or vulgar might have had some difficulty in extracting from his speech what really lay at the heart of it, and that is the principle of noncolonization.

Noncolonization implied that the American hemisphere was not open to further colonization by European powers; although it required that Latin America should be released from exclusive trade practices, it was chiefly directed against British pretensions in the Far West.[21] Adams knew that commercial England was opposed to forcible intervention in Latin America, and that her navy could and would

[17] *Memoirs,* V, 250–252, for the whole conversation, as hilarious as it is important. Italics inserted.

[18] The British government did not wish to call attention to the Hudson's Bay Company which, about to merge with the Northwest Company, promised to become the great power in the Oregon country; it therefore instructed Stratford Canning—Castlereagh to S. Canning, April 10, 1821—not to contest Adams' remarks. Bemis, *Adams and Foreign Policy,* p. 493.

[19] E.g., Christopher Hughes to Albert Gallatin, Stockholm, November 16, 1821: "I suppose you have highly *relished* and *approved* the meek *spirit,* kind *temper,* and good taste . . . [of] our Boston Demosthenes. Gallatin Papers, NYHS.

[20] Adams to Robert Walsh, July 10, 27, 1821; to Edward Everett, January 31, 1822; *Writings,* VII, 113, 127, 197.

[21] He was opposed, of course, to Russian claims north of 55° north, and told the Russian Minister that the U.S.A. would "contest the right of Russia to *any* territorial establishment," *Memoirs,* VI, 104; but he never took Russia as seriously as he did Great Britain.

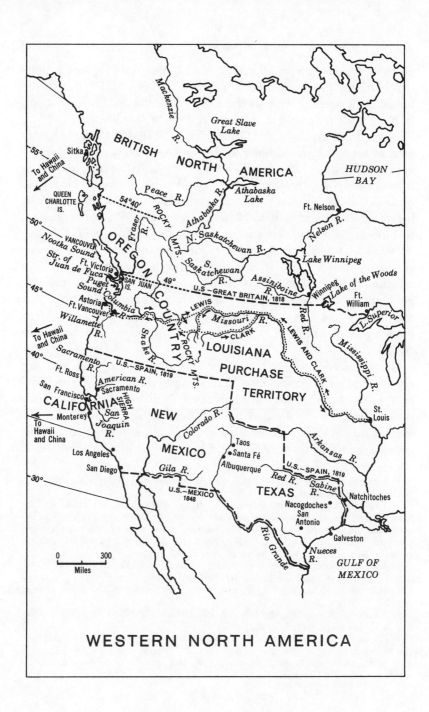

WESTERN NORTH AMERICA

sink any expedition—French or Holy—long before it reached its destination. He was suspicious, however, of her designs upon Cuba, and at length in 1823 he instructed the new Minister to Spain, Hugh Nelson, to this effect:

> The annexation of Cuba to our federal republic will be indispensable to the continuance and integrity of the Union itself. . . . It is obvious however that for this we are not prepared. . . . But there are laws of political as well as physical gravitation; and if an apple severed by the tempest from its native tree cannot choose but fall to the ground, Cuba, forcibly disjoined from its unnatural connection with Spain, and incapable of self-support, can gravitate only towards the North American Union, which by the same law of nature cannot cast her off from its bosom. . . . You will not conceal from the Spanish Government the repugnance of the United States to the transfer of the island of Cuba to any other power.[22]

This great reiteration of the no-transfer principle completed his verbal defenses against the British Empire; needless to say, he did not believe that the United States was in any position to go to war with Great Britain over Cuba.[23]

By now a great change had taken place in the history of the British Foreign Office. Lord Castlereagh, if not exactly a man of the world, was a tremendous grandee, who moved among the courts and courtiers of Europe with all the prestige, not only of statesmanship but also of birth, and whose diplomacy was a matter of intricate personal relationships in the highest quarters. Although every student of his later career knows that he was to some extent the servant of English commercial and industrial interests, and was already breaking with the very Concert he had labored to create, he was (very naturally) most unwilling to accept this solution. He would have done anything to avoid it, and he still hoped against hope that he could bring the Conference of Verona to accept his concept of the balance of power— his dream, that is to say, of a perpetual stalemate. But it was not to be. In the summer of 1822 he was grossly overworked. Parliament had proved unusually troublesome; and, although outwardly unruffled, he was in fact extremely sensitive to the mounting hatred of radical and

[22] Adams to Nelson, April 28, 1823; *Writings*, VI, 372–73, 381. It was then feared that Britain might ask for Cuba in return for her support of Constitutionalist Spain.

[23] *Memoirs*, VI, 138.

romantic Englishmen. He was considered the very image and agent of oppression; though in actual fact he was something more fearful—a man who did not recognize oppression when he saw it. He was now heard to complain that his mind was worn out; in two dreadful interviews with George IV and the Duke of Wellington he began to accuse himself of every crime, and at last, shut up in his country house, with every razor and pistol kept out of sight, the poor madman succeeded in cutting his throat with a small penknife. This tragic event took place on August 12, 1822.[24] On September 9 his great rival, George Canning, who was preparing to go into exile as Governor General of India, was offered the post of Foreign Secretary, together with the leadership of the House of Commons.

Canning was then, and still remains, a somewhat enigmatic figure. If Lord Castlereagh had at length got out of his depth in his effort to maintain the conference system, it is still arguable whether George Canning had much depth out of which to get. The man who perceived that Singapore was the *unum necessarium* for the maintenance of British rule in India can hardly, it is true, be accused of shortsightedness. The man who, before his death in 1827, had discredited the Holy Alliance must, surely, be granted his share of force. And yet, then as now, one could not be certain that his successes were other than superficial: and perhaps, even today, the best one could say for him (it is, of course, a good deal) is that his remarkable opportunism responded, with a curious fidelity, to the beginnings of a movement toward industrial laissez faire.

It says much for Lord Liverpool that he was so eager and so determined to unite his fortunes with this ambiguous man. Canning

[24] E. L. Woodward, *The Age of Reform* (Oxford, 1938), p. 189, says that in 1821 the Foreign Office staff consisted only of twenty-eight persons, whose training was "rudimentary." Webster, *Foreign Policy of Castlereagh*, II, 484–485; Peter Quennell (ed.), *The Private Letters of Princess Lieven to Prince Metternich* (New York, 1938), pp. 189–190; Earl Stanhope, *Notes of Conversations with the Duke of Wellington* (London, 1888), p. 272. Shelley wrote these terrible lines in *The Mask of Anarchy* (1819): "I met Murder on the way—/ He had a mask like Castlereagh—/ Very smooth he looked, yet grim;/ Seven blood-hounds followed him." Thomas Hutchinson (ed.), *The Complete Poetical Works of Shelley* (Oxford, 1904), p. 364. When Byron, in Italy, heard the news, he composed the following epitaph: "Posterity will ne'er survey/ A nobler grave than this/ Here lie the bones of Castlereagh;/ Stop, traveller, and p——" Kaufmann, *British Policy*, p. 135 n. Castlereagh, in private, was a most affectionate man and his friends were devoted to him.

had been born a Whig, but the Whigs looked down on him because his disinherited father had died in poverty and his mother had become an actress in order to support the family. Canning had been rescued by an uncle from his disheveled existence, but he was never forgiven by the Whigs. "I regard the son of an actress," said Earl Grey, years later, "as being *de facto* incapacitated from being premier of England."[25] Such ineffable contempt as this, together with the influence of Burke and Pitt, drove Canning into the Tory fold. He was one of the leading young writers for the *Anti-Jacobin;* he was Under Secretary of State before he was thirty; he first became Foreign Secretary when he was thirty-five. Certainly the Tories had been kind to this energetic convert. From 1810 until 1822, however, he was usually in eclipse. The most brilliant orator in the House of Commons,[26] he never (it was said) made an important speech without also making an important enemy. His nicknames[27] were cutting and faintly juvenile, as was his wit; he seemed, indeed, always to be revenging upon society the slights it had inflicted upon his mother. On the other hand, he could be charming and convivial when he pleased: in nonultra London (with the aid of an unexceptionable marriage) he carried all before him until he stopped going out.[28] In politics, however, he was called a faithless colleague, a tireless intriguer; even his cousin, Stratford Canning, could say no more of him than that "he is, in the main, an honest man."[29] No evidence has been unearthed to support these

[25] Temperley, *Canning,* p. 33; J. A. R. Marriott, *George Canning and His Times* (London, 1903), pp. 4, 5.

[26] "I never saw Canning but once," said Disraeli, who heard him make his last speech in the Commons. "I remember as it were but yesterday the tumult of that ethereal brow. Still lingers in my ear the melody of that voice." Temperley, *Canning,* p. 441.

[27] Lord Westmorland, the hard-drinking Lord Privy Seal, became "le sot [sceau] privé"; the shrill voiced Mr. Wynn, when a candidate for the Speakership, was "Mr. Squeaker"; the bulky Duke of Buckingham was the Ph.D. or Phat Duke, etc., etc. Temperley, *Canning,* p. 234. "We shall see," said Sydney Smith, when Canning first became Foreign Secretary, "whether the nation can be saved by schoolboy jokes." Josceline Bagot, *George Canning and His Friends* (2 vols., London, 1909), I, 48.

[28] Temperley, *Canning,* p. 233, shows that he had a circle of devoted friends and that even Lord Holland and Lord Byron acknowledged his charm. Kaufmann, *British Policy,* p. 35, gives a brilliant description of Canning. See also Vicomte de Marcellus, *Politique de la Restauration* (Paris, 1835), pp. 15–17.

[29] Marriott, *Canning,* p. 13.

accusations and insinuations: though not overburdened with scruples, Canning was no monster of duplicity. He was pre-eminently an opportunist, which is quite another thing.

It may well have been his opportunism which so strongly attracted Lord Liverpool and incurred the hatred of George IV and the Ultras in his own party. Translated into politico-economic terms, this opportunism was the very instinct of Liberal Toryism, which never achieved a philosophy but merely felt its way toward one. Canning also had a well-deserved reputation for fiscal cleverness: it had recommended him to the Borough of Liverpool, which he represented in Parliament for twelve years; and it was the basis of his intimacy with William Huskisson.[30] He favored the repeal of the Navigation Laws, but hoped to replace them with a scheme for imperial preference; advocated Catholic Emancipation; disliked the obsolete tariff system; and even, toward the end of his life, was preparing for an attack upon the Corn Laws. His later career amply demonstrates that he had glimpsed the vital importance of free competition to a powerful industrial economy. And yet, with all his shrewdness, he was no friend to parliamentary reform, the essential first step toward economic freedom. And his feelings for the mass of his countrymen, sunk so deep in so much misery, were a repulsive combination of eighteenth-century optimism and Malthusian despair; for if he was a disciple of Burke, he lacked Burke's flashes of compassionate insight.

Such was the man who, for the rest of this study, must be considered the most conspicuous external influence upon the foreign policy of John Quincy Adams. At first, at Verona, the Duke of Wellington (not Canning's choice) discovered that he was quite unable to drive a wedge between the neo-Holy Allies and royalist France. Unaccustomed to being left out in the cold, the Duke returned with a new grudge against Canning, whom he had never liked, and endeavored, with the aid of George IV, the Austrian and Russian ambassadors, and Madame de Lieven, to humiliate the Foreign Secretary into resignation. But Canning, with the unflinching support of Lord Liverpool, was immovable.[31]

[30] J. W. Croker to Robert Peel, August 25, 1822; *Croker Papers* (3 vols., London, 1884), I, 213. Gallatin to Clay, August 31, 1827, writes that Canning was "influenced by Mr. Huskisson in all that related to commerce or commercial consideration." *Senate Docs.,* 22 Cong., 1 sess., III, 132.

[31] *Letters of Princess Lieven,* pp. 273, 274, 283–84. "My Lord Liverpool,"

None the less, he was in serious difficulties. He had given an activist impulse[32] to the policy of Castlereagh; he had detached Great Britain, informally but firmly, from the Quadruple Alliance. But a French army stood poised upon the Spanish frontier, against the wishes of everyone, for even the neo-Holy Allies wanted nothing more than an ambassadors' conference in Paris to express, as they put it, a moral solidarity between themselves and the French.[33] Canning endeavored to mediate, but in vain: on April 6, 1823, the French army, under a Bourbon prince, crossed the Bidassoa, and plunged into Spain. All Canning could do was to speed his good wishes to the constitutionalists from the floor of the House of Commons; but (contrary to his expectations) the French met with no resistance, the constitutionalists with their prisoner king withdrew to Seville, and the end was clearly in sight.[34]

There was little to be done at this juncture by a nation which, even if it had been in a mood to make war on France, had no troops in readiness for such a venture. Even threats would be harmful, because empty. "Menace not intended," Canning once told the British Ambassador to France, "is an engine which Great Britain could never condescend to employ." In the meantime, in May, his defiance of France and the Holy Allies, and his speech in the Commons wishing well to the revolutionaries in Spain, had become known in Washington.[35] "The course you have taken in the great politics of Europe,"

Wellington blurted out at a dinner party, "is nothing less than a political prostitute."

[32] *Cambridge History of British Foreign Policy,* II, 622; Canning to Wellington, September 27, 1822; Temperley, *Canning,* p. 64.

[33] Wellington to Canning, September 21, 1822; Wellington, *Despatches, Correspondence, and Memoranda,* I, 288 ff.

[34] Stapleton, *Official Correspondence,* I, 73–74; *British and Foreign State Papers,* X, 64–70. By suppressing a revolution by force, the French had drifted into the Holy orbit, and at his own dinner table, where he was entertaining the Russian and Austrian Ambassadors, the Prussian Minister, and the French chargé, George IV mocked at Canning for his apparent diplomatic defeat. "There is nothing more contemptible than half-measures and half-tones. I hate them. *Don't you, Mr. Canning?" Letters of Princess Lieven,* p. 273. The Comte de Villèle, the leading figure in the French Cabinet, never intended to develop a mass attack upon Spanish America; but the French Council of State had approved the chimerical idea of sending Spanish princes to South America, with the backing of the French fleet and army. Temperley, *Canning,* p. 72; Dexter Perkins, *The Monroe Doctrine, 1823–1826* (Cambridge, 1927), pp. 111 ff.

[35] For Canning's speeches of April 14 and April 30, 1823, see Woodward, *Age*

wrote Stratford Canning, *"has had the effect of making England almost popular in the United States. . . . Even Adams has caught something of the soft infection.* On the whole, I question whether for a long time there has been so favorable an opportunity . . . to bring the two countries nearer together."[36] In June, Adams himself suggested that the United States and Great Britain should now "compare their ideas and purposes together, with a view to the accommodation of the great interests upon which they have hitherto differed."[37] One cannot blame Stratford Canning for presuming that by "accommodation" Mr. Adams meant "compromise." Reporting his conversation to Rush in July, however, Adams hinted that what he meant was that Great Britain should now submit to the American theory of neutral rights.[38] The British predicament at Verona and in Spain had stimulated his neomercantilist nerve—his desire, in this instance, to extract advantages without an equivalent concession.

George Canning, having received Stratford Canning's report on the "soft infection," became very affable in his dealings with Minister Rush. In July he asked him to transmit to Monroe and Adams copies of a speech of April 16, in which he had said: "If I wished for a guide in a system of neutrality, I should take that laid down by America in the presidency of Washington and the secretaryship of Jefferson." The speech was covered with corrections in Canning's own hand—the speech, but not the history. He had forgotten, if he had ever known, Jefferson's farewell report as Secretary of State, with its demands for a system of restrictions and regulations against Great Britain's "unnatural monopoly" of American exchanges.[39] But that Canning should even have used such language was astonishing: to men such as he

---

of *Reform,* p. 198; Temperley, *Canning,* p. 88; Webster and Temperley, "British Policy in the Publication of Diplomatic Documents under Castlereagh and Canning," *Cambridge Historical Journal,* I (1924), 164–165; Kaufmann, *British Policy,* p. 149; Hansard, 2 ser., VIII, 1480.

[36] Stratford Canning to George Canning, May 8, 1823; Dexter Perkins, *Monroe Doctrine,* p. 60.

[37] Adams, *Memoirs,* VI, 151.

[38] Adams to Rush, July 28, 1823; Monroe, *Writings,* VI, 359.

[39] Bemis, *Adams and Foreign Policy,* p. 378; John C. Miller, *The Federalist Era* (New York, 1960), pp. 142–143. In August, 1823, in Liverpool, at a banquet where Christopher Hughes (now chargé at Stockholm) happened to be present, Canning said: "The force of blood again prevails, and the mother and the daughter stand together against the world." *Speeches of George Canning* (6 vols., London, 1886), VI, 414.

Jefferson was usually an Ananias, not an analogue. And then, on August 16, in the course of a long interview, Rush just happened to mention the pleasure he derived from the thought that England would never allow France to interfere with the emancipation of the Spanish colonies, or remain passive if France attempted to obtain territory there by conquest or cession. Canning listened attentively, and then he asked what the American government would say to going hand in hand with England in such a policy. No concert of *action,* said Canning, would be necessary: if it were simply known that the two nations held the same opinions, would not that deter the French?

Rush's answer was admirably cool. He would communicate this proposal to his government as informally as it had been presented to him. The chief concern in Washington, he continued very shrewdly, was the precise situation in which the British government stood toward the Spanish American revolutionaries. Were they taking, did they think of taking, any step toward the recognition of those states? Canning's answer was neither precise nor candid. His government, he said, contemplated a preparatory step only—one which would leave Great Britain free "to recognize or not according to the position of events at some future period." Rush's report on this conversation reached Washington on October 9.[40]

In August it had become all too clear that the French would defeat the Constitutionalists and release King Ferdinand VII. Their plan for establishing Bourbon monarchies in Latin America was already well known. From Canning's point of view, if a new *pacte de famille* was to be formed between the French and Spanish Bourbons, it could not be allowed to extend to Ferdinand VII's former colonies.[41] With his European diplomacy in danger of collapse, he had to regain prestige in the field of Spanish America; and here, for want of anyone else to turn to, he sought the co-operation of the United States. Such was the motive behind his proposal to Rush on August 16.

[40] Rush to Adams, August 19, 1823; Monroe, *Writings,* VI, 361 ff.; Rush, *Residence at the Court of London* (Philadelphia, 3rd ed., 1872), pp. 399 ff. Canning later described these overtures as a "flirtation." Canning to Bagot, January 22, 1824; *Canning and His Friends,* II, 125.

[41] Canning, always a monarchist, was not opposed to Spanish princes in the New World, at least in Mexico and Brazil, as "a cure for the evils of universal democracy," but he wished France to have no part in their selection. Canning to A' Court, December 31, 1823; Stapleton, *Canning and His Times,* pp. 394–395.

This is the conventional view, and there is much to be said for it, and much with which to support it. Canning hoped to come to an understanding with America in the matter of "hands off" in Cuba. He feared that the French might attempt to revive their old colonial Empire and their old sea power: who, if not the purchasers of Louisiana, would be the most eloquent opponents, with England, of such an ambition? And then he wished "to prevent the drawing of the line of demarcation which I most dread—[hemispheric] America versus Europe."[42] Add to these reasons his need for prestige, and his concern for Latin American trade, and one can well believe that his overture to the United States was a valid diplomatic gesture.

Yet, as the overture grew more urgent, it is hard to believe that these reasons, though present and active, were quite sufficient to account for its urgency. Stratford Canning had already informed him that the American government had no designs upon Cuba, then or in the near future, and this was true. He could hardly have convinced himself that the United States meant a great deal to the reactionaries of Europe. He knew that British sea power was anything but "a menace nor intended . . . which Great Britain could never condescend to employ." Indeed, as the natural defender of Latin America, British fleets—along with cheap British manufactures—must have a more favorable influence than any recognition of independence, necessary though such a recognition might be. As for the "line of demarcation," Lord Liverpool had already suggested that it was more easily drawn by tariffs than erased by declarations. Had the United States yet shown any urgent desire to advance beyond the Tariff of 1816? Might it not—would it not—as part of Mr. Adams' "accommodation" withdraw its absurd pretension implied in the word "elsewhere"? Was

[42] *Idem.* See also Canning to John Hookham Frere, January 8, 1825: "The great danger was the division of the world into European and American, Republican and Monarchical." Temperley, "The Later American Policy of George Canning," *American Historical Review,* X (1906), 781. The Polignac Memorandum (see next chapter) in his opinion obviated that particular danger. In 1822, he told the Cabinet of his suspicions concerning a seizure of Cuba by the United States; Cabinet Memo of November 15, 1822, in. C. K. Webster, *Britain and the Independence of Latin America* (2 vols., London, 1938), II, 393. In January, 1823, Stratford Canning informed him that there was no foundation for these suspicions, and in March Lord Liverpool told Rush that Great Britain would never agree to a change in Cuban sovereignty, or seize the island herself; Adams, *Writings,* VII, 373 n.; Bemis, *Adams and Foreign Policy,* pp. 373–374.

it not still a friendly market? Thus it is at least permissible to suggest, when considering the great events now to be outlined, that Canning made his overture to the United States not merely as a conscious diplomatist in search of prestige but also as the partly unconscious servant of British coal and iron, of British spindles and furnaces.

On August 20, he wrote an "unofficial and confidential" note to Richard Rush. In it he set forth five "opinions and feelings."

(1) We conceive the recovery of the Colonies by Spain to be hopeless.

(2) We conceive the Question of the Recognition of them, as Independent States, to be one of time and circumstance.

(3) We are, however, by no means disposed to throw any impediment in the way of an arrangement between them and the mother country by amicable negotiations.

(4) We aim not at the possession of any portion of them ourselves.

(5) We could not see any portion of them transferred to any other Power with indifference.

If these opinions and feelings are as I firmly believe them to be, common to your government with ours, why should we hesitate mutually to confide them with each other; and to declare them in the face of the world? . . . Do you conceive that under the power which you have recently received, you are authorized to enter into negotiation, and to sign any Convention upon this subject? . . . Nothing would be more gratifying to me than to join you in such a work, and I am persuaded, there has seldom, in the history of the world, occurred an opportunity, when so small an effort, of two friendly Governments, might produce so unequivocal a good and prevent such extensive calamities.[43]

"So small an effort" strikes the observer of today as somewhat less than perceptive. Mr. Canning may have been granted some insight, although a faulty one, into the mind of Minister Rush; he may also have known the sort of bait that might be tempting to James Monroe; but of the "feelings and opinions" of Mr. Adams he had been vouchsafed no glimpse at all. Only (1) and (5) could have been entirely acceptable to Adams.

Mr. Rush, in his reply, balked only at (2). The paramount consideration, he said, must be the recognition of the Latin American states by the powers of Europe, "and especially, I may add, by Great

[43] Canning to Rush, August 20, 1823; Monroe, *Writings,* VI, 365–366; Manning, *Diplomatic Correspondence,* III, 1478–1479.

Britain." He therefore refused to commit himself, and on September 8 he assumed that negotiations on this point would now come to an end.[44]

And yet, as he waited day after day for some final word from Canning, he began to doubt. Could it be that the Foreign Secretary proposed to continue his pleas, and with even more warmth? And if so, why so? As he turned the matter over in his mind, he wrote a letter to James Monroe which is one of the most revealing documents in this whole transaction.

He could not, he told the President, bring himself to believe that the Tories had changed their attitude toward political freedom, although he suspected that they would continue to liberalize their foreign-trade policy, and that Liverpool and Canning would become even more intimate and friendly in their dealings with the United States. He did not impute sinister motives to them; he believed that neither Whigs nor Radicals would offer such good terms; he merely wished to observe (or so it seems to us) that a government which had little respect for civil liberties might appear almost high-minded in its quest for economic advantages.[45]

His predictions to Monroe were amply fulfilled. When Canning returned to London in September, he renewed his overtures. The United States, he told Rush, was now "confessedly" the leading power upon the American continent. "Had not a new epoch arrived in the relative position of the United States toward Europe? Were the great political and commercial interests which hung upon the destinies of the new continent, to be canvassed and adjusted . . . without some proper understanding between the United States and Great Britain, *as the two chief commercial and maritime states of both worlds?* He hoped not, he would wish to persuade himself not." He even went so far as to say that if he were invited to the new Congress, he would refuse to appear unless a similar invitation were sent to the United States. But he received the same answer: if he would guarantee an

---

[44] Rush to Canning, August 23, 1823; Canning to Rush, August 23, 1823; Rush to Canning, August 27, 1823; Rush to Adams, August 28, 1823; Canning to Rush, August 31, 1823; Rush to Adams, September 8, 1823. Monroe, *Writings,* VI, 366 ff.; Manning, *Diplomatic Correspondence,* III, 1483, 1485–1486.

[45] Rush to Monroe, September 15, 1823; Monroe, *Writings,* VI, 374–377.

immediate recognition, Rush would agree to a joint declaration. This remarkable interview took place on September 18.[46]

Eight days later, summoning Rush to his home at Gloucester Lodge, Canning made a final effort. Would "a promise by England of *future* acknowledgement" satisfy his scruples? To Rush this vagueness could only mean that the United States was to accept British leadership, not merely in Spanish America, but everywhere. His answer was the same as before. When they met again on October 8 and October 9, not a word could Canning be brought to say upon the subject of co-operation: he merely expressed a desire that all his communications on this subject, verbal or written, should be treated as entirely confidential. "That no act will result from them," Rush wrote to Adams, "is my present belief."[47]

An act did result from them, but one which neither Rush nor Canning could have predicted. Canning, of course, was in daily expectation of the fall of Cadiz—it fell on September 30, but the news did not reach London until October 10—and he had already begun a series of momentous conversations with the Prince de Polignac, the French Ambassador, which must be noticed in due course. In the meantime, Rush's two reports on Canning's August overtures had found their way to the City of Washington. Returning from Massachusetts on October 11, Mr. Adams was gravely presented with them by President Monroe, who then left for his farm in Virginia.[48]

One cannot examine the preliminary stages in the formulation of the Monroe Doctrine without remarking upon the curious role which was played there by time itself. When the reports reached Monroe and John Quincy Adams, they were reports upon an offer which had in fact already been withdrawn. While Canning labored to charm and possibly to entrap the American Minister in August and September, Washington was deserted. When it began to fill up again, and resume

---

[46] Rush to Adams, September 19, 1823; *ibid.*, VI, 377 ff. For an analysis of Canning's diplomacy at this anxious time as something more than "mere hazard and emotional reflex," see Kaufmann, *British Policy*, esp. Chaps. 6, 7, 8, although he does less than justice to the economic motive behind it. A Cabinet in those days gave a great deal of freedom to the Foreign Secretary, but Canning was not free from the surveillance of Liverpool or the thinking of Huskisson.

[47] Rush to Adams, October 2, October 10, 1823; Monroe, *Writings*, VI, 386–390.

[48] Bemis, *Adams and Foreign Policy*, p. 382.

its connection with the transatlantic world, Canning had turned else-where. Yet Monroe and Adams examined the two Rush reports, just as if calendars and distances had never interposed themselves between Washington and London. As far as they were concerned, and they had no choice, the conversations were still continuing, in some timeless August. Monroe therefore transmitted his copies of the reports to Jefferson, with a request that he should send them on to Madison; these two venerable and affectionate mentors were to advise him as to whether or not he should close with Canning's (now nonexistent) offer. "My own impression," he said, "is that we ought to meet the proposal of the British govt."[49]

Jefferson's nostalgic answer, uttered out of the twilight of the Virginia Dynasty, is full of interest: the year might almost be 1803, and the crisis centered around an alien New Orleans: "By acceding to her proposition, we detach her from the bands [of despotism], bring her mighty weight into the scale of free government, and emancipate a continent at one stroke, which might otherwise linger long in doubt and difficulty. Great Britain is the nation that can do us the most harm of any one, or all on earth; and with her on our side we need not fear the whole world."[50] Madison was more cautious and mis-trustful. He did not think that England had undergone, or could undergo, some miraculous conversion. None the less, she had offered co-operation at a "particularly fortunate" moment and "for an object the same as ours. With that co-operation we have nothing to fear from the rest of Europe. . . . There ought not, therefore, to be any backwardness, I think, in meeting her the way she has proposed."[51]

With these two letters in his pocket, Monroe returned to Washington on November 4. He was now prepared to go all the way with Great Britain.

When the Cabinet met on November 7, it was expected to pass upon the Canning overtures, together with a note which Adams had received on October 16 from the Baron de Tuyll, the Russian Minister.[52]

[49] Monroe to Jefferson, October 7, 1823; Monroe, *Writings*, VI, 324.

[50] Jefferson to Monroe, October 24, 1823; *Writings*, Ford (ed.), XII, 318–319.

[51] Madison to Monroe, October 30, 1823; Madison, *Works*, Cong. ed., III, 339.

[52] This Cabinet had undergone some changes. Crawford was very ill, having been mistreated for some disease—possibly erysipelas—with some nostrum—

This note declared that the Tsar would receive no agents from the South American states, and that he congratulated the United States upon their *neutral* attitude to South America.[53] With no further information to guide them, the Cabinet members had many reasons for anxiety and even dejection: for surely the overtures and the Russian note, in combination, could mean only one thing: Canning suspected that the Holy Allies were about to make some positive effort to restore his former colonies to Ferdinand VII.

We can now see how valuable the interposition of time and space may be to a diplomacy which is conducted by a strong and supremely courageous mind. Undisturbed by daily or hourly information, with no knowledge of what was actually taking place in Europe, Mr. Adams insisted, November 7, that the note from de Tuyll had presented the United States with a splendid opportunity, both to take a stand against the Holy Allies and also to decline the overtures of Great Britain. Would it not be more candid and dignified, he asked, to make an explicit declaration of American principles to France and Russia than "to come in as a cockboat in the wake of the British man-of-war?"[54] These words were the effect of long thought, and also the enunciation of settled policy.[55] To Adams, as a continentalist, no less than as a neomercantilist, the British Empire was the great rival. And so the first response of the Cabinet in November 1823—a response entirely dictated by Adams—was an unequivocal rejection of Canning's request: although Monroe occasionally wavered toward the British thereafter, it was also the final response.[56]

---

possibly calomel, or perhaps lobelia; he was bedridden, half-paralyzed, and nearly blind. Mrs. Harrison Smith, *The First Forty Years of Washington Society,* Gaillard Hunt, ed. (Washington, 1906), p. 162; J. E. D. Shipp, *Giant Days,* 174 n. Smith Thompson had resigned from the Navy Department and ascended to the Supreme Court; his place was taken by Samuel L. Southard of New Jersey, supposedly a Calhoun supporter, but actually given to following the lead of Adams, C. M. Wiltse, *Calhoun: Nationalist,* p. 278. Bemis, *Adams and Foreign Policy,* p. 385.

[53] W. C. Ford, "John Quincy Adams and the Monroe Doctrine," *American Historical Review,* VIII (1902), 32.

[54] *Memoirs,* VI, 177–179. Here Calhoun and Monroe are shown as willing to make a pledge, as part of the joint declaration, never to take Cuba or Texas.

[55] Adams to Rush, July 22, 1823; cited in Van Alstyne, *Rising American Empire,* p. 96.

[56] On November 13, the fall of Cadiz was known in Washington; for

On November 16, Rush's dispatch arrived, saying that Canning had apparently lost interest in a joint declaration; and while this eased the tension, it could not check the momentum which Canning's overtures had imparted to the policy of Adams.[57] On November 17, the kindly, bustling de Tuyll was unhappily obliged to read to Adams an extract from dispatches just received from Count Nesselrode. It was a panegyric upon the collapse of revolution in Europe, and it ended with the vainglorious remark that the Tsar wished "to guarantee the tranquillity of all the states of which the civilized world is composed."[58]

Did this mean that Alexander proposed to return Latin America, by force, to Ferdinand VII? This was the construction which Calhoun was tempted to put upon it. He was now quite confirmed, he said, in his views concerning the Holy Allies. "It quite confirms me in *mine*," retorted Adams, to whom Alexander's words were mere sound and fury. On November 19, Monroe was again wavering toward discretionary powers for Rush, and again Adams opposed him with all his strength.[59] When the Cabinet met on November 21 and the instructions for Rush were discussed, Monroe had been persuaded. No more was said about a joint declaration: it had become a dead issue. Nor was any voice raised against Adams' proposed reply to de Tuyll. He wished, he said, to assert in a moderate and conciliatory manner his government's dissent from the principles set forth in the second extract; to offer instead the principles upon which his government was founded; to disclaim any intention, either to propagate these principles by force or to interfere with the politics of Europe; and then to announce "our expectation that European powers will equally abstain

Monroe's and Calhoun's agitation, and Adams' firm response, see *Memoirs*, VI, 185–186. The Holy Alliance, said Adams, who had now been shown the Jefferson and Madison letters, and was quite unimpressed, "will no more restore Spanish dominion on the American continent than the Chimborazo will sink beneath the ocean."

[57] Two dispatches came from Rush on this day, (1) referring to Canning's offer of a recognition at "some future day," No. 334, of October 2; (2) No. 336 of October 10, saying that Canning "said nothing of Spanish affairs." No. 336 eased the tension, No. 334 supplied the momentum. In Monroe, *Writings*, VI, 386, 388, the date of arrival is given as November 19; in *Memoirs*, VI, 187, as November 16. If we accept Monroe's date, it would account for Calhoun's anxiety; but Adams is usually accurate.

[58] *Memoirs*, VI, 190; Ford, "John Quincy Adams," pp. 34 ff.

[59] *Memoirs*, VI, 190.

from any attempt to spread their principles in the American hemisphere or to subjugate by force any part of these continents to their will."[60]

Thus ended the first stage in these famous discussions, in which the Secretary of State, on the basis of a diplomatic experience which none of them could rival, imposed his own policy upon his discouraged colleagues.

At this point, one must return to London and recall what Canning had accomplished in his interviews with the Prince de Polignac. They began on October 3 and ended in the famous memorandum of October 9–12, 1823. In this memorandum, the British government was described as unwilling to interfere in any *practicable* negotiations between Spain and the colonies, but that "the junction of any Foreign Power in an enterprise of Spain against the Colonies, would be viewed by them as constituting an entirely new question, and one upon which they must take such decisions as the interests of Great Britain would require." To this very strong language there were appended certain trading conditions, themselves even stronger. (1) Ever since 1810 the trade with the Spanish colonies had been open to British subjects, and the ancient coasting laws of Spain were, "as regarded them at least, racially repealed." (2) Great Britain asked for no exclusive right to this trade, which was now free to all the world; but if her claim were disputed, she would immediately recognize the independence of the Spanish American states. In reply, Polignac disclaimed any intention, on France's part, to seize any portion of the Spanish possessions in America. All she asked was the right to trade in Spanish America upon the same terms as Great Britain; and, in any event, he declared, she *"abjured any . . . design of acting against the colonies by force of arms."*[61]

This was, no doubt, as much a trade agreement as a warning to the Holy Allies against aggressive action in Spanish America.[62] But

[60] *Ibid.,* VI, 194.

[61] Monroe, *Writings,* VI, 413–419; *British and Foreign State Papers,* XI, 49–53; Temperley, *Canning,* pp. 115–117; *Cambridge History of Foreign Policy,* II, 633–637.

[62] I.e., the influence of the Count de Villèle, who "favored strengthening the monarchy by stimulating the French economy," Hoffmann, p. 130, and who was eager to expand trade through access to South American markets, was

its language was decisive. With Great Britain and France opposed to forcible intervention, the Allies were helpless and the Alliance itself was virtually dissolved. This was a great personal triumph for Canning, whose language reflected it;[63] but, while the memorandum was known to the Allies by October 21, and was circulated to all European governments at the beginning of November, it was not verbally communicated to Rush until November 24, and not circulated to him until December 13. Was it possible that Canning's government still hoped, through its chargé d'affaires in Washington, to extract from Monroe and Adams the joint resolution which it had not obtained from Rush? If so, it was grossly deluded; for the answer it received was the Monroe Doctrine of December 2, and the Doctrine has become all the more resonant in history because it was written without any knowledge of the Polignac memorandum.

Nor should one forget how much of this special resonance was due to President Monroe. Adams had intended that his statement of foreign policy should be confined to diplomatic correspondence only: but Monroe thought otherwise, and he was a man who, once his mind was made up, was not easily deflected from his purpose. And so, on November 21, when the joint declaration was buried once and for all, the President produced a sheaf of papers containing (he said) a statement of American policy which he proposed to incorporate in his Annual Message on the State of the Union. In a tone of "deep solemnity and high alarm" he began to read. At first, his draft was little more than repetition of a sketch of foreign affairs which Adams had presented the week before; but the Secretary of State, listening with some complacency, was suddenly shocked to hear the President departing from his text—lecturing the French on their invasion of Spain—excoriating the principles upon which it had been founded—calling for an acknowledgment of the independence of revolutionary

---

now coming out of eclipse; and that of d'Artois and the ultraroyalists was declining.

[63] Canning now compared—at Plymouth, October 28—the quiescence of Great Britain to the sleep of a battleship: "one of those stupendous masses, now reposing on their shadows in perfect stillness—how soon, upon any call of patriotism, or of necessity, it would assume the likeness of an animated thing, instinct with life, etc., etc." Temperley, *Canning*, p. 119. Perkins, *Monroe Doctrine*, pp. 68–69.

Greece—demanding from Congress an appropriation sufficient to send a Minister there.[64]

Of the two men, Adams was the more visionary; but he was, as it were, at this time a practical visionary. He earnestly besought the President not to take so strong a line; not to issue a call to arms for the sake of the Spanish Constitutionalists, whom the British had abandoned, and the revolutionary Greeks, whom the Tsar had taken up; not to create a diplomatic rupture with France, with Spain, and perhaps even with Russia. He failed to perceive, or at any rate to approve, the fact that Monroe's language was simply ethical: informed, that is to say, with the innocent spirit of Old Republicanism, which believed that America could convert the Old World, not with fleets and subsidies, but with the magic of words and the force of example. On the next day, alone with the President, Adams begged him "to make an American cause and adhere inflexibly to that." Two days later, Monroe showed him his revised paragraphs on Greece, Spain, and South America. They were, said the Secretary, now "quite unexceptionable," quite in keeping with the spirit of Monroe's whole administration, which would "hereafter, I believed, be looked back to as the golden age of this republic." It would now end with the Holy Allies the aggressors, and the administration in peace and amity with the whole world.[65]

Having thus extracted from the President's proposed message all that was typically Virginian, Adams proceeded to inject into it some of the harshness of New England, and to give Monroe and the Cabinet an example of the language of "peace and amity." On November 25, he submitted his proposed draft upon "the Communications recently received from the Minister to Russia." But the Cabinet would have none of it. Its language (said Calhoun) was so aggressively and self-righteously hostile as to offend not only the Emperor of Russia but

---

[64] Bemis, *Adams and Foreign Policy*, p. 388.

[65] *Memoirs*, VI, 197, 199. For the innocence of Old Republicanism see, for example, Jefferson to John Dickinson, March 6, 1801, where the restoration of Republican government will be (he hopes) "a standing monument and example for the aim and invitation of the people of other countries" so that "the inquiry which has been excited among the mass of mankind by our revolution and its consequences, will ameliorate the condition of man over a great portion of the globe." *Writings* (Ford, ed.), IX, 202.

Great Britain as well. Would the country support its government (said Wirt) in a war for South America; and, in any case, should one use warlike language when the choice of peace or war rested with Congress?[66]

To these constitutional scruples Adams reluctantly yielded; he permitted "the cream of my paper" to be skimmed from it: but it took several remonstrances from Monroe before this was done. In its final shape, as read to de Tuyll on November 27, his note declared that the United States would remain neutral between Spain and her colonies so long as Europe took the same position; and it went on to say that the Tsar's remarks about restoring tranquillity were, in the opinion of the President, "not intended to embrace the United States of America, nor any portion of the American Hemisphere." It ended with a grand reiteration of the No-Transfer principle.[67]

This note, together with the instructions to Rush regarding Canning's overtures and the relevant passages in the President's forthcoming message were (Adams assumed) "the various parts of one system." The instructions, dated November 29, said that only if Great Britain acknowledged the independence of the Spanish American states would the United States move in concert with her.[68] By the time they reached Minister Rush he had, of course, received his copy of the Polignac memorandum, together with a note from Canning referring somewhat wistfully to his late overtures. When Rush duly communicated his instructions of November 29, Canning replied that late events had put an end to the state of things which had prompted him to make his first approaches.[69]

Had Canning missed an opportunity for some Anglo-American entente? To ask this question is to misunderstand the character of

[66] *Memoirs*, VI, 201, 203. One of the paragraphs, Wirt said, was "a hornet." It is a pity that it has not survived; one cannot sting posterity.

[67] Ford, "John Quincy Adams," pp. 39–40. As leading authorities have shown, the No-Transfer Principle, though not included in the President's message, was joined to the Monroe Doctrine by Hamilton Fish, Grant's Secretary of State. Bemis, *Adams and Foreign Policy*, p. 395, citing Dexter Perkins, *Monroe Doctrine, 1867–1907* (Baltimore, 1937) p. 25. John A. Logan, Jr., *No Transfer: An American Security Principle* (New Haven, 1961) p. 250. *Memoirs*, VI, 222.

[68] Adams to Rush, November 29, 1823; Manning, *Diplomatic Correspondence*, I, 210–212.

[69] Canning to Rush, December 13, 1823, Rush to Adams, February 9, 1824 (referring to an interview of February 2); Monroe, *Writings*, VI, 409, 426.

the Foreign Secretary, the nature and limitations of Liberal Toryism, and the intentions of Adams. Six days after the Monroe Doctrine had been given to Congress, Adams sent some supplementary instructions to Rush which hinted, in diplomatic language, that the British government should now revise its concept of maritime rights in accordance with the wishes and views of the United States.[70] But Canning was an imperialist, to whom such hints, from such a quarter, were impertinent and insulting. As for Liberal Toryism, it was an economic innovator, which strove to release the energies of British coal and iron without departing from its fundamental belief that society was a compact between the living and the dead. It endeavored, that is to say, to place certain Benthamite doctrines within the framework of the thinking of Burke. In such a predicament, it could make no more advances; and even had it wished to do so, the Monroe Doctrine would have discouraged them.

The Doctrine itself, as delivered on December 2, begins as follows:

At the proposal of the Russian Imperial Government, made through the Minister of the Emperor, residing here, a full power and instructions have been transmitted to the Minister of the United States at St. Petersburg, to arrange by amicable negotiation, the respective rights and interests of the two Nations on the North West Coast of this Continent. A similar proposal has been made by His Imperial Majesty, to the Government of Great Britain, which has likewise been acceded to. . . . The occasion has been judged proper, for asserting as a principle in which the rights and interests of the United States are involved, that the American Continents, by the free and independent condition which they have assumed and maintain, are henceforth not to be considered as subjects for future colonization by any European Power. . . . [71]

The wording of this paragraph and its doctrine of noncolonization were both the work of John Quincy Adams. The message now dealt at length with a number of domestic issues before returning to the subject of foreign affairs. It then proceeded as follows, and the language was Monroe's:

It was stated at the commencement of the last session, that a great effort was then making in Spain and Portugal, to improve the condition of the

[70] Adams to Rush, December 8, 1823; Bemis, *Adams and Foreign Policy,* App. 2, p. 578.
[71] Richardson, *Messages and Papers,* II, 209.

people of those countries; and that it appeared to be conducted with extraordinary moderation. It need scarcely be remarked, that the result has been, so far, very different from what was then anticipated. Of events in that quarter of the Globe, with which we have so much intercourse, and from which we derive our origin, we have always been anxious and interested spectators. The Citizens of the United States cherish sentiments the most friendly, in favor of the liberty and happiness of their fellowmen on that side of the Atlantic. In the wars of the European powers, in matters relating to themselves, we have never taken any part, nor does it comport with our policy, so to do. It is only when our rights are invaded, or seriously menaced, that we resent injuries, or make preparation for our defense. With the movements in this Hemisphere we are of necessity more immediately connected, and by causes which must be obvious to all enlightened and impartial observers. The political system of the allied powers, is essentially different in this respect from that of America. This difference proceeds from that, which exists in their respective Governments, and to the defence of our own, which has been achieved by the loss of so much blood and treasure, and matured by the wisdom of their most enlightened citizens, and under which we have enjoyed unexampled felicity, this whole nation is devoted. We owe it therefore to candor, and to the amicable relations existing between the United States and those powers, to declare that we should consider any attempt on their part to extend their system to any portions of this Hemisphere, as dangerous to our peace and safety. With the existing Colonies or dependencies of any European power, we have not interfered, and shall not interfere. But with the Governments who have declared their Independence, and maintained it, and whose Independence we have, on great consideration, and on just principles, acknowledged, we could not view any interposition for the purpose of oppressing them, or controuling in any other manner, their destiny, by any European power, in any other light, than as the manifestation of an unfriendly disposition towards the United States. In the war between these new governments and Spain, we declared our neutrality, at the time of their recognition, and to this we have adhered, and shall continue to adhere, provided no change shall occur, which in the judgment of the competent authorities of this Government, shall make a corresponding change, on the part of the United States, indispensable to their security.

The late events in Spain and Portugal, show that Europe is still unsettled. Of this important fact, no stronger proof can be adduced, than that the allied powers should have thought it proper, on any principle satisfactory to themselves, to have interposed by force, in the internal concerns of Spain. To what extent, such interposition may be carried, on the same principle, is a question, in which all Independent powers, whose Governments differ from theirs, are interested; even those most remote, and surely none more so than the United States. Our policy in regard to Europe, which was adopted at an early stage of the wars which have so long agitated that quarter of the Globe . . . [nevertheless] remains the same, which is, not to interfere in the internal concerns of any of its powers; to consider the Government *de facto;* as the legitimate for us; to cultivate friendly relations with it, and to preserve those relations by a frank, firm and manly policy, meeting in all instances, the just claims of every power; submitting to injuries from none. But, in regard to those continents, circumstances are eminently and conspicuously different. It is impossible that the allied powers, should extend their political systems, to any portion of either continent, without endangering our peace and happiness, nor can anyone believe, that our Southern Brethren, if left to themselves, would adopt it of their own accord. It is equally impossible, therefore, that we should behold such inter-position in any form with indifference. If we look to the comparative strength and resources of Spain and those new Governments, and their distance from each other, it must be obvious that she can never subdue them. It is still the true policy of the United States, to leave the parties to themselves, in the hope, that other powers will pursue the same course."[72]

Thus, the Monroe Doctrine, as it appeared in the message, was concerned with two principles:

(1) Noncolonization, which forbade any European power, in the future, to form new colonies in North or South America. (2) Nonintervention, which precluded the United States from taking part in the wars of European powers, since their political systems were distinct from those of the American hemisphere. Conversely, nonintervention regarded as "unfriendly" any attempt on the part of any European power to oppress or to control the destiny of the independent states of the New World. It can be seen that this principle in effect committed the United States to a leading role in world politics.

And to these must be added, from the note to de Tuyll, no-transfer, which forbade the transfer, by one European power to another, of any possession in the New World.

The word "forbade" had no great force behind it. If he had been supported (as he was not) by a resolution of Congress, Monroe could not have made good his language without the support of the British

---

[72] Richardson, *Messages and Papers,* II, 217–219. Bemis, *Latin American Policy,* pp. 63–64, quotes the original manuscript copy in the Senate Archives, and this version is followed here.

fleet. He himself believed that he was endeavoring to quiet an immediate crisis; and although his words encompassed the future, they did so rather in terms of hope than of certainty; they were virtuous but not inflexible. He would no doubt have been as surprised as gratified could he have known the part they would ultimately play in American foreign policy. But it was this very flexibility which gave the Doctrine its permanence: it could be used or neglected as circumstances allowed; and it was not, indeed, until Polk's first Annual Message of 1845 that it was called upon again, and then only as regards the North American continent.[73] None the less, merely considered as one of the American scriptures, as a glowing passage in the literature of self-determination and of republicanism, the message—even if it had never been permitted to become a doctrine—would command respect. And as an example of presidential leadership—for it must be recalled that Monroe had not yet heard of the Polignac memorandum—it was singularly direct and courageous.

This kind of courage made no impression upon the continental European powers. Their statesmen dismissed the message as "blustering," "monstrous," "arrogant," and so forth; and no formal protests were ever issued. "The document in question," de Tuyll was informed, "merits only the most profound contempt. His Majesty therefore invites you to preserve the passive attitude which you have deemed proper to adopt."[74] Since the great autocratic powers were now painfully digesting the Polignac memorandum, this dyspeptic language was only to be expected, nor was it altogether uncomplimentary, for they all assumed that the Doctrine would have some influence upon the progress of republicanism and the rise of popular governments.[75] Its reception in Latin America, among liberal thinkers, was at first cordiality itself.[76] A Virginian President might well have congratulated himself upon this verbal triumph.

It is only when we consider the reaction of Great Britain that another and more pointed story begins to reveal itself. At first, it seems, George Canning was much pleased. His overtures had supplied the original momentum, and Europe was according him a degree of in-

[73] Richardson, *Messages and Papers*, IV, 398.
[74] Perkins, *Monroe Doctrine*, p. 166.
[75] *Ibid.*, p. 168.
[76] *Ibid.*, p. 178.

fluence upon the United States which was no mean consolation for the actual fact that these overtures had been coldly turned down. "The Congress," he said, "was broken in all its limbs before, but the President's speech gives it the *coup de grâce*."[77]

None the less, on second thoughts and more careful reading, he became thoroughly disgusted with the noncolonization aspect of the Annual Message, and so did Mr. Huskisson. "The unoccupied parts of America," said the president of the Board of Trade, "are just as much open as heretofore to colonization by Great Britain as well as by other powers."[78] Canning found himself on a sudden quite unable to continue his plans for a joint representation with the United States at St. Petersburg against Russia's pretensions on the northwest coast.[79] "It is Mr. Monroe's declaration in his famous message," Christopher Hughes wrote three years later, "that it was time for the old world to be taught, that the new was no longer to be regarded as open to future colonization that sticks in their [the British] throats. I know, to use the words of a great British employee, 'there was not a man in the British councils whose blood did not tingle at his fingers' ends, on reading that proposition of President Monroe.' "[80]

Here, however, he did somewhat more than justice to Monroe. The noncolonization passage had been written originally by Adams and had been placed in the message in deference to his opinions. The nationalism of Monroe was more accommodating: it had permitted him, at first, to suggest that a joint declaration with England would be quite in order; and if his suggestion had been adopted, there would

[77] Stapleton, *Canning and His Times*, p. 395. Of course, what really delivered the *coup de grâce* was Canning's refusal on January 30, 1824, to send a British representative to attend it. *British and Foreign State Papers*, XI, 58–62. Chateaubriand said in January, 1824, that the Monroe Doctrine was made "in virtue of an understanding between the British and American Governments." Canning denied this, but most equivocally. Webster, *Great Britain and Independence*, II, 131–134.

[78] Anna Lane Lingelbach, "William Huskisson as President of the Board of Trade," *American Historical Review*, XLIII (1938), 769.

[79] Bemis, *Adams and Foreign Policy*, pp. 522, 524. In 1821 a Russian ukase, dated September 4/16, prohibited all foreign vessels from coming within 100 Italian miles of the northwest coast between the Bering Straits and 51° north, and granted whaling and fishing rights exclusively to Russian subjects. This question was easily settled by the Convention of April 5/17, 1824. *American State Papers, Foreign Relations*, IV, 861–864.

[80] Hughes to Gallatin, January 19, 1827; Gallatin Papers, NYHS.

have been no Monroe Doctrine at all. It will be recalled that Jefferson, a convinced agrarian, was much in favor of a joint declaration; that Madison, at best a moderate agrarian, was willing to go along with Great Britain, but was far more mistrustful of her motives; and that Calhoun, who was a South Carolina slaveholder but also, at the time, a nationalist, wavered between submission to Canning and a confused belligerence. From Adams' diary we know that Southard consistently supported him in his refusal to make a declaration with Canning, and Southard was eventually to become a pillar of the Whig party. As for Adams, whose Presidency was to be an honest if mistaken commitment to economic nationalism, he had from the beginning asked the President to "make an American cause and to adhere inflexibly to that."

Monroe, whose administration was marked by a gradual abandonment of agrarian principles, was easily persuaded to take this course; moreover, in the domestic portion of his famous message, he himself issued a plea for further protective tariffs. Thus the Liverpool government was answered on two fronts; for if Mr. Canning was warned in effect to keep away from the Columbia River and its basin, Lord Liverpool and Mr. Huskisson were told that they must not look for open markets in the United States. It remained only for Richard Rush, when he began negotiations in 1824, to insist that the word "elsewhere" meant equal trading rights with Great Britain in every part of the British Empire: he had also been instructed to lay a claim to the Oregon country at least as high as 51°.[81] From all these points of view it might be said that the Monroe Doctrine, with its surrounding claims and negotiations, was more of a challenge to the industrial British, whose fleet sustained it, than it was to the Holy Allies or the legitimist French, against whom it was ostensibly directed.

Canning perceived, however, that its immediate effect was in his

---

[81] Van Alstyne, *Rising American Empire*, p. 97. Rush submitted this proposition first in December, 1823. Adams to Rush, July 22, 1823, *ASPFR*, V, 447–448. Adams permitted him as a last resort to fall back to 49° N. L. The reader is referred to Chapter XXV, "The Oregon Question," in Bemis, *Adams and Foreign Policy*, 510 ff., where these problems are discussed in a lucid, thorough and masterful fashion. In 1824, the House of Representatives brought in a bill, and passed it 113–57, calling for a military post at the north of the Columbia and (as originally worded by Representative Floyd of Virginia) for the creating of a territorial government, with no restriction of northern boundary. The bill was killed in the Senate on March 1, 1825: *Register of Debates*, 18 Cong., 2 sess., I, 712.

favor; that it had added some force to the Polignac memorandum; that a Congress on Spanish America was now impossible; and that the neo-Holy Allies had been reduced to impotence. It was now time for him to counteract, in some more public fashion, whatever influence the Doctrine might still exercise upon the Spanish American states. In this he was much assisted by a memorial from Sir James Mackintosh, in favor of recognizing their independence: it was presented on June 15, 1824, and bore some of the great City names—Montefiore, Baring, Ricardo, Benjamin Shaw.[82] There followed a report from his commissioner to Buenos Aires, Woodbine Parish, which showed that the thirty-nine British commercial houses already there controlled almost all the export and import trade, and that half the public debt was in British hands.[83] This was quite enough for Lord Liverpool, already a sick man, but still wielding his customary quiet power. Lords Westmorland, Bathurst, and Eldon protested against a recognition; the Duke of Wellington would not speak to Liverpool except in Cabinet, and threatened to resign; and George IV remarked that his Foreign Secretary was a scoundrel.[84] Once more the hopes of Madame de Lieven and Metternich were revived. But it was all useless; Lord Liverpool was immovable; and Colombia, Mexico, and the United Provinces (Buenos Aires) were recognized by Great Britain on December 31, 1824. In return she asked (and needed) no more than equal opportunity.[85]

This was made known to Parliament in the King's speech on February 7, 1825. Lord Eldon was obliged to read it, which he did with a very ill grace; for George IV declined to be present on so detestable an occasion. (He had a bad attack of gout, he explained, and he had also, unaccountably, mislaid his false teeth.)[86] More than a year and a half later, George Canning came down to the House of Commons to defend his toleration of a continued French occupation of Spain. He

[82] Kaufmann, *British Policy,* p. 176 n., points out that Canning professed not to be too impressed by the efforts of British merchants to guide his foreign policy.

[83] *Idem,* where this report is called decisive as to Lord Liverpool. See also E. J. Pratt, "Anglo-American Commercial and Political Rivalry on the Plata, 1820–1830," *Hispanic American Historical Review,* XI (1931), 305.

[84] *Letters of Princess de Lieven,* p. 339.

[85] Kaufmann, *British Policy,* p. 202, for specific instances of Canning's unwillingness to accept special favors in Latin America.

[86] Temperley, *Canning,* p. 152.

based his explanation upon a new and somewhat anarchical concept of the balance of power, and concluded it with two sentences which seemed to abolish history . . . the heroism of Bolívar, San Martín, Sucre, and their armies, the recognition of Spanish America by the United States, the President's message. "Contemplating Spain," he said, "such as our ancestors had known her, I resolved that if France had Spain, it should not be Spain 'with the Indies.' I called the New World into existence to redress the balance of the Old." Having uttered these vainglorious words, he sank back exhausted. We are told that there was a silence, then a single mocking laugh, and then a great cheer.[87]

For the time being, no doubt, Canning was right. The Polignac memorandum, sedulously circularized throughout Latin America, and backed by British manufactures and loans and men-of-war, was of far more consequence to the former Spanish colonists than the Monroe Doctrine, which had little as yet to offer but promises growing yearly more lukewarm. It is not, indeed, through such comparisons as these that the Doctrine should be examined. Nor yet (except for the immediate history of these times) should one comment upon its vein of economic nationalism, nor even upon its expressed aversion to European politics. Its enduring claim to attention and veneration lies in its valiant committal of the United States to a leading position in *world* politics. For if the committal was decidedly premature, in 1823, surely the valor was not.

[87] Woodward, *Age of Reform,* p. 201; Temperley, *Canning,* pp. 380–381. His concept of the balance of power rarely went beyond his famous statement to the British Ambassador in St. Petersburg, which is a somewhat crude but vigorous prevision of laissez faire. ". . . things are getting back to a wholesome state again. Every nation for itself and God for us all." Canning to Bagot, January 3, 1823; Stapleton, *Official Correspondence,* p. 389.

CHAPTER 7

Mobility and Consolidation

THE President's message was received very cordially in the United States, but without any great enthusiasm: the press as a whole—the few exceptions were of Federalist and New England origin—took the President's words at their face value and rather offhandedly assumed that the United States could resist the Holy Alliance on its own. In Congress a resolution committing the United States explicitly to nonintervention was never brought to a vote, and a request for further information on Latin American affairs was quietly dropped when Monroe let it be known that such information would not be to the public good. There was a debate upon the building of further sloops of war, in which no mention was made of the Spanish-American struggle, nor (which is even more significant) were any additional sloops of war voted.[1] As a nationalist manifesto the Monroe Doctrine remained for the time being an expression of individual statesmanship, not of collective feeling. Still less was it a summons to collective action.

Indeed the nationalism of the 1820's—in so far as one may refer to it at all—was becoming obscurely introspective and egalitarian. The eyes of the nation were turning westward—that is to say, toward the problems and challenges of internal development; these inevitably touched upon the problem of inner satisfaction, of democratic initia-

---

[1] Perkins, *Monroe Doctrine,* pp. 145, 147; Adams, *Memoirs,* VI, 224. *Annals of Congress,* 18 Cong., 1 sess., I, 2204; *Register of Debates,* 19 Cong., 1 sess., II, 2446.

tive, of the curbing of privilege and the conquest of elites. One has merely to look at some picture of the more remote past, for example, at Colles' road *Survey* of 1789, to see that the barbaric network of communications, which Colles so carefully charts, would more naturally foster a republican than a democratic way of life.[2] How difficult it must have been in those days, when the world moved so slowly and so painfully, even to crawl to the polls in bad weather or poor health; how difficult to learn, by physical contact, what lay beyond one's own neighborhood! And the early movement of internal trade, counterclockwise, down the Ohio and the Mississippi, up the coast, across the Alleghenies, was infinitely slow and cumbersome. By the War of 1812, there had been improvements, especially in turnpikes in the East, but the War of 1812 was a fruitful, not to say a frightful, lesson in poor communications. America, as it moved on into the postwar years, while full of pioneering vigor, was still parochial. It could lie at the mercy of governmental cliques at any level, and its social mobility, though very marked, was certainly checked by the physical problems involved in moving at all. De Tocqueville's fear of the tyranny of majority opinion (his suspicion, that is, of a growing American *sameness*), uttered in the 1830's, would have been very exaggerated if it had been set forth in the 1820's.

In the 1820's, however, the impulse toward internal improvements became very marked, and it was accompanied by a strange political restlessness, an obscure dissatisfaction. It would be too much to say that an improvement in communications—roads, canals, rivers, steamboats—was the visible cause of a more egalitarian or more assertive democracy. But the two seem to run parallel, with the promise inherent in all parallels—that they would meet somewhere in the future. One of the indications of this, ironically enough, was Marshall's decision in *Gibbons* v. *Ogden*, which, written by a judge to whom political restlessness was anathema, was the very herald of political restlessness. Until this decision was rendered in 1824, the Livingston-Fulton steamboat monopoly, in spite of the most ingenious efforts to circumvent it, ruled over all the waters of New York State.[3] The founders of this

[2] Christopher Colles, *A Survey of the Roads of the United States of America: 1789*, Walter W. Ristow, ed. (Cambridge, 1961). This traces the major roads from Albany, New York, south to Yorktown, Virginia.

[3] 9 Wheaton, 1. For the preliminaries, which are extremely interesting and not

monopoly, before their deaths, had apparently got the Mississippi itself in their grip; but here the American spirit was too much for them and their heirs, and the unlicensed steamboat was moving with some freedom upon the western waters long before Marshall decreed that it might go where it pleased in New York, upon interstate occasions, and with no more than a federal coasting license.[4] None the less, *Gibbons* v. *Ogden* was as creative in the West as in the East. The counterclockwise movement in internal trade was gradually reversed, and the effect upon interior prices in the West became very noticeable.[5] It is, however, as a democratic engine, as a purveyor of social as well as economic mobility, that the steamboat won its place as the greatest and most-loved adventure in American history. From the first it was an eccentric symbol of the new democracy; it moved against the current, it was always in danger from its own mechanism, it was a prey to snags and sawyers and uncharted shiftings in the river bed; but it was singularly independent. Although Congress began to make regular appropriations for the removal of snags and the improvement of river beds, the steamboat asked no more help than that.[6] Having triumphed over monopoly, in 1824, with the aid of the Supreme Court, it proceeded on its own unsubsidized momentum to triumph over space and loneliness.

The proponents of internal improvements at the federal expense turned a blank gaze upon the steamboat, as well they might; and they did not exactly welcome another spectacular event which, in 1824,

---

without comedy, see Livingston *v.* Ogden and Gibbons (1819), 4 Johnson, Ch. 48; *In re Vanderbilt* (1819), 4 Johnson, Ch. 57; Ogden *v.* Gibbons (1819), 4 Johnson, Ch. 176; Livington *v.* Tompkins (1820), 4 Johnson, Ch. 570; Livingston *v.* Gibbons (1820), 4 Johnson, Ch. 570; Livingston *v.* Gibbons (1821), 5 Johnson, Ch. 250; North River Steamboat *v.* Hoffman (1821), 5 Johnson, Ch. 300; Gibbons *v.* Ogden (1820), 7 Johnson, Ch. 488; Gibbons *v.* Livingston (1822), 6 N.J. Law, 236; Gibbons *v.* Ogden (1822), 6 N.J. Law 285; Gibbons *v.* Ogden (1822), 6 N.J. Law 582.

[4] *Acts of Territory of Orleans, 1811* (Act of April 19, 1811), pp. 112–118, bestowed on the Livingston-Fulton monopoly the same exclusive privilege conferred by the New York statute. In 1817 the heirs sought to enforce their rights in the U.S. District Court for the Territory of New Orleans, losing their case finally in 1825. Charles Warren, *The Supreme Court in U.S. History,* I, 598 n. In February, 1825, North River Steamboat *v.* Livingston, 3 Cowen 713 ff., the N.Y. Supreme Court declared the *intrastate* monopoly to be unconstitutional. See esp. Savage, C. J., pp. 739–756.

[5] Taylor, *Transportation Revolution,* p. 160.

[6] *Ibid.,* p. 68; Dangerfield, *Era of Good Feelings,* p. 324.

when *Gibbons* v. *Ogden* was settled, was very close to fulfillment. The Erie Canal owed much to the promotional genius of De Witt Clinton and nothing at all to the federal government. It was, to be sure, singularly blessed by geography: there was a most fortunate propinquity between the upper reaches of the Hudson and the one real break in the Appalachian system, since the Mohawk Valley led by imperceptible gradations to the Finger Lakes district, whence the Oswego and the Genesee flowed northward into Lake Ontario. As soon as the necessary legislation was passed in 1816 and 1817 the Canal, with the additional Lake Champlain canal, became the child of good fortune. The necessary $8 million were raised from land sales, taxes on salt and auctions, lotteries, appropriations, and tolls; no fraud or privilege marred this complicated bookkeeping. The engineers learned as they went and invented as they went; machines were devised for pulling up trees, and a new kind of plow was contrived for cutting their matted roots. At no point along the 363 miles was the canal more than six hundred feet above sea level, and in one famous stretch of sixty-nine and a half miles east of Syracuse there was not a single lock. The very stone that was dug up could be used for construction. Only the human beings who labored in the virgin forest and among the foul swamps were punished by violated nature with fevers and agues and typhus, and with diabolical pestilences that never found a name. But human labor was, alas, cheap; there was never a lack of victims; and by 1823 the eastern section, from Rome to the Hudson, was complete, and the two other sections, from Rome to the Seneca River, and from the Seneca River to Lake Erie, were demonstrably beyond the chance of failure. By 1824 it was becoming clear enough that the trans-Allegheny route was to be shifted away from the Potomac and the slaveholding South; the portentous future of New York City was already inscribed upon the great stone aqueducts and the memorable fills. How natural for the citizens of Ohio to dream of canals connecting Cincinnati with the Maumee, Portsmouth with Cleveland, and all with the system created by New York! How natural, too, for Indiana to contemplate a new highway connecting the headwaters of the Maumee with those of the Wabash! In this way, too, with the steamboat forging up river, the great movement of internal trade could be clockwise as well as counterclockwise; and the productive energies of the nation were such that, even when the railroad became a competitor, the downriver traffic of the Mississippi would hardly suffer, since there was room for all.[7]

Other states, with less feasible schemes, were anxious to follow the example of New York. But geography and poverty were both against them, and federal aid presented itself as the best answer to their need. The growing urgency of this need, or demand, or dream, could be charted federally: from Madison's veto in 1817, which was accepted with equanimity; to the House's decision in 1818 that Congress had an appropriating but not a jurisdictional power; to Calhoun's report in 1819, which shelved the constitutional question but praised the defensive value of a judicious national system of roads and canals; to the Cumberland Road bill of 1822, which Monroe returned unsigned.[8] The Cumberland Road bill specifically stated that Congress had a right to establish turnpikes on the Road, with gates and tolls, and to enforce the collection of tolls by penalties for evasion: in other words, that it had a jurisdictional right after all. No one doubted the importance of the Cumberland Road, although many wondered how Congress had come to build it in the first place; but the bill of 1822 opened, to thoughtful minds, alarming vistas of future federal invasions of the states, invasions armed with contracts and subsidies and penalties and all the panoply of consolidation. A year later, Monroe formulated his Doctrine without too much misgiving, because foreign affairs were constitutionally delegated to Executive leadership; his domestic nationalism was altogether more cautious. When he returned the bill, on May 4, he accompanied his message with an immense paper called "Views of the President of the United States on the Subject of Internal Improvements." He now admitted that "Congress have an unlimited power to raise money, and that in its appropriation they have a discretionary power, restricted only by the duty to appropriate it to the purposes of common defense and of general, not local, national, not State, benefit." The paper was solemn, dry, and

[7] Taylor, *Transportation Revolution*, p. 34; Edward C. Kirkland, *A History of American Economic Life* (New York, 1932), pp. 272–278; Ellen C. Semple, *American History and its Geographic Conditions* (Baltimore, 1903), pp. 267–271; F. A. Shannon, *Economic History of the People of the United States* (New York, 1934), p. 178; John A. Krout, "New York: Early Engineers," *New York State Historical Society Quarterly*, XXVI (1945), 269 ff.

[8] Turner, *Rise of the New West*, pp. 228–231; *Annals of Congress*, 15 Cong., 1 sess., I, 1249 ff.; *American State Papers, Miscellaneous*, p. 534; Babcock, *American Nationality*, Chap. XV; Richardson, *Messages and Papers*, II, 142–143.

extremely able. No one could have read it then, or can read it now, without perceiving the legal and constitutional jungle into which a government of the 1820's might have floundered unless it had been guided by Monroe's restrictions. And yet the restrictions themselves were far from clear, for who could really tell the difference, even then, between general and local, national and state benefit?[9]

As a last and final argument, Monroe resorted to the Old Republican solution of a constitutional amendment. This had two advantages. On the one hand, if the voting in the House was any criterion, the amendment would be long delayed; on the other, if it should be passed, it could be so written as to delimit, once and for all, the jurisdictional powers of Congress. In 1824, in the meantime, Congress passed a General Survey Bill, the evident purpose of which was to prepare the way for a program of appropriations for internal improvements on a national scale, and of subscriptions to the stock of companies engaged in these enterprises.[10] Monroe experienced no qualms about signing this bill; it was a logical extension of his own views; it was all promise and no performance. But there is much danger in such actions; and the student of these years will notice, without too much surprise, that Monroe's last deed as President was to sign a bill authorizing Congress to subscribe $300,000 to the Chesapeake and Delaware Canal Company.[11]

In this way, he moved into ground which was subsequently occupied by Andrew Jackson. Jackson's Maysville veto was based partly on the fact that the Maysville Road lay within a single state, and partly (no doubt) upon his suspicion of federal grants to private corporations. His attitude toward internal improvements, however, was rather expedient than constitutional; he conceived that serious abuses might arise if the government entangled itself in local schemes; and a national plan, to his way of thinking, could be considered only when the national debt had been extinguished. None the less, like Monroe, he is known to have approved the appropriation of federal funds for the

[9] The "Views" are in Richardson, *Messages and Papers,* II, 144–183.

[10] Turner, *Rise of the New West,* pp. 232–233; 4 U.S. Statutes at Large, 629. (The bill called for surveys of such roads and canals as Monroe considered of importance for commercial, military, or postal purposes.) He had already signed a bill (the first of such) for the improvement of harbors. 3 U.S. Statutes at Large, 780, March 3, 1823.

[11] 4 U.S. Statutes at Large, 124.

building of roads and canals; and thus, while employing the language of strict construction, he managed in practice to swallow his own words.[12]

In 1824, of course, the "Transportation Revolution" was just beginning to revolve; but one need only study the House voting to see how much reason there was for federal caution. The vote of the western states, with the exception of two members from Tennessee, was in favor of the Cumberland Road bill of 1822; so too were the districts along the line of the Potomac and the Ohio, or tributary to the road in Pennsylvania and western Virginia. Pittsburgh, fearful that her trade would be diverted to Baltimore, the lands along the Susquehanna, which on the contrary looked to Baltimore, and the greater part of New York, opposed the bill.[13] When the General Survey bill was passed in 1824, the situation was less confused but still far from clear: New England was divided against it by 26 to 12; the Middle States were in favor by 37 to 26, with New York opposed by 7 to 24; while western Virginia, western North Carolina, and a considerable fragment of South Carolina and Georgia voted for it. Thus the entire west, including the southwest, together with Pennsylvania and the Potomac Valley, acted as a unit in favor of internal improvements; but a formidable opposition was already emerging in New England, New York, and the Old South.[14]

When the General Survey bill was debated, the leadership of the internal improvements bloc in the House was naturally committed to Henry Clay, who had just returned to Congress and had been triumphantly elected Speaker. With all his skill and all his vigor, Clay condemned the Virginia Dynasty for its vetoes of 1817 and 1822. "A new world has come into being since the Constitution was adopted," he said. "Are the narrow, limited necessities of the old thirteen states, of indeed, parts only of the old thirteen states, as they existed at the formation of the present Constitution forever to remain the rule of interpretations?"[15] To the modern reader, such words are more harsh than excessive. The history of the 1820's, however examined—in terms of population increase, economic diversification, industrial enterprise,

---

[12] Taylor, *Transportation Revolution*, p. 20; Glyndon G. Van Deusen, *The Jacksonian Era* (New York, 1959), p. 52.

[13] Turner, *Rise of the New West*, p. 231.

[14] *Ibid.*, p. 235.

[15] *Annals of Congress*, 18 Cong., 1 sess., I, 1315.

agricultural surpluses, the north-south direction of the great rivers—
echoes and re-echoes with the call for better communications between
east and west, and with the need for economic mobility come the obvious political and cultural pressures—enlargement of suffrage, better
education, the right of the individual to move with the times.

In the General Survey debates Clay's vision, for the last time, encompassed the whole West and brought it into focus. The House vote
on the General Survey bill was recorded on February 10, 1824, and
immediately a new debate began on a new and more ambitious tariff
bill. The issue was comparatively simple: should the nation content
itself with the prevailing and comparatively free exchange of raw
materials for foreign manufactures, or should it attempt to relieve
distress in the agricultural and industrial areas by creating a home
market based on protection? The western farmer was not unwilling to
accept the home-market argument at this time: when voiced outside
of Congress, by Hezekiah Niles, for example, in his respected and
popular *Weekly Register,* it had all the fascination of irrelevance and
abstraction. Niles was in the happy position of being able to invent
his own statistics, of being able to prove, for example, that the annual
export of animal and vegetable food in 1823 amounted to $9,622,300,
whereas the 500,000 persons "employed in or fed by the products of
manufactures" consumed animal or vegetable foods of domestic
origin to the amount of $13,700,000. "So we see," argued Niles, "by
the force of plain practical arithmetic, that the support of the 500,000
manufacturers of whom Mr. Floyd speaks so indifferently consumes
about one half more than the whole exports of the products of 15
states, and more than seven-eighths of all the exports raised by the
free agriculturalists of the United States."[16] This plain practical arithmetic ignored certain facts, such as that the planting states produced
the great export surpluses, that the volume of the export trade at the
time was far larger than that of the internal trade, and that the 500,-
000 "manufacturers" were not confined to a factory system but were
largely engaged in household manufactures and subsisted themselves
to a considerable extent upon produce of their own raising.[17]

Indeed, the industries of the United States in 1824, whether "in-

[16] *Niles' Register,* XXVI, 65–66.
[17] Taylor, *Transportation Revolution,* p. 173, gives a comparison of the
volumes of internal and of foreign trade in the 1820's.

fants" or not, were still in that condition where protection was as likely to stifle their initiative as hasten the day when they would actually be able to provide a home market. The iron industry suffered chiefly from poor communications: the supplies of bituminous coal could not be moved, except at ruinous expense, to the regions where the industry was located. But there were other and less sensible reasons for its inertia.[18] The woolen industry was still sunk deep in the household manufacturing stage; it was unfamiliar with the new machinery; its methods were out of date. It suffered terribly in the lean years of 1819–21. Yet by 1824 the survivors, who did not receive much protection, were so situated that four years later they did not need the protection they then received.[19] The textile industry was already in a healthy condition in 1824. Lowell started production in 1822; Nashua was founded in 1823; Waltham was flourishing. The Providence-Pawtucket region had learned how to use the tremendous water power of the Fall River, and its factories were creeping up the Blackstone into Massachusetts, or along the Pawtucket toward Connecticut. Outside New England and the Hudson, Mohawk, and Delaware valleys, progress was slow; but within this region the industry had moved out of the household manufacturing stage because hand spinning wheels could not make good cotton warp.[20] It is true that the deluge of British goods in 1816 and the panic and depression of 1819–21 had threatened American industry with ruin, and that the whole period up to 1830 was a difficult one. This might excuse and perhaps justify a call for protective tariffs. Yet it is extremely difficult today to show that protective tariffs, throughout the ante-bellum period, ever did anything for the industries they were supposed to protect.[21] It would be more plausible to argue that time, technology,

---

[18] As, for example, blacksmiths and farmers still preferred charcoal iron. Puddling was not introduced generally until 1830–40; the use of anthracite coal for blast furnaces was unknown until 1836. Stanwood, *American Tariff Controversies,* I, 172–173; Taussig, *Tariff History,* pp. 55 ff.; Chester W. Wright, *Economic History of the United States* (New York, 1941), pp. 391 ff.; Kirkland, *American Economic Life,* pp. 319–321.

[19] *American State Papers, Finance,* V, 792–832.

[20] Kirkland, *American Economic Life,* pp. 332–334; Shannon, *Economic History,* p. 252; Wright, *Economic History,* p. 388; Caroline F. Ware, *The Early New England Cotton Manufacture* (Boston, 1931), pp. 60–63, 64, 67, 70, 78.

[21] Taylor, *Transportation Revolution,* p. 366, ably summarizes the arguments

and the competitive and inventive urge were all that was really needed. Or one could say, with some justice, that as in England, so in America, an Industrial Revolution would have first to be founded upon good communications between the raw materials and the factories that used them. In this sense, the call for internal improvements represented a healthy expansionist instinct, and the demand for protective tariffs a desire to centralize too swiftly and thus to compound for greed and mediocrity.

As the House set about its task of building a new tariff wall in 1824 there was, as usual, some doubt as to the materials of which it was to be composed, and no certainty that, once built, it would stand up at all. The home-market argument and the infant-industry argument did not always agree. The wool growers, for example, demanded a high duty on imported wool, whereas the woolen manufacturers contended that nothing more was necessary than a high duty on imported woolens. The ironmasters protested that they could not survive without a swinging tariff on Scottish pig iron, though Scottish pig iron was held to be uniquely adapted to the manufacture of the small castings used in machinery. Even free-traders made exceptions in their own cases—as the whale fishery of Massachusetts, which asked for a high duty on tallow in order to protect whale oil from candles, and the sugar growers of Louisiana, who would put up with nothing less than an ad valorem duty of 62.07 per cent on foreign sugars.[22]

The wings of the protectionist army in Congress were very strong in 1824, but it so happened that the center was very weak. Massachusetts was beginning to divert her capital from shipping and commerce to industry; but the financiers, merchants, and shipowners of Boston were not yet ready to abjure the old faith. They said that the proposed duties on iron, hemp, and flax would embarrass the shipbuilders, and that the duty on molasses would play havoc with New England's rum

---

in this respect. He suggests, citing Wolfgang F. Stolper and Paul A. Samuelson, "Protection and Real Wages," *Review of Economic Statistics,* IX (1941), 58–73, that protection may have "helped somewhat" toward raising real wages; otherwise he accepts the view of Guy Stevens Callender, *Selections from the Economic History of the United States, 1765–1860* (Boston, 1909), p. 488, that "no important industries can be said to have been created or prevented from growth by that legislation." The present writer does not dismiss the possibility of a stultifying effect.

[22] *Niles' Register,* XXVI, 29 ff.; *Annals of Congress,* 18 Cong., 1 sess., II, 1751 ff., 1859; Gray, *History of Agriculture,* II, 746.

industry and its basic exchange of fish, provisions, and lumber for the molasses of the West Indies.[23] Daniel Webster was, then and thereafter, the most trustworthy barometer for the climate of opinion in State Street; and on April 1 and 2, he made what has been called, with some truth, the finest free-trade speech ever made in the eighteenth or any other Congress.[24] A year later the great firm of W. & S. Lawrence of Boston turned from importing to domestic manufactures and carried State Street with it. In 1828, standing up in the Senate, Webster took back every word that he had uttered in the House in 1824.

On the protectionist side, however, there was a weakness less obvious than the abstention of Massachusetts, and that was the inability of the protectionists to realize that South Carolina, the intellectual leader of the cotton kingdom, was still in two minds about the constitutional right to levy duties for protection. Later in the year, when her legislature met, South Carolina made this abundantly clear; for her Senate then declared that tariffs for protection were unconstitutional and inoperative, and her House retorted that state legislatures had no right to question the acts of the federal government.[25] If they had been more alert, the protectionists might have observed and exploited this division in the 1824 debates; for Representative James Hamilton argued that neither the power to lay and collect imposts nor the power to regulate commerce gave Congress any right to protect domestic manufactures, whereas one of his colleagues, George McDuffie, was forced to confine himself to the statement that protective tariffs had an unjust and unhealthy effect upon the exchange of domestic cotton for foreign manufactures. McDuffie had once written a pamphlet called "A Defence of a Liberal Construction of the Powers of Congress," and he was fresh from lecturing the House upon the theme that the Constitutional Convention "did not regard the State governments . . . as in any respect more worthy of confidence than the General Government." McDuffie was a nationalist, and his great mentor, John Caldwell Calhoun, was still wavering between protection and free trade. In December, 1825, the South Carolina House of Representatives

---

[23] *Report of the Committee of Merchants and Manufacturers on the Proposed Tariff, January 1824* (Boston, 1824).

[24] *Annals of Congress,* 18 Cong., 1 sess., II, 2026–2082.

[25] Ames, *State Documents,* IV, 6.

changed its mind and officially condemned the protective tariff, with the same compulsive effect upon Mr. Calhoun that the conversion of W. & S. Lawrence had had upon Mr. Webster—the same as to compulsion, though not direction. In 1826, Calhoun became a free trader.[26]

Under these circumstances, the debate of 1824 was little more than a confused sea of doctrines and interests, and Speaker Clay, scouring those waters like a dove of peace, was hard put to it to find a patch of dry land. He had already done his best in creating a Committee on Manufactures, with a fanatical protectionist as its chairman, and he had seen to it that the Committee on Agriculture was not unfriendly to protection.[27] On the floor he did as well as, indeed, much better than might have been expected even from an acknowledged master: his speech of March 31 stands out from the bulk of his printed oratory because it is still readable, and has survived the loss of his ephemeral magic—the strange posturings and glidings, the punctuating pinches of snuff, the pointed finger, the unforgettable smile, and all the music of that wonderful voice. His peroration might dismay the economist, but it is extraordinarily moving. "I appeal to the South," he cried, "to the high-minded, generous and patriotic South—with which I have so often co-operated, in attempting to sustain the honor and to vindicate the rights of our country. . . . Of what does it complain? A possible temporary enhancement in the objects of consumption. Of what do we complain? A total incapacity, produced by the foreign policy, to purchase, at any price, necessary foreign objects of consumption. In such an alternative, inconvenient only to it, ruinous to us, can we expect too much from southern magnanimity?"[28]

Southern magnanimity, alas, retorted with a dry analysis of the

[26] *Annals of Congress,* 18 Cong., 1 sess., I, 1372; Ames, *State Documents,* IV, 4; *Niles' Register,* XXIX, 293.

[27] The tariff was to some extent the child of persistent and successful lobbying. "There has been more outdoor than indoor legislation with regard to the bill," said James Hamilton of South Carolina. "All sorts of pilgrims have travelled to the room of the Committee on Manufactures." Stanwood, *American Tariff Controversies,* I, 237. That the Commitee on Agriculture was also not deaf to the prayers of these devout men may be seen in *Annals of Congress,* 18 Cong., 1 sess., II, 1857–1859, where its report is a faithful résumé of the home-market argument.

[28] *Annals of Congress,* 18 Cong., 1 sess., II, 1962–2001; Clay, *Works,* Colton (ed.), VI, 293.

proposed tariff upon foreign hemp and foreign cotton bagging. Mr. Clay's state, and Mr. Clay's district, were deeply involved in the production of hemp. In southern opinion, dew-rotted hemp from Kentucky was altogether inferior to water-rotted hemp from Russia. "We much prefer," said Brent of Louisiana, "paying forty cents per yard for the foreign article to making use of the bagging of Kentucky at twenty-five cents." In 1824, Clay's American System of tariffs, internal improvements, and central banking was fully matured; he was prepared to stand or fall on it; and an answer such as this was fearfully damaging. So too was Churchill C. Cambreleng's remark that the system would give "our capitalists . . . the exclusive privilege of supplying our country with manufactures." Somehow or other, and try as he would to give it a liberal veneer, Clay's American System was beginning to look like consolidation at its brassiest.[29]

In the event, the tariff bill scraped by with a vote of 107 to 102. An analysis of the vote shows that the grain, wool, and manufacturing states (Massachusetts excepted) favored the bill, and that planting, navigation, and fishing states opposed it. Although severely amended in the more conservative Senate, the bill was a distinctly protective piece of legislation. It did not satisfy the high protectionists, who were insatiable, but an average rate of 37 per cent for all the new duties was high enough to appease any rational appetite and not too high to be intolerable. Only the woolen manufacturers, who had been given 33⅓ per cent on imported woolens, were rocked back on their heels with a 30 per cent duty on imported wool. All in all, if it had represented the extremest limit of advance, the bill might have been called a decent compromise; for while it quieted the fears of the protectionists, it would never have excited or excused a call for nullification. It was signed by James Monroe on May 22, 1824.[30]

The real victim was Clay's American System. The delegations from

<hr/>

[29] *Annals of Congress*, 18 Cong., 1 sess., II, 1515, 1569.

[30] *Niles' Register*, XXVI, 113; Turner, *Rise of the New West*, p. 242; 4 U.S. Statutes at Large, 25–30. Some of the chief duties were pig iron raised from 50 cents to 56 cents a hundredweight, hammered bar iron from 75 cents to 90 cents, rolled bar iron from $1.50 to $3.00, hemp from $15 a ton to $35. Cotton fabrics received a duty of 33⅓ per cent instead of 25 per cent. Dewey, *Financial History*, pp. 191–192, summarizes the arguments for protection. See also Samuel Rezneck, "The Rise and Early Development of Industrial Consciousness in the United States, 1760–1830," *Journal of Economic and Business History*, IV (1932), 787 ff.

the Northwest, it is true, had accepted his "home market" by a vote of 18 to 0, and Kentucky by 11 to 0; but Tennessee was opposed by 7 to 2, and the whole Southwest had turned against him. For "Glorious Harry of the West" this represented a severe defeat, and worse was to follow. Whatever the Kentucky delegation might do, it cannot be said to have reflected the feelings of Kentucky at this time. One must look beyond Congress for these; nor is it inappropriate that, virulent, suggestive, and eccentric, they should have been manifested in a border state whose interests radiated in every direction.

The historian of these years is confronted with a political unrest which, as has been suggested, seems to run parallel with the demand for greater social and economic mobility; and Kentucky, high-spirited Kentucky, affords a good example of this. Kentucky could claim, to be sure, that she had been especially hard hit by the Panic of 1819; and she had some reason to complain that the two branches of the Bank of the United States, at Lexington and at Louisville, had behaved more like usurers than like banks. *McCulloch* v. *Maryland* had deprived her reformers of their best chance to strike back. They had, however, already turned to their own legislature, which, on December 21, 1820, produced an act prohibiting the sale of property by court order for less than three-quarters of its value, as assessed by a jury of the debtor's neighbors, unless the plaintiff would accept payment in notes of the Bank of Kentucky or the Bank of the Commonwealth. If he refused such payment, the debtor might replevy for two years. The Bank of the Commonwealth had a nominal capital of $2 million, but it went into business with nothing more substantial than a legislative appropriation of $7,000 for books, paper, and plates for printing. By May, 1822, its paper was worth little more than 50 cents on the dollar. It is doubtful, therefore, that the Act of December 21, 1820, had done more than afford the debtor some temporary relief, with the fair certainty that in the course of time his holdings under execution would pass into the hands of the few men who had saved some money for investment. The creditor, on the other hand, could either accept as composition about half what he had lent or wait two years with the prospect of getting nothing at all.[31]

[31] Arndt M. Stickles, *The Critical Court Struggle in Kentucky* (Bloomingdale, 1929), pp. 24, 26; *National Gazette*, Philadelphia, May 4, 1822; *Niles' Register*, XXXIII, 96; Robert M. McElroy, *Kentucky in the Nation's History*

It is not surprising that creditors should have described this act as a flagrant violation of contract: stay laws and replevin laws usually bore this character. Nor was it exactly unbecoming in the Kentucky Court of Appeals to declare the act unconstitutional, but it may have been unwise.[32] Kentucky creditors, as often as not, were citizens of some other state. The response, at any rate, was to change the whole nature of the controversy from something legal to something irresponsible, vital, and rebellious. On December 24, 1824, the Relief party succeeded in passing a bill through the legislature creating a new Court of Appeals.[33] From this event there arose two parties, both calling themselves Republican for national purposes—an Old Court party, supported by the larger landowners, the professional men, and the two branches of the Bank of the United States, and a New Court party, which represented the debtor and (perhaps) the innovator.[34] There were also, of course, two Courts of Appeal, one of which refused either to resign or to do business, the other created by a legislative majority in a fit of temper.[35] The circuit judges, with four exceptions, were careful to send cases in appeal to both courts; the people were not so circumspect. "It is about this time," we are told, "that . . . the term 'lynch law' first appeared in Kentucky." It is

---

(New York, 1909), p. 385; Lewis Collins, *History of Kentucky,* rev. and enlarged by his son R. H. Collins (2 vols., Covington, 1878), I, 30.

[32] Chief Justice John Boyle did this in the case of Blair *v.* Williams, and Associate Justices William Owsley and Benjamin Mills in Lapsley *v.* Brashears and Barr; 4 Littell 34–46, 46–87.

[33] *Kentucky Acts of 1824,* pp. 44–48. The bill was skillfully drawn up by George M. Bibb, not a member of the legislature, and one of the ablest lawyers in the state. It was steered through the House by John Rowan, member from Jefferson and Oldham counties, a man of "magnificent and commanding presence" but with gloomy, rugged, iron features which chilled one at a look. Stickles, *Court Struggle,* p. 51. His chief opponent was Ben Hardin of Nelson County, whose wit (said John Randolph of Roanoke, when Hardin was in Congress) was "like a butcher knife whetted on brickbat." R. G. Swemm (ed.), *Letters on the Condition of Kentucky in 1825, reprinted from the Richmond Enquirer* (New York, 1916), pp. 3, 15, 23, 27; Arndt M. Stickles, "Joseph R. Underwood's Fragmentary Journal of the New and Old Court Contest in Kentucky," *Filson Club Historical Quarterly,* XIII (1939), 308.

[34] Stickles, *Court Struggle,* p. 71.

[35] The New Court Chief Justice was William T. Barry, later Postmaster General in Andrew Jackson's Cabinet, a good criminal lawyer, and a man of high ideals. Stickles, *Court Struggle,* p. 60. *National Intelligencer,* February 22, 1825, and McMaster, *History,* V, 163, for Old Court's refusal to do business.

certainly true that the New Court justices went armed to church in Frankfort, and even Hezekiah Niles believed that something like civil war was in the making.[36]

In the end, Kentuckians decided—in the elections of 1825 and 1826 —that it would be better to submit appeals to a conservative court than to live in a state of judicial anarchy: in both elections they returned Old Court majorities to the legislature. By the end of 1825, the Old Court was in business again; by the end of 1826, the New Court had ceased to act.[37] But this was not the conclusion, nor submission to custom the moral, of this singular controversy. It had taught the Kentucky debtors, the most characteristic citizens of that state, that there was "something wrong with the administration" of the federal government. The Supreme Court had deserted them in *Mc-Culloch* v. *Maryland,* and in *Green* v. *Biddle* (1823) had exposed them to the mercies of the land laws of Virginia.[38] A year later, the Federal District Court decreed that every judgment it issued in execution of debt should be paid in silver and gold, and that no replevy should obtain for more than two months.[39] This was very severe treatment, and in 1825 the New Court majority in the legislature instructed Henry Clay to vote for Andrew Jackson when the presidential election was thrown into the House of Representatives. But Clay disobeyed them, and went on to become Secretary of State under John Quincy Adams. Thereafter, he and his President notoriously bestowed their patronage upon Old Court men. Clay's American System, with all its careful qualifications, was a summons to consolidation; but what kind of consolidation was this? When things grew easier for the Kentucky debtor, that was because good times were gradually returning;

[36] Stickles, *Court Struggle,* p. 69; Philip Lindsley, "A Kentucky Judicial Episode," *Green Bag,* XVI (1904), 522; *Niles' Register,* XXVIII, 277.

[37] In all, the New Court decided seventy-eight cases, which will be found in 2 T. B. Monroe's *Kentucky Reports;* the last was Handley and Hathaway v. Rankins, October 28, 1825.

[38] Green v. Biddle, 8 Wheaton 11, declared the Kentucky Acts of 1797 and 1812 unconstitutional, since they impaired the contract between Virginia and Kentucky, made at the time of separation, whereby all land disputes were to be settled by the laws of Virginia. For a very able discussion, with particular reference to the occupancy laws, see Paul W. Gates, "Tenants of the Log Cabin," *Mississippi Valley Historical Review,* XLIX (1962), 3–31.

[39] McMaster, *History,* V, 415. The Act of 1820 was repealed in 1823, and a law substituted declaring that all property sold in execution must fetch at least three-quarters of its value in gold and silver. Stickles, *Court Struggle,* p. 40.

he had received no help from the federal government. In 1828, Kentucky deserted Adams and Clay, her favorite son, and gave her electoral vote to Andrew Jackson. The American System, *qua* system, was moribund; and Clay, although he remained one of the most loved and most fascinating figures in public life, never regained the trust he had once received from the individualists of the West.[40] As for the Tariff of 1824, which Monroe signed and Clay steered through the House, it was received in Great Britain as a flat coda to the hands-off policy of the Monroe Doctrine, either as that or as a means of coercing concessions in the West Indies; and the British subsequently did their part in destroying the neomercantilist system of John Quincy Adams. In 1824, both at home and abroad, a planned consolidation did not seem to be the answer to the expansionism and the individualism of America.

[40] For the American System, see Clay, *Works,* Colton, ed., VI, 74–80, 108–110, 117–135, 218–237, 254–294; VII, 388–391, 393–415, 437–486. The formulation of this System may be said to have begun with his address of 1816 on the Bank of the United States. It reached its climax in his tariff of 1824. It was completed by his great apologia—and epitaph—of February, 1832.

CHAPTER 8

The Election of 1824

I N 1824, with a new President to be elected, the congressional caucus
passed from the scene, as if to make way for governments more responsive to the majority, and to the restless individuals who composed
it. The passing of the congressional caucus took place some two and
a half months before the signing of the General Survey Bill; and
might be said to express, in terms of political mobility, precisely what
the bill was trying to adumbrate in the realms of physical and social
movement.

Of the five candidates who had presented themselves to the electorate, William H. Crawford was said to be Thomas Jefferson's choice.
The heroic Crawford, who had been stricken by some unknown malady
(possibly erysipelas) in 1823, and was now half paralyzed and sometimes almost blind, would occasionally heave his great frame out of
bed and make a dazed appearance in Washington. His friends protested that he would soon be himself again; he was quite of the same
mind, and by the fall of 1824 he was once again endeavoring to perform his duties at the Treasury.[1] His supporters, who now called them-

---

[1] Asbury Dickens to Van Buren, Washington, October 28, 1824. "For some
time past Crawford has been attending to all his duties, and transacts business
every other day at his office. His conversation displays its usual frankness and
vigour and vivacity. His good humor continues unabated. . . ." In intellect he
"is as eminent as he ever was." Martin Van Buren to B. F. Buller, December
27, 1824: "He [Crawford] has never appeared half so interesting and respectable
to me as he has this winter, & especially these last few days. . . . [He has] a

selves Radicals, relied upon a program which seemed to be composed partly of an addiction to economy, partly of an aversion to Calhoun and Adams.[2] If there was any radicalism to be discerned in the Radical program, it would have taken a most penetrating eye to discover it; and it has now become totally invisible. In fact, the supporters of Crawford reposed their chances of success upon party regularity, slim chances in a period of disintegrating one-party rule, and they expected to hoist their candidate into the Presidency by means of the congressional caucus.

But the congressional caucus, which surrendered the final choice of a presidential candidate to a group of congressmen in Washington, was already an antiquated piece of machinery, unable to sustain such an effort. It had been under attack in 1816; it had not been employed when Monroe sought a second term; and its survival has been attributed, in part, to an exaggerated fear of Federalist conspiracy and Federalist revival. When it met on February 14, 1824, it duly nominated Crawford for President and Albert Gallatin for Vice-President; but only sixty-six Congressmen cared or dared to put in an appearance. Some of the absentees, said Senator Lowrie of Pennsylvania, a Caucus supporter, had been "afraid of their constituents"—a terrible and a true admission.[3] The friends of the other candidates—John

---

continued but slight impediment in his speech." Both in Van Buren Papers, LC. For evidence less Crawfordite see John McClean to John W. Taylor, October 25, 1824; John W. Taylor Papers, NYHS. Also, so Southard told Adams in 1825, one day in the "winter" of 1824 Crawford used "extremely improper" language toward Monroe on a matter of customs appointments, and, upon Monroe's objecting, raised his cane and said: "You damned infernal old scoundrel." Whereupon the undaunted President, seizing the fire tongs and uttering a "retaliatory epithet," put himself in a posture of defense. Crawford then apologized and left the room. Adams, *Memoirs,* VII, 81.

[2] "He [Crawford] is called the 'radical' candidate by way of derision. Jefferson was called the democratic or jacobinical candidate in '98 and '99 by the same sort of people who now talk about '*radicals.*' If they go on they will make it a popular epithet, as they said *yankee;*—and afterwards, *democrat*—& lately *bucktail.*" Erastus Root to Van Buren, January 3, 1823. Van Buren Papers. The Crawfordites, by adopting the name Radical, evidently adopted Root's point of view along with it, but not before 1823.

[3] Nathaniel Macon refused to attend because "it produces so much electioneering among the members of Congress that it seems to border on intrigue & bargain, and is not known to the Constitution." Nathaniel Macon to Martin Van Buren, May 9, 1823. John Taylor of Caroline wrote to Martin Van Buren that "if the habit of choosing presidents by Congressmen, instead of the electors

Quincy Adams, John Caldwell Calhoun, Henry Clay, and Andrew Jackson—were not above using state legislative caucuses to attain their ends, but all had set their newspapers, their committees of correspondence, and their circulating letters to work in a successful effort to make the congressional caucus unusable.

It was doomed in any event. If the legislative caucus was still to be found in some states, it was giving way to "mixed" caucuses, to "pure" state conventions, to public meetings; and expressions of preference for this presidential candidate or that were already being made by grand and petit juries and by militiamen on muster days.[4] The voice of the people had, at any rate, condemned the Republican caucus in Washington long before it committed *felo de se* on February 14, 1824. The friends of Crawford continued the battle and, if their candidate had been a well man, might have put up a better showing than they did; but as the caucus candidate, he had probably lost whatever chance he had. A Senate debate in March, with Rufus King leading the attack upon this "new, extraordinary, self-created central power, stronger than that of the Constitution," ended without a vote; it was at best an obituary performance, and not too accurately worded at that. It was not because he was new, but because he was old, that

provided for by the Constitution, should induce the country to compare it with the eight years' rotation habit, it may not be unprofitable." Taylor to Van Buren, May 12, 1823. Van Buren Papers, LC. John W. Taylor wrote John Quincy Adams, May 28, 1823: "The Albany Caucus of the 22d, ult. recommending a congressional nomination was gotten up by Gen Root & many at the time expressed their disapprobation & more have since—The members of the next Legislature may and probably will entertain different [i.e., anti-Caucus] sentiments—Those of the last [,] at least a majority of them [,] with equal facility might have been induced by the same political leaders to pass resolutions denouncing congressional caucuses." John W. Taylor Papers, NYHS; Livermore, *Twilight of Federalism*, p. 149; M. Ostrogorski, *Democracy and the Organization of Political Parties* (2 vols., New York, 1902), II, 31; Lowrie to Gallatin, February 21, 1824, Gallatin Papers, NYHS. In October, after much ill-natured comment as to his foreign birth and aristocratic leanings, and after receiving a letter from Lowrie (which, said Lowrie, cost him the utmost pain to write), Gallatin retired from the contest. His nomination, he told Van Buren, was "a misfortune founded on a miscalculation." Lowrie to Gallatin, September 25, 1824, Gallatin Papers; Gallatin to Van Buren, October 2, 1824, Van Buren Papers.

[4] Ostrogorski, *Democracy and Political Parties*, II, 36–39; Sydnor, *Southern Sectionalism*, pp. 164–165.

"King Caucus" had been obliged to put an end to himself in so public a manner.[5]

Indeed, the significance of the caucus fiasco lies in the aptness with which it symbolized other, less dramatic, and more enduring phenomena. One may look for these—though their appearance is somewhat obscure—in the Constitutional Conventions of Connecticut (1818), Massachusetts (1820), and New York (1821). Here the main problem, however variously discussed, was one of bringing the majority of individual citizens into a more direct and managing relation with government.[6] The Connecticut Convention of 1818 overthrew the Congregationalist establishment, an event of the utmost importance, even though its other reforms were somewhat mild.[7] The Massachusetts Convention of 1820 was more concerned with unequal representation than with suffrage qualifications.[8] The New York Convention of 1821, while it abolished the two anomalous Councils of Appointment and Revision, shows how mistaken Van Buren and his Bucktail reformers were when they balked at complete manhood suffrage and, even more, when they gave the governor the appointment, and not the people the election, of justices of the peace.[9] These conventions spread upon their journals a warning against the continuance of political elites, a kind of writing on the wall. If Van Buren misread or ignored it, as

[5] *Annals of Congress*, 18 Cong., 1 sess., pp. 355–362, 382, 412.

[6] Connecticut, *Journal of the Proceedings of the Convention & Delegates . . .* (Hartford, 1901); Massachusetts, *Journal of the Debates and Proceedings in the Convention of Delegates . . . begun and holden at Boston, November 15, 1820* (New ed., Boston, 1853); New York, *Reports of the Proceedings and Debates of the Convention of 1821 . . . assembled for the purpose of . . . amending the Constitution* (Albany, 1821).

[7] Jarvis Means Morse, *A Neglected Period of Connecticut History* (New Haven, 1933), pp. 3–7.

[8] Massachusetts, *Journal of Debates*, pp. 304–321; Chilton Williamson, *American Suffrage from Property to Democracy, 1760–1860* (Princeton, 1961), p. 192; Arthur M. Schlesinger, Jr., *The Age of Jackson* (Boston, 1945), p. 15.

[9] New York *Reports*, pp. 135, 140, 142. (The free Negro vote was now tragically restricted, and remained so until after the Civil War, to those seized or possessed of a freehold worth $250. *Ibid.*, pp. 180, 181, 184; Litwack, *North of Slavery*, p. 91.) Charles Z. Lincoln, *The Constitutional History of the State of New York* (5 vols., Rochester, 1906), I, 665; Lee Benson, *The Concept of Jacksonian Democracy* (Princeton, 1961), p. 9. In 1826 the Van Burenite reformers were obliged to concede, by constitutional amendment, both universal suffrage and the popular election of justices. *Ibid.*, p. 11.

he certainly did in 1821 and 1824, that is because it had as yet (in New York) little respectability: it was more in the nature of a *graffito*. When Henry Clay, in 1825, mistook the New Court movement in Kentucky for some temporary aberration, he was equally deluded: he could not perceive that this vulgar debtor's foray, so briefly inscribed upon the statute books, might have an influence upon his whole future as a leader in the West.

It used to be held that manhood suffrage was the real legacy from the West at this time. "The wind of democracy blew so strongly from the West," Frederick Jackson Turner wrote in one of the most captivating of his works, "that even in the older states of New York, Massachusetts, Connecticut, and Virginia Conventions were called which liberalized the constitutions by strengthening the democratic basis of the state."[10] Actually the demand for manhood suffrage was influenced less by the New West than by common sense and hard experience; for the history of suffrage in the United States reveals, from the beginning, how difficult it was to prevent a man from voting if his mind was set on doing so. If the West had an influence, and of course it did, it could be used in either direction: Connecticut conservatives lauded the taxpaying qualification in the Ohio constitution, for example, while eastern reformers pointed to the universal (white) manhood suffrage which Missouri had granted when she entered the Union.[11] Western constitutions were not original, and in their suffrage requirements seem to have been borne forward by a wave coming out of the East and from the depths of post-Revolutionary history.[12]

Indeed, the most potent influence of the West during this decade, although the whole West adhered to the general government when it voted for internal improvements, as did the Northwest when it called for protective tariffs, was actually centrifugal. After the great land boom collapsed in 1819, a Senate Committee on Public Lands, all of

[10] *The Frontier in American History* (New York, 1920), p. 250.

[11] Williamson, *American Suffrage,* p. 210. It should be noted that Vermont established manhood suffrage in 1777 and Maryland in 1802.

[12] One should not forget, however, that such waves have a backwash. There is great merit in the Turnerian argument that manhood suffrage in the western state reciprocally hastened its consummation in the older ones because they feared that liberal western suffrage would otherwise lure too many of their citizens away.

whose members but one were from the West, brought in a thoughtful report recommending the abolition of the credit system, which notoriously encouraged the speculator and not the settler.[13] This was accomplished by the famous Act of April 2, 1820, which also reduced the minimum purchasable tract to eighty acres, and the minimum cash payment to $1.25 per acre. A farm of eighty acres could now be purchased for $100. This was the first effort to legislate for the settler rather than the Treasury, and on September 30, 1822, the debt on public lands (which had stood at $16,794,795.14 in 1818) was calculated at $10,544,454.16.[14] By the apportionment of 1822 the western representation in Congress was increased to forty-seven representatives, who, with a delegation of eighteen in the Senate, continued to press for more democratic land laws until, in 1830, the pre-emption laws changed the status of squatter from one of public pest to one of public benefactor. He could now purchase his lands, however valuable they might be, at the minimum price and before anyone else could bid for them at the public auction.[15] This was no Homestead Law, but it represented a single victory over eastern capitalists, western speculators, southern planters, and federal conservatism. The pressure of old reforming drives, of the unforgotten Panic of 1819, of better

[13] Benjamin A. Hibbard, *A History of the Public Land Policies* (New York, 1939), p. 98, citing *Annals of Congress*, 15 Cong., 2 sess., p. 216.

[14] *American State Papers, Finance,* III, 718, and *Public Lands,* III, 561; Hibbard, *Public Land Policies,* pp. 94–95; Ernest L. Bogart, *Economic History of American Agriculture* (New York, 1923), p. 48.

[15] The Act of 1820 made some provision for pre-emption, but only for those who had made a payment on land and had then relinquished part of it. Hibbard, *Public Land Policies,* p. 151. As regards the squatter, Congress temporized again and again; but the real measure of centrifugal western influence after the reapportionment of 1822 may be gauged by the fact that the House Committee on Public Lands in 1824 spoke against the squatter, whereas the House Committee in 1828 was entirely on his side. "It is just and proper that he who renders a benefit to the public, who by his enterprise and industry has created to himself and his family a home in the wilderness, should be entitled to his reward." *American State Papers, Public Lands,* III, 619; V, 401. In 1830 this influence clashed with the centripetal House Committee on Manufactures, which in a classical report opposed as unfair the House Committee on Public Lands, when it favored price reduction and relinquishment of public lands to the states. *Ibid.,* V, 445–447, Hibbard, *Public Land Policies,* pp. 148–191; Bogert, *American Agriculture,* pp. 48 ff.; Percy Bidwell and John I. Falconer, *History of Agriculture in the Northern United States, 1620–1860* (Washington, 1941), pp. 95 ff.

communications—the irresistible impulse toward internal development
—gave the 1820's a democratic urgency which political leaders could
not always interpret so well.

Indeed, the presidential election of 1824 appears at first to be singularly irrelevant to the dissatisfied and troubled spirit of the times.
All the candidates avowed themselves Republicans; all offered, with
different degrees of emphasis, much the same program, or so it seemed.
John Caldwell Calhoun, who presented himself to the electorate in
the chimerical shape of a man of southern principles and northern
policies,[16] had given up the contest in March. A nominating convention at Harrisburg, Pennsylvania, strongly anticaucus, and diligently
canvassed beforehand by the friends of Calhoun, came out for Jackson
as President and Calhoun as Vice-President. The Secretary of War
at once accepted the verdict, and declared that he would run for the
Vice-Presidency, which was certainly his for the asking.[17] He was
young; he could wait: forever as it happened. Of the two remaining
Cabinet members, Crawford had the caucus like an albatross around
his neck, his Radicalism offered nothing more than a watery dilution
of Old Republican doctrine, and he had used his Treasury patronage
to build up something like an exclusive machine. John Quincy Adams
was strong for internal improvements but evasive on the tariff; he
relied chiefly upon his record at the State Department, which, if it
did not satisfy the extreme expansionists, had earned him the respect
of conservative men everywhere.[18] This was not true of Andrew

[16] "It is true, Mr. Calhoun is a southern man, but he forms the remarkable
exception to this class of citizens—whilst he has the principles of the South—
he holds the policy of the North, in other words he unites them." Thomas L.
McKenney to Philip Milledoler, December 13, 1821; Milledoler Papers, NYHS.
McKenney was Superintendent of Indian Trade under Calhoun until his office
was abolished through western fur trade influences in 1822.

[17] Sydnor, *Southern Sectionalism,* pp. 164–165; Wiltse, *Calhoun: Nationalist,*
pp. 283–284; Klein, *Pennsylvania Politics,* pp. 153 ff. The convention met on
March 4, 1824. George M. Dallas, Calhoun's Pennsylvania manager, had in
fact conceded defeat on February 18. *National Intelligencer,* February 24, 1824.

[18] For Adams on internal improvements, see Bemis, *Adams and the Union*
(New York, 1956), p. 25; and for his advocacy of a "cautious" protective tariff,
see *ibid.,* p. 26. It is noteworthy that John Taylor of Caroline had now with-
drawn most of his objections to Adams; Taylor to Monroe, April 29, 1823,
Monroe Papers, LC. This letter was written in a mood of profound mistrust of
Crawford, who had recently been accused in the "A.B." letters (written by
Ninian Edwards of Illinois) of willful mismanagement of public funds in his
dealings with banking institutions in the West. The accusation was *not* well

Jackson, whose disputatious term as governor of Florida, coming on top of his Seminole adventure, was not likely to appeal to cautious minds: for this very reason, and because his political views were so much more obscure than his military achievements, he compelled the imagination of men who were not only dissatisfied but also unsure as to the causes of their dissatisfaction.

In 1822, Jackson's friends had secured him a nomination from the legislature of Tennessee, but this did not mean very much to him. "As the Legislature of my state has thought proper to bring my name forward," he wrote, a little sarcastically, "without consulting me, I mean to be silent—and let the people do as seemeth good unto them."[19] Indeed, he took very little interest in the campaign until— it was quite in character—he had a highly personal reason for doing so: until he discovered that Governor Carroll of Tennessee, ostensibly his friend, had been working in secret for the election of Henry Clay. Then at last his wrath blazed up and the campaign became a vendetta, in the arts of which he had long been skilled. "Should the people take up the subject of my nomination in the south and west," he said, ". . . they will soon undeceive Mr. Clay's friends [.] If the people of Alabama, Mississippi, and Louisiana, follow the example of Pennsylvania, they will place Clay and Crawford where they ultimately will be, *Dehors the political combat*."[20] This was in 1823, and the "people" of Pennsylvania were the small farmers, miners, rivermen, and mechanics who had held a mass meeting at Harrisburg in February, and had conveyed their nomination to him in a letter from one H. W. Peterson, a barkeeper. Jackson, breaking his former silence on such matters, replied in person: the Presidency, he said, should not be sought, but it could not with propriety be declined. This infectious answer was published in the Harrisburg *Commonwealth* and did not cease to spread.[21] In 1824, a visiting New England schoolteacher wrote from Cincinnati:

---

founded. The "A.B." letters, fifteen in all, appeared in the Washington *Republican* from January 20 to March 3, 1823, and in its semiweekly issue between March 5 and April 9, 1823. Wiltse, *Calhoun: Nationalist,* p. 426, n. 35. For the origins of the Edwards-Crawford enmity, see White, *The Jeffersonians,* p. 127; it was over land-office nominations in Illinois.

[19] Jackson to A. J. Donelson, August 6, 1822; *Correspondence,* III, 174.
[20] Jackson to John Coffee, March 10, 1823; *ibid.,* III, 192.
[21] Marquis James, *Andrew Jackson: Portrait of a President* (Indianapolis,

Strange! Wild! Infatuated! All for Jackson! . . . It [is] like an influenza, and will pass off like it. . . . If the influenza passes off in season the patients will vote coolly and dispassionately for the best man—Mr. Adams. . . . But should no hope in the last case be left, I regard Mr. J. as the most independent of the southern gentry, one on whom they will be least likely to unite; and if they unite, one from whom they will gather the least flatteries, therefore I believe I would vote for him sooner than for [Clay or Crawford].[22]

This letter expresses, with great shrewdness, the essential appeal of General Jackson: he was independent. Moreover he possessed, to a degree even greater than Henry Clay, what might be called the public personality; he could attract to himself, like a magnet, all kinds of uncommitted opinions. When he at length got himself elected to the Senate, a position he detested but one which was necessary to his political fortunes, he carried all before him in Washington. Everybody expected, he said, "to see me with a tomahawk in one hand and a scalping knife in the other."[23] Instead, as had always been the case when he chose to do so, he fascinated society with his high fine manners, with his Christian courtesy and forgiveness. As a senator, his record was uninspiring. He voted but did not speak for the General Survey Bill and maintained a noncommittal attitude towards the tariff although he voted for the Tariff of 1824. It was his military legend, his valiant character, and the fact that he had no clearly defined ideas which, in combination, accounted for his popularity. But popularity alone could not prevail in those days, when the election could be cooked in the legislatures, hampered by district systems, or clogged by taxpaying qualifications and the detritus of decaying political machines. Moreover, the voters were bewildered by the absence of political platforms: the old Republican party was breaking up, but there was nothing as yet to take its place.[24]

1937), p. 44; Jackson to H. W. Peterson, February 23, 1823; *Correspondence*, III, 189.

[22] Henry D. Ward to Ephraim Cutler, April 14, 1824, in Harry R. Stevens, *The Early Jackson Party in Ohio* (Durham, 1957), p. 109.

[23] Jackson to G. W. Martin, January 24, 1824; *Correspondence*, III, 222.

[24] The legislatures still chose presidential electors in Vermont, New York, Delaware, South Carolina, and Georgia. District tickets prevailed in Maine, Massachusetts, Maryland, Tennessee, Missouri, and Illinois. McMaster, *History*, V, 75 n.; Ostrogorski, *Democracy and Political Parties*, II, 19–21. Only in Illinois, Indiana, Missouri, Vermont, New Hampshire, New Jersey, Alabama,

Only in one instance, but that a most suggestive one, does the election of 1824 reflect with some composure the otherwise distracted features of the times. Henry Clay, unlike his three opponents, did offer a recognizable program—one to which he had so far committed himself that he could not qualify it to suit the uncommitted mind. The American System was connected more with him than with anyone else. It has been said, with some justice, that the Second Bank of the United States was not an issue in this campaign;[25] nor was it, openly. But in Ohio, which (next to Kentucky, where he was not yet embroiled in the Court battle) was Clay's great stronghold, the Bank had not been forgiven. When the popular vote of Ohio was recorded, Clay won a very close victory over Jackson; but if Hamilton County (with Cincinnati at its heart) had not gone so heavily against him, the figures would have looked much better.[26] Cincinnati considered that she had been raped by the Bank in 1819, and Cincinnati did not forget that Clay had acted as attorney for the Bank on several occasions, or that the Bank was one of the three pillars of his American System.[27]

A study of the electoral vote reveals a larger and more telling picture. Clay won the electoral votes of Kentucky, Ohio, and Missouri, three states which were then committed to internal improvements and the protective tariff. He had no chance in New England and New York, which were opposed to internal improvements, and he made no showing in the Southwest, which was opposed to the protective tariff. It is often said that the election of 1824 was inconclusive, but in this one respect it could hardly have spoken more clearly. Its sec-

---

Maryland, and Kentucky was there neither a property nor a tax-paying qualification.

[25] Bemis, *John Quincy Adams and the Union*, p. 25 n.: "The Bank of the United States did not come under discussion in 1824."

[26] The figures for Hamilton County, computed as accurately as possible, by Dr. Harry R. Stevens, in the absence of original returns in the official records of the Secretary of State, are Clay, 696; Jackson, 2,679; Adams, 1,217. Stevens, *Early Jackson Party*, App. I.

[27] Clay had become legal counsel for the Bank in 1819, and its legal counsel in Ohio in 1820; and on November 5, 1820, had accepted the legal superintendency of the Bank in Ohio and Kentucky. "He incurred . . . a good bit of resentment among many groups in Ohio." *Ibid.*, p. 37; Eugene H. Roseboom and Francis P. Weisenburger, *A History of Ohio* (Columbus, 1958), p. 94; Clay to Langdon Cheves, November 14, 1819, and March 15, 1820; *Papers of Henry Clay*, II, 720, 794–95.

tionalism was delusive: it was a solid defeat for the American System and for consolidated, as compared to piecemeal, federal planning.[28]

The popular figures were: Jackson, 153,544; Adams, 108,740; Crawford, 46,618; Clay, 47,136. In the electoral college, Jackson's ninety-nine consisted of all the votes of New Jersey, Pennsylvania, North Carolina, South Carolina, Alabama, Mississippi, Tennessee, and Indiana, seven of Maryland's eleven votes, three of Louisiana's five, two of Illinois' three, and one of New York's thirty-six. Adams' eighty-four consisted of the solid vote of New England, twenty-six of New York's thirty-six, one of Delaware's two, three of Maryland's eleven, two of Louisiana's five, and one of Illinois' three. Crawford's forty-one included all the Virginian and Georgian vote, two of Delaware's three, five from New York, and one from Maryland. Clay's thirty-seven came from Kentucky, Ohio, and Missouri, with four from New York.[29] The geographical distribution in the electoral college, like the popular vote itself, made Jackson the favorite candidate; but the verdict now lay with the House of Representatives.

This constitutional procedure took the election one step farther from the people: the House would have to choose between Jackson, Adams, and Crawford, with each state having one vote. Illinois would be as powerful as Pennsylvania, Delaware as New York, Rhode Island as Virginia. In such a situation, only angels would have refrained from bargaining. And, but for New York, the result might have been even less "popular" than it was: in New York Clay had been mysteriously deprived of the four electoral votes which would have placed his name before the House, and had his name been before the House, Mr. Clay would possibly have been just skillful enough to create a majority in his favor.

The electoral vote of New York, where the choice of presidential electors was still in the hands of the legislature, has long been accepted as too dark for accurate scrutiny: its background, which is more important, is fortunately open to inspection. The legislature in 1824

---

[28] In Ohio, Clay received 19,255 votes; Jackson, 18,489 (or, 18,457); Adams, 12,280. In Kentucky, Clay received 17,321; Jackson, 6,455; and Adams none. In Missouri Clay received 1,401; Jackson, 987; and Adams, 311. Clay received no votes at all, popular or electoral, in New England. In Pennsylvania he ran a poor last to Jackson (36,100), Adams (5,440), and Crawford (4,206) with 1,609. McMaster, *History*, V, 75.

[29] *Ibid.*, pp. 75, 76.

was controlled by a group of efficient men, headed by United States Senator Martin Van Buren, the brains of the Bucktail faction: in an addled moment, they had set their faces against giving the choice of presidential electors directly to the people, and the very scarecrows in the fields had borne, that spring, cards stitched to their coats with the word "Regency" inscribed on them.[30] Having committed this error, the newly christened and infatuated "Albany Regency" went on to perpetrate a far grosser one. On the last day that the legislature was in session, it passed a resolution removing De Witt Clinton from the office of Canal Commissioner, which he had occupied with such devotion and success.[31] The effect of this despotic move was to make Clinton governor and James Tallmadge lieutenant governor in the November elections over the Regency choices of Samuel Young and Erastus Root.[32]

[30] Dennis T. Lynch, *An Epoch and a Man; Martin Van Buren & His Times* (New York, 1929), p. 266; Hammond, *Political Parties,* II, 143 ff. W. L. Marcy to Martin Van Buren, December 14, 1823, says that the "enlightened republicans" were against a change in the electoral law, but that "the current of public opinion was so strong that it cannot be resisted." On January 11, 1824, Marcy says that the demand for a change in the electoral law is growing very strong; but he is sure that if the election is given to the people "in a general ticket," they will vote for Clinton. He thinks that those who oppose a change would, if it cannot be resisted, "go for the districting system." Van Buren Papers, LC. This does not coincide with Ostrogorski's view, *Democracy and Political Parties,* II, 21, that a general ticket came to be associated with power falling into the hands of the few and with state and congressional caucuses.

[31] Martin Van Buren, *The Autobiography of Martin Van Buren, American Historical Association, Annual Report, 1918,* II (1920), 144, calls this a "very unexpected and badly devised step" of which he "had no knowledge, being in Washington." However, W. L. Marcy to Martin Van Buren, January 11, 1824, warned him that Judge Roger W. Skinner, one of the Regency, "now and then indulges his spleen against *certain persons* for keeping Clinton in the board of Canal Commissioners." Van Buren Papers, LC. See also Holmes Alexander, *The American Talleyrand* (New York, 1934), p. 204. The resolution to remove Clinton, passed on April 12, 1824, was introduced in the New York Senate by Bowman of Monroe County, but was handed to him by Silas Wright, Jr., one of the Regency leaders. Bennett Champ Clark, *John Quincy Adams* (Boston, 1932), p. 212. In the Clinton Papers, NYPL, there is a resolution of the citizens of the Village of Geneva attacking his removal by a majority of the Legislature as "malignant," and "showing a contempt for public opinion and a disregard for the public interests."

[32] Clinton's majority was 16,906; Tallmadge's, 32,409. Tallmadge represented the reforming "People's party." Hammond, *Political Parties,* II, 175. Root, who was pro-Caucus, but who vigorously opposed disenfranchisement of the Free Negro, deserved a better fate in this election.

The Regency's candidate for President was William H. Crawford, but it had long been accepted that the election for governor would have a great if not decisive influence upon his fortunes.[33] And so it came about after much maneuvering, more clever than decent: Adams received twenty-six electoral votes, Crawford five, Clay four, and Jackson one. Thus Clay lost his chance of making the subsequent election in the House even more of a wizard's sabbath than it actually became.

But he was, in any event, now cast in a congenial role. "It is in fact very much in [his] power," William Plumer ruefully told his father, "to make the President."[34] The friends of Jackson, Adams, and Crawford watched him in dismay as—gay, insouciant, and somehow menacing—he wandered from boardinghouse to boardinghouse, from banquet to banquet, not a candidate but a kingmaker.[35] With his immense prestige and his admitted mastery as Speaker, what might he not accomplish? He was not personally on good terms with Adams; he had openly broken with Jackson over the Florida question; for the Radicalism of Crawford he had no appetite at all. Even before December 16, however, when the vote of Louisiana reached Washington and the results could finally be tabulated, he had told his friend and lieutenant, Thomas Hart Benton, who had become a Jacksonian, that he could not follow his example.[36] Did this mean that he was leaning toward Adams? Certainly it did. On December 17 and 23, according to the Diary, Representative Robert P. Letcher of Kentucky called upon Adams; receiving, on the first occasion, the Secretary's assurance that he "harbored no animosity" against the Speaker; imparting, on the second, the thought that everything depended upon the first ballot, and that this could be secured for Adams if Kentucky, Ohio, Missouri (all Clay states), Indiana, and Illinois could be persuaded to vote for him. "Impracticable," said Adams, but he com-

[33] Benjamin F. Butler to Van Buren, March 27, 1824. Crawford will receive the "united vote of the State . . . provided we succeed in the Govs election." Van Buren Papers, LC.

[34] William Plumer, Jr., to William Plumer, Sr., December 16, 1824; Brown (ed.), *Missouri Compromises*, p. 123.

[35] "I found myself transformed from a candidate before the people, into an elector for the people." "Mr. Clay's Address to his Constituents," Clay, *Works*, Colton (ed.), VI, 302.

[36] James, *Jackson*, p. 105; Thomas Hart Benton, *Thirty Years' View*, I, 48.

pleted his entry with the ominous words *"Incedo super ignes."* On January 1, 1825, he agreed with Mr. Letcher that the time had come for him to have a conversation with Mr. Clay, and that very night, seated at a banquet for Lafayette, the two agreed to a conference in the near future.[37] By now it was presumed that Clay was looking for the State Department, and therewith the succession.[38]

The two men met on the evening of January 9, a Sunday, and with a wonderful if pathetic irony Adams noted in his Diary that he had already been to church and had heard the Reverend Mr. Little discourse on Ecclesiastes vii, 23—*"I said I will be wise; but it was far from me."* His Diary is otherwise silent about what took place.[39] We have every reason to suppose that the two men came to an understanding; but surely it must have been an understanding only, an implicit but not an overt bargain, not the Presidency for the State Department in so many words. Clay would have thought such a bargain naïve and Adams would have considered it sinful. But once the conference had taken place, Adams began to receive visitors, and here he went as far as anyone could go without actually committing himself, and a good deal farther than his own conscience could possibly

[37] Adams, *Memoirs,* VI, 447, 452, 453, 457.

[38] However, as late as December 27, 1824, Van Buren could write: "If Clay's friends go with [Crawford] (which is probable but not certain) he will have the highest vote on the first ballot, & if he does he will keep ahead." Van Buren to B. F. Butler, December 27, 1824; Van Buren Papers, LC. It is typical of this election that Van Buren had no moral objection to the delegations of Kentucky and Ohio (which states had not voted for him) swinging their votes to Crawford. For a later New York opinion, Ebenezer Sage to John W. Taylor, January 28, 1825: "Mr. Clay will do all he can [for Adams] and perhaps Mr. Adams if he should become President will make him Secre[y] of State." John W. Taylor Papers, NYHS.

[39] Adams, *Memoirs,* VI, 464–465. Adams merely writes that Clay arrived at six and stayed all evening, and that "he wished me, as far as I might think proper, to satisfy him with regard to some principles of great public importance, but without any personal considerations for himself. In the question to come before the House between General Jackson, Mr. Crawford and myself, he had no hesitation in saying his preference would be for me." He also adds that Clay told him of some "gross" approaches by Crawfordites; and that certain friends of Adams, without Adams' authority, had urged "considerations personal to himself." Here the Diary stops. Bemis, *Adams and the Union,* p. 40 n., quotes J. Q. A. to G. W. Adams, November 28, 1827: "I will appeal to yourself whether your interruptions in your diary . . . have not been most frequently owing to a sense of shame. . . ." *Verb. sap.?*

have approved. The visitors were bargain hunters to a man, and Mr. Adams did not show them the door.[40] On January 24, Clay and a majority of the Ohio and Kentucky delegations "unequivocally avowed" their intention to vote for Adams, and on January 28 the Philadelphia *Columbian Observer* printed an accusation, said to have been written by a congressman from Pennsylvania, that Clay had been offered the State Department if he could deliver these votes.[41] At this unhappy moment, when everything was once more in solution, Daniel Webster made his appearance at the State Department, with the postdated draft of a letter he had written to the Federalist Henry R. Warfield, a lame-duck congressman from Maryland. Webster had the massive impudence to read from this draft. He confidently expected, he had written to Warfield, that Adams (if elected) would demonstrate "by some one clear and distinct case" that he did not propose to continue the Dynasty's proscription of Federalists.[42] Adams replied that he "approved altogether the general spirit" of the Warfield draft; and Webster departed, to use his influence with the Maryland delegation, with the solitary representative from Delaware, and with Stephen Van Rensselaer of New York.[43]

In the end, it was upon the shoulders of Stephen Van Rensselaer that the burden of this election was placed. Van Rensselaer was no

[40] They were William Plumer of New Hampshire, John Scott of Missouri, the Federalist John Reed of Massachusetts, and W. C. Bradley of Vermont. The Federalists of Delaware and Maryland would not give their support to Adams without the influence of Daniel Webster, who was known to be hankering after the post of Minister to London; and Mr. Plumer was told that Webster's wishes "might be gratified hereafter." James, *Jackson,* p. 118; Adams, *Memoirs,* VI, 469. Plumer called on January 17.

[41] On January 31 Clay published a card in the *National Intelligencer,* calling upon the writer to reveal his identity. He immediately unmasked himself as Representative George Kremer, "a manager of some originality and boldness" from a Pennsylvania Dutch district. Klein, *Pennsylvania Politics,* p. 184; *Memoirs,* VI, 476. His manners and dress were so deplorable that Clay could not bring himself to duel with him. This incident was so damaging that Adams really lost his head: he visited Van Buren, and promised the New York senator that the gentleman he had recommended for the consulate at Santiago "would be nominated, but *perhaps not till after the election in the House.*" *Memoirs,* VI, 487. Italics inserted.

[42] Livermore, *Twilight of Federalism,* pp. 174–176; *Memoirs,* VI, 492–93.

[43] Webster called on February 3. Van Rensselaer called the next day, and received the same answer as Webster; this he imparted to the Federalist John Lee of Maryland, who had believed that Jackson would be more liberal to Federalists. Warfield called on February 5. *Memoirs,* VI, 493, 497.

Atlas. He was a kindly, upright, simple old Federalist gentleman, who suffered from a congenital inability to hurt other people's feelings, and in the course of the campaign he had managed to give the impression that he favored all the candidates.[44] Toward the end, however, it was generally believed that he was wavering between Jackson and Crawford.[45] The New York delegation was known to be split 17 to 17; a deadlock would produce no vote at all; and since Adams needed to win on the first ballot, because Maryland intended to desert him on the second and would take other states with her, the vote of New York was essential to him. The connection between Van Rensselaer and Webster now offered some hope that the New York tie would be broken in Adams' favor, and so it came about. On February 9, Van Rensselaer cast his vote for Adams, attributing this action (so Van Buren remembered his saying) not to Webster but to some higher source.[46] His correspondence after the election, and a memorandum of Rufus King's, give a very different impression, or rather two different impressions;[47] we shall never know what really took place in his mind.[48] In any event, the crucial vote was cast, and when the tellers, Daniel Webster and John Randolph, announced the result of

[44] Livermore, *Twilight of Federalism,* p. 178.

[45] He had already received a stern letter from De Witt Clinton, rather more than hinting at an "odious" Adams-Clay bargain. Clinton to Van Rensselaer, February 1, 1823; MS., N.Y. State Lib. Since Clinton supported Jackson— Hammond, *Political Parties,* II, 188–89—this supports Adams' assertion in *Memoirs,* VI, 470, that Clinton was working on New York, "particularly Gen. Van Rensselaer," to vote for Jackson.

[46] *Autobiography,* p. 152. He told Van Buren that, as New York began to ballot, he bent his head in prayer, and saw at his feet an Adams ballot, which he took to be a sign from Heaven.

[47] Van Rensselaer to Clinton, February 10 (misdated March 10), 1825: "Dear Sir, the long agony is over. M. Adams was elected on the first ballot. Mr. Clay's combination could not be resisted and to allay the excitement we agreed to vote for Adams." Clinton Papers, NYPL. Rufus King wrote that Van Rensselaer called on him on February 11 and explained that, having received Adams' assurances during his visit on February 4, he considered himself thereafter as pledged to that gentleman. Memorandum of February 12, 1824, Rufus King Papers, NYHS.

[48] J. Gales to Albert Gallatin, February 28, 1825: "Not five minutes before the vote was taken, he was firm against him [Adams], but finally gave way to the fears with which it was attempted to alarm him." Gallatin Papers, NYHS. Fear, responsible fear, may actually be the answer: the notion that an election in the House might be dragged out indefinitely and result in Calhoun's being elected President by default was current as early as October, 1824. So "N" to Samuel Smith, October 17, 1824; Van Buren Papers, LC.

this first ballot, Adams had received the vote of thirteen states, Jackson of seven, and Crawford of four.[49] "It was impossible to win the game, gentlemen," said John Randolph, "the cards were packed."[50]

Two days later, Adams called on Monroe and told him that the State Department had been offered to Henry Clay. Monroe felt that this precluded him from offering any advice; but the next day he sent Major General Jacob Brown to Adams, "to make known to him, the public sentiments." Brown, in turn, did not feel that he could announce himself as Monroe's emissary, and he merely suggested that De Witt Clinton would make the best Secretary of State. On February 14, Adams called on the President again, to inform him that Clay had accepted his offer; and Monroe, courteous to the last, said not a word of criticism.[51]

When the news was known officially, Andrew Jackson agreed with Randolph that the cards had been packed, but his language was more direct. "So you see," he wrote, "the Judas of the West has closed the contract and will receive the thirty pieces of silver. [H]is end will be the same."[52] From then onward, perhaps for all his life, Henry Clay had to refute the charge that the State Department had been obtained by "bargain and corruption." Nowadays, we would admit that "corruption" is not a word that one should use lightly about men like Adams and Clay. As a distinguished scholar puts it: "The implicit but certainly not corrupt bargain between Adams and Clay was the least questionable of several deals . . . that Adams made to secure election in the House of Representatives."[53] It was these personal "deals" that

[49] For Adams: Maine, New Hampshire, Vermont, Massachusetts, Rhode Island, Connecticut, New York, Maryland, Louisiana, Kentucky, Missouri, Ohio, Illinois. For Jackson: New Jersey, Pennsylvania, South Carolina, Alabama, Mississippi, Tennessee, Indiana. For Crawford: Virginia, Delaware, North Carolina, Georgia.

[50] Mrs. Harrison Smith, *The First Forty Years of Washington Society,* Gaillard Hunt, ed. (New York, 1906), p. 181.

[51] *Memoirs,* VI, 508–09; *American Historical Review,* XLII (1937), 273–276.

[52] Jackson to W. B. Lewis, February 14, 1825; *Correspondence,* III, 276. Jackson's own refusal to engage in any *personal* bargaining appears in Klein, *Pennsylvania Politics,* pp. 176, 180. Moore (ed.), *Works of James Buchanan* (12 vols., Philadelphia, 1908–11), I, 263–267; James T. Curtis, *Life of James Buchanan* (2 vols., New York, 1885), I, 41–44; Philip S. Klein, *President James Buchanan* (University Park, Pa., 1961), p. 52.

[53] Bemis, *Adams and the Union,* p. 58. Bemis gives a very complete and objective survey of Adams' "deals" in *ibid.,* Chap. III.

tormented the conscience of Adams, who could not forgive himself for conniving, for electioneering, for behaving like anyone else. He truly believed that Jackson's election would be a calamity; that he himself would make a worthy President; that Clay, whose foreign and domestic politics now so nearly approached his own, would add both stability and symmetry to his administration. His conscience refused to be assuaged by these considerations. When a Committee of the House called upon him to inform him that he was President-elect, sweat poured from his stricken face as he listened to the words of Daniel Webster, the committee's chairman.[54] He asked permission to use a precedent set by Thomas Jefferson, and to answer in writing. If it were possible, he wrote, by declining the office to bring about an immediate election, with a clearer result, he would gladly do so. But this was not constitutionally permissible, and therefore he accepted office.[55] In his Diary he admitted that the election had not been conducted "in a manner satisfactory to pride or just desire; not by the unequivocal suffrages of a majority of the people; with perhaps two-thirds of the whole people adverse to the actual result."[56]

To Clay, who was more earthy, it was a matter of genuine surprise that the "bargain and corruption" cry did not die away.[57] He never could see that to accept an office which still was supposed to carry the succession with it, after having delivered the votes of Kentucky, Ohio, and Missouri, could only (as Clinton said) "convey the most odious implications."[58] He honestly believed that in justice to himself and his friends, and for the good of the American System, it was his duty to take what was offered. He had, no doubt, been made the scapegoat for a kind of political management of which he was simply the most conspicuous example; and yet, a popular man himself, he seems to have turned his back upon the debtors, the small farmers, the men with little property or none, now looming upon the verge of political history and determined to get in. How else could one describe his espousal of the Old Court party and his bland dismissal of the fact

[54] See Margaret B. Smith, *First Forty Years,* p. 186, who had the story from "one of the committee."

[55] Richardson, *Messages and Papers,* II, 292–293.

[56] *Memoirs,* VII, 98.

[57] For example, Clay to Crawford, February 18, 1828; *Works,* Colton (ed.), IV, 193.

[58] Cf. note 45, *supra.*

that the Kentucky legislature had instructed its delegates in Congress to vote for Jackson? Kentucky had given Jackson only 6,455 votes to Clay's 17,321, but to Adams she had given no votes at all. It is not surprising that the cry of "bargain and corruption" had grown quite irrepressible by the time that Mr. Adams, sad and drawn after two sleepless nights,[59] was driven to the Capitol for his inauguration.

[59] *Memoirs,* VI, 518.

CHAPTER 9

The Perilous Experiment

O N November 25, 1825, the new President read to his Cabinet
the draft of his first Annual Message. In it he recommended
to Congress the founding of a national university, the financing of
national scientific explorations, the establishment of a uniform standard
of weights and measures, the building of an astronomical observatory,
the creation of a Department of the Interior, a reform of the patent
laws, and the inception of a program of internal development on a
huge scale. The draft ended with a frank admission that "the Constitution under which you are assembled is a charter of limited
powers," and then with the statement that these limited powers were,
for practical purposes, almost unlimited. "If the power to exercise
exclusive legislation," ran this eloquent but fatal passage—

If the power to exercise exclusive legislation in all cases whatsoever over
the District of Columbia; if the power to lay and collect taxes, duties, imposts, and excises, to pay the debts and provide for the common defense and
general welfare of the United States . . . and to make all laws which shall
be necessary and proper for carrying these powers into execution—if these
powers and others enumerated in the Constitution may be effectually brought
into action by laws promoting the improvement of agriculture, commerce,
and manufactures, the cultivation and encouragement of the mechanic and
of the elegant arts, the advancement of literature, and the progress of the
sciences, ornamental and profound, to refrain from exercising them for the
benefit of the people themselves would be to hide in the earth the talent

committed to our charge—would be treachery to the most sacred of trusts. The spirit of improvement is abroad upon the earth. It stimulates the heart and sharpens the faculties not of our fellow-citizens alone, but of the nations of Europe and of their rulers. While dwelling with pleasing satisfaction upon the superior excellence of our political institutions, let us not be unmindful that liberty is power, that the nation blessed with the largest portion of liberty must in proportion to its numbers be the most powerful nation upon earth, and that the tenure of power by man is, in the moral purposes of his Creator, upon condition that it shall be exercised to ends of beneficence, to improve the condition of himself and his fellow-men. While foreign nations less blessed with that freedom which is power than ourselves are advancing with gigantic strides in the career of public improvement, were we to slumber in indolence or fold up our arms and proclaim to the world that we are palsied by the will of our constituents, would it not be to cast away the bounties of Providence and doom ourselves to perpetual inferiority?[1]

Few presidential programs have been summed up with such cogency; few have offered such evidence of careful thought, keen intelligence, and lofty vision; few have betrayed so strange an inattention to the known susceptibilities of its audience. To accuse the new Congress of a disposition to slumber in indolence was not tactful in a newly elected President; and it was even less tactful to warn that body against being palsied by the will of its constituents, when thousands of these constituents already believed that their will had been palsied by the election of the President. But tactlessness is not the only, nor is it the heaviest charge that could be brought against this message. When Adams described a cautious reading of the enumerated powers as "treachery to the most sacred of trusts," he must have realized that many Americans, including his predecessor in office, still wondered whether any other kind of reading might not be treachery. When he summoned the nation to an orgy of internal development— physical, intellectual, scientific—was it exactly wise to cite the example of "the nations of Europe and their rulers," the very example which, Americans believed, they had fought two wars to escape and to transcend? His bitterest enemies could not have resurrected, with a more untimely magic, the buried rumor that "all Adamses are monarchists"; or have informed the public, with a more sinister gusto, that if the

---

[1] Richardson, *Messages and Papers,* II, 296–297.

first presidential Adams had signed the Alien and Sedition Acts, the second had even stronger views about consolidation and central government.[2]

Had he listened to the advice of his Cabinet, Adams would never have submitted such a message to Congress. But the Cabinet had been chosen, in part, more to conciliate Republican opinion than to counsel the President. Calhoun's friend, Samuel L. Southard of New Jersey, had been retained in the Navy Department. The War Department had been given to James Barbour of Virginia, a follower of Crawford, although the motive behind this choice might have had something to do with splitting the powerful Crawford interest in Virginia. William Wirt remained as Attorney General. John McLean of Ohio, no friend to Adams, was kept on as Postmaster General, in which office—though it did not carry Cabinet rank—he dispensed an invaluable patronage.[3] It is as plain to us as it must have been to Adams that such a group configured the perpetuation of an old elite: and Southard, Barbour, and Wirt now betrayed that instinct for survival which, as might be expected, is somewhat highly developed in such entities. All three listened to the draft with profound dismay. But this was not all, or nearly all. For even Henry Clay, father of the American System, did not care to stand sponsor for a national university, a new executive department, or a modernization of the patent laws. His political instincts, dormant during the late election, were now thoroughly aroused: he "approved the general principles," he said, but "scrupled a great part of the details." Only Richard Rush of Pennsylvania, an ardent protectionist, who had been recalled from London to take up Crawford's duties at the Treasury, gave his blessing to "near the whole."[4] With Rush in the Treasury, Clay in the State Department,

---

[2] "Orgy" is justified on the grounds that Adams departed completely from the Jeffersonian view that a constitutional amendment was needed to define and delimit the federal power. His position was weakened when his friend John Bailey of Massachusetts introduced such an amendment to the House of Representatives, against his advice. Bemis, *John Quincy Adams and the Union*, p. 75.

[3] *Ibid.*, p. 56; *Memoirs*, VI, 510; Wiltse, *Calhoun: Nationalist*, pp. 313, 317–318.

[4] *Memoirs*, VII, 58–64. Southard was silent during the discussions, but silence here cannot be construed as consent. The Treasury was first formally offered to Crawford, and then to Rush, "the only sheerly political appointment [Adams] made." J. H. Powell, *Richard Rush: Republican Diplomat* (Philadelphia, 1942), p. 181.

and Adams in the White House, the new administration might have been said to rest upon a geographical basis which ran from New England, through Pennsylvania, and on into the industrial regions of the Ohio Valley. Even this basis, it now appeared, might not be strong enough to support such a verbal mass of consolidation.

But Adams persisted. He told his Cabinet, it is true, that it was quite immaterial to him whether he should present his views in a first or a final Annual Message. He said only that, in one message or the other, "I should feel it my indispensable duty to suggest them." Why then did he choose the first? His own reason was that the approval of Rush was decisive: "thus situated [he wrote], the perilous experiment must be made."[5] It may be perhaps doubted that this was the only explanation for his choice. Fortunately, we know something of what was in his mind when he wrote the message.

The great effort of my administration [he explained some years later] was to mature into a permanent and regular system the application of all the superfluous revenue of the Union into internal improvement which at this day would have afforded high wages and constant employment to hundreds of thousands of laborers, and in which every dollar expended would have repaid itself fourfold in the enhanced value of the public lands. With this system in ten years from this day the surface of the whole Union would have been checkered over with railroads and canals. It may still be done half a century later and at the limping gait of State legislature and private adventure. I would have done it in the administration of the affairs of the nation. . . . When I came to the Presidency the principle of internal improvement was swelling the tide of public prosperity, till the Sable Genius of the South saw the signs of his own inevitable downfall in the unparalleled progress of the general welfare in the North, and fell to cursing the tariff and internal improvement, and raised the standard of free trade, nullification, and state rights. I fell and with me fell, I fear, never to rise again in my day, the system of internal improvement by means of national energies. The great object of my life, therefore, as applied to the administration of the government of the United States, has failed. The American Union, as a moral person in the family of nations, is to live from hand to mouth, and to cast away instead of using for the improvement of its own condition, the bounties of Providence.[6]

[5] *Memoirs*, VII, 63.
[6] Adams to the Reverend Charles Upham, February 2, 1837, quoted by

The "permanent and regular" system which he presented to Congress and the nation in his first Annual Message had been advanced as a theory by George Washington in the days of the Potomac Company. It had then been taken for granted by George Washington and those who thought as he did that the American nation, if it hoped to generate a truly national energy, would have to be the product of a social system resting upon converging highways: in general, upon the rivers which, with their tributaries, drained the Mississippi Valley; in particular, upon the Ohio and the Potomac, joined by a canal. This would have made the future city of Washington, founded at the juncture of these rivers with ocean navigation, "a capital of the first magnitude," the center of American exchanges, industry, and education, "whose influence, incidentally, should convert Virginia because of her resources of iron and coal into an industrial community, and thus into a free state."[7]

As the basis for a system, the theory lacked only the sanction of history and geography, which had already doomed it before the election of John Quincy Adams: by the Presidency of Washington, which forced the great man to sever his connection with the Potomac Company; by the invention of the cotton gin, which decreed that Virginia should become a slave-selling and not an industrial state; and by the existence of a natural break in the Appalachians, producing in the course of time—and without federal aid—a more viable and less costly highway in the Erie Canal.

It was quite in keeping with the family pieties that Brooks Adams, in a savagely defensive essay, should have called his grandfather an "idealistic philosopher," in whom there was not a trace of the politician, and it is here, indeed, that he offers us a valuable clue to the rashness of John Quincy Adams. "Idealistic" is a term which can mean almost anything; and Brooks Adams intended it to cover the reasoning of a man who sincerely believed that his benign Creator thought according to certain fixed laws, that these were scientific laws,

Brooks Adams in Henry Adams, *The Degradation of the Democratic Dogma* (New York, 1919), p. 11.

[7] Dorfman, *Economic Mind*, I, 256–257, for Washington's hope that a great industrial empire would rise close to Alexandria. Brooks Adams, in Henry Adams, *Degradation*, pp. 17–22, gives a plausible version of J. Q. Adams' extention of this hope.

and that they could "be discovered by human intelligence and when discovered . . . adapted to human uses."[8] Thus the Creator's plan for America and for mankind had first been glimpsed by George Washington and his partners, and first adapted to human use in the Annual Message of 1825. In his great prolegomenon to this message, his extraordinary *Report on Weights and Measures* of 1821, Adams had sometimes resorted to language that was nothing if not millennial. "If the Spirit of Evil is, before the final consummation of things, to be cast down from his dominion over men, and bound in the chains of a thousand years, the foretaste here of man's eternal felicity . . . then the metre will surround the globe in use as well as multiplied extension; and one language of weights and measures will be spoken from the equator to the poles."[9] A statesman who could lecture Congress in this way might well have believed that he had made, as it were, a scientific covenant with his God to regenerate the American people. Under these circumstances, how could he wait until a final message before showing America the path to salvation?

The thought was an intoxicating one, and it was followed, with a depressing punctuality, by the usual consequences of intoxication. Science and education were Adams' passions, and these might have been safely presented to the Congress and the people in general terms: they were, after all, both complementary and essential to internal development. But Adams had committed himself to the public lands as a source of revenue for his federal system of internal improvements; and while he was careful in his message not to suggest an enhancement in the price of these lands, and never thereafter, as President, opposed those laws which would have the effect of lowering it, there were people who perceived at once that he was arguing for a very careful stewardship of the public domain. The alarm excited in 1825 was well summed up by James K. Polk in 1830. "The policy . . . is, to sell your lands high, prevent thereby the inducements to emigration, retain a population of paupers in the East, who may, of necessity, be driven into manufactories to labor at low wages for their daily bread. The second branch of the system is high duties . . . first, to protect the manufacturer, by enabling him to sell his wares at higher prices,

[8] Brooks Adams, in *ibid.*, pp. 11, 31, 32.
[9] *Report of the Secretary of State Upon Weights and Measures* (Washington, 1821), p. 48.

and next to produce an excess of revenue. The third branch of the system is internal improvements, which is to suck up the excess of revenue."[10]

Needless to say, this is not what Adams had in mind. He would have scorned the thought that he had set himself up as the leader of the nation's industrial interests. Nor did he see high tariffs as revenue producers, but as a necessary means toward the realization of national self-containment and independence; and his allusion to tariffs in his message had been extremely cautious.[11] But what he withheld with one hand he bestowed with the other. His Secretary of the Treasury, along with the 1825 *Report on the State of the Finances,* had submitted a letter which was little less than a protectionist dithyramb. "By a flourishing state of manufactures," wrote Richard Rush, "we shall see rising up a new class of capitalists, rivaling in the extent and usefulness of their operations, and in the amount of their gains, the wealthiest of our merchants. . . . When to the complete establishment of manufactures, the internal improvements of the country shall have been superadded, the farmer of the United States cannot but perceive that the measure of his prosperity is made potentially full."[12] Two years later, Rush's economic nationalism grew so flagrant that he issued a report which was a frank denigration of the pioneer as a consumer of capital and a drain on the labor market.[13] Of this report Adams wrote, in private, "It will, of course, be roughly handled in and out of Congress. But the policy it recommends will outlive the blast of faction and abide the test of time."[14]

In effect, Adams believed that he could foster the spirit of competition and yet make it subserve the moral principle that all should labor for the common good. He hoped that he was about to solemnize

---

[10] *Register of Debates,* 21 Cong., 1 sess., pp. 698–699.

[11] He had merely alluded to "laws promoting the improvement of . . . manufactures." Richardson, *Messages and Papers,* II, 296.

[12] *A Letter From the Secretary of the Treasury Enclosing the Annual Report on the State of the Finances* (Washington, 1825).

[13] "Report on the State of the Finances," December 8, 1827, 20 Cong., 1 sess., No. 786; *American State Papers, Finance,* V, 638.

[14] *Memoirs,* VII, 36. When New York protectionists urged him to mention tariffs in this Third Annual Message, he declined. "I added, however, that the Report of the Secretary of the Treasury upon the finances would with my entire approbation recommend the protection of the manufacturing interest in the most effective manner." *Ibid.,* VII, 365.

a lasting marriage between the democratic ideal of equality and his scientific plans for a collective administration. The reception given to his message suggests that the American people regarded such a marriage as, at best, an unnatural and, at worst, a foolish affair. They greeted it either with rage or with ridicule. The rage could be anticipated, since Old Republicanism had not yet expended all its moral force.[15] The ridicule was galling and, to Adams, it must also have been depressing in the extreme. An astronomical observatory, for example, could and should have been considered an essential part of the equipment of any civilized government: all the American people did was to seize upon his phrase "those light-houses of the skies" and make it a national joke. The message, the very interpretation of his Creator's will, was not acted upon in Congress.[16] From then onward the Presi-

[15] "Their [the Federalists'] younger recruits . . . now look to a single and splendid government of an aristocracy, founded on banking institutions, and moneyed incorporations under the guise and cloak of their favored branches of manufactures, commerce and navigation, riding and ruling over the plundered ploughman and beggared yeomanry. This will be to them a next blessing to the monarchy of their first aim." Jefferson to W. B. Giles, December 26, 1825, *Writings,* Ford (ed.), XII, 427. Crawford to Clay, February 4, 1828, says that he remembered the message as "being replete with doctrines which I hold to be unconstitutional." Clay, *Works,* Colton (ed.), IV, 192; *Niles' Register,* XXV, 190; Richmond *Enquirer,* December 28, 1825; Madison to Thomas Ritchie, December 18, 1825, Madison, *Works,* III, 506. Francis Preston Blair, Clay's supporter in the *Kentucky Argus of Western America,* on reading the message switched his allegiance to Jackson. Wiltse, *Calhoun: Nationalist,* p. 321.

[16] Even although there was a rage for internal improvements, the response of Congress to Adams' invitation was entirely lacking in the system he had called for: whether this piecemeal response was hostile, or timid, or bold, cannot be decided. Only the $2,500,000 appropriated to the upkeep and extension of the Cumberland Road—for which there were precedents—shows any decision. Exclusive of land grants and Cumberland Road appropriations, the moneys voted for small projects and for subscriptions to the stock of canal companies amounted in all to somewhere between $2,300,000 and $2,600,000. *Statement of Land Grants Made by Congress to Aid in the Construction of Railroads, Wagon Roads, Canals and Internal Improvements, Compiled from the Records of the General Land Office by Order of the Secretary of the Interior* (Washington, 1908), pp. 22–27; E. C. Nelson, "Presidential Influence in the Policy of Internal Improvements," *Iowa Journal of History and Politics,* IV (1906), 33 ff.; P. B. Trescott, "Louisville and Portland Canal Company, 1825–1874," *Mississippi Valley Historical Review,* XLIV (1960), 692; John Lalor (ed.), *Cyclopaedia of Political Science* (1883), II, 570; *Reports of Committees of the House of Representatives,* 21 Cong., 2 sess., No. 77, pp. 37–67; Sydnor, *Southern Sectionalism,* pp. 180–181; Bemis, *Adams and the Union,* p. 75; Taylor, *Transportation Revolution,* p. 21. Under Jackson, at best an equivocator on internal

dent, a truly good man, began to ask himself whether he had been abandoned, not only by Congress and the American people but also by his Creator. He began to experience those "agonizing doubts" which, he confessed in his old age, "I can neither silence nor expel."[17]

To the reader of today, the language of the summarizing paragraph seems both axiomatic and mild, suggesting only that Adams, born into another century and another complex of events, might not have been unsympathetic to the claims of social democracy. But the audience he was addressing, inside the Congress and out of it, was an audience still struggling to produce a political democracy; and his hint (for it was scarcely more than that) that he proposed to substitute an economy of conservation for an economy of waste was quite enough to set such an audience by the ears. He was, in fact, the last man to sympathize with the spendthrift dynamics of political democracy; and when he called his message a "perilous experiment," he may even have been anticipating its failure, as a necessary and inevitable compensation for his victory over Jackson in the House of Representatives.

At any rate, he sternly refrained from taking any steps which might perhaps have given him a chance to impose its views upon the country. Only the most downright use of patronage and the power of dismissal would have done that, and Adams could not bring himself to use these expedients until it was too late for them to be useful.[18] The election of 1828 was lost by default in 1825. No doubt, when Adams offered De Witt Clinton the post of Minister at London, he was acting

---

improvements, $10,582,882 was appropriated. For the most astute analysis of the rage for internal improvements and the difficulty of responding to it either with or without a constitutional amendment, see James Madison to Martin Van Buren, September 20, 1826; Van Buren Papers, LC.

[17] Brooks Adams, in Henry Adams, *Degradation*, pp. 33, 34; *Memoirs*, XI, 340–341. This position is disputed by Bemis, *Adams and the Union*, p. 106, n. 42.

[18] Toward the end, he began to compromise with his conscience: "The right must . . . yield to the expedient." *Memoirs*, VIII, 5. Possibly, as Wiltse, *Calhoun: Nationalist*, p. 327, suggests, Adams did not bother too much about what was going on behind his back. His presidential dismissals, however, according to C. R. Fish, *The Civil Service and the Patronage* (Cambridge, 1904), p. 72, amounted in all to twelve! Fish, "Removal of Officials by Presidents of the United States," American Historical Association, *Annual Report*, 1899, I, 70–72, shows that Jefferson removed in his eight years 109 presidential officers, Madison 27, and Monroe 27. J. Q. A.'s dismissals in four years were therefore about equal to Madison's and Monroe's in eight; and how different the circumstances! White, *Jeffersonians*, p. 379.

in accordance with the nonpartisan language of his Inaugural Address; and when Clinton turned down this formal offer, and the post was given to Rufus King, this was no more than an acknowledgment of the promise made to Daniel Webster.[19] To the President's friends in New York, however, such maneuvers were an outrage; and when the vacant federal judgeship in the Northern District was given to Alfred Conkling, a Clintonian, they scarcely knew whether they were standing on their heads or on their heels. "Mr. Adams is pursuing a steady course," wrote Tallmadge to Weed, "but will he succeed to keep old friends and buy up old enemies? He began by an attempt on Clinton— who sniffed at him—I suppose the price was too low. Next he selected King—a minister recalled by Jefferson for cause as the head of the Federalist Party—their candidate against Tompkins—against whom all republicans are committed on handbills to rise up against him— and who is now without influence in either party—Next comes Conklin (sic) for District Judge, a quondam federalist, now a mere page to Clinton. . . ." When Weed received this agitated and incoherent missive, he traveled to Washington, to plead the cause of New York; and in Washington the President received him with chilling politeness, whereas Henry Clay was all warmth and understanding.[20]

Clay, in fact, was conspicuously a fellow sufferer. When he warned the President that the principal customhouse officers at Philadelphia and Charleston were hostile to the administration and were appointing hostile subordinates, when he murmured that the friends of the administration were being forced to contend not only with their enemies but with the Administration as well, the only answer he received from Adams was that he saw no reason "sufficient to justify a departure from [my] principle . . . of removing no officer for merely preferring another candidate for the Presidency." Even as an elite, the administration could not survive such a principle as this. John McLean of Ohio, for example, had been retained in office in spite of his known

[19] Adams to Clinton, February 18, 1825; Clinton Papers, NYPL. For the appointment of King, see Adams, *Memoirs*, VI, 523.

[20] Tallmadge to Weed, September 3, 1825, MS., N.Y. State Lib.; Weed, *Autobiography*, pp. 177–181 (Vol. I of Harriet A. Weed [ed.], *Life of Thurlow Weed* [2 vols., New York, 1883–1884]). The anger at the appointment of Rufus King was not confined to New York. Livermore, *Twilight of Federalism*, p. 188. In De Witt Clinton's immense Diary, really an appointment book, entry for July, 1825, Clinton mentions the Kentucky New Court contempt for King; MS., NYHS.

enmity to Adams, and his extensive patronage was now being openly bestowed upon men who felt as he did. When Clay demanded Mc-Lean's removal, Adams replied that he was a notably efficient administrator, which was true; that he had committed no decisive offense, which was doubtful; and that "I will not dismiss, or drop from Executive offices, able and faithful political opponents to provide for my own partisans."[21]

To refrain from judging one's own cause in one's own favor—that certainly was becoming in a philosopher, whether "idealistic" or not; but to Clay, the supreme politician, it could only have suggested that philosophers in government must either cease to be philosophers or cease to govern. Nothing in Clay's career is more agreeable to contemplate than his gentle, courteous, and loyal relations with a President who seemed so bent on ruining himself and all who had mixed their fortunes with his.

[21] *Memoirs,* VII, 163–164, 343, 349, 364.

CHAPTER 10

George Canning's Revenge

M R. ADAMS had somehow hoped that the various features of his national program—the Department of the Interior, the roads and canals, the Patent Office, and all the rest—might be included in one "very short act, expressing in very general terms the objects committed to it."[1] How such an act could be written, or if written how it could be passed, might have baffled a far more sanguine mind than his. A sympathetic, indeed a subservient Congress was necessary, and the Nineteenth Congress was neither the one nor the other. In the election of a Speaker, it is true, the President's candidate—John W. Taylor of New York—had received a majority of two votes over three other candidates.[2] This showed (Taylor thought) that the opposition was still uncertain and divided; but it also suggested—although Taylor refrained from saying so—that Adams' control of the House was already somewhat shaky.[3] Nor was Taylor the kind of Speaker who could bring order and discipline to bear upon his fellow legislators: he was by no means a strong man, he was distrusted and disliked by the southern members, and he had never really seen eye to eye even with the Adams faction in his own state.[4] Over the Senate Adams had, from

---

[1] Bemis, *John Quincy Adams and the Union*, p. 75.
[2] *Register of Debates*, 19 Cong., 1 sess., II, Pt. I, 795. Taylor, 99; Louis McLane of Delaware, 44; John W. Campbell of Ohio, 42; Andrew Stevenson of Virginia, 5. This was on the second ballot.
[3] Taylor to Tallmadge, December 28, 1825; John W. Taylor Papers, NYHS.
[4] Taylor recommended to Adams, admittedly on an understanding with

the beginning, no real control at all. Under these circumstances, a short act, expressing the national program in very general terms, was mere fantasy; and the President, who had approached the Nineteenth Congress with such a very bold program, was left—inside as well as outside Congress—with no means of implementing it.

The program itself was not only bold, it was also vatic. It drew a picture of the contemporary scene in terms of a future which was almost, if not quite, millennial. "Man has always yearned for a moral law," the President's grandson wrote, "which should reflect the thought of a supreme, benevolent being, by whose means even-handed justice should be done. Such was the vision which Mr. Adams harbored. . . . Never since the world was made had any community been so favored as was the American by the gift of Providence of what was practically, for them, an unlimited store of wealth, which for many generations would raise them above the pressure of any competition which would be likely to engender war. The only serious problem for them to solve, therefore, was how to develop this gift on a collective, and not a competitive or selfish basis. Dominant private interests as a motor would be fatal. . . ."[5]

The problem was rather more than serious: in the 1820's, it was insoluble, indeed invisible. The lines of Mr. Adams' picture dissolved as soon as they had been drawn. As Secretary of State he had labored, both diligently and brilliantly, both as a practical man and a man of vision, to ensure the future of the Republic as it strode westward; but the Monroe Doctrine was the conceptual peak of this suggestive nationalism. Economically, the Doctrine had gone as far as it could go with the Tariff of 1824; territorially, it was still astray in the mysteries of Oregon. For the time being it had said all that could be said, and it had been accepted because of its obvious (if somewhat delusive) appeal to a traditional isolationism. Anyone who had read the democratic omens in the 1820's with any degree of prudence might have

Clinton, the very appointment of Alfred Conkling which so disgusted Tallmadge and Weed. The best Taylor could say for his candidate was: "His professional attainments are respectable, and his moral character is fair." Taylor to Adams, August 22, 1825, *ibid.*

[5] Brooks Adams in Henry Adams, *Degradation of the Democratic Dogma,* pp. 80–81. Prejudiced as Brooks Adams was against agrarian individualists, he is the more able (as here) to give a remarkable, not to to say alarming, insight into his grandfather's program.

known that the postwar nation would accept isolationism, but not in the neomercantilist form suggested by the Message of 1825.

The nationalism which followed the Peace of Ghent had to be isolationist, and was well expressed by such a foreign policy; but once Lord Liverpool and George Canning had declared their independence of the Concert of Europe (by recognizing Mexico, Colombia, and Buenos Aires in 1824), the time had come to temporize with the British Empire. A withdrawal of the "elsewhere" clause, an acceptance of British overtures as contained in their "American Trade Act" of 1822, would have been the wiser course. Could the United States afford, was it powerful enough, to act on its own?

The answer is painfully obvious, when one considers the problem of Cuba, as it presented itself to Adams and Clay in March, 1825. By then it was a matter of almost common belief that Mexico and Colombia, once they had removed all traces of Spanish rule from their own territories (an event which was predicted for the fall of 1825), hoped to invade Cuba. Even if they were disposed toward caution— which seemed more unlikely than was actually the case—would not the behavior of Ferdinand VII force them to act? For that infatuated monarch, whose regime now reposed upon a painful foundation of French bayonets, had instituted a series of raids out of Cuba, in the weird hope that they would bring his former colonists to heel.[6]

Adams and Clay were placed in a most awkward dilemma. If Mexico and Colombia actually invaded and occupied Cuba, would they be strong enough to hold the island? That was the real danger; since, if they were not strong enough, it might well be taken over by some European power more dangerous than Spain. Yet the United States could not openly invoke the no-transfer principle against Mexico and Colombia. It was anti-European; and to urge it against new *American* powers would place the United States in the most odious light. Moreover the principle rested upon a congressional resolution of 1811 which referred only to territories contiguous to the United States. If a Mexican-Colombian invasion took place, would Congress extend the principle to Cuba and sanction a military intervention in order to expel two sister republics? And would not such

---

[6] Kaufmann, *British Policy,* p. 205, points out that Mexico and Colombia replied with privateering raids into European waters, the success of which may have encouraged them to contemplate an invasion of Cuba.

a measure produce the utmost ill will in Latin America, and almost certainly provoke an international quarrel? Only a racial uprising in Cuba would justify so hazardous an enterprise.[7]

Adams proposed to deal with this potential crisis in three ways: first, by asking Mexico and Colombia to exercise patience and forbearance; second, by counseling Spain to make peace with her revolted colonies; and third, by suggesting that the Tsar Alexander and (should he refuse) Great Britain and France should bring pressure to bear upon Ferdinand VII and his advisers. Was it not obvious, he and Clay argued, that Spain, so far from winning this unhappy war, must lose both Cuba and Puerto Rico if she continued it?[8]

This policy, which proved quite abortive, only showed that the United States had lost the initiative in hemispheric affairs; and, to make matters worse, the French decided in May to make a little trouble on their own. At the end of that month, Governor Count Donzelot of Martinique furnished a convoy for Spanish troops on their way to Havana; and this suspicious action was rendered even more suspect when (on the plea of collecting a debt from Haiti) the French squadron in the Caribbean was suddenly reinforced with twenty-eight vessels. It is commonly accepted today that French commercial interests were growing most uneasy with their country's expensive and profitless occupation of Spain; that they were looking for some reestablishment of trade relations with Latin America; and that these heavy naval movements were conducted in the spirit of an Autolycus not an Alexander. In effect, they were a fishing expedition for minor and marginal advantages: no conquest of any kind was ever intended.

[7] Clay to Henry Middleton (Minister to Russia) December 26, 1826, makes it clear that the United States would intervene by force only if the Mexican and Colombian attack was so cruelly conducted as to bring on a race warfare in Cuba, with possible repercussions in our own slave states. William R. Manning (ed.), *Diplomatic Correspondence of the United States Concerning the Independence of the Latin-American Nations* (3 vols., New York, 1925), I, 265.

[8] For this policy see (1) Clay to Joel R. Poinsett, newly appointed (as a sop to Calhoun) Minister to Mexico, March 26, 1825. Manning, *Diplomatic Correspondence,* I, 229–233. (For Calhoun's proposal of an extensive reorganization of the Cabinet in his own favor, see Bemis, *Adams and the Union,* p. 56.) (2) Clay to Henry Middleton, Minister to Russia, May 10, 1825. *Diplomatic Correspondence,* I, 244 ff. Alexander's reply, long delayed, was that he could not act except in accordance with the views of Spain. *Ibid.,* III, 1875. (3) Clay to Rufus King, May 11, 1825, and to James Brown (Minister to France) May 13, 1825. *Ibid.,* I, 250–252.

To Canning, so much nearer to these events, their meaning was naturally a little obscure; and certainly a government which had prefaced its invasion of Spain in 1823 by announcing that it intended nothing more than the prevention of an epidemic of yellow fever from crossing into France could as easily mount an invasion of Cuba on the plea of collecting a debt from Haiti. He made a stern protest to Paris[9] which did produce the assurance that Donzelot would be disavowed, but the French squadron was not reduced in size.

Canning now offered the timeworn device of a joint renunciation by Great Britain, France, and the United States of any design to occupy Cuba. Such a joint renunciation could be easily evaded, nor did it bind other interested parties; but the nation that first proposed it would, had it been accepted, have seized the initiative in Latin American affairs. It was coolly turned down by Minister Rufus King, who had no instructions and, indeed, never received any. A few days later, France also declined this disingenuous and somewhat mocking overture.[10]

The doctrines of no-transfer, noncolonization, and nonintervention had, however, become for the time being purely verbal. The emergence of Latin American states with minds of their own and a disposition to transfer, colonize, and intervene, George Canning's defiance of the Concert of Europe, the failure of French policy in Spain, the imbecile persistence of Ferdinand VII and his advisers, the growing coolness of Great Britain, even Adams' unpopularity at home—all these, in their several ways, emphasized the helplessness of a great diplomat. When France still maintained her enlarged squadron in the Caribbean, Adams had no choice but to maintain an impolitic silence or utter impolitic threats. On October 25, he committed himself, and

[9] Granville to Canning, June 6, 1825; Canning to Granville, July 12, 1825. C. K. Webster (ed.), *Great Britain and the Independence of Latin America, 1812–1830* (2 vols., London, 1938), II, 183, 185. Dexter Perkins, *Monroe Doctrine,* p. 201 n. The American policy at this point only permitted a mild remonstrance: see esp. Brown to Clay, July 15. Manning, *Diplomatic Correspondence,* II, 1412–1416.

[10] Clay to King: "I am not . . . now ready to communicate to you the instructions of the President," May 10, 1825. *Senate Docs.,* 22 Cong., 1 sess., III, No. 132, pp. 2–3. Canning to King, July 28, August 17, 1825. Manning, *Diplomatic Correspondence,* III, 1553, 1560. King to Canning, August 24, 1825. Webster, *Great Britain and Latin America,* II, 526. Granville to Canning, August 29, 1825. *Ibid.,* II, 196.

Clay dispatched to Minister Brown in Paris a most uncompromising discourse, which Brown was to communicate to the French government. His government, said Clay, expected in the future to be given due warning before France reinforced her Caribbean fleet, and he added that the United States would never consent to the occupation of Cuba "by any other power than Spain under any contingency whatsoever."[11]

A copy was transmitted to Canning, who read it with delight.[12] He was now invited by Clay, through King, to issue a similar warning to the French government. He replied, with a gleeful sarcasm not lacking in vulgarity, that he had already done this in the summer and saw no reason to repeat himself "at the suggestion of a third power, and as subsidiary to the declarations of that power."[13] He wished to show (1) that he could handle France quite on his own and (2) that the United States was inspired by self-interest, not by any friendship to the Latin American states. Could not the words "any other power than Spain" be made to apply directly to Mexico and Colombia? In this latter respect, Adams and Clay certainly gave him such assistance as was in their power. On December 20, Clay sent identical notes to Mexico and Colombia asking for a suspension of their plans against Cuba. The British Minister in Washington, Charles Vaughan, was so little in Canning's confidence that he innocently reported that he had approved (fortunately for him not in writing) the two notes. He received a tremendous wigging, in the course of which Canning revealed that, suspicious though he was of the United States, he no longer feared its intervention. "If they think [he wrote] that particular interests of their own require that a certain operation of war should not be undertaken by one of the belligerents, it is a question, and a very nice one for them, how they will prevent the undertaking of it." That was indeed the question.[14]

[11] Clay to Brown, October 25, 1825. Manning, *Diplomatic Correspondence,* I, 260–261.

[12] "It is as pert a paper," he said, "as a French Minister can wish to hear." Canning to Granville, December 28, 1825. Stapleton, *Canning and His Friends,* p. 609. Perkins, *Monroe Doctrine,* p. 202, shows that by October, 1825, Canning had lost all fear of French designs upon Cuba.

[13] King to Canning, January 9, 1826; Canning to King, January 13, 1826. Webster, *Great Britain and Latin America,* II, 538, 540–41.

[14] Logan, *No-Transfer,* p. 184; Kaufmann, *British Policy,* p. 210; W. R. Manning, *Early Diplomatic Relations Between the United States and Mexico*

As it turned out, both Adams and Canning had overestimated the belligerence of Colombia and Mexico. These two countries really preferred to submit their case to a congress or conference which was to meet in Panama, and they put out feelers to the United States with regard to a possible attendance at this gathering. The Mexican note, delivered on November 3, made a fairly pointed reference to the principles of the Monroe Doctrine as a protection against European interference in Latin America. The Colombian note, delivered on November 2, suggested that the United States might assist in a discussion of the following topics: the clarification of international law, the possibilities of an inter-American alliance based upon Monroe's noncolonization principle, the abolition of the slave trade, and the attitude to be adopted towards the black republic of Haiti.[15] It might have seemed from these notes that the United States had, after all, not lost the initiative; but Colombia hinted, with an ominous tact, that there were some affairs to be discussed which would be of interest only to Latin American belligerents. It was this hint which prompted Adams and Clay, more than a month later, to send their ambiguous request for a suspension of plans against Cuba. In his First Annual Message, however, Adams had already referred to the coming congress, and had said that ministers would be commissioned in order to confer at Panama upon subjects not incompatible with the neutrality of the United States.[16] On December 26, he submitted to the Senate the names of Richard C. Anderson of Kentucky and John Sergeant of Pennsylvania as Envoys Extraordinary and Ministers Plenipotentiary to the Assembly of American Nations; and in his accompanying message he spoke only of commercial relations and fraternal friendship. The United States, he said, would take no part in deliberations of a belligerent character, nor would it contract any alliances.[17]

As a recent study puts it, with admirable dryness, "to those who . . . have been persuaded . . . that true democracy implies legislative

---

(Baltimore, 1916), p. 142; Clay to José María Salazar, December 20, 1825, Manning, *Diplomatic Correspondence*, I, 263; Vaughan to Canning, December 21, 1825; Canning to Vaughan, February 6, 1826, Webster, *Diplomatic Correspondence*, II, 536, 543.

[15] Bemis, *Adams and Foreign Policy*, pp. 546–547; *American State Papers, Foreign Relations*, V, 835–839. Adams, *Memoirs*, VI, 542.

[16] Richardson, *Messages and Papers*, II, 302.

[17] *Ibid.*, II, 318–320.

direction of foreign affairs, the debates on the mission to Panama should be instructive."[18] In the Nineteenth (as in the Twentieth) Congress the "friends" of Adams, Jackson, Calhoun, and Crawford, the *disjecta membra* of the Era of Good Feelings, together with a handful of surviving and hopeful Federalists, were rearranging their agreements and differences into some semblance of a new two-party system. To the friends of the administration the Panama issue was, on the whole, an embarrassment. To its enemies, with a few exceptions, Panama was a chance to make trouble. In the Senate, for example, the opposition raised the ghost of that defunct alliance between northern and southern democrats, supported by a New York-Pennsylvania-Virginia axis, which had brought in Jefferson in 1800; and while the northern element in this still somewhat spectral combination made a great play with the no-transfer principle, protesting that it should have been uttered with far more vigor against both Europe *and* Latin America, the southern faction saw nothing but emancipation in the objectives of the Panama meeting, and heaped a variety of insults upon the Latin Americans.[19] Against this extremely damaging and quite irrelevant criticism, the friends of the administration had little to offer but expostulations and votes.

Eventually, on March 14, 1826, the Senate consented to the nominations of Richard C. Anderson (27 to 17) and of John Sergeant (28 to 18) as Envoys Extraordinary and Ministers Plenipotentiary to the Assembly of American Nations.[20] On April 22, the House, where Adams could still count upon a substantial if lukewarm majority, agreed to appropriate the $40,000 necessary to sustain their mission, and did so by a vote of 134 to 60.[21]

Adams had been, from the beginning, acutely aware of the perils that lurked in the invitations of Mexico and Colombia, with their

[18] Logan, *No-Transfer*, p. 188.

[19] *Ibid.*, p. 190, where the opposition's no-transfer argument is shown to be disingenuous. Cf. Carl Schurz, *Life of Henry Clay* (2 vols., Boston, 1887), I, 273. For Southern attacks on Latin Americans, see *Register of Debates,* 19 Cong., 1 sess., II, Pt. 1, pp. 112, 166, 208, and especially 290 ("an ignorant and vicious people": White of Tennessee); also 150 for the characterization of John Sergeant as "an acknowledged abolitionist." Sergeant was a Federalist, a protectionist, and had been an antislavery leader in the Missouri Debates: a political, but not a tactful choice.

[20] *Register of Debates in Congress,* 19 Cong., 1 sess., II, Pt. 1, p. 150.

[21] *Ibid.*, Pt. 2, p. 2514.

suggestion of a multilateral alliance. In his message to the House of March 15, 1826 (requesting the appropriation of $40,000), he made it clear that he was not looking for confederates but for converts. He hoped that the South Americans at Panama might be persuaded to endorse his high neutralist concept of the freedom of the seas, and perhaps his plans for a full commercial reciprocity; and even here his hopes seemed not excessive.[22]

But in the midst of this cautious discourse he committed himself to language that was nothing if not bold. He had studied the Farewell Address with minute and devoted attention; and in his message of March 15, he wished to remind the House that Washington had not rested his case upon a simple *caveat* against entangling alliances and political connections. There was nothing in the Address to preclude a friendly understanding with the Latin American states; there had been no Latin American states when the Address was written. Did not the counsel of Washington, "like all the counsels of wisdom," accept the circumstances prevailing at the time? But did it not also accept the principle of change? Had not Washington predicted (said Adams) that

by our union and rapid growth, with an efficient Government, the period was not far distant when we might defy material injury from external annoyance; when we may take such an attitude as will cause our neutrality to be respected, and, with reference to belligerent nations, might choose peace or war, as our interests, guided by justice should counsel. . . .[23] We were then the only independent nation of this hemisphere, and we were surrounded by European colonies, with the greater part of which we had no more intercourse than with the inhabitants of another planet. These colonies have now been transformed into eight independent states, extending to our very borders, seven of them Republics like ourselves, with whom we have an immensely growing commercial and *must* have and have already important political connections; with reference to whom our situation is neither distant nor detached. . . .[24]

[22] Richardson, *Messages and Papers*, II, 329–340. One should add that his allusion to Haïti, pp. 335–336, was caution itself.

[23] Richardson, *Messages and Papers*, I, 222. (For the Hamiltonian authorship of this passage, see Felix Gilbert, *To the Farewell Address* [Princeton, 1961], pp. 131–134; and for J.Q.A.'s possible influence on the Address see S. F. Bemis, "John Quincy Adams and George Washington," *Massachusetts Historical Society Proceedings*, LXVII [1945], 365–84.)

[24] *Messages and Papers*, II, 337–338.

Since there were many to whom these political connections were either invisible or undesirable, this language was certainly incautious; but the President now took a position which, if slightly more conventional, was even more intrepid.

The rapidity of our growth [he continued] and the consequent increase of our strength, has more than realized the anticipations of this admirable political legacy. Thirty years have nearly elapsed since it was written, and in the interval our population, our wealth, our territorial extension, our power—physical and moral—have nearly tripled. Reasoning upon this state of things from the sound and judicious principles of Washington, must we not say that the period he predicted as then not far off has arrived; that *America* has a set of primary interests which have none or a remote relation to Europe; that the interference of Europe, therefore, in these concerns should be spontaneously withheld by her upon the same principles that we have never interfered with hers, and that if she should interfere, as she may, by measures which have a great and dangerous recoil upon ourselves, we might be called in defense of our own altars and firesides to take an attitude which would cause our neutrality to be respected, and choose peace or war as our interest, guided by justice, should counsel.

The acceptance of this invitation [to Panama] therefore, far from conflicting with the counsel of the policy of Washington, is directly deducible from and conformable to it. Nor is it less conformable to the views of my immediate predecessor as declared in his annual message to Congress of the 2d. December, 1823. . . .[25]

It was a peculiarity of Adams' thinking that he believed he could measure the growth of morality; and while we can only lament that he has not bequeathed to posterity his means of performing so difficult a feat, we can be fairly sure that his immediate audience was not impressed by it. Indeed, a ratio of increase of nearly three to one in more material assets—population, wealth, territorial extension—could not have reassured a peaceable House and nation to the extent of agreeing with the President that the period predicted by Washington had at length arrived. None the less, Adams had returned to a position which the most isolationist among his hearers could at any rate understand; for they at least would say that if his words were deducible from the Farewell Address, then "America" could not possibly be stretched into meaning "the Americas," and his reference to political

25 *Ibid.,* p. 338.

connections with the Latin American states had been canceled as soon as made. What the Minister of Colombia would think when he read Adams' words may easily be guessed: the President's language could only have implied that the United States, if it acted to restrain Europe, would act unilaterally, in accordance with its own interests and sense of justice. And it may well be true that the foreign policy of Adams, so well constructed for continental purposes, was by no means adjusted to hemispheric occasions.

What is even more to the point, however, is the effect which this message undoubtedly had upon the House. Adams had deliberately wedded the Farewell Address to the Monroe Doctrine: that is to say, he had given the Doctrine almost the status of public law. He was attempting to raise it into a system. In the debates that followed, no friend of the administration, and few of its enemies, cared to attack the Monroe Doctrine. Its generalizations were grave and noble, but they had been designed to meet an immediate crisis; they could be revived or not as events demanded; and no one was quite ready to accept them as a permanent pledge of future action. We are left wondering why Adams was so ready to give them this bold and (at the time) exceptional interpretation.[26]

The historian should hesitate before putting into Adams' words meanings for which he has offered no certain evidence, but it does seem that the operative phrase in the Farewell Address was, for him, "efficient government." He had offered the nation an efficient government in his First Annual Message; and this efficient government, designed to create a self-sustaining continental bastion, was to approach the outer world with commercial reciprocity, the freedom of the seas, and a unilateral interpretation of the Monroe Doctrine.[27] In this way it could persuade the outer world to act peaceably; or, conversely, could cause its neutrality to be respected, at any time, by going to war. Since the nation did not accept his idea of efficient government,

[26] For an analysis of this debate, see Perkins, *Monroe Doctrine,* Chap. VI.

[27] The advances of five of the new states—Chile, Colombia, Brazil, Mexico, and the United Provinces—either for actual alliance or for provisional assistance were declined in language that must have seemed very chilling. Bemis, *Latin American Policy,* p. 68. Adams to José María Salazar, August 6, 1824, and Clay to John M. Forbes, chargé d'affaires at Buenos Aires, January 3, 1828 —in Manning, *Diplomatic Correspondence,* I, 224–226, 292—testify to this rejection of a multilateral Doctrine.

and (as it transpired at Panama) Latin America did not appear to be much taken with his concepts of maritime law, he must be said to have crammed down his contemporaries' throats a somewhat indigestible slice of futurity. Always a man of vision, he had now become a visionary; and the fate of visionaries in high places is rarely a happy one. In short, an addiction to "perilous experiments" had made it impossible for this honest man to speak, at this interesting moment, in such suitably equivocal terms as would oblige his audience, and not himself, to swallow his words.

As for the Panama Congress, it was doomed from the start.[28] Of the American nations invited only Colombia, Mexico, Peru, and Guatemala sent delegates. The ministers of the United States were *sent,* in so far as congressional appropriations could do it, but they never appeared. The Congress was to meet in June, 1826; and John Sergeant, who knew something about Panamanian summers, absolutely declined to venture his life upon the Isthmus during the hot months. The brilliant and charming Richard Anderson, on the other hand, came down from Bogotá; but he was slain by some tropical disease as his steamboat lay grounded at Cartagena.[29]

It was a tragic and useless sacrifice. One of the Peruvian delegates announced in the press: "This will probably be the last attempt to ascertain whether Mankind can be happy. Companions! The field of glory is before us. Our names are about to be written either in immortal praise or in eternal opprobrium."[30] But fever haunted the little city where this feast of words was spread before the delegates; and

[28] Whether Simon Bolívar was opposed to the presence of the United States or favored it in the hopes of creating "an all-inclusive multilateral pact in support of Non-Colonization" is discussed in Bemis, *Adams and Foreign Policy,* p. 549 and Logan, *No Transfer,* p. 186.

[29] Clay to Sergeant, May 5, 11, 1826; Sergeant to Clay, May 8, 13, 1826. Additional instructions to Anderson gave him the option of proceeding to Panama at once or sending a note there to suggest a meeting in some more salubrious spot; Clay to Anderson, May 20, 1826. These instructions arrived too late. All cited in Bemis, *Adams and Foreign Policy,* pp. 557–558. The administration's tolerance of Sergeant's defection (cf. Adams, *Memoirs,* VII, 126–127), and its willingness to have Anderson stay in Bogotá, suggest that—as a result of the Senate and House debates and because of Adams' latent but controlling isolationism—it had grown cool to the Panama Congress even before it opened in June.

[30] H. W. V. Temperley, "The Later American Policy of George Canning," *American Historical Review,* XI (1906), 786.

the delegates, like the guests at another haunted banquet, stayed not upon the order of their going. Having concocted, in some haste, four treaties for mutual defense and a common army, and having agreed to meet again in Tucubaya when their respective governments had ratified their work, they went their ways. Only the government of Colombia bothered to ratify anything.

The single personage to gain any satisfaction out of these abortive proceedings was a man who had been invited in the capacity of an observer, not a participant. He was Edward J. Dawkins, the agent of George Canning. According to his instructions, he was to warn the delegates of Great Britain's opposition to any project that would place the United States at the head of an American confederacy; and he was also to suggest that Great Britain's principles of maritime law— paper blockades, the right of search, free ships do *not* make free goods, a loose definition of "contraband," and all the rest—would be of more service to Latin America than the idealism of Mr. Adams' freedom of the seas. In other words, he was to make what mischief he could.[31] He was, it is true, unable to persuade the delegates to assent to British maritime law; but then he noted with satisfaction that the Mexicans and Peruvians would have nothing to do with the freedom of the seas, while the Guatemalans were divided. And when it came to reciting the opprobrious speeches of American senators, or drawing attention to the marked discrepancy between Adams' Message to the House and the aspirations of the Congress of Panama, or proving that Great Britain had persistently endeavored to reconcile Ferdinand VII to the new states[32]—here Mr. Dawkins was very successful indeed. The climax came when he repeated to Pedro Gual of Colombia the language of his instructions from Canning: "We have uniformly refused to join with the United States in remonstrating with Mexico and Colombia

[31] J. Fred Rippy, *Rivalry of the United States and Great Britain over Latin America* (Baltimore, 1929), p. 229; Webster, *Diplomatic Correspondence,* II, 403–409.

[32] Minister Everett had written to Clay from Madrid a report that Great Britain had no desire to see the war ended, and this imprudent dispatch had been given a wide circulation in the United States. Everett to Clay, October 20, 1825; *Sen. Docs.* No. 68, 19 Cong., 1 sess., Ser. 127, pp. 84–85. Dawkins showed Pedro Gual of Colombia a set of British dispatches between London and Madrid, which proved just the opposite. Dawkins to Canning, July 7, 1826; Webster, *Diplomatic Correspondence,* I, 413–420.

against the supposed intention [to invade Cuba]. We should indeed regret it, but we arrogate to ourselves no right to control the military operations of one belligerent against another."

Thus Mr. Dawkins became the velvet glove, concealing, not exactly a mailed fist, but a mailed handshake—the friendly, inexorable grip of ready loans and cheap manufactures. British trade with Latin America (Cuba excepted) was at least three times greater than that of the United States; and with Cuba removed from the political scene, as it effectually was at Panama, British commercial predominance was complete. Already the heiress of imperial Spain, but asking for no political ties or exclusive privileges, Great Britain was to enjoy this predominance for many years. Except for the fact that a refusal to attend the Congress would have been undiplomatic, the administration's Panama diplomacy had merely emphasized its isolation: not only abroad, but also and more so at home.

One incident will serve to illustrate this. The chief contriver of opposition in the Senate was Martin Van Buren, still a Crawford Radical. In February, 1826, he had made himself responsible for two mischievous and apparently aimless resolutions, requesting the President to state whether all documents submitted by him on the Panama mission might be made public, or only a portion of them; and if only a portion, *which* portion.[33] A courteous reply would have exposed Van Buren; but the President, sorely tempted, could not refrain from using his sharp pen. "I deem it my indispensable duty," he wrote, "to leave to the Senate itself the decision of a question, involving a departure hitherto, as I am informed, without example . . . and upon the motives for which, not being informed of them, I do not feel myself competent to decide."[34] There were angry protests, barely subdued by administration votes.[35] And then John Randolph of Roanoke, who had recently been forced to transfer his peculiar gifts from

[33] Resolutions agreed to by 23–20 on February 15, 1826; *Register of Debates,* 19 Cong., 1 sess., II, Pt. 1, p. 142.

[34] Richardson, *Messages and Papers,* II, 327, February 16, 1826. The "departure" was from the usage of making all communications on Executive business confidential.

[35] Rowan of Kentucky, Woodbury of New Hampshire, and Holmes of Maine submitted resolutions chiding the President; they were negatived by votes of 24 to 19 and 24 to 20. *Register of Debates,* 19 Cong., 1 sess., II, Pt. 1, pp. 143–146.

the House to the Senate, delivered, on March 30, one of the strangest of all his speeches.[36]

It began appropriately enough with the words: "Our name is Legion." And, with his shrill voice, his slim and boyish figure, his wrinkled and desiccated face, the virulence of his invective, the violence of his gestures, Randolph was indeed beginning to resemble not so much a man possessed as a demon in need of dispossession. He had long hated the Adams family, and the centralizing policies of the fifth President seemed to him even more dreadful than the "monarchism" of the second. "The cub," he said, "is a greater bear than the old one."[37] In his speech of March 30, he appeared to be verging upon that madness of which, in fact, he stood in constant fear. It was an immense rambling oration, full of dire insinuations, which at length came to a head in the monstrous suggestion that the Mexican and Colombian invitations had been either forged or doctored by Mr. Clay in the State Department! Even then, he said, he would not have opposed the President's right to a confidential communication with the Senate, if the President had not impugned the Senate's motives.

That moment [he shrilled] did I put, like Hannibal, my hand on the altar and swear eternal enmity against him and his politically. . . . Here I throw the gauntlet to him and the bravest of his compeers to come forward and defend these miserable dirty words: "Involving a departure, hitherto, as I am informed, without example, from that usage, and upon the motives for which, not being informed of them, I do not feel myself competent to decide." Amiable modesty! . . . After twenty-six hours exertion, it was time to give in. I was defeated, horse, foot and dragoons—cut up—and clean broke down—by the coalition of Blifil and Black George—by the combination, unheard of till then, of the puritan with the blackleg.[38]

Mr. Clay at once challenged Randolph to a duel; the Virginian replied "in superlatively decorous language"; and the two met on

[36] This speech of March 30 is in *ibid.*, pp. 390–401.

[37] Henry Adams, *John Randolph* (Boston, 1882), pp. 19, 26; William Cabell Bruce, *John Randolph of Roanoke* (2 vols., New York, 1922), I, 74; H. A. Garland, *The Life of John Randolph* (2 vols., New York, 1850), II, 248.

[38] A week before this speech, he had told Josiah Quincy: "There are Blifil and Black George characters in every age." Josiah Quincy, *Figures of the Past,* M. A. de W. Howe, ed. (Boston, 1833), p. 180. Any reader of *Tom Jones* would agree, however, that Black George is more agreeable than Blifil. So Clay was, to Randolph, less hateful than Adams.

April 8. After a first and harmless exchange of shots, Clay put a bullet through the skirts of Randolph's long white flannel overcoat, and Randolph, firing into the air, hurried forward to shake his opponent's hand. "You owe me a coat, Mr. Clay," he said. How true, but then he owed Mr. Clay a reputation. "The puritan . . . the blackleg" were long remembered.[39]

Mr. Adams, too, joined in this unseemly dispute. Next to Van Buren, Calhoun was the chief contriver of opposition; and on May 1 an article appeared in the Washington *National Journal,* an Adams newspaper, attacking the Vice-President for his silence during Randolph's libelous speech. (Calhoun had already explained that he was not a member of the Senate, but only its presiding officer, and that senators alone could call a senator to order.) The article was signed "Patrick Henry," but the style was unmistakable. Calhoun replied with a sarcastic piece signed "Onslow," which was published in the *Intelligencer* on May 20; and "Patrick Henry" retorted with a second gasconade in the *National Journal* on June 7. Thus the public, already instructed in high-toned politics by the Clay-Randolph duel, was given an even more edifying lesson in this exacting art by the President and Vice-President of the United States, as they blazed away at each other in the public newspapers.[40] On the whole, even before the Panama Congress met, the administration's Panama policy may be said to have gone up in smoke.

This policy was, when all is said, little more than a skirmish on the edge of a larger and more significant battle. This battle had been already joined as early as 1823, when Richard Rush opened a general negotiation with Stratford Canning and William Huskisson in London. A slave-trade convention, signed on March 13, 1824, came to nothing because of crippling amendments in the United States Senate; discussions of the northeast boundary between Maine and New Brunswick and the northwest boundary between the Rockies and the Pacific were equally futile. The "northwest angle of Nova Scotia" and the "northwesternmost head of the Connecticut River" remained as obscure as they had been in 1783; the Oregon country was left open to citizens of both nations.[41] Rush then turned to the freedom of the

[39] Benton, *Thirty Years View,* I, 71–77; Clark, *John Quincy Adams,* p. 245.
[40] Wiltse, *Calhoun: Nationalist,* pp. 333–334.
[41] Bemis, *Adams and Foreign Policy,* pp. 475–476, 521–522, 528. Van

seas, which, in the mind of Secretary Adams, had become a humane and noble concept. He had engrafted the traditional American theories ("free ships, free goods," no impressment, no paper blockades, severely limited definitions of "contraband") upon a grander stock—he was asking that eventually all privateering should be abolished and that all property on the seas, neutral or belligerent, should be exempt from capture by public cruisers.[42] Was it, however, at all likely that the world's greatest sea power would regard this peaceful system as anything but a challenge?

And so at last negotiations drifted down to an explicit issue, the West Indian trade itself. Stratford Canning and William Huskisson were quite ready to offer a reciprocal suspension of duties, if the Americans would abandon their claim to equal trade—a reasonable solution, and one quite in keeping with the friendly spirit of the British Act of 1822. But neither Rush nor his successor, Rufus King, was authorized to agree to it. Adams, it seems, was counting upon the pressure of West Indian interests in Parliament to force the British government's hand. An indirect supply through the French, Danish, and Swedish islands would have been attacked as awkward, unnatural, and expensive. So far he had reasoned correctly: what he appears not to have perceived is that British statesmen were less colonially minded than they had been.[43] Moreover, West Indian slave labor was beginning to trouble the utilitarian conscience.[44] India and Canada, the termini of the Empire, were of a different order: the former was already a great market for cheap cotton goods;[45] the latter was treasured for her lumber, fish, and furs, and a convinced imperialist like Can-

---

Alstyne, *Rising American Empire,* p. 97, shows that Canning had some hopes that the Hudson's Bay Company, as it trapped Oregon, would make that country less "open" to citizens of the United States. Canning's great objective was, of course, the whole Columbia River basin.

[42] Cf. "John Quincy Adams' Project of a Convention for Regulating the Principles of Commercial and Maritime Neutrality." Bemis, *Adams and Foreign Policy,* App. 3. John G. C. Hutchins, "The American Maritime Industries and Public Policy," *Harvard Economic Studies,* LXXXI (1941), 253.

[43] Woodward, *Age of Reform,* p. 350.

[44] John Morley, *The Life of William Ewart Gladstone* (3 vols., London, 1909), I, 22 ff.

[45] Hansard, 2 ser., XII, 1198: statement of March 25, 1825, showing that British cotton goods were by that time underselling native manufactures in India.

ning could even dream of the Columbia River and the trade to China.[46] But an expanding industrial economy, with a taste for free trade, and its future all before it, is not given to "colonialism"; and it may well be that when Adams believed that Lord Liverpool's government would yield on the West Indies trade, he had miscalculated the importance of the West Indies to Lord Liverpool's government.

In fact, the system of colonial preferences had by now become less responsive to planting than to shipping interests, and was not to be sacrificed to the American carrying trade. In 1818 and 1820, the American navigation laws had made a great impression upon the British, as they struggled to adjust themselves to peace. But much had happened since then. On the British side, there had been the parliamentary attack upon their own navigation laws, the friendly American Trade Act of 1822, the great free trade budgets of 1822 and 1823, and Canning's brief "flirtation" with the United States. And how had the Americans answered? With the "elsewhere" Act of 1823, the Monroe Doctrine, the crippling of the Slave Trade Convention, and the Tariff of 1824. It was time for the British to strike back.[47]

The first blow was struck on June 27, 1825, when an act was passed for "further regulating the trade of His Majesty's possessions in America and the West Indies, and for warehousing goods therein."[48] It invited the countries of Europe, Africa, and western Asia to compete with the United States in the West Indies, and established five free warehousing ports which would take from the United States some part of its trade with South America. Obviously the chief purpose of this act was to suggest that the British West Indies could be supplied from sources other than the United States. Its secondary purpose was to confront the Monroe Doctrine (which threatened political hegemony)

[46] Van Alstyne, *Rising American Empire,* p. 98, points out that neither Canning nor Adams had any idea of the expansionist potential of the small, underpopulated, and economically retarded Canadian colonies on the St. Lawrence; but Canning had a very keen sense of their value as a producer of naval stores, etc. Canning's earlier dream of the Columbia as an artery for trade with China had been abandoned as impractical long before the Oregon question became acute in the administration of Polk. See Merk, "British Government Propaganda and the Oregon Treaty," *American Historical Review,* XL (1935), 38 ff.

[47] For Lord Liverpool's hostility at this time, see Brock, *Liberal Toryism,* p. 111, and Benns, *American Struggle,* p. 105.

[48] 6 Geo. IV, c. 73.

with a commercial hegemony in Latin America, something more easily accomplished at the Congress of Panama. It was not a strong act, and merely shows that the diplomacy of Canning was not independent.

On July 5, 1825, there followed three more acts, which almost defied analysis,[49] but which—where they did not simply testify to the fearful prolixity of Admiralty lawyers—had a convulsive but not *quite* inscrutable relation to early nineteenth-century liberalism.

The first of these, "An Act to regulate the trade of the British possessions abroad," was simply a repetition of the Act of June 27, except for its fourth section, in which a distinction was made between nations with colonies and nations without them, the latter being required to place the commerce and navigation of the United Kingdom on the footing of "most favored nation" in its ports.[50] The United States was the only such nation having any considerable trade with British possessions, so that the fourth section—though not so demanding as the American "elsewhere" clause—must be considered a direct blow at President Adams. Its preamble, however, appeared to be very liberal as regards the export trade between British colonies and European countries.

The second act of July 5, "An Act for the encouragement of British shipping and navigation," was more discouraging than otherwise, since its effort to explain what should be the law of navigation for the British Empire was too imprecise to be useful.[51] Only in its eleventh section did it condescend to speak clearly: here it forbade the *importation* of goods into British possessions in Africa, Asia, or America in foreign ships, unless these ships were of the country of which the goods were the produce and from which they were imported. This was a hit at the American carrying trade, and also a modification of the liberalism displayed in the preamble to the first Act of July 5.

The third Act of this memorable day, "An Act to repeal the several laws relating to the Customs,"[52] did away with some 450 statutes on

[49] So Gallatin to Clay, October 27, 1826. *Sen. Docs., 22* Cong., 1 sess., III, No. 132, pp. 14–15.

[50] 6 Geo. IV, c. 114. Since the United States had different arrangements with different countries—commercial treaties as well as separate and reciprocal acts —it would have been difficult to place Great Britain upon this footing. Benns, *American Struggle,* pp. 109, 111.

[51] 6 Geo. IV, c. 109.

[52] 6 Geo. IV, c. 105.

customs and navigation, dating back as far as the reign of Richard II. This harmless and rather antiquarian work was, however, violently interrupted at the 359th section, where the Act of June 24, 1822—the act which had been so favorable to the United States—was rudely repealed. Since this third act of July 5 was to come into force on July 25, 1826, United States shipping would be banned from the West Indies after that date! Unless it had already been banned by the first act of July 5, which was to come into force on January 6.

The historian who endeavors to make sense out of this heaving confusion must fall short of an exact explanation; but, on the assumption that parliamentary statutes are not entirely frivolous or futile, one might suggest that an effort to liberalize the navigation laws had somehow collided with a determination to use these laws illiberally against the United State, as a punishment for its stubbornness during the negotiations of 1824. In other words here was a response to Adams' policy of protectionism at home and commercial reciprocity abroad.[53]

When the four acts of June 27 and July 5 (never officially communicated) were read and studied in Washington, it was assumed that the reprisals which they appeared to threaten would be withdrawn by order in council.[54] But the British remained silent. In April the Senate began to complain that the grain-growing states were being victimized by the administration's obstinacy, and these complaints were being coupled with eulogies of Mr. Huskisson for "opening the eyes of the world to the advantages of a free trade."[55] At this the protectionist administration took counsel, and it was at length agreed—possibly through the pressure of Henry Clay—that the word "elsewhere" must be offered up as a sacrifice to Ceres.[56] The sacrifice was painful, needful, democratic, enlightened, and too late. It was entrusted to Albert Gallatin, who was induced to take Rufus King's place in London. He was instructed to accept what the British had asked in 1824—a reciprocal suspension of alien and discriminatory duties, and a withdrawal of the claim to equal trading rights with

[53] I am deeply indebted to F. Lee Benns' admirable monograph for guidance through this opaque legislation, but even Benns has not quite elucidated it. The suggestion of a collision between a liberalizing and a punitive policy is my own.
[54] Since the Act of June 27 was repealed on May 26, 1826—7 Geo. IV, c. 648—it is probable that the British were still open to offers on that date.
[55] *Register of Debates*, 19 Cong., 1 sess., II, Pt. 1, pp. 576, 579.
[56] Adams, *Memoirs*, VI, 540.

Great Britain and her Empire in the West Indies.[57] Gallatin, one of
the most brilliant negotiators in American history, loyally set out on
this thankless task, arrived in England in August, 1826, and was at
once greeted with an order in council interdicting trade in United
States vessels with all British colonies except those in North America,
and with these the trade, whether inland or seaborne, was subjected
to a heavy countervailing duty. "It was an unhappy coincidence," said
George Canning. It was nothing of the sort. The British government
explained that it had shown a "liberal disposition" toward the United
States, and had been much put out by an obstinate refusal to recipro-
cate; and that it had issued its well-timed order with great reluctance.[58] Nor was Gallatin permitted simply to extract the sting from
the word "elsewhere"; Canning now declared that he would not resume the negotiations where Rush and King had left them unless the
Congress first humiliated the administration by repealing the Act of
1823.[59]

No doubt the British would have behaved less vengefully if there
had not been a severe financial panic in the winter of 1825–26. A
gradual return of prosperity after 1822, a sharp rise in prices between
1824 and 1825, overtrading, timid banking, all contributed to this
brief but spectacular collapse.[60] The shipping interest, which had
grossly extended its operations, now turned all its fury upon the government, whose relaxation of the navigation laws was described as
"a qualification . . . for entry into Bedlam."[61] Liberal Toryism never
recovered from this blow, and Huskisson at the Board of Trade was
particularly hard hit. In the end he bowed to the storm and, taking
refuge behind the August order in council, the only government measure of which anyone seemed to approve, he uttered an oblique but

[57] American State Papers, Foreign Relations, VI, 248, 262.

[58] Adams, Memoirs, VII, 150; Bemis, Adams and the Union, p. 122.

[59] Benns, American Struggle, pp. 119, 122; Gallatin to Clay, August 19, 1926,
Sen. Docs., 22 Cong., 1 sess., III, No. 132, p. 6. For Clay's lack of information
on the Northeast boundary question, see Clay to Gallatin, private, June 21,
1826; Gallatin Papers, NYHS. On July 5 Adams directed him to leave Gallatin
"a large measure of discretion." Bemis, Adams and Foreign Policy, p. 476. For
the Oregon question, like the Northeast question left undecided, see American
State Papers, Foreign Relations, VI, 650 ff.

[60] Brooks Adams, The Law of Civilization and Decay (1934 ed.), p. 312.
Lord Overstone, Tracts and Other Publications (London, 1858), p. 325.

[61] Hansard, 2 ser., XVII, 599, 619.

significant tirade. It was not insincere, at that. Noncolonization and the Tariff of 1824 had, in turn, profoundly distressed him. He had perceived, however dimly or partially, the menace of Adams' neo-mercantilist system; and at the end of a long speech defending the reduction of tariff schedules, he admitted that a new and "formidable" rival had just arisen in America's (protected) textile industry, and that only by admitting raw materials as cheaply as possible into English ports could this rival be crushed.[62] His language was no doubt exaggerated, but it was extremely important. Not much attention has been paid to it, either in his own time, or in ours.

Its importance, needless to say, does not really lie in its reference to the Tariff of 1824 or to any predictable and stiffer schedules. What really matters is that the whole quarrelsome Anglo-American world, at this moment, had a tendency to concur in at least one sentiment—and that was a suspicion of the economic nationalism of Mr. Adams. If Huskisson was losing allies to the shipping interests in the Commons, he was beginning to gain them among the opposition in the Nineteenth Congress.

According to the Act of 1823, Adams might have issued a retaliatory interdict upon British shipping: he preferred instead to seek support in the Congress. The Senate Committee on Commerce, February 21, 1827, duly reported a bill designed to make the British recede from their order. It was attacked as not conciliatory, as not in accord with the friendly British Act of 1822, which—said Smith of Maryland— "gave us all that we wanted." The Maryland senator insinuated that Monroe's administration had drafted the Act of 1823 by stealth and imposed it on the Senate without an explanation. "Few of us understood what was the real meaning of the word 'elsewhere.' "[63] The Senate received with complacency this reflection upon its intelligence, and on February 24, 29 to 19, accepted Smith's humiliating amendment to the committee's bill.[64] "You may rest assured," wrote Martin

---

[62] *Ibid.,* pp. 620 ff.; speech of May 7, 1827. The temperate Gallatin wrote: "He has been compelled, on account of the opposition of the shipping interests, to take in some respects, some retrograde steps." Gallatin to Clay, July 20, 1827; *Sen. Docs.,* 22 Cong., 1 sess., III, No. 132, p. 25.

[63] *Register of Debates,* 19 Cong., 1 sess., III, 399–402.

[64] *Ibid.,* pp. 403–417.

Van Buren, "that Mr. Adams' re-election is out of the question."[65]

One can, however, detect in the debate upon the committee's bill and the Smith amendment a note of genuine bewilderment. The British proposals in 1822 had been more than reasonable; why then had Adams, as Secretary and President, refused to entertain them? His enemies in the Senate scarcely deigned to look for an answer and his friends could never find one. Not being privy to his Diary, how could they tell that all this was part of a "perilous experiment" that had failed—and failed because it was at once too visionary and too rigid? At length James Hamilton of South Carolina was reduced to describing the administration as "a set of drivellers."[66]

In the House, in these last days of the Nineteenth Congress, there was still a majority willing to support the President in a grave emergency; but the effect of this majority's support was that the House declined to compromise with the Senate, by votes of 71 to 47 and 75 to 67. The Congress then adjourned, leaving Mr. Adams to the mercies of the British.[67]

According to the Act of 1823, Adams had now no choice but to issue a proclamation closing American ports against all British vessels coming from any British colony in the Western Hemisphere. After two or three Cabinet meetings, he did so; but the accompanying Treasury orders were lenient, and the interdict was only nominal.[68] Clearly the last hope was Gallatin in London, but Gallatin could do nothing. Concessions that would have been accepted in 1824 were now angrily turned down. "I only encountered," he wrote, "irritation, not yet extinguished, on account of the United States not having met, especially in 1823 and 1824, the overtures of Great Britain."[69] This mild language does not conceal the completeness of his defeat. When he left London at the end of 1827, the order in council was still in force and still popular. In America, as Van Buren had predicted, the West Indies controversy doomed the administration, for Adams' loss of

[65] Van Buren to H. Bleecker, February 25, 1827. *MS.*, N.Y. State Library.

[66] *Register of Debates,* 19 Cong., 2 sess., III, 399–402. Webster, now the leader for the administration in the Senate, explicitly refused to discuss the "elsewhere" clause. *Ibid.,* p. 1524.

[67] *Ibid.,* pp. 1503–1506, 1515–1517, 1522–1527, 1528–1530.

[68] Richardson, *Messages and Papers,* II, 376; proclamation of March 17, 1827. Adams, *Memoirs,* VII, 236.

[69] Gallatin to Clay, October 3, 1827; *Sen. Docs.,* 22 Cong., 1 sess., III, 31.

the West Indies trade in 1826 and his subsequent failure to regain it became one of the few explicit issues in the presidential campaign. And now, one by one, the victors, who had triumphed at the cost of their liberal principles, departed from the scene: Lord Liverpool and George Canning died in 1827, William Huskisson in 1830.[70] Canning and Huskisson lived to hear themselves and their following described in the Commons as "a crowd of visionary theorists, of political economists, and the professors of what are called the liberal principles of the present day."[71] Such was the verdict of Tory England upon these heralds of a new industrial order.

As for the verdict of democratic America upon the neomercantilism of President Adams, its most succinct, if least gratifying expression will be found in certain words of Martin Van Buren, when, as Secretary of State in the next administration, he began to repair the damage which had been done to the West Indies trade. The repair was easy, when both sides were willing to make concessions. While the United States abandoned Adams' claim that it should be granted exceptional privileges without a fair equivalent, the British made some important modifications in their navigation laws. What could not be achieved in 1824 under an economic nationalist was easily managed under a democratic one. But the language which prefaced this sensible accommodation is surprising. "To set up the acts of the late Administration," wrote Van Buren, "as the cause of the forfeiture of privileges which would otherwise be granted to the people of the United States would, under existing circumstances, be unjust in itself, and could not fail to excite their deepest sensibility."[72] This language, according to Daniel Webster, was "derogatory to the character and honor of the

---

[70] Charles C. F. Greville, *The Greville Memoirs: Reigns of George IV and William IV*, Henry Reeves ed. (London, 3 vols., 4th ed., 1875), I, 89, II, 48. Adams, when he heard of Canning's death, described him as "an implacable rancorous enemy of the United States," *Memoirs*, VII, 328. The antiprotectionist Gallatin, however, said that he missed Canning's "sagacity, quickness, self-confidence and decision." Gallatin to Clay, August 31, 1827: *Sen. Docs.*, 22 Cong., 1 sess., III, No. 132. The contrast in judgments is instructive.

[71] Hansard, 2 ser., XVII, 560; speech of W. Peel, May 4, 1827. Greville, however, wrote after Canning's death, "The march of Liberalism (as it is called) will not be stopped, and this he knew." *Greville Memoirs*, II, 42.

[72] Van Buren to Louis McLane, July 20, 1829; *Sen. Docs.*, 21 Cong., 2 sess., I, No. 20, p. 11.

United States."[73] And so, no doubt, it was; but that was not its intention. It was intended only as an unflattering epitaph upon premature centralization: and an unflattering epitaph it remains to this day.

[73] Webster, *Writings,* J. M. McIntyre, ed. (18 vols., Boston, 1903), III, 357.

CHAPTER 11

Abominations

O N December 4, 1827, the President's Third Annual Message was presented to a new (the Twentieth) Congress. Adams had composed it "in such agony of mind . . . that I am ashamed of it, and am almost afraid to read it to my confidential advisers."[1] It was anything but confident; and, except for a brief panegyric on internal improvements, hardly betrayed an idea. Mr. Adams was obliged to confess that, even in the realm of foreign relations, where he was most at home, he had little to report but defeat and frustration. The British still refused to negotiate on the West Indies trade; the French declined to pay their bill for depredations committed during the Napoleonic Wars; the Panama Conference had come to nothing. A forlorn stepchild of the Virginia Dynasty, the President had saved himself from resembling a mere public anachronism by offering two small concessions. He asked for a further relaxation of the land laws, not in terms of reduced prices (he would never have urged that) but as regarded the remission of forfeitures; and he inserted a chilly little plea for "the amelioration in some form or the modification of the diversified and often oppressive codes relating to insolvency."[2]

These concessions may have been small and quite verbal, but they were still significant. By admitting the pioneer and the debtor into his

---

[1] Adams, *Memoirs,* VII, 362.
[2] Richardson, *Messages and Papers,* II, 378–392.

message, the President at least acknowledged the existence of a spirit essentially hostile to his neomercantilist policies. This spirit had arisen out of the Panic of 1819, which was now interpreted both as a calamity and as a symptom of growth, just as the lessons which economists and publicists were extracting from it were directed not only toward the relief of needless distress, but also toward the release of needful energy. Thus strict land laws and stern insolvency codes could be condemned as a check upon individual enterprise; and even a President whose sympathy with the debtor and the bankrupt was avowedly small, and who believed that individual enterprise should be managed in the national interest, was obliged to make his obeisance in the temple of Rimmon. In short, the new nationalism—introspective, individualistic, egalitarian—required that every public servant should speak its confusing language, and Mr. Adams had condescended so far as to attempt to do so. But the attempt was cold and grudging; it was not a language that pleased him; for even when he spoke most vehemently or acted (as in the West Indies quarrel) most unrestrainedly, he spoke and acted for a very different kind of nationalism. Conservation, careful stewardship, controlled expansion, rational planning: upon these restrained and centralizing terms the nation was to advance into the future. He now confessed, in private, that he himself had failed. "General Jackson," he wrote on December 17, "will be elected. . . . But it is impossible that his Administration should give satisfaction to the people of this Union. He is incompetent both by his ignorance and by the fury of his passions. He will be surrounded by incompetent men . . . they will crumble to pieces, and the Administration will go to wreck and ruin. Then, too, will come the recoil of public opinion in favor of Mr. Clay, and it will be irresistible."[3] He would not admit that the American System—as a *system*—was already obsolete.

This does not mean that majority opinion, now manifestly inclining toward Andrew Jackson, was in favor of unrestricted laissez faire: as far back as Jefferson's Second Inaugural it had been admitted, even by the great philosopher of minimal government, that government should become the encourager and promoter of industry.[4] And if the Panic and depression of 1819–21 had taught Americans anything, it had taught them that men could never be left "free to regulate their

[3] Adams, *Memoirs,* VII, 383.
[4] Richardson, *Messages and Papers,* I, 379.

own pursuits of industry and improvement."[5] After the Panic, the
individual states had been expected to act vigorously for the relief of
distress; and even the federal government had been supposed to play
its part, and had endeavored to do so.[6] The results had not been especially encouraging, and the strange flowering of economic thought[7]
which accompanied the recession and its aftermath was now directed
toward a larger speculation concerning the character of national
growth. It is obvious that this thought would continue to revolve
around the two poles of positive and negative government, and this
would be especially true of the federal government; yet even here it is
noticeable that the extreme negativists had begun to believe in negative *action*. As early as 1820, for example, a great Virginian particularist had stated that the Second Bank of the United States ought to be
abolished instanter; but at the same time he had contrived to argue
that the national currency should be centrally controlled.[8] Indeed,
those who were most directly opposed to one another—the hard-money
men and the believers in inconvertible paper, the protectionists and
the free traders—were usually looking for regulation of some kind;
but this was given a peculiar intensity, the febrile "note" of the late
1820's, by the fact that the whole national community had been in-
jured by the Panic of 1819. Thus one could conceive of the nation,
if one so desired, as a nation of individuals, to whom the winds of
economic distress had not been tempered; and one could maintain
that the future growth of the nation was to some extent a matter of
the fostering and release of individual enterprise.

Here John Quincy Adams' ideals of planned collective enterprise,
however mild and even axiomatic they may seem to us in retrospect,
were at a considerable disadvantage. In Pennsylvania, for example,
the majority opinion favored one aspect or another of the American
System; yet regional and local jealousies were so acute that the American System was never able to form a party. This was partly but not
chiefly due to political ineptitude—the Jacksonians, after all, were
in little better shape. At the heart of the administration's failure to

[5] *Ibid.*, I, 323; from Jefferson's First Inaugural.
[6] Murray N. Rothbard, *The Panic of 1819* (New York, 1962), *passim*.
[7] Dorfman, *Economic Mind*, I, 362–404.
[8] Rothbard, *Panic of 1819*, pp. 138–139, citing Spencer Roane as "Am-
phictyon" in Richmond *Enquirer*, April 18, 1820.

create an organization lay the belief that Adams was an aristocrat, who favored only privileged elites, and that Jackson was a democrat, who somehow or other did not.[9] There was a strong element of superstition in this Jacksonian faith: some Pennsylvania Germans, it was said, voted for the General long after the General was dead. But, whether superstitious or not, the faith could become a faith in the individualist, of whom Jackson was the supreme example: as if the will power of self-made men, by a process of simple addition, made up the will power of the nation. But first the self-made man must be given the opportunity to make himself.

In Illinois, the obscurity of state politics could best be understood on these terms. After the proslavery men, some of whom were Jacksonians, had been defeated in the convention battle of 1824—had been forbidden, that is to say, to construe opportunity in Missourian terms—the main political effort was to get rid of Governor Ninian Edwards and his son-in-law, the popular Representative Daniel P. Cook. They were accused by the "friends" of Jackson (who were not themselves exactly guiltless in this respect) of having opposed a reduction in the price of public lands, because this would injure their own large holdings in real estate. Partly for this reason, Cook was defeated for Congress in the fall elections of 1826. The other reason was that he had voted for Adams when the Presidency was thrown into the House of Representatives. Thus Adams was connected—as he had been in the Kentucky Court battle, already described—with an old political order, able but "aristocratic," and bent on exacting a personal allegiance as the price of its services.[10] In Kentucky, of the eight delegates who had gone against their instructions and voted for Adams

[9] Philip S. Klein, *Pennsylvania Politics, 1817–1832* (Philadelphia, 1940), p. 250; *Pennsylvania Archives*, 4 Ser., V, 667, 747. For the steps which the Jacksonians took to get themselves into better shape see Robert V. Remini's extremely able and, indeed, definitive study *The Election of Andrew Jackson* (Philadelphia and New York, 1964), chapters 3 and 4.

[10] Ninian Edwards to John McClean, June 24, 1828; "The Edwards Papers," E. B. Washburne (ed.), *Chicago Historical Society's Collection*, III, 1884, 352. W. H. Brown, "Memoir of the Late Hon. Daniel P. Cook," in N. W. Edwards, *History of Illinois from 1778 to 1833* (Chicago, 1870), p. 273. John Marshall of Shawneetown to Ninian Edwards, September 2, 1826; Brown, "Memoir," p. 255. Elihu B. Washburne, *Sketch of Edward Coles, in Collections of the Illinois State Historical Library* (C. W. Alvord, ed.) Biographical Series, No. I. "Correspondence of Edward Coles," *Journal of Negro History*,

in the House, four did not choose to run and one was defeated in the election of 1826.

In Massachusetts, the political divisions within the state also entered the national picture as divisions between the principle of order and the principle of change. Although Adams had never been forgiven for his apostasy from Federalism in 1808, the merchants, the professional men, and the big new banker-industrialists like Nathan Appleton and Amos and Abbot Lawrence were quite content for things to remain as they were. Their particular protégé, Daniel Webster, was now directing the administration forces in the United States Senate. In 1826 and 1827, however, the leaders of the urban and rural democracy, David Henshaw and Marcus Morton, organized the Friends of Jackson as a political party in the Commonwealth. This might have been expected; what was more surprising was the fact that leading members of the old Salem aristocracy, like George and Theodore Lyman, and former Hartford Conventionists, like Harrison Gray Otis, were also expressing a preference for Jackson.[11] These gentlemen were equally out of place as allies of Henshaw and Morton or as followers of the western hero; the Lymans, for example, denounced all western migrants as "the refuse of society";[12] and their Jacksonian sympathies can be explained only in two ways. Either they believed that Jackson would dissolve the Dynasty's proscription against admitting Federalists to office or they hoped that he would lead the nation back into a simpler and purer world than anything that could be discerned in the messages of Adams. As Arthur H. Cole has reminded us, their commercial philosophy would have been happier with that state of "local independence and self-determination in business affairs" from which the economy was visibly departing in the late 1820's.[13] They, too, were individualists.

No doubt the refusal of the national one-party system to resolve itself into two distinct parties had something to do with the ferment

---

III (1918), 158 ff. Edward Coles to Rev. Thomas Lippincott, September—, 1860; *Journal of the Illinois State Historical Society*, III (1911), 61. McMaster, *History*, V, 187–188. The anticonventionists won by 6,640 to 4,972.

[11] Arthur B. Darling, *Political Changes in Massachusetts, 1828–1842* (New Haven, 1925), pp. 2 ff.

[12] R. G. Thwaites (ed.), *Early Western Travels*, I, 60, 61.

[13] W. B. Smith and A. H. Cole, *Fluctuations in American Business, 1790–1860* (Cambridge, 1935), p. 40. See also Marvin Meyers, *The Jacksonian Persuasion* (Stanford, 1957), p. 43.

which so violently and yet so obscurely animated the congressional elections of 1826. The administration, however pure its motives in this respect, noticeably suffered from its inability to organize a strong party—to extend its patronage, rather than its promises, to gentlemen in search of opportunity. An effective organization, at all levels of political action, might possibly have rescued Adams' internal improvements program from that mass of local jealousies which (more, perhaps, than distrust of the administration) prevented Congress from acting on it with enthusiasm.[14] As it was, the administration commanded little respect, especially in the remoter parts of the Union; and this was most disagreeably illustrated in the State of Georgia, still a weird satrapy of the Cotton Kingdom. In Georgia the class conflict between the cotton planters, under the educated George Michael Troup, and the small subsistence farmers, led by the illiterate John Clark, had distracted everyone to such an extent that when, in 1824, the Clark faction wrested the election for governorship from the legislature and gave it to the people, the people at once bestowed the governorship upon George Michael Troup.[15] But when the two factions were united they were truly formidable, and they were quite united in their desire to expel the Creeks and Cherokees from those lush cotton lands which, lying between the Flint and Chattahoochee Rivers, blocked Georgia's advance into the beckoning West.

On February 12, 1825, United States Commissioner Duncan G. Campbell and a handful of Creek chieftains perpetrated the Treaty of Indian Springs, which took from the Creeks 4,700,000 acres of their best land without an adequate return; and this fraudulent affair, which delighted Georgia, had first been proclaimed and then nullified by the Adams administration.[16] In its place a somewhat more humane

[14] See Chapter 9, n. 16, and Julius Rubin, *Canal or Railroad? Imitation and Innovation in the Response to the Erie Canal in Philadelphia, Baltimore, and Boston,* American Philosophical Society, *Transactions,* New Series, Vol. 51, part 7 (Philadelphia, 1961), *passim.*

[15] Amanda Johnson, *Georgia as Colony and State* (Atlanta, 1938), p. 209; U. B. Philips, "Georgia and State Rights," American Historical Association, *Annual Report, 1901* (Washington, 1902), II, 104. Paul Murray, "Economic Sectionalism in Georgia, 1825–1855," *Journal of Southern History,* X (1945), 293–307.

[16] 7 U. S. Statutes at Large 237; *American State Papers, Indian Affairs,* II, 563–564. Adams signed the treaty March 5, 1825, before he had heard rumors of its fraudulence.

treaty, called the Treaty of Washington, was submitted to the United States Senate on January 23, 1826, and publicly proclaimed in April.[17] In December, 1826, declaring that a treaty once proclaimed could not be annulled, the Georgia Assembly protested against this "violation" of state rights by the general government. Governor Troup went further. He ordered the major generals of militia commanding the Sixth and Seventh Divisions to get ready to repel a hostile invasion; and he warned James Barbour, the Secretary of War, that any federal attempt to interfere with the Treaty of Indian Springs would be met by force.[18] At this the administration, whose concern for the Indians was not acute, ingloriously yielded, and the Creeks and Cherokees were abandoned to their doom.

No doubt, had Georgia indulged in a fateful skirmish with the United States, she would have been disavowed by the rest of the South; but when her bluff succeeded, Alabama and Mississippi also began to take an extreme state-rights position toward the Indians within their borders. The controversy was, in fact, truly ominous, not because it bore any resemblance to nullification, a different and more sophisticated affair, but because it demonstrated how easily the acquisitive impulse, when thwarted, could ally itself with the doctrine of state rights.

In any case, there was a great deal of confusion behind the fall elections of 1826. Their signs and portents, except in the case of Georgia, were not too legible, and they were only transcribed into actualities when the Twentieth Congress assembled in December. On December 3, the administration's Speaker, John W. Taylor of New York, was defeated for re-election by the hostile Andrew Stevenson of Virginia, the vote standing at 104 to 94; while the Senate chose for its printer the ebullient Duff Green of Missouri, whose *United States Telegraph,* published in Washington, invariably abused the President. For the first time in American history (Adams noted) an administra-

[17] *U.S. Sen. Docs.,* 57 Cong., 1 sess., No. 452; *American State Papers, Indian Affairs,* II, 731–734; Richardson, *Messages and Papers,* II, 324–326, 345.
[18] *Acts of Georgia 1826,* p. 277; *American State Papers, Indian Affairs,* II, 731–734; Troup to James Barbour, February 17, 1827, in Edward J. Harden, *Life of George M. Troup* (Savannah, 1859), p. 485; Richardson, *Messages and Papers,* II, 370–373; R. S. Cotterill, *The Southern Indians* (Norman, 1954), pp. 221–222, 234; Sydnor, *Southern Sectionalism,* p. 184.

tion only two years old had lost its control of both Houses of Congress.[19]

The defeat of Taylor was due partly to his Missouri record, partly to scandal,[20] and partly to the victory of De Witt Clinton in New York's gubernatorial election of 1826.[21] Clinton had supported Jackson in 1824, and his victory in 1826 was almost enough to convince Van Buren that Jackson was the man to follow:[22] by the middle of 1827 the Regency was said to be willing to join forces with Clinton.[23] The effect of all this upon the New York delegation had been to divide it irreparably when it cast its vote for the Speakership. Moreover Adams himself had done nothing to assist the unfortunate Taylor in New York.[24] The news of the Speakership election was followed into New York by the text of the Third Annual Message, and the shock which

[19] Adams, *Memoirs,* VII, 367, 369. He calls the *Telegraph* "a scurrilous and abusive print." *Ibid.,* VII, 370. Sam Houston wrote, "Desperation is their [the administration's] only hope." Houston to Jackson, January, 1827; Jackson, *Correspondence,* III, 329.

[20] Taylor, a mild philanderer, had been unfairly accused of gross sexual irregularities. Taylor to R. M. Livingston, May 3, 1826; John W. Taylor Papers, NYHS. Adams, *Memoirs,* VII, 369, was not willing to give him the benefit of the doubt.

[21] The draft of an article by Taylor, dated December 27, 1827, attributes his defeat to divisions in the New York delegation; John W. Taylor Papers.

[22] Van Buren to Thomas Ritchie, January 13, 1827; Van Buren Papers, LC.

[23] J. Schermerhorn to Van Buren, July 15, 1827, asks Van Buren to "accede to the nomination of Gov. Clinton as V. President & give him your support. . . . I view Gov. C. and his friends, if they cannot essentially aid the election of the Gen., they certainly can defeat it. . . . Gen. J. is apprized that I have written to you on the Presidential question. . . ." Van Buren Papers. By November, 1827, Van Buren was writing to Jackson asking him not to come to Washington, since this would "impair our good prospects"; *ibid.* In December, 1826, there were still rumors to the effect that Van Buren would make his peace with Adams. W. L. Marcy to Van Buren, December 27, 1826; *ibid.* In April, 1827, John W. Taylor still believed that Van Buren's re-election to the Senate was not a Jacksonian portent, but that Clinton "has descended to play second fiddle" to him. Taylor to Charles Miner, April 16, 1827; John W. Taylor Papers, NYHS. All this would make it at least probable that Van Buren's mind was not made up until the early summer of 1827.

[24] Tallmadge to Taylor, January 17, March 4, 1826; John W. Taylor Papers. The final blow was the appointment of Judge Samuel Rossiter Betts— who proved to be a most distinguished admiralty lawyer—to the federal judgeship for the Southern District of New York, a post which was earmarked for either James Tallmadge or Henry Wheaton, both staunch Adams men. Tallmadge to Taylor, December 4, 1826, shows that Tallmadge had written to Adams directly about this; *ibid.* See also Taylor to Tallmadge, December 23, 1826, and Tallmadge to Taylor, February 3, 1827; *ibid.*

this administered to the administration party was said to have been extreme. It had been confidently expected that the President would have something eloquent to say in favor of protective tariffs, but on this central topic the Message had said no word! "This state is becoming outrageously tariff-mad," wrote Ebenezer Sage, "and Mr. Adams' silence on that subject in his late messuage [was Mr. Sage attempting a pun?] is considered . . . an electioneering matter and that he is with the Boston merchants—his best friends here find a great difficulty in getting over the thing, the more so as they had promised us that he would unquestionably recommend the American System."[25]

The President, as has been shown, preferred to leave the tariff to the vividly, indeed virulently protectionist report of his Secretary of the Treasury, Richard Rush. Some premonition warned him that it would be better not to recommend it directly, or, as he put it, not to "interfere improperly for the purpose of exercising an influence over the House."[26] And indeed, if the failure of his West Indies policy was the most discernible single influence in his subsequent overthrow, the tariff may be said to have provided its *mise en scène*.

The propagandists had already done their work so well that farmers everywhere, outside the South and the Southwest, were almost sure that protection would be in their interest. Massachusetts capital had also gone over to the cause, otherwise Daniel Webster, a perfect barometer of opinion among men of wealth, would not have driven a bill through the House, in the late Congress, giving the New England woolen manufacturer all the protection he needed.[27] In due time

[25] Sage to Taylor, February 17, 1828; John W. Taylor Papers. Also Ambrose Spencer to Taylor, January 12, 1828, in which Spencer says that the agriculturists of New York are favorable to "the American System as now understood," because they believe it will enhance prices; *ibid*. Tallmadge to Taylor, December 18, 1827, tells of a meeting at Dutchess County, which passed pro-tariff resolutions and where "it was difficult to calm the murmurs against Mr. Adams for omitting the Tariff in his speech"; *ibid*. See also Charles Buller to A. C. Flagg, Genesee, December 15, 1827: "The silence of the message on the tariff affords striking proof of the heartlessness and policy of the man"; A. C. Flagg Papers, NYPL.

[26] Adams, *Memoirs,* VII, 362. See Chapter 9, n. 12, *supra*.

[27] By an ingenious system of minimum valuations, the ad valorem of 33⅓ per cent on imported woolens was nominally retained, but imports of the value of $1 a square yard—the most important—were subjected to a duty of 83⅓ cents a yard. Taussig, *Tariff History*, p. 82. Stanwood, *Tariff Controversies*, I, 254 ff. The agitation *for* this bill began at the Exchange Coffee House, Boston, in September, 1826. *Niles' Register,* XXXI, 105.

the bill came before the Senate, much to the embarrassment of Martin Van Buren. Van Buren had already decided that effective opposition to Adams would be achieved through "the most natural and beneficial combination . . . that between the planters of the South and the plain republicans of the North."[28] Here he looked back to the days when New York and Pennsylvania supported Jefferson; but the national party which he now had in mind was a very loose cohesion of disparate interests. Could it, under such a challenge as this, be made to cohere? The plain republican farmers of western New York were much in favor of a high tariff, but this was simply not the case with the planters of the South. Van Buren solved his personal dilemma by not voting at all;[29] and many other senators took the same heroic course and stayed away. When the roll was called in the Senate, the result was a tie. It was then that Vice-President Calhoun, whose tariff views were still not generally known, showed the iron in his composition and killed the woolens bill with his casting vote.[30]

Such a narrow defeat only inspired the protectionists. In the summer of 1827 the Pennsylvania Society for the Promotion of Manufactures called a convention together at Harrisburg in order "to take into consideration the present state of the wool growing and wool manufacturing interests, and such other manufacturers as may require encouragement." It was attended by delegates from thirteen of the twenty-four states—an interesting assembly of wool growers, manufacturers, politicians, and editors. After five days, an agreement was actually made between the growers of wool and the manufacturers of woolens, and with this agreement the early tariff movement reached its height.[31]

[28] Van Buren to Thomas Ritchie, January 13, 1827; Van Buren Papers, LC.
[29] Van Buren, *Autobiography*, p. 169, says that he was absent because he had promised a friend to go on a visit to the Congressional Cemetery!
[30] *Register of Debates*, 19 Cong., 2 sess., p. 496.
[31] Stanwood, *Tariff Controversies*, I, 264. There were no delegates from Indiana or Illinois, but delegates came from Virginia, Delaware, and Maryland. For a list of delegates, see *Niles' Register*, XXXII, 388–396. If the "wool growers" were also wool manufacturers—Taussig, *Tariff History*, p. 83, and Wiltse, *Calhoun: Nationalist*, p. 354—their agreement becomes easy to understand. This agreement was: An ad valorem duty on imported woolens of 40 per cent, rising gradually to 50 per cent, and 20 cents a pound on import wools, rising by $2\frac{1}{2}$ cents per annum until it reached 50 cents. The Convention also asked for minimum valuations on imported woolens of 50 cents, $2.50, $4.00, $6.00. Thus imported woolens valued at the most usual price—$1.00 a yard—

The Convention was neither for Adams nor against Jackson: it believed that neither candidate could win if he openly opposed the protective principle. It enjoyed the backing of respectable journalists; but its economic report had been poorly put together, and only after the report had been written did it discover hanging around its doors a singular personage called Georg Friedrich List, editor of the German-American weekly *Readinger Adlinger,* who certainly could have done the job. List had been professor of "administration and politics" in the University of Tübingen, but his views on tariffs had aroused the venom of the authorities of Württemberg, and he had been forced to make a run for it. European savants were a rare commodity in those days, and List was soon writing a series of letters on the philosophy of the American System for the Philadelphia *National Gazette.* "We appear to have imported a professor from Germany," sneered James Hamilton of South Carolina, "in absolute violation of the American System."[32]

There were others who, if less pungent than List, were more sophisticated. Daniel Raymond's Ricardian views upon banks of issue were, no doubt, a little *too* subtle for the ordinary protectionist; but his anonymous pamphlet *The American System* was eloquent, widely read, and fortunate enough to exacerbate Governor William B. Giles of Virginia, whose writings always did more harm to his friends than his enemies.[33] Another leading protectionist was a Boston lawyer, Willard Phillips, who had been somewhat of a rake at Harvard, but who had subsequently repented his sins in a course of plain living and high thinking. His *Manual of Political Economy* was, with some justice, greatly admired.[34] Nor should one forget, among those who put their brains at the service of protection, the humbler but highly popular efforts of Hezekiah Niles in his *Register* and of Mathew Carey. A native of Dublin, a friend of Irish revolution, Carey had been obliged

---

would be treated as if they were $2.50 a yard, and subjected to a most punitive ad valorem.

[32] Dorfman, *Economic Mind,* II, 575 ff.; *Dictionary of American Biography,* XI, 292.

[33] Daniel Raymond, *Thoughts on Political Economy* (2 vols., Baltimore, 1820), see esp. I, v, vi. For subsequent editions see Dorfman, *Economic Mind,* II, XXII, n i. Thomas Ritchie to Martin Van Buren, March 11, 1828: "What think you of Gov. Giles's message & writings? His friends . . . must manage him better"; Van Buren Papers, LC.

[34] Dorfman, *Economic Mind,* II, 585–593.

to flee to America; and in America he became known as a pious Catholic, a warm humanitarian whose disinterested affections embraced both the workingman and the banks of issue, and a copious editor and publisher of—among other productions—his own economic writings. These, said McDuffie of South Carolina, were "statistical nonsense." The time was soon to come when the protective tariff could have been described in the same terms.[35]

Van Buren had not allowed his own hand-picked delegate, Samuel Young, to attend the Convention at Harrisburg. He was not sure whether the Convention might not advance the fortunes of Henry Clay. He preferred, in any case, a more practical if more devious course. He had already gone traveling in the South, accompanied by a notorious free-trader, Churchill C. Cambreleng of New York: his object had been to bring the Crawford Radicals into the Jacksonian fold; and at the bedside of the dying Crawford it had been agreed that, in return for Crawford's influence, Van Buren would accomplish the ruin of John Caldwell Calhoun. This would be done after the presidential election of 1828, and it would be done by letting the General know that Calhoun had endeavored to disgrace him after the Seminole campaign of 1818.[36] At the end of May, Van Buren returned from the South, plump, smiling, enigmatic. The President, who had been following his movements with a glum surmise, reported that in character no less than appearance he much resembled Aaron Burr.[37]

Van Buren's position had become a very delicate one. Possibly the most famous economist in the South at this moment was Thomas Cooper, an ex-Englishman and ex-Pennsylvanian (and by this time ex-materialist) who, after a six years' residence in South Carolina, was already exclaiming that "We of the South . . . hold our plantations as the serfs and operatives of the North."[38] His ingenious twisting

[35] *Dictionary of American Biography,* III, 489–490; *Niles' Register,* XXXII, 173; Dorfman, *Economic Mind,* I, 384–386.

[36] Wiltse, *Calhoun: Nationalist,* p. 363. Calhoun had gone over to Jackson in 1826 and had been well received by the General. Calhoun to Jackson, June 4, 1826; Jackson to Calhoun, July 26, 1826. Jackson, *Correspondence,* III, 304–305, 307–308.

[37] Adams, *Memoirs,* VII, 272.

[38] Dorfman, *Economic Mind,* II, 527 ff., and iii, n. 26. For an extensive portrait of this somewhat chameleonlike personage, see Dumas Malone, *The Public Life of Thomas Cooper* (New Haven, 1926).

of Ricardo's theory of rent in favor of the conservative landowner had, like his stern free-trading views, recommended him in the best quarters, and as the scientific president of South Carolina College he was already an oracle in Calhoun's state.[39] It may have given Van Buren some discomfort to receive, in July, 1827, two letters from Thomas Cooper, accusing him of a fondness for high protective tariffs.[40] On the other hand, and this was more important, his abstention from voting on the woolens bill had made a very bad impression upon the protectionists of New York.[41]

The defeat of Adams was undoubtedly the chief business before the Twentieth Congress, and the Speaker had seen to it that the more important House committees were packed with the President's enemies. John Randolph, now too ill to do any work, was even made chairman of the Ways and Means Committee; and if the chairman of the Committee on Manufactures was an Adams man, Rollin Mallary of Vermont, the majority was composed of Jacksonian protectionists. The petitions and memorials which flooded into Washington showed a leaning against a higher tariff; the lobbyists did not. When at length, on March 4, 1828, Mallary reported a tariff bill out of his committee, he announced that it did not represent his own views, and that he proposed to amend it so as to bring it more in line with the report

[39] He had recently published his *Lectures on the Elements of Political Economy* (Columbia, 1826).

[40] Thomas Cooper to Martin Van Buren, July 5, 31, 1827; Van Buren Papers, LC. The second letter threatens Van Buren with the prospect, should a woolens bill be passed, that "in one twelve month from that period, South Carolina will be an independent State and her ports will be free ports." It also says that Van Buren "with all your reputation for management" has *hitherto* been on the side "of plain good sense and honesty of intention." Both letters, however, betray an uncertainty as to whether Van Buren was *finally* committed to protection: precisely the uncertainty which Van Buren would have preferred to maintain in free-trade circles.

[41] W. L. Marcy to Van Buren, January 29, 1828: "There was last Spring a more than half formed opinion that you were hostile to the tariff; this opinion was settling down into a conviction accompanied with some excitement and was doing infinite mischief to the cause of General Jackson in this state. . . ." Marcy adds that there is a "manufacturing excitement rageing all over the State (except the city of New York)" and that "if Jackson's friends do not do all that mortal man can do for the success of such a measure [a high protective tariff] we shall have a difficult and doubtful contest at the next election"; Van Buren Papers, LC.

of the Harrisburg Convention. It had been the work, he said, of Silas Wright of New York.[42]

Wright was an upright man, but he was also a strict partisan; and he would not have worked out a bill that did not concur exactly with the views of his chief, Van Buren. The bill was remarkable for its assault upon imports of raw materials. Pig iron and rolled bar iron were heavily protected, although no one had asked for an increase in the existing duties. Foreign hemp was burdened with a duty of $45 a ton instead of the existing $35, and this was to be raised by an annual $5 until it reached $60. Since domestic hemp was used in the manufacture of cotton bagging and common ropes, and was already secure from foreign competition, the only purpose in this was to make cordage and cables more expensive. There was also a heavy duty on sail duck, without the customary drawback on the small quantities re-exported in vessels for their own use. Iron, hemp, and sail duties struck most conspicuously at the shipbuilders of New England. To this there was added a double duty—10 cents a gallon—on imported molasses, a slap at New England's rum distilleries, rendered all the more spiteful and stinging because the usual drawback on exports was no longer permitted.[43]

But it was the treatment of wool and woolens which revealed the inner meaning of this singular bill. Imported raw wool was now subjected to a most ingenious mixture of specific and ad valorem duties. The purpose of this was to put a heavy tax on the coarse wool (not grown in America, but imported from Asia Minor and South America) which was used in the manufacture of carpets and cheap cloths, and at the same time to give a substantial protection to the higher grades of domestic wool. This gratified the farmer and hurt the manufacturer. To make things worse, imported woolens were now subjected to certain "specific and unambiguous" duties, which imposed a comparatively harmless tax of 40 cents on woolen goods at $1 a square yard, the usual price of cheap imported woolens. These goods were in great demand in the South, where they clothed the slave, so that the tariff deprived the woolen manufacturer of New

[42] Wiltse, *Calhoun: Nationalist,* pp. 367–368; *American State Papers, Finance,* V, 778–845; *Register of Debates,* 20 Cong., 1 sess., IV, Pt. ii, pp. 1749–1754. Mallary was himself a protectionist.

[43] *American State Papers, Finance,* V, 784–792; Taussig, *Tariff History,* pp. 90–91, 93.

England of this southern market, or at least forced him into an uneven competition with the traditional British imports. To make this competition a little more even, and thus more favorable for the Southern slaveholder, the Jackson men then reduced the specific duty on raw wool from 7 cents to 4 cents a pound.[44] The whole treatment of wool and woolens in the bill was, therefore, such as to favor the protectionist farmer in the middle and western states, and extend at least some consideration to the slaveholding consumer in the South. Only the New England manufacturer was left out. This was the original meaning of the Tariff of 1828, and it was quite as coarse as the imported wool and woolens to which the tariff gave such a genial reception.

Recent scholarship has indicated, suggestively if not conclusively, that the classical interpretation of the Tariff of 1828 is not the correct one.[45] It was always assumed that the tariff was deliberately written so as to defeat itself. The northern and southern Jacksonians, in other words, were to oppose all amendments to the bill, but at the final vote the Southerners were to reverse themselves and vote against it. Since New England would do the same, the bill would be defeated; and the southern wing of the Jackson party could claim a victory in the South, while the northern wing could blame its defeat upon the administration. If this interpretation is incorrect, it follows that Van Buren really wished the tariff to succeed, and for three reasons: because he was sure the South would never vote for Adams, because the protectionist feeling in New York was too strong to be resisted, and because he wished to secure the middle and western states for Jackson. He had, in short, always believed that a victorious tariff would be more likely to favor Jackson than a defeated one. This theory goes against the opinions of Clay, McDuffie, Calhoun, and Van Buren himself at a later stage in his career; for these opinions tend to show that the tariff was not marked for survival, but that protectionist sentiment was so strong that the plotters were hoist with their own petard.[46] On the

---

[44] Taussig, *Tariff History,* p. 92. In *Register of Debates,* 20 Cong., 1 sess., IV, Pt. ii, pp. 1878–1899, John Davis of Massachusetts said that "the dollar minimum falls at the point most favorable . . . for the British manufacturer."

[45] Cp. Robert V. Remini, "Martin Van Buren and the Tariff of Abominations," *American Historical Review,* LXIII (1958), 903–917.

[46] Clay to J. J. Crittenden, February 14, 1828 (cited *ibid.,* p. 909), believed there was a plot long before the crucial voting had taken place. For McDuffie's

other hand, the correspondence of Van Buren and his lieutenants at the time, the tone of the Regency press, and the behavior of the Regency-dominated New York legislature all suggest that Van Buren did intend to push the tariff through at all costs.[47]

However this may be, and it is not a matter of very great significance, the facts are that an unamended tariff bill passed through the House by a final vote of 105 to 94.[48] New England voted 23 to 16 against the bill: a closer vote than might have been expected, but one that was predicated upon the belief that the bill would be severely amended in the more conservative Senate. And this, indeed, is what happened. The crucial amendment in the Senate was one to change the specific duties on woolen goods into ad valorem duties, which would—according to the method then used for assessing the dutiable value of European goods—have raised the tax on all classes of woolens to $49\frac{1}{2}$ per cent.[49] This provision was just sufficient to satisfy New England; and it was because he voted *for* it that Van Buren was subsequently accused by southern Jacksonians of breaking his word and ensuring the passage of the bill, which was endorsed in the Senate by a final vote of 26 to 21. The whole South opposed it, with the exception of Bouligny of Louisiana; the middle and western states supported it; and New England, under Webster's leadership, approved it by 6 to 5. In the House it met with little further resistance, and so the "Tariff of Abominations" became law.[50]

---

view, given years later, see *Cong. Globe,* 28 Cong., 1 sess., p. 747; Calhoun, *Works,* III, 47–51; Van Buren, "Notes," August 4, 1840; Van Buren Papers, LC. This was also the view of James Hamilton, who said "Resist we will . . . and our friends at the north, who love us yet, in spite of our probable rebellion must . . . in some degree thank themselves for attempting to play 'brag' with the *Blackleg* on this most foul and corrupting subject." Hamilton to Van Buren, July 3, 1828. I.e., Clay had defeated the plot.

[47] Remini, "Van Buren." See the same author's *Martin Van Buren and the Making of the Democratic Party* (New York, 1959) Chapter 12, and his more temperate and succinct account in *The Election of Andrew Jackson,* pp. 171–178.

[48] *Niles' Register,* XXXV, 53–55, gives an analysis of the vote. For New England speeches against the bill, see especially John Anderson of Maine, *Register of Debates,* 20 Cong., 1 sess., IV, Pt. ii, pp. 1772–1784; Jonathan Hunt of Vermont, *ibid.,* pp. 1784–1789; Isaac Bates of Massachusetts, *ibid.,* pp. 1998–2014; Peleg Sprague of Main, *ibid.,* pp. 2054–2079; Ralph J. Ingersoll of Connecticut, *ibid.,* pp. 2123–2131.

[49] Taussig, *Tariff History,* p. 100.

[50] *Ibid.,* p. 101. It was on May 9, 1828, that Daniel Webster made his ex-

The present writer would venture to repeat that the problem of Van Buren's intentions is not really central to the history of the Tariff of 1828, although it is of some importance to biographers of Van Buren. What really matters is that the Tariff of Abominations, a rather strong title for a quite impracticable piece of legislation, is an almost perfect mirror in which to observe the transient features of the Jacksonian revolution. Nothing else reflects, with such weird fidelity, the powerful democratic nationalism which opposed itself to the economical nationalism of John Quincy Adams. For the Tariff of 1828 was economic only as regards its subject matter. Otherwise it gave an eccentric, a peculiar testimony to the convulsive effect of growing pains. It revealed a passion for the haphazard, the piecemeal, and the *ad hoc*. Everyone wanted something.[51] The essence of any *political* tariff may well be the whetting of appetites: so that the Tariff of 1828, although designed to favor the grower over the fabricator, became in the end an undisguised hunt for special advantages. It was less a serious effort at economic protection than it was a monstrous *battue,* in which advantages were not so much sought for as shot down. It showed that the central government was expected to give assistance, but never to plan the assistance that it gave. Nothing could be less in keeping with the custodial philosophy of President Adams, or less adjusted to the centralizing system of Henry Clay. As for the South, in so far as South Carolina could speak for the South, it now endeavored to define a decisive answer.

When the bill was passed, and had received the signature of a President who could find no constitutional reasons for imposing his veto, there was a meeting of the South Carolina delegation at the

planation—never thereafter forgotten—that he was about to deny everything he had said in his great House free-trade speech of 1824, because New England had built up her manufacturing enterprise on the understanding that protection was now a settled policy of government. *Register of Debates,* 20 Cong., 1 sess., IV, Pt. ii, pp. 750–770; see also pp. 726–727, 730, 734, 783, 786. The bill was signed by the President on May 19.

[51] Thomas Hart Benton, for example, mockingly asked for a duty on indigo, in gratitude to those Southerners who had voted to protect hemp; but he was quite serious when he moved for duties on furs and lead. Levi Woodbury of New Hampshire, an antiprotectionist, swallowed his principles and asked for a duty on manufactured silks. Mahlon Dickerson of New Jersey wanted a 50 per cent ad valorem on imported vermicelli. The duty on pig and rolled bar iron was voted, although no ironmaster had ever asked for it. Stanwood, *Tariff Controversies,* I, 283; *American State Papers, Finance,* V, p. 784.

house of Senator Robert Y. Hayne. Here it was agreed to do nothing of a violent nature until after the election. Vice-President Calhoun was not present, but his influence was undoubtedly predominant. Even after his vote against the woolen bill, he had been called a "nationalist" and a "moderate" in his own state; and although he wished to preserve, both then and for the rest of his life, the character of a nationalist, he perceived that the designation of "moderate" would do him immense harm. South Carolina was in no mood for moderation. As a result of the British financial panic in the winter of 1825–26, cotton had sunk to an average of 12 cents in 1826 and of 8.8 cents in 1827. On the heels of this decline there came the Tariff of 1828, threatening to raise the price of everything which the planter bought.[52] It was believed, however, that Jackson would modify the tariff, and it was still supposed that Calhoun would be his successor. Retiring to his home in the South Carolina uplands, Calhoun began to compose a document which was afterward known as *The South Carolina Exposition and Protest*. It was to be published in December, and anonymously. Calhoun's style, needless to say, was anything but anonymous.

The *Exposition* opened with a conventional disquisition on the tariff: it was an unjust tax upon the South's exchanges; it was levied for the benefit of northern profiteers; and it would provoke such a retaliation from the outer world as to deprive the planter of his international market. Moreover, since the South was responsible for two-thirds of the nation's exports, but was politically no more than one-third of the nation, the tariff was a clear case of oppression by the majority. This much was to be expected, but Calhoun's remedies had at least the merit of surprise.

Throwing away his shield of the natural law, a respectable but cumbersome device, he advanced to the attack brandishing a strange assortment of weapons which he had filched from the armories of John Taylor of Caroline, Robert Turnbull, Judge Spencer Roane and

[52] Wiltse, *Calhoun: Nationalist,* p. 356. One of the great agitators in South Carolina was Robert J. Turnbull, whose *Crisis* had already been published in October, 1827. For its effect on South Carolina, see James Hamilton, *An Eulogium on the Public Services and Character of Robert J. Turnbull, Esq.* (Charleston, 1834), p. 15, and D. F. Houston, *A Critical Study of Nullification in South Carolina* (Cambridge, 1896), p. 50. For Calhoun's dilemma, see also Turner, *Rise of the New West,* p. 323.

the Virginia and Kentucky Resolutions. There was, he said in effect, no division of sovereignty between states and the general government. Government was one thing, sovereignty another. Government was strictly limited; sovereignty resided in all its amplitude in the people of the several states. Thus the Constitution itself was merely a compact between sovereign states. The "compact" theory was certainly nothing new; but this was not true of the uses to which Calhoun proposed to put it. Any state, he said, could peacefully prevent the operation of any federal law within its boundaries until a decision had been made by the amending power—that is to say, by three-fourths of the states. Like his subsequent theory of concurrent majorities, this would have reduced the nation to immobility, if not to disunion, if any state had *successfully* maintained it.

Calhoun had, in many respects, one of the most original minds in the Union; but it was a stern, metaphysical, conventual mind, which was simply not accessible to the ordinary man. Calhoun's arguments concerning government and sovereignty seemed either unintelligible or perverse, and his "compact" theory was not only embarrassing to moderates of the state-rights school, it was also—to nationalists of any description—a shocking reminder of the Hartford Convention. In its published form, the *Exposition* was an example of the twisted cleverness to which the sectional spirit could drive a southern intellectual, but there was one paragraph in it—a paragraph too extreme to be printed—which was not sectional at all:

The [protective] system [he writes] has not been sufficiently long in operation with us, to display its real character in reference to the point now under discussion. To understand its ultimate tendency, in distributing the wealth of society among the several classes, we must turn our eyes to Europe, where it has been in action for centuries,—and operated as one among the efficient causes of that great inequality of property which prevails in most European countries. No system can be more efficient to rear up a moneyed aristocracy. Its tendency is, to make the poor poorer, and the rich richer. Heretofore, in our country, this tendency has displayed itself principally in its effects, as regards the different sections,—but time will come when it will produce the same results between the several classes in the manufacturing States. After we [the southern planters] are exhausted, the contest will be between the capitalists and operatives; for into these two classes it must, ultimately, divide society. The issue of the struggle here must be the same as it has been in Europe. Under the operation of the system, wages must sink more rapidly than the necessaries of life, till the operatives will be reduced to the lowest point,—when the portion of the products of their labor left to them, will be barely sufficient to preserve existence.[53]

In other words, Calhoun was endeavoring to preserve his character as a nationalist by pointing out that the nation was composed, not of sections, but ultimately of classes. Had he pursued this argument to its logical conclusion, he must have announced that the nation should either do away with protection for the good of the whole economy or face the prospect of a proletarian revolution. In the long run, however, in spite of his originality, and because he was a slaveholder, this kind of historical "necessity" did not appeal to him; he began to argue that a revolution was impending, but that it need never take place. If the capitalists of the North and the planters of the South would pool their *class* interests—if the capitalists would sanction slavery, and the planters assist in suppressing labor agitation—then the nation would rise above the need for sectional disputes. Van Buren's suggested alliance between the plain republicans and the planters was distinctly unpleasant,[54] but Calhoun's specific was nothing less than unholy. It has been brilliantly described as "an arresting defense of reaction, a sort of intellectual Black Mass." All this, however, was in the future. It must be admitted that in 1828 when Calhoun wrote the *Exposition* he had, in the recesses of his mind, at least a logical answer to the democratic nationalism which both revealed and caricatured itself in the Tariff of 1828. In other words, Calhoun was endeavoring to preserve his character as a nationalist by pointing out that the nation must think of itself, not in terms of sections, but in terms of classes. The protective principle threatened the whole national com-

[53] Calhoun, *Works,* VI, 1–59, gives the full text of the *Exposition and Protest.* For helpful discussions, see Turner, *Rise of the New West,* pp. 326–330, and Wiltse, *Calhoun: Nationalist,* pp. 390–397. An illuminating study will be found in Richard Hofstadter, *The American Political Tradition* (New York, 1948), pp. 67–91, from which the "intellectual Black Mass" quotation, *infra,* is taken and to which the reader is referred.

[54] Van Buren to Thomas Ritchie (a copy), January 13, 1827. Supporting his case for a revival of "old party distinctions," Van Buren says that it was not until these were broken down under "the amalgamating policy of Mr. Monroe" that the clamor against southern influence and Negro slavery began in the North, Van Buren Papers, L.C. For Van Buren's highly exaggerated ideas of what he called Monroe's "fusion policy" see Remini, *Martin Van Buren,* chapter 2, esp. p. 24.

munity, he said, because it was bound to create an American proletariat—a proposition which, in 1828, was at least arguable. Moreover it cannot be said to reveal the reactionary mania which, in his later years, altogether deformed Calhoun's thinking. Had this paragraph been admitted, the *Exposition* would have been the most chilling of all responses to the Tariff of 1828.

CHAPTER 12

The Election of 1828

THE Tariff of 1828 may possibly have given satisfaction to the wool and hemp growers of the West and Northwest; otherwise it was little more than a series of absurd or spiteful or optimistic variations on the twin themes of expansion and opportunity. In the old South and the new Southwest, where the price of cotton had been sinking precipitously, except for a brief upsurge in 1824–25, it was naturally abominated; and this was, of course, especially true of the Old South, where production costs were higher, and where exhausted soils spoke for themselves. Calhoun's *Exposition and Protest,* in its printed form, was an extravagant gloss upon the fact that the planter of the Old South must look to Liverpool and not to Washington for relief; that he lay at the mercy of an international market, and could not endure to see it tampered with by a group of northern and western expansionists who had seized control of the machinery of central government. In the West, on the other hand, in so far as the new West had achieved an identity, there was a fairly continuous advance from 1823 onward, in spite of much discouragement: not merely in terms of population, although the popular figures are startling,[1] but

[1] By 1820 one quarter of the population of the U.S.A. was already living west of the Alleghenies: U.S. *Census* (1820). Between 1820 and 1830, ratios of increase show: Ohio from 581,434 to 937,903, or 60 per cent; Indiana from 147,178 to 343,031, or 58 per cent; Illinois from 55,211 to 157,445, or 170 per cent; Missouri from 66,586 to 140,455, or 125 per cent. Kentucky increased from 564,317 to 687,917; Tennessee from 422,823 to 681,904; Alabama

(after 1827) in the less spectacular arithmetic of foodstuff prices and of land sales.[2] The Northeast, and particularly New England, was the scene of a fundamental transformation in which capital was being shifted from commerce to industry, and upon which the promise of a national market was already beginning to dawn. One cannot think of the 1820's in the North and West without realizing that the adjustment to the collapse of 1819 to 1821 had been painful indeed, but that the economy was now hovering on the edge of a new boom. The Era of Good Feelings, so called, had not really survived the Panic of 1819; it had been succeeded, domestically, by an Era of Introspection, in which American democracy looked westward for its national path to the future, but *inward* for the terms upon which that future was to be realized. The excitement, the irritability, the hope, and the fear of this period, so oddly and yet so dramatically mirrored in the Tariff of Abominations, now reappeared in the presidential election of 1828.

How far the appearance was appearance only is still debatable. In 1828 the President, who had never forgiven himself for his success in 1824, hugged to his bosom the gnawing certainty of defeat; most of his colleagues were of a like mind; but was his defeat in that year quite as popular as it is said to have been? The one-party muddle of 1824 was, it is true, vanishing: there were now two parties, each with a modest organization in the nation's capital and in most of the states, one calling itself the "friends" of Adams, the other the "friends" of Jackson. Each was a loose cohesion of interests; but in doubtful states, and even in a presidential year, neither was mature enough to give this cohesion a coherence. The nation had a choice, as it never had in 1816 or in 1824, but it was a choice between stereotypes, such as Aristocracy and Democracy, behind which there lay a preference either for economic or for democratic nationalism, either for controlled or for piecemeal expansion, either for the American System as a whole or for the American System in detail. Even in the South, where particularism was again in fashion, and democracy was being linked to white supremacy, the shaky posture of cotton in the world market at once called for and failed to justify an extreme state-rights

---

went from 127,091 to 309,527; and Mississippi from 75,448 to 136,621. *Historical Statistics of the U.S.,* p. 13.

[2] Douglass C. North, *Economic Growth of the United States, 1790–1860* (Englewood Cliffs, N.J., 1961), pp. 136–137, esp. Chart I–XI, p. 137.

position. The particularist could not look to Washington, if Washington were to become a prey to industrial capitalists and federally minded democrats; on the other hand, he did not know exactly what Jackson stood for. In the South, as elsewhere, Jackson represented opportunity, change, the dissolution of the status quo.

In actual fact, however, there were aspects of the national life and growth upon which neither the administration nor the Jackson party cared to reflect; and it was because they did not consider these aspects that the Jacksonians, in 1828, were at best simulacra of that profound democratic nationalism which sought to express itself in the presidential election. The grievances which lay at the very heart of expansion were concerned with free education, abolition of imprisonment for debt, a more equitable militia system, a mechanics' lien law, and, in general, with equality of opportunity in every sense of the term.

Probably the greatest and most widespread of these was the demand for a reform in public education; and this is all too easy to understand when one considers that education was not an intellectual but a strictly practical concept, a means of grasping the skirts of opportunity as they flaunted themselves along the roads and canals, in the wake of the upriver steamboat, and especially at every new industrial and commercial gateway to the fuller life. Free education had always been one of the expressed concerns of America; but free education, although its conditions varied from state to state, was hopelessly inefficient. At the more genteel levels of society, it was connected with pauperism; more generally, the taxpayer offered it only verbal support; but the chief reason for its failure was administrative indifference. Land and money were usually expended upon academies and colleges for the children of the well-to-do; and, in spite of the nation's expressed ideals, the children of the poorer classes were educated as paupers or not educated at all.[3]

It was natural that this grievance should find its most effective

---

[3] In New England, some attempt had been made to provide free schooling for all classes; but New York was probably the most advanced state in the Union in this respect, and in New York it was known that 25,000 children between the ages of five and fifteen were not attending any school at all. McMaster, *History*, V, pp. 343 ff.; William Boume, *History of the Public School Society of the City of New York* (New York, 1870), III; John R. Commons and associates, *History of the Labor Movement in the United States* (4 vols., New York, 1918–1935), I, 181–182.

voice in urban districts. Between 1820 and 1830 the percentage of
urban population had risen from 4.9 to 6.7 of the total, while the
number of cities with over 8,000 inhabitants had grown from eleven
to twenty-four.[4] Urbanization, even in this exiguous form, meant a
more variegated life, just as it also meant the entrance of the workingman into American history, not as a journeyman, but as a wage earner
without property.[5] As a wage earner, he began to demand shorter
working hours and better pay; as a journeyman, who hoped to become
in time an independent employer, he asked for better educational
facilities. Opportunity was becoming more various and more enticing;
but if his children were required to labor in factories from sunup to
sundown, often without the chance of even one child in a family
being withdrawn for education, how were they to acquire that practical knowledge which alone could exploit the varieties of opportunity?

Thus the "Transportation Revolution," which implied not only a
more closely knit nation but also the advance of capitalism all over
America, was likely to provoke specific grievances in those areas where
capital was most concentrated, where America was least obviously a
land of pioneers, and where expansion turned inward and became
introspection. The Boston house carpenters' strike of 1825, the Philadelphia journeymen carpenters' strike of 1827, the formation of a
Mechanics' Union of Trade Associations in Philadelphia in that year,
the Workingmen's Party Convention of 1828—these represented
questions concerning the nation's future which neither national party,
in 1828, was prepared to answer.[6]

[4] These figures, *ibid.*, I, 176–177, are probably too low. See Taylor, *Transportation Revolution*, p. 7, and *Historical Statistics of the U.S.*, 14, Sec. A,
181–194. The meaning of "urban" is susceptible to different interpretations. In
Historical Statistics of the U.S. the number of places with over *5,000* inhabitants is shown to have increased from 34 to 56, and those with over
10,000 from 13 to 23. Here the number of places between 10,000 and 25,000
had exactly doubled itself—from 8 to 16.

[5] The journeyman is usually described, and indeed described himself, as being
now caught between the merchant-capitalist (who supplied the raw materials,
financed the production expense, and marketed the finished product) and the
merchant-employer (who had sunk to the status of a small contractor, making
his profits out of wages and work). Commons, *History of Labor*, I, 158.

[6] *Ibid.*, I, 159–160; Boston *Columbian Centinel*, April 20, 1825; Philip S.
Foner, *History of the Labor Movement in the United States* (New York,
1947), pp. 102–124; *Mechanics' Free Press* (organized 1828), April 19,

Among the many grievances set forth by the Mechanics' Union and the Workingmen's party, imprisonment for debt was emphasized as a cruel, outmoded, and irrational restraint upon communication; for if a man were imprisoned for debt, how could he work his way back into good relations with his creditor? It was an affront, not merely to common sense, but to mobility and opportunity; and it bore, of course, most heavily upon the very poor man or woman. In the same egalitarian and opportunistic spirit the union and the party attacked the power of the state legislatures to create corporations by special charter, a power which was not responsive to men with little capital or political influence, and which tended, therefore, to make business enterprise itself a preserve for small cliques of wealthy capitalists, who would raise prices and force down wages. This was particularly evident, it was thought, in the case of bank charters; for bankers did not extend credit to the small enterprisers who were most in need of it, and their depreciated paper was purchased by employers at a discount and forced upon wage earners at its face value. Workingmen were usually "hard money" men, opposed to banks of issue and sometimes to banks of any kind; and although we now know that "hard money" sentiments were not confined to the East, but flourished in the West as well,[7] it was the workingman of the East who made out the most striking case for hard money. He, too, was notoriously in need of a mechanics' lien law, which would oblige employers who went bankrupt to pay their workmen at least a moiety of what was due them, and prevent employers from declaring themselves bankrupt, as they often did, solely to avoid the payment of wages.

August 25, 1828; Edward Pessen, "The Workingmen's Movement in the Jackson Era," *Mississippi Valley Historical Review*, XLIII (1956), 428–443.

[7] E. T. Randall, "Imprisonment for Debt in America—Fact and Fiction," *Mississippi Valley Historical Review*, XXXIX (1952), 89–102, argues that this was less severe than is generally supposed; but cf. Richard B. Morris, "Measure of Bondage in the Slave States," *ibid.*, XLI (1954), p. 219–240, for the harsh treatment of white debtors in the South. Rothbard, *Panic of 1819, passim,* takes the position that "hard money" and "soft money" sentiments flourished side by side throughout the Union. Hammond, *Banks and Politics in America, passim,* inclines to the view that agrarians everywhere were usually "hard money" men and the business community was normally inflationist. In any event, the once-accepted idea of a "soft money" West is now no longer acceptable without serious modification; but the Eastern "hard money" mechanic was still the more vocal at this time.

The attack upon special charters of incorporation was, in its way, a recognition of the fact that the character of the corporation was changing: it was becoming disconnected from the idea of public utility and attaching itself more and more to that of private advantage.[8] General laws of incorporation, it was thought, would give the corporation a more public character, at least in the sense that it would be more available to the small enterpriser. Indeed, every grievance of the 1820's seemed to favor the creation of a public world which would be responsive to the individual citizen. In this respect, John Quincy Adams' planned economy might have been the answer, if it had not talked of restraint rather than reform. The reform demanded in the late 1820's was designed to create a public world where more people would have a chance to do more things; its advocates expected administration, at any level, to advance this kind of opportunity; but they did not care for that paternalistic state which might, given the time, have emerged from the plans of John Quincy Adams. As it was, all that they could see in his idea of a system of communications financed by the sale of public lands was, in fact, a scheme for creating a pool of cheap labor in the manufacturing states; the national bank, although it was now wisely managed under Nicholas Biddle, was racked between two different interpretations—it was either a government monopoly or it was the apotheosis of a system of depreciated paper; and the protective tariff, a more rational construct than the Tariff of 1828, was held to be "most prone to reduce the wages of workmen." But the Jacksonians, although they employed an egalitarian language, do not appear to have been interested, in 1828, in egalitarian reforms. In New York State, for example, they offered themselves to the public as a state-rights party; they were silent about the private banks with which the Regency was allied; and it was not until

[8] Oscar Handlin and Mary Plug Handlin, *Commonwealth: A Study in the Rise of the American Economy, Massachusetts, 1774–1861* (New York, 1947), pp. 172–173. See also A. B. Street, *The Council of Revision in the State of New York* (Albany, 1859), p. 425, which gives Chief Justice Lansing's idea of the quasi-public nature of a corporation, where he argues against the incorporation of the Manhattan Company in 1799; i.e., what a corporation might *not* do should be set forth in the severest detail in any charter. The charter of the Manhattan Company is a good early example of the new or private character of charters; ostensibly a water company, the Manhattan Company was actually a bank with very wide powers.

all was over that their President spoke against imprisonment for federal debt.[9]

It was in New York State, where the Anti-Masonic party was founded, that the ambiguous spirit of the times found its most characteristic expression. The alleged and probable murder of a defecting Mason in 1826 was a very nasty affair; but the idea of huge secret "conspiracy" of Masons, whose purpose was to run the nation in their own interests, could only have made an impression in a time when the common man was first seriously demanding his share in the benefits of expansion. The fact that Adams was not a Mason, and that Jackson was one, did not really confuse the issue: it showed that the Anti-Masons were not interested in either side; and although they supported Adams in New York, in 1828, they became a separate and militantly reforming party once the election was over.[10] Their history proves that it was not so much their reforming impulse as the complications created by their attack on Masonry which silenced them after a brief and a spectacular career.

Under all these circumstances, it was perhaps to be expected that the subterranean battle between restraint and reform should not have found an expression in the presidential election of 1828; or rather, to put it another way, that it should have expressed itself only in the most limited and frustrated manner. The campaign became an exchange of personalities, which only compounded confusion. The friends of Adams, for example, took their stand upon the President's long experience in the management of public business; the friends of Jackson pointed out that too much of this experience had been acquired in the corrupting atmosphere of foreign courts. Adams had already been accused, on the grounds that he had purchased a billiard table and a set of chessmen for the White House, of consorting with gamblers and spendthrifts;[11] and as Madame du Deffand once re-

[9] Lee Benson, *The Concept of Jacksonian Democracy* (Princeton, 1961), pp. 30 ff.

[10] *Ibid.*, pp. 15 ff. If the issue was not confused, proponents of the two candidates certainly were. For example, W. L. Marcy to Van Buren, January 29, 1828: "The antimasonic excitement in the West [of New York State] will be turned in favor of Mr. Adams." Van Buren Papers, LC. Whereas L. B. Langworthy to John W. Taylor, July 10, 1828, says: "The antimasons are doing Mr. A. more harm than anything you can imagine." John W. Taylor Papers, NYHS.

[11] *Register of Debates*, 19 Cong., 2 sess., II, Pt. ii, pp. 2655–2656. The

marked, when she was told that the martyred St. Denis had picked up
his head and walked a whole mile, "in such a case, it is the first step
that counts." The Nineteenth Congress having made the first step,
it was easy to go on from there and describe his character as a very
compost of European vices. Nor was this all. Adams was a highly educated man; he was also an intellectual; but he was anything but popular in his approach to the arts of government. The President who
implored the Congress not to be paralyzed by the will of its constituents, or who vented his sarcasms on the Senate at a critical moment
in his foreign policy, was a somewhat outstanding example of intellectual impatience. If the attack on him had been wholly concentrated
upon his behavior in (for example) the West Indies controversy, where
he had pursued an idea too hard and too far, it might have been
justified: an intellectual in office is always vulnerable. Instead it took
the form of "John Quincy Adams who can write/and Andrew Jackson who can fight." If this comparison was stupid, and it was, it
none the less gave a sort of shape to the activist impulse of democratic
nationalism; but it also expressed the fears and insecurities which
moved in the underworld of egalitarian reform. Anti-intellectualism
is usually a child of fear. It is worth recalling that Anti-Masonry was
founded upon the belief in a "conspiracy" that did not exist.

In such a climate, Andrew Jackson had most of the advantages.
He was a hero; that is to say, a man of action, and a child of nature.
At the height of this strange campaign, when to betray an idea was
almost to commit a felony, he was far too shrewd to attempt to do
so. His earlier call for a "judicious" tariff was a masterly example of
how to avoid an issue.[12] It is odd (though not surprising) that the
more worldly Van Buren should have feared that his impulsive General would speak out of turn:[13] the General's impulses had rarely been
purposeless, and they had never been self-defeating. This did not

---

billiard table cost the public $61, the chessmen $21. The point, if any, is that
chess in those days *could* be a gambling game. Adams' standards of entertainment at the White House were, of course, in accordance with his ideas of what
was due to the dignity of the office of President. For a description see Francis
Boott Greenhough (ed.) *Letters of Horatio Greenhough* (Boston, 1887), p. 36.
His personal life, however, was always more Spartan than otherwise.

[12] This had been made in 1824; the actual wording was "a judicious examination and revision" of the tariff, and this was Jackson's last word on the
subject. Jackson to L. H. Coleman, April 26, 1824; Parton, *Jackson*, III, 35.

[13] Van Buren to Jackson, November 24, 1827; Van Buren Papers, LC.

mean that he was insincere, or merely an opportunist; but it did mean how readily he grasped the fact that in the confusion of 1828 a truly national figure could not be committed in advance. It is not unlikely that those Federalists who preferred him to Adams did so not merely because they believed that he would relax the political proscription against them,[14] but also because they believed that he would lead America back into a simpler, less vulgar,[15] less corrupt and conniving world than the American System seemed to offer. For the American System, even if one superimposed upon it all Adams' severe ideas of federal control and national self-restraint, was primarily a system for the industrial capitalist. Jackson was, indeed, a giant figure; but whether in 1828 he was really an egalitarian, or really a reformer, or to what extent he was either, are to this day questions which have not found a precise answer.

To his opponents,· he seemed a very slippery contestant, a political Proteus. As a Westerner, he was a democrat but not a particularist; as a planter and slaveholder, he might possibly be more a particularist than a democrat; as the old Hero, he was a nationalist without a program. It is rightly regrettable, but not unintelligible, that in these rather desperate circumstances, the "friends" of Adams should have descended to the basest kind of personal attack. If the anti-intellectualism of the Jacksonians strikes us as offensive and dangerous, the methods employed by the Adamsites were blankly disgraceful. To call Jackson a military tyrant was one thing—the "Coffin Handbill" is just within the bounds of permissible invective—to accuse him and Mrs. Jackson of having lived together in willful adultery was quite another.[16] Neither Adams nor Clay was responsible for this infamous

[14] Livermore, *Twilight of Federalism, passim,* but especially pp. 162–164, for Jackson's "Drayton Letter" of October, 1816, suggesting to Monroe the appointment of a Federalist to the War Department. See also Jackson to A. J. Donelson, April 11, 1824, Bassett, *Correspondence,* III, 246–247; Gallatin to W. Lowrie, May 22, 1824, Gallatin Papers, NYHS; Jefferson to R. Rush, June 5, 1824, *Writings,* Ford (ed.), X, 304–305.

[15] Marvin Meyers, *The Jacksonian Persuasion,* 73, n. 77.

[16] The "Coffin Handbill," put out by John Binns of the Philadelphia *Democratic Press,* accused the General of "murdering" six militiamen for desertion during the War of 1812. Marquis James, *Andrew Jackson: Portrait of a President* (Indianapolis and New York, 1937), p. 159. For the scurrilities in this campaign, see Bemis, *John Quincy Adams and the Union,* pp. 140–142. The slander concerning Jackson's "adultery" was being whispered around in

accusation, which broke Mrs. Jackson's heart and hastened her death; but they knew of it, and they let it go on—Adams because he was puritanical enough both to believe it and to think it justifiable, Clay because he was too desperate to behave as he normally would have done. In reply, the Jacksonian *United States Telegraph* put forth some nonsensical story about premarital relations between President and Mrs. Adams, but the General's response to this was crushing. "I never war against females," said Jackson, "and it is only the base and cowardly that do." No more was heard about Mrs. Adams.[17]

The election is said to have demonstrated the extent to which Jackson profited by the people's new access to the polls. In the campaign of 1824, six states chose their electors in the legislature and seven others by districts and not by a general ticket. In 1828, only two states gave the choice to the legislature, and only four retained the district system. The nation was verging upon (white) manhood suffrage, the population had increased: the election returns should therefore show how momentous the "Jacksonian Revolution" really was.[18]

The election was held between October 31 (Pennsylvania, Ohio) and November 14 (Tennessee); and when it was all over it was known that Adams had carried all New England, New Jersey, Delaware, and Maryland, that he had lost New York by a close margin, and that the rest of the country had declared for Jackson. The electoral

---

1825—cf. "Anonymous" to John W. Taylor, January 22, 1825; John W. Taylor Papers, NYHS. It was picked up by the presumably respectable Charles Hammond (see *Dictionary of American Biography,* VIII, 202) in 1826; repeated by the administration's *National Journal* in 1827; refuted by the Washington *United States Telegraph;* and answered by Hammond with the unforgivable question: "Ought a convicted adulteress and her paramour husband be placed in his highest offices in this free and christian land?" Washington *National Journal,* March 26, 1827; Washington *United States Telegraph,* June 22, 1827; Charles Hammond, *A View of General Jackson's Domestic Relations* (Cincinnati, 1828). The villains were Charles Hammond and Peter Force, editor of the *National Journal.* The truth was that Jackson had married Rachel Robard in 1791, believing (as she did) that she had been legally divorced in Virginia. Two years later they had discovered, to their horror, that the divorce had never been final. They had at once remarried.

[17] *United States Telegraph,* June 16, 1827; Jackson to Duff Green, August 13, 1827, in James, *Jackson,* p. 158. Green had the weird idea that Mrs. Jackson's honor would be "vindicated" if a similar charge could be laid against Mrs. Adams.

[18] McMaster, *History,* V, 75, 518.

vote—178 to 83—and the popular vote—647,276 to 508,604—offer a resounding proof of Jackson popularity.[19] But was it an overwhelming one? At any rate, it was *not* a demonstration of the transforming energies of manhood suffrage. In states where the victory of one or the other candidate was taken for granted, the new voters apparently did not bother to go to the polls: this was the case in all the South below the Potomac, and in all the new West,[20] whose influence was once held to have been decisive, but should be better described as portentous. In New England again, where Adams' victory had been conceded, there was a significant increase in voter participation only in New Hampshire—the one state where the Adams' conservative "amalgamation" policy had produced a violent division.[21] It was, in fact, only in the middle states and in the old West that the contest between economic and democratic nationalism, between controlled and piecemeal expansion, was really fought out at the polls. In Kentucky, for example, a defeat for the American System meant a disavowal of Henry Clay: here a number of the Old Court party, which Adams and Clay had favored to the detriment of Clay's popularity with the New Court reformers, was now known to be friendly to Jackson;[22] and the voting was keen and the contest bitter. If the two national parties had been better organized, would the voting itself have been more national in scope?

The question is irrelevant, because the *mise en scène* was simply not favorable to meticulous organization. The election of 1828, if one removes the clutter of state and local issues, reveals only a Jeffersonian

---

[19] *Ibid.*, pp. 518–520, for a tabulation of the results. Richard Rush, vice-presidential candidate on the Adams side, obtained the same number of votes as Adams. Calhoun lost the seven votes of Georgia to William C. Smith of South Carolina, so that his electoral vote was 171.

[20] A most interesting, careful, and scholarly discussion of this will be found in Richard P. McCormick, "New Perspectives on Jacksonian Politics," *American Historical Review*, LXV (1960), 288–301, to which I am much indebted. The argument that the nation was still more involved in the local and state issues than in national ones—an involvement which makes an analysis of the presidential election of 1828 a somewhat baffling enterprise—is certainly supported in this article.

[21] Livermore, *Twilight of Federalism*, pp. 224–227. Cf. also Levi Woodbury to Van Buren, July 1, 1828. "Our opponents [i.e., the Adams supporters] are talented—wealthy and cunning—they include almost all the old leaders of both parties"; Van Buren Papers, LC.

[22] W. B. Lewis to Van Buren, August 8, 1828; Van Buren Papers.

world in decay. There were Adams Republicans and Jackson Republicans, Adams Federalists and Jackson Federalists: the terms National Republican and Jacksonian Democrat were not yet current. It was as if the old Republican philosophy had become deeply split. On the one hand, there was Jefferson's faith in an aristocracy of intellect and virtue—government by an intelligent but disinterested elite; on the other, there was the Jeffersonian trust in the moral character of the people. Thus, the federal "civil service" under the Virginia Dynasty had become honest and efficient but it was also exclusive:[23] it was opposed by the concept of rotation in office, which assumed that any man of ordinary intelligence could do as well.[24] The cry of "aristocracy," so often and successfully raised against Adams, was aimed not only at those moneyed elites whom Adams was supposed to favor, and whom the American System actually did favor, but also at the bureaucratic elite. The cry of "democracy," when it was applied to Jackson, meant that Jackson was a gigantic symbol of Jefferson's belief in the uncommonness of the common man. The Jeffersonian world, in short, was being dissolved by economic opportunities with which it was unable to cope in Jeffersonian terms; and these opportunities were destined to be carried into the agrarian West by the very Transportation Revolution that Adams had hoped to control in the national interest. Even Adams' neomercantilism was, in a severe way, a distortion of the realism in Jefferson's natural philosophy, its insistence upon the categorical, whereas the "democracy" of Jackson was a response to the nominalism in Jefferson's idea of American history— its vision of an American world of discrete particulars. One need only repeat that in 1828 the realism behind the national sentiments of the Era of Good Feelings had already worked itself out in the Transcontinental Treaty, *McCulloch* v. *Maryland,* the Monroe Doctrine, the Navigation Act of 1823 and the Tariff of 1824; whereas the Panic of 1819 had produced a new kind of nationalist, to whom expansion had become unlimited opportunity, who spoke for the small entrepreneur, and who had no program at all. The Tariff of 1828 was a good example of this kind of nationalism: it was, in its piecemeal character,

---

[23] White, *Jeffersonians,* Chap. XXXV.

[24] "The duties of all public officers are, or at least admit of being made, so plain and simple that men of intelligence may readily qualify themselves for their performance." Andrew Jackson, First Annual Message, December 8, 1829; Richardson, *Messages and Papers,* II, 449.

an absurd distortion of the nominalist position. Thus the nation in 1828 was in a peculiarly introspective mood, wondering what kind of national existence would emerge from the agonized passing of the Jeffersonian world; and here the democratic nationalists, who were profoundly discontented with the *status quo,* were at once more hopeful and more introspective than their opponents.

On November 7, Martin Van Buren, who had got himself elected governor of New York as a "proper" step toward Cabinet rank,[25] was writing to the free-trade Jacksonian, Churchill C. Cambreleng, in a mood of discreet elation.[26] He was soon to be warned that Jackson's administration was doomed in advance; that the General was feeble, sick, and an ignoramus; that the Cabinet, where he was to be Secretary of State, was incompetent and divided.[27] Indeed, it was generally believed that Jackson intended only to serve for one term: he was a national figurehead in the election of 1828 and its aftermath—at best a symbol of change, tremendous but transient. When the returns were all in, the administration professed to be horrified by a defeat which it had in fact predicted; but Adams was convinced that the nation would soon come to its senses. He himself refused to attend the inauguration of a man who had accused him of bargain and corruption, and whom (alas) he continued to stigmatize as an adulterer and an illiterate barbarian. Abuse was easier than prediction where Jackson was concerned, but prediction did not come easily for anyone after that election. For example, Adams was sure that he had been thrust into the outer darkness of retirement and of poverty—not, of course, of oblivion. The *Report* and the Diary would take care of his memory. He could not have guessed, no one could have guessed, that he would soon begin a long, embattled, and honorable career in the

[25] J. Clark to Van Buren, April 18, 1828, advised him to run for governor, as a Jacksonian. This would make "justices, constables, & all the minor active men in the towns familiar with your name. . . . After an election should you wish to go into the Cabinet you could go as well from the governor's chair as from the Senate & I think with much more propriety;" Van Buren Papers, LC.

[26] Van Buren to C. C. Cambreleng, November 7, 1828: "If a man who has had the Philistines upon him & has come out gloriously can condescend to do a favor for one who is only Governor elect (as it is supposed) etc., etc."; Van Buren Papers. This mood of discreet elation was undoubtedly tempered by the fact that the governorship race was an exceedingly close one, and the final canvass could not have been made on this date.

[27] Van Buren, *Autobiography,* pp. 229–231.

House of Representatives. All he could tell himself in 1829 was that his great services as Secretary of State had been most ungenerously repaid, that his presidential schemes had been idly mocked or deliberately flouted, that his reputation was in tatters; and it was an embittered man who, on March 4, while Jackson was being carried to his inauguration and his fame, rode out from a hired dwelling on Meridian Hill and on into the empty city. On his way back, a gentleman called Dulaney hailed him "and inquired of me whether I could inform him how he could see John Quincy Adams."[28] One cannot tell whether this question came too late or too soon.

[28] Adams, *Memoirs,* VIII, 105.

Bibliographical Essay

Bibliographies

The Harvard Guide to American History, Paul H. Buck, Oscar Handlin, Frederick Merk, Samuel Eliot Morison, Arthur M. Schlesinger, and Arthur M. Schlesinger, Jr., compilers (Cambridge, 1954), is as complete as could be wished for up to the year of publication. Samuel Flagg Bemis and Grace Gardiner Griffin, *Guide to the Diplomatic History of the United States, 1775–1921* (Washington, 1921), is the standard bibliography in its field. These should be supplemented by Grace Griffin, *Writings on American History,* which gives an annual account of printed articles, documents, and books; and by the list of articles on historical subjects in the *American Historical Review.*

Manuscript Collections

Adams Family Papers, Massachusetts Historical Society
Nicholas Biddle Papers, Library of Congress
James Buchanan Papers, Pennsylvania Historical Society and Library of Congress
Henry Clay Papers, Library of Congress
De Witt Clinton Papers, New York Public Library and Columbia University
Edward Coles Papers, Chicago Historical Society
Ninian Edwards Papers, Chicago Historical Society
A. C. Flagg Papers, New York Public Library
Albert Gallatin Papers, New-York Historical Society
John Holmes Papers, Maine Historical Society
Andrew Jackson Papers, Library of Congress
Rufus King Papers, New-York Historical Society
William Lowndes Papers, Library of Congress

John B. C. Lucas Papers, Missouri Historical Society
James Madison Papers, Library of Congress
James Monroe Papers, Library of Congress and New York Public Library
Harrison Otis Papers, Massachusets Historical Society and New York Public Library
William Plumer Papers, Library of Congress
Tallmadge Family Papers, New-York Historical Society
John W. Taylor Papers, New-York Historical Society
Martin Van Buren Papers, Library of Congress
Daniel Webster Papers, Library of Congress
William Wirt Letterbook, Library of Congress

The reader should also consult, although its esoteric arrangement may present some difficulties, *The National Union Catalog of Manuscript Collections, 1959–1961* (Ann Arbor, 1962).

Newspapers

Among the important newspapers published during this period are:

Albany *Argus*
Boston *Columbian Centinel*
Boston *Commercial Gazette*
Boston *New-England Palladium and Commercial Advertiser*
Charleston *Gazette and Commercial Daily Advertiser*
Charleston *Courier*
Frankfurt *Argus of Western America*
Nashville *Constitutional Advocate*
New York *American*
New York *Columbian*
New York *Daily Advertiser*
New York *Enquirer*
New York *Evening Post*
Niles' Weekly Register (Baltimore)
Philadelphia *Franklin Gazette*
Philadelphia *National Gazette*
Philadelphia *Poulson's American Daily Advertiser*
Philadelphia *United States Gazette*
Pittsburgh *Gazette*
Richmond *Enquirer*
Washington *Gazette*
Washington *National Intelligencer*
Washington *National Journal*
Washington *Daily Telegraph*

Collections of Documents: General

American State Papers: Documents, legislative and executive, of the Congress of the United States (38 vols., Washington, 1832–61). The relevant volumes on Finance, Foreign Affairs, Military Affairs, and Public Lands are especially pertinent. J. D. Richardson (ed.), *Compilation of the Messages and Papers of the Presidents, 1789–1897* (10 vols., Washington, 1907); Hunter Miller (ed.), *Treaties and Other International Acts of the United States* (8 vols., Washington, 1931); *Statutes at Large of the United States of America, 1789–1873* (17 vols., Boston, 1850–1873). Judicial reports (Supreme Court) relevant to the period are Willam Cranch, *Reports of Cases Argued and Adjudged in the Supreme Court of the United States* (9 vols., Washington, 1804–17), and Henry Wheaton, *Reports of Cases Argued &c. . . .* 1816–1827 (12 vols., Philadelphia, 1816–27). The debates in Congress are reported, far from perfectly, in J. D. Gales (comp.), *Debates and Proceedings in the Congress of the United States, 1789–1824* (42 vols., Washington, 1834–56), commonly known as *Annals of Congress,* and *Register of Debates in Congress, 1825–1837* (29 vols., Washington, 1825–37), sometimes known as *Congressional Debates.* Among lesser and more eclectic collections, H. V. Ames (ed.), *State Documents on Federal Relations* (Philadelphia, 1906), will be found to be very useful. Especially recommended is Helen T. Catterall (ed.), *Judicial Cases concerning American Slavery and the Negro* (4 vols., Washington, 1926–37). For Latin American affairs during this period, two collections are indispensable, not least because they complement each other: Charles K. Webster (ed.), *Britain and the Independence of Latin America* (2 vols., London, 1938), and William R. Manning (ed.), *Diplomatic Correspondence of the United States concerning the Independence of the Latin-American Nations* (3 vols., New York, 1925).

Published Correspondence, Diaries, and Memoirs

The new and great Jeffersonian edition, Julian P. Boyd (ed.), *Papers of Thomas Jefferson* (Princeton, 1950–) has, alas, not yet reached this period; nor have the definitive *Papers of James Madison,* William T. Hutchinson and William M. E. Rachal (eds.) (Chicago, 1962–), come within hailing distance of these years. We have Paul L. Ford (ed.), *The Writings of Thomas Jefferson* (10 vols., New York, 1892–99), and Andrew A. Lipscomb (ed.), *The Writings of Thomas Jefferson* (20 vols., Washington, 1903–4); and Gaillard Hunt (ed.), *The Writings of James Madison* (9 vols., New York, 1900–1910), and *Letters and Other Writings of James Madison* (4 vols., Congressional ed., Philadelphia, 1865). There appears to be no promise of a definitive Monroe, and the reader is somewhat slenderly served by Stanislaus Hamilton (ed.), *The Writings of James Monroe* (7 vols., New York, 1898–1903).

Worthington C. Ford (ed.), *The Writings of John Quincy Adams* (7 vols., New York, 1913–17), is extremely useful but stops short of Adams' Presidency; and the wonderful *Memoirs, Comprising Portions of his Diary from 1795–1848,* Charles Francis Adams (ed.) (12 vols., Philadelphia, 1874–77), while rich for every other aspect of this period, is relatively thin for the Presidency. The other presidential figure is admirably and objectively handled in John S. Bassett (ed.), *Correspondence of Andrew Jackson* (6 vols., Washington, 1926–35). The second volume of Lester J. Cappon (ed.), *The Adams-Jefferson Letters* (2 vols., Chapel Hill, 1959), gives a charming view of the elder Adams' mind in his last years.

Richard K. Crallé (ed.), *The Works of John C. Calhoun* (6 vols., New York, 1851–56), is the chief printed source; but the student should also consult J. Franklin Jameson (ed.), "Correspondence of John C. Calhoun," in the American Historical Association's *Annual Report for 1899,* II (Washington, 1900). Calvin Colton (ed.), *The Life, Correspondence and Speeches of Henry Clay* (10 vols., Federal Edition, New York, 1904), is more concerned with speeches than life or correspondence. It is now fortunately being superseded by James F. Hopkins (ed.) and Margaret W. M. Hargreaves (assoc. ed.), *The Papers of Henry Clay* (10 vols., Lexington, 1959–), of which the first three volumes are in print, carrying us up to the end of 1824. This is a fine edition. Charles R. King (ed.), *The Life and Correspondence of Rufus King* (6 vols., New York, 1894–1900), displays lacunae at important moments—as e.g., the Missouri Compromise—but as a general conspectus will pass muster. This is not true of Henry Adams (ed.), *The Writings of Albert Gallatin* (3 vols., Philadelphia, 1879), which does not do justice to a great collection. Fletcher Webster (ed.), *The Writings and Speeches of Daniel Webster* (18 vols., Boston, 1903), is ample. *The Autobiography of Martin Van Buren* in American Historical Association, *Annual Report, 1918,* II (Washington, 1920), is indispensable, although it is somewhat chilly and—for the Tariff of 1828—possibly furtive.

Thomas Hart Benton, *Thirty Years View* (2 vols., New York, 1854), is vigorous, but must be used with due caution. John B. Moore (ed.), *The Works of James Buchanan* (12 vols., Philadelphia, 1908–11); Dorothy C. Barck (ed.), *The Letters from John Pintard to His Daughter Eliza Noel Pintard Davidson* (4 vols., New York, 1940–41); and George S. Hilliard (ed.), *Memoir and Correspondence of Jeremiah Mason* (Cambridge, 1873) are all valuable for the Federalist dilemma in these years, as is William Kent (ed.), *Memoirs and Letters of James Kent LLD* (Boston, 1898). Gaillard Hunt's edition of Margaret B. Smith, *The First Forty Years of Washington Society* (New York, 1906), is admirable for background.

General Works

Henry Adams, *History of the United States of America During the Administrations of Jefferson and Madison* (9 vols., New York, 1889–91), is still essential; the last volume, of course, only concerns this period. Edward Channing, *A History of the United States* (6 vols., New York, 1912–25), is justly praised for its insights. John B. McMaster, *A History of the Republic of the United States* (8 vols., New York, 1883–1913), is full of industrious and indeed valuable research; but its noncommittal method is distinctly frustrating.

Among works which embrace this period is Frederick Jackson Turner's *The Rise of the New West* (New York, 1907), a jewel of historiography, still bright after many years; it should be supplemented, for the years up to 1818, by K. C. Babcock, *The Rise of American Nationality* (New York, 1906). The period is also covered in John A. Krout and Dixon R. Fox, *The Completion of Independence* (New York, 1944), in terms of social history; in George Dangerfield, *The Era of Good Feelings* (New York, 1952); in Shaw Livermore, Jr., *The Twilight of Federalism: The Disintegration of the Federalist Party, 1815–1830* (Princeton, 1962), which is a scholarly investigation of Federalist politics; in Robert V. Remini, *Martin Van Buren and the Making of the Democratic Party* (New York, 1959); and in Philip S. Klein, *Pennsylvania Politics: 1817–1832* (Philadelphia, 1940), which, though confined to one state, conveys with great skill and learning the ambiguity of the whole period. On nationalism in general, see Boyd C. Shafer, *Nationalism: Myth and Reality* (New York, 1955), and, for the United States, Merle E. Curti, *The Roots of American Loyalty* (New York, 1946).

For various aspects of economic history, there are, general: Chester W. Wright, *Economic History of the United States* (New York, 1941); Edward C. Kirkland, *A History of American Economic Life* (New York, 1932); and F. A. Shannon, *Economic History of the People of the United States* (New York, 1934); Davis R. Dewey, *Financial History of the United States* (rev. ed., 1934); Bray Hammond's learned, instructive, and dramatic *Banking and Politics in America: From the Revolution to the Civil War* (Princeton, 1957); Esther R. Taus, *Central Banking Functions of the United States Treasury, 1789–1941* (New York, 1943); Frank W. Taussig, *The Tariff History of the United States* (rev. ed., 1931); Edward Stanwood, *Tariff Controversies in the Nineteenth Century* (2 vols., 1903), which supplements Taussig's classic; Arthur H. Cole's invaluable *Wholesale Commodity Prices in the United States, 1700–1861* (Cambridge, 1938); Walter B. Smith and Arthur H. Cole in their equally invaluable *Fluctuations in American Business, 1790–1860* (Cambridge, 1935); Joseph Dorfman's great mine of information, *The*

Economic Mind in American Civilization (2 vols., New York, 1946); Louis Hartz, *Economic Policy and Democratic Thought: Pennsylvania, 1776–1860* (Cambridge, 1948); and Oscar Handlin, *Commonwealth: A Study of the Role of Government in the American Economy, Massachusetts, 1774–1861* (New York, 1947), a most suggestive work. To these we must add two indispensable works: Norman S. Buck, *The Development of the Organization of Anglo-American Trade* (New Haven, 1925), and L. H. Jenks, *The Migration of British Capital to 1875* (New York, 1927).

For transportation and related problems, no book could be more welcome for this period than George R. Taylor's fine *The Transportation Revolution, 1815–1860* (New York, 1951), with its remarkably comprehensive bibliography, covering every aspect of American economic life; one might add, as pertinent to this period, U. B. Phillips, *A History of Transportation in the Eastern Cotton Belt to 1860* (New York, 1908), and E. C. Kirkland, *Men, Cities and Transportation, A Study in New England History, 1820–1900* (2 vols., Cambridge, 1948); two outstanding studies by R. G. Albion, *The Rise of New York Port, 1815–1860* (New York, 1939), and *Square-Riggers on Schedule* (Princeton, 1938); Louis C. Hunter, *Steamboats on the Western Rivers* (Cambridge, 1949), also outstanding; Vernon G. Setzer, *The Commercial Reciprocity Policy of the United States, 1774–1829* (Philadelphia, 1937); and F. Lee Benns, *The American Struggle for the West India Carrying-Trade, 1815–1830* (Bloomington, 1923). These two important works carry one into the realm of foreign policy, Benns' seminal study, in particular, being to my mind quite essential to an understanding of the administration of John Quincy Adams.

For agriculture, the period is admirably served by three general studies: Percy Bidwell and John I. Faulkner, *History of Agriculture in the Northern United States, 1620–1680* (Washington, 1941); Lewis C. Gray, assisted by Esther K. Thompson, *History of Agriculture in the Southern United States, to 1860* (2 vols., Washington, 1933); and Paul W. Gates, *The Farmer's Age* (New York, 1960). Ernest L. Bogert, *Economic History of American Agriculture* (New York, 1923), is an extremely useful supplement to these works.

For public land policies and movements, Bogert, *supra;* Benjamin A. Hibbard, *A History of the Public Land Policies* (New York, 1924); Paysan J. Treat, *The National Land System* (New York, 1910); Shoshuke Sato, *History of the Land Question in the United States* (Baltimore, 1886); and *American State Papers, Public Lands* should be consulted, together with the extremely interesting graphs in Buckingham and Cole's *Fluctuations.*

For manufactures: Victor S. Clark, *History of Manufactures in the United States* (3 vols., New York, 1929), is by far the best general study; and one should add two exemplary special studies, Caroline F. Ware, *The Early New*

England Cotton Manufacture (Boston, 1931), and Arthur H. Cole, *The American Wool Manufacturer* (2 vols., Cambridge, 1926); and for the South there is Broadus Mitchell, *William Gregg, Factory Master of the Old South* (Chapel Hill, 1928), which is good for the struggling cotton industry in the South in these years.

For labor: John R. Commons and associates, *History of Labour in the United States* (4 vols., New York, 1918); Philip S. Foner, *History of the Labor Movement in the United States* (New York, 1947); and the wage statistics in Volume II of Jurgen Kuczynski, *A Short History of Labor Conditions under Industrial Capitalism* (3 vols., London, 1943). Labor, in terms of a labor movement, is of course barely discernible in this period, but such traces as are visible have been well charted in Edward Pessen, "The Workingmen's Movement in the Jackson Era," *Mississippi Valley Historical Review,* XLIII (1956) 428 ff.

Statistics: *Historical Statistics of the United States: Colonial Times to 1957* (Washington, 1960) serves to remind us, rather abruptly, that the years before 1820 in this book are not rich in statistical material. Contemporary works are Timothy Pitkin, *A Statistical Review of the Commerce of the United States* (New Haven, 1935); George Watterson and Nicholas Biddle Van Zandt, *Tabular Statistical Review of the United States* (Washington, 1828); and J. Marshall, arranger, *A Digest of the Accounts . . . Printed Pursuant to the . . . Recommendations of the Select Committee of the House of Commons,* March 1, 1833 (London, 1833).

Biographies

This period is relatively rich in biographical works. John Quincy Adams has been particularly well served by two definitive studies: *John Quincy Adams and the Foundations of American Foreign Policy* (New York, 1949) by Samuel Flagg Bemis, and the same author's *John Quincy Adams and the Union* (New York, 1956). Although the first of these is, in effect, a masterly work in the field of diplomacy and the second in that of political history, both give an enduring picture of the man himself. Bennett Champ Clark, *John Quincy Adams* (Boston, 1932), is simple, conventional, but a charming tribute to a great statesman. William M. Meigs, *The Life of John Caldwell Calhoun* (2 vols., New York, 1917), is a sound and reliable biography. C. M. Wiltse, *John C. Calhoun: Nationalist* (Indianapolis and New York, 1944), is particularly valuable for the administrative history of Monroe's two terms; its overenthusiastic interpretation of Calhoun as a protector of minorities has been corrected by Richard Hofstadter in *The American Political Tradition* (New York, 1948). For Henry Clay there is Glyndon Van Deusen, *The Life of Henry*

Clay (Boston, 1937), the most thorough account. Bernard Mayo, *Henry Clay* (Boston, 1937), ends unfortunately in 1812; but for the early years of the great Kentuckian it is both a dazzling and a deep work. Clement Eaton, *Henry Clay and the Art of American Politics* (Boston, 1957), is brief but rewarding; and the reader may be moved by the eloquence of Carl Schurz, *Life of Henry Clay* (2 vols., Boston, 1892). Albert Gallatin was treated rather formally by Henry Adams, *Life of Albert Gallatin* (Philadelphia, 1879), but has at last found a worthy biographer in Raymond Walters, Jr., *Albert Gallatin* (New York, 1957). One should still read James Parton's heroic *Life of Andrew Jackson* (3 vols., Boston, 1859–1885), but J. S. Bassett, *The Life of Andrew Jackson* (2 vols., New York, 1911), is *the* scholarly and judicious account of the General, which is well supplemented by Marquis James's more dramatic *Andrew Jackson: The Border Captain* and *Andrew Jackson: Portrait of a President* (Indianapolis, 1933 and 1937). John W. Ward, *Andrew Jackson: Symbol of an Age* (New York, 1955), is a pleasing and in some respects profound study of contemporary reactions to a living myth. Although one should not yet discount William C. Rives, *History of the Life and Times of James Madison* (3 vols., Boston, 1859–68), the definitive work is now Irving Brant, *James Madison* (6 vols., Indianapolis, 1948–61), the last volume of which—a little hastily—traverses this period. Daniel C. Gilman, *James Monroe* (Boston, 1883, 1895), was the only life of Monroe until W. P. Cresson, *James Monroe* (Chapel Hill, 1946), which, but for its author's death before completion, would have been more adequate than it is. Lucius Wilmerding, *James Monroe: Public Claimant* (New Brunswick, 1960), is a probing but oversevere account of Monroe's notion of his monetary deserts. George T. Curtis, *Life of Daniel Webster* (2 vols., New York, 1870), and Claude M. Fuess, *Daniel Webster* (2 vols., Boston, 1930), will between them furnish all we need to ask; possibly a more polemical study is still needed, possibly *requiescat in pace*.

Kenneth W. Porter, *John Jacob Astor, Business Man* (2 vols., Cambridge, 1931), is particularly interesting for the China trade and fur trade in this period. It is outstanding for these years, because they are not rich in business biographies, but the reader should consult the same author's *The Jacksons and the Lees* (Cambridge, 1937) for the cleavage between manufacturing and commerce in Massachusetts; Edward Gray, *William Gray of Salem, Merchant* (Boston, 1914); Hamilton A. Hill, *Memoir of Abbott Lawrence* (Boston, 1884); William R. Lawrence (ed.), *Extracts from the Diary and Correspondence of the Late Amos Lawrence* (Boston, 1859); and Frances R. Morse, *Henry and Mary Lee* (Boston, 1926). William N. Chambers, *Old Bullion Benton, Senator from the New West* (Boston, 1956), is scholarly throughout, and here particularly valuable for the Missouri background to the Compromise. Thomas P. Govan, *Nicholas Biddle: Nationalist and Public Banker* (Chicago, 1959), is felicitous and able. E. D. Shipp, *Giant Days, or the Life and Times of William H. Crawford* (Americus, 1909), is thin, but all that we are ever likely to get. Raymond Walters, Jr., *Alexander James Dallas* (Philadelphia, 1943), is a well-balanced and important biography. W. E. Dodd, *Life of Nathaniel Macon* (Raleigh, 1903), is a happy and useful example of this charming historian's work. Albert J. Beveridge, *The Life of John Marshall* (4 vols., Boston, 1916–19), is a monumental and durable work, which subsequent legal historiography has revised but not defaced. Samuel Eliot Morison, *The Life and Letters of Harrison Gray Otis* (2 vols., Boston, 1913), is a classic portrayal of the mind of New England Federalism. Charles Greer Sellers, Jr., *James K. Polk, Jacksonian, 1795–1843* (Princeton, 1957), is extremely useful for Tennessee politics in this period. William Cabell Bruce, *John Randolph of Roanoke* (2 vols., New York, 1922), provides a thorough, strange, and rather terrifying explanation of this bizarre *tertium quid*. Henry Adams, *John Randolph* (Boston, 1882), though often criticized for unfairness, seems to me a most penetrating study. Philip H. Simms, *Life of John Taylor* (Richmond, 1932), should be read as an introduction to E. T. Mudge's brilliant *The Social Philosophy of John Taylor of Caroline* (New York, 1939). Neither Denis T. Lynch, *An Epoch and a Man, Martin Van Buren and His Times* (New York, 1929) nor Holmes Alexander, *The American Talleyrand* (New York, 1935) seems adequate for this stage in Van Buren's career; but the gap is well filled by Robert V. Remini's *Martin Van Buren*, cited above, although this is political history rather than biography. John A. Garraty, *Silas Wright* (New York, 1949) is important; as is Jabez D. Hammond, *Life and Times of Silas Wright* (1848), reprinted as Vol. III of Hammond's admirable *History of Political Parties in the State of New York* (3 vols., New York, 1852).

Chapter 1: Madison and Monroe

William Appleton Williams, *The Contours of American History* (Cleveland and New York, 1961), although his interpretation of mercantilism may seem somewhat broad, is exceedingly suggestive for the concept of the corporate state as it dawned upon the minds of Madison, Monroe, and Calhoun; and, in general, for a distinction between the Hamiltonian and the "new Republican" points of view. The opening chapters of Arthur M. Schlesinger, Jr., *The Age of Jackson* (Boston, 1945), particularly Chapter 3, should be consulted; like the rest of this gifted book, they are at once scholarly, vivid, and controversial: in this instance, one asks whether Schlesinger has paid enough attention to the mere problem of adjustment from a world at war to a world at peace. Adrienne Koch, *Jefferson and Madison:*

The Great Collaboration (New York, 1950), supplies, though too briefly, a corrective. Jeffersonian ambivalence, in terms of directly opposed ideas within one ideological framework, is examined in Roland Van Zandt, *The Metaphysical Foundations of American History* ('s-Gravenhage, 1959), a book whose haughtiness verges upon *hubris,* but a challenging book. Two very important monographs, Kenneth L. Brown, "Stephen Girard, Promoter of the Second Bank of the United States," *Journal of Economic History,* II (1942), 125, and Raymond Walters, Jr., "Origins of the Second Bank of the United States," *Journal of Political Economy,* LIII (1945), 115, are of great assistance. On the formidable character of the Second Bank, as compared to other national banking institutions, see Bray Hammond, "Jackson, Biddle, and the Second Bank of the United States," *Journal of Economic History,* VII (1947), 1.

The tariff issues are covered in Taussig and Babcock, and can be examined in the debates in *Annals of Congress,* and the internal improvements issue can be extracted from the *Annals* and set off against the wholly admirable explanation in Taylor, *Transportation Revolution.*

Chapter 2: Secretary Adams, General Jackson, and the Transcontinental Treaty

A good introduction to the transcontinental problem will be found in R. W. Van Alstyne, *The Rising American Empire* (New York, 1960), and Henry Nash Smith, *Virgin Land* (Cambridge, 1950). The reader should also consult Samuel Flagg Bemis, *The Latin American Policy of the United States* (New York, 1943), and, as for every aspect of diplomatic policy in this period, the same author's *John Quincy Adams and the Foundations of American Foreign Policy* (New York, 1949). John A. Logan, Jr., *No-Transfer: An American Security Principle* (New Haven, 1961) is a compendious study, useful for the whole period.

A special study of the Treaty will be found in Philip Coolidge Brooks, *Diplomacy and the Borderlands: The Adams-Onís Treaty of 1819* (Berkleley, 1939), which is especially strong in Spanish archival research; and with this should be consulted Charles C. Griffin, *The United States and the Disruption of the Spanish Empire, 1810–1822* (New York, 1937).

The Adams-Onís negotiations are in *American State Papers, Foreign Relations,* IV; Adams, *Memoirs,* IV; and Adams, *Writings,* VI.

For the Seminoles, see especially R. S. Cotterill, *The Southern Indians* (Norman, 1954); Edwin C. McReynolds, *The Seminoles* (Norman, 1957); John R. Swanton, "Early History of the Creek Indians and Their Neighbors," Bureau of American Ethnology, *Bulletin 73* (Washington, 1922); Charles J. Kappler, *Indian Affairs, Laws, and Treaties* (3 vols., Washington, 1892–

1913), II, 108–109; *American State Papers, Indian Affairs,* I; and a brief background in Roy H. Pearce, *The Savages of America* (Baltimore, 1953).

Jackson's military campaign is in *American State Papers, Indian Affairs,* I; *Military Affairs,* I; and *Correspondence,* II. The rather (for this period) otiose mystery of the Rhea letter is explored in Richard R. Stenberg, "Jackson's Rhea Letter Hoax," *Journal of Southern History,* II, (1936), 480–496.

For British and European reactions to Jackson's activism and Adams' diplomacy, see Richard Rush, *Memoranda of a Residence at the Court of London* (Philadelphia, 1845 ed.), and the Gallatin Papers for the years 1818 and 1819.

Chapter 3: The Panic of 1819

Murray N. Rothbard, *The Panic of 1819* (New York, 1962), covers not only the Panic but also the nation's effort to counteract the subsequent depression. An earlier assessment is Samuel Reznack, "The Depression of 1819–1822, A Social History," *American Historical Reivew,* XXXIX (1933), 28 ff.

A. H. Cole, *Wholesale Commodity Prices,* cited above, stresses the short supply of specie and the early break in prices.

For the Second Bank of the United States and its role in the Panic, see especially Walter B. Smith, *The Second Bank of the United States* (Cambridge, 1953); Bray Hammond, *Banks and Politics;* and two earlier books, still vigorous, though to some extent superseded, Ralph C. Catterall, *The Second Bank of the United States* (Chicago, 1903), and J. T. Holdsworth and D. R. Dewey, *The First and Second Banks of the United States* (Washington, 1910). A contemporary work, William M. Gouge, *A Short History of Paper Money and Banking in the United States* (Parts I and II, Philadelphia, 1833), has been attacked as journalistic, but is extremely perceptive. The reader should also consult Albert Gallatin, *Considerations on the Currency and Banking System of the United States* (New York, 1831).

For the immediate and long range effects of the Panic, see Harry R. Stevens, *The Early Jackson Party in Ohio* (Durham, 1957); Charles R. Sydnor, *The Development of Southern Sectionalism* (Baton Rouge, 1948); William A. Sullivan, *The Industrial Worker in Pennsylvania* (Harrisburg, 1955); Richard C. Wade, *The Urban Frontier* (Cambridge, 1959); James A. Kehl, *Ill Feeling in the Era of Good Feeling* (Pittsburgh, 1956); Beveridge, *Marshall;* and Benton, *Thirty Years View.*

For arguments for and against the Bank, see especially Dorfman, *Economic Mind,* I, 368 ff.

For John Marshall and Marshall's Court see Beveridge, *Marshall,* and Edward S. Corwin, *John Marshall and the Constitution* (New York, 1919);

for corrective points of view, consult W. Melville Jones (ed.), *Chief Justice John Marshall* (Ithaca, 1956), especially the essays by Charles Fairman and Donald G. Morgan, and Allison Dunham and Phillip B. Kurland (eds.), *Mr. Justice* (Chicago, 1956), especially the essay by W. C. Crosskey. Fred Rodell, *Nine Men* (New York, 1955), despite a deplorably "popular" style, should also be read. Felix Frankfurter, *The Commerce Clause* (Chapel Hill, 1937), is indispensable. Max Lerner, "John Marshall and the Campaign of History," 3 *Columbia Law Review* (1939), stresses the relation between constitutionalism and capitalism. By far the best examination of *McCulloch* v. *Maryland* is Harold J. Plous and Gordon Baker, "McCulloch versus Maryland, Right Principle, Wrong Case," 9 *Stanford Law Review* (1957).

Chapter 4: The Missouri Compromises

For the philosophy of John Taylor of Caroline, see Mudge, *Social Philosophy*. For his reformism, see Avery O. Craven's excellent "The Agricultural Reformers of the Ante-Bellum South," *American Historical Review,* XXXIII (1928), and, of course, Taylor's *Arator* (Georgetown, 1814).

For the general southern background to the Missouri controversy, Clement C. Eaton, *The Growth of Southern Civilization, 1790–1860* (New York, 1961); T. P. Abernethy, *The South in the New Nation* (Baton Rouge, 1961); Sydnor, *Southern Sectionalism;* and Wilbur J. Cash, *The Mind of the South* (New York, 1941), an unusually stimulating work. For additional lights on the Trans-Mississippi West as discussed in this chapter see Ray A. Billington, *The Far Western Frontier, 1830–1860* (New York, 1956), Chapter 2, and W. Eugene Hollon, *The Southwest Old and New* (New York, 1961), Chapter 5.

The institution of slavery has not been examined here, but the reader should in any case consult Helen T. Catterall (ed.), *Judicial Cases,* cited above; Carter G. Woodson, *The Negro in Our History* (Washington, 8th ed., 1945); John C. Hurd, *The Law of Freedom and Bondage* (2 vols., Boston, 1861); Dwight L. Dumond, *Anti-Slavery* (Ann Arbor, 1961); and Kenneth M. Stampp, *The Peculiar Institution* (New York, 1956), as an especially effective antidote to such sympathetic works as U. B. Phillips, *American Negro Slavery* (New York, 1918). The literature is, of course, immense.

Proslavery sentiment in the Northwest can be usefully studied in Theodore C. Pease, *The Frontier State, 1818–1848* (Springfield, 1918); "Correspondence of Edward Coles," *Journal of Negro History,* III (1918); William H. Brown, "Memoir of the late Honorable Daniel P. Cook," in N. W. Edwards, *History of Illinois from 1778 to 1833* (Springfield, 1870); and Margaret C. Norton (ed.), *Illinois Census Returns* (Springfield, 1934).

Glover Moore, *The Missouri Controversy, 1819–1821* (Lexington, 1953), is the best work on the Compromises themselves; and the reader should consult Robert Ernst, "Rufus King, Slavery, and the Missouri Crisis," *New-York Historical Society Quarterly* (1962), pp. 357–82. Earlier and useful studies are H. A. Trexler, *Slavery in Missouri* (Baltimore, 1914); Everett S. Brown (ed.), *The Missouri Compromises and Presidential Politics, 1820–1825, from the Letters of William Plumer, Junior* (St. Louis, 1926); Homer C. Hockett, "Rufus King and the Missouri Compromise," *Missouri Historical Review,* II (1908); Frank H. Hodder, "Side Lights on the Missouri Compromises," American Historical Association, *Annual Report for the Year 1909* (Washington, 1911); Floyd C. Shoemaker, *Missouri's Struggle for Statehood, 1804–1821* (Jefferson City, 1916); and James A. Woodburn, "The Historical Significance of the Missouri Compromise," American Historical Association, *Annual Report for the Year 1893* (Washington, 1894).

For Jefferson's attitude toward a "separate creation" of Negroes, see Daniel Boorstin's captivating *The Lost World of Thomas Jefferson* (New York, 1948), Chap. III.

Early L. Fox, *The American Colonization Society* (Baltimore, 1919), has been superseded by P. J. Staudenraus, *The African Colonization Movement* (New York, 1961), which is excellent for this period.

Herbert Aptheker, *Negro Slave Revolts* (New York, 1943) is the best as it is the most sympathetic study.

The nationwide attitude toward the free Negro is evident enough in the Missouri debates in *Annals of Congress,* and the northern free Negro can be studied in Helen T. Catterall, *Judicial Cases,* particularly; also in J. C. Hurd, *Law of Freedom and Bondage;* Henry W. Farnam, *Chapters in the History of Social Legislation in the United States to 1860* (Washington, 1938); and New York, *Reports of the Proceedings of the Convention of 1821* (Albany, 1821). A recent study, Leon F. Litwack, *North of Slavery: The Negro in the Free States, 1790–1860* (Chicago, 1961), is somewhat thin for these years but very useful, not least for its bibliographical essay.

Chapter 5: Toward the Monroe Doctrine
Chapter 6: The Monroe Doctrine

The classic work on the Monroe Doctrine is Dexter Perkins, *The Monroe Doctrine, 1823–1826* (Cambridge, 1927). The subject is also explored in (especially) Samuel Bemis, *John Quincy Adams and the Foundations of American Foreign Policy;* Arthur P. Whitaker, *The United States and the Independence of Latin America, 1800–1830* (Baltimore, 1941); Frederic L. Paxson, *The Independence of the South American Republics, A Study in Recognition* (Philadelphia, 1916); Edward L. Tatum, *The United States and Europe, 1815–1823* (Baltimore, 1936); and, far more *ex parte,* in

Charles K. Webster, *The Foreign Policy of Castlereagh, 1815–1822* (London, 1925), and Harold W. V. Temperley, *The Foreign Policy of Canning, 1822–1827* (London, 1925). A brilliant study, both for style and content, is William R. Kaufmann, *British Policy and the Independence of Latin America, 1801–1828* (New Haven, 1951). One should also consult Julius W. Pratt, *A History of American Foreign Policy* (Englewood Cliffs, 1955); Robert H. Ferrell, *American Diplomacy, A History* (New York 1959); and Alexander DeConde, *A History of American Foreign Policy* (New York, 1963).

Documentary collections: *American State Papers, Foreign Relations,* IV and V; W. R. Manning (ed.), *Diplomatic Correspondence,* already cited; Charles K. Webster (ed.), *Britain and the Independence of Latin America,* also cited; Charles Vane, Marquess of Londonderry (ed.), *Correspondence, Despatches, and Other Papers of Viscount Castlereagh* (12 vols., London, 1848–53); *Despatches, Correspondence and Memoranda of the Duke of Wellington,* ed. by his son (8 vols., London, 1867–80), and *Supplementary Despatches, Correspondence and Memoranda* (15 vols., London, 1858–72).

For correspondence and memoirs there are Hamilton (ed.), *Writings of James Monroe,* esp. Vol. VI; Adams, *Memoirs,* V and VI; E. J. Stapleton (ed.), *Some Official Correspondence of George Canning* (2 vols., London, 1887); and Capt. Josceline Bagot (ed.), *George Canning and His Friends* (2 vols., London, 1900), which gives us a very good picture of Canning's wit and charm.

W. R. Brock, *Lord Liverpool and Liberal Toryism* (Cambridge, 1941), is excellent for the Earl's domestic policies but unfortunately slights America; a consultation of Hansard, 2 series, I and VI, will show how much. The reader should also consult Anna L. Lingelbach's admirable "William Huskisson as President of the Board of Trade," *American Historical Review,* XLIII (1938).

Chapter 7: Mobility and Consolidation

In general, consult Taylor, *Transportation Revolution,* and Monroe's "Views" in Richardson, *Messages and Papers,* II, 144–183.

On the Tariff of 1824, see Turner, *Rise of the New West,* Taussig, Stanwood, and Kirkland; also Hopkins and Hargreaves (eds.) *The Papers of Henry Clay,* III.

A fruitful relationship between the Transportation Revolution and egalitarian movements is developed in Lee Benson, *The Concept of Jacksonian Democracy* (Princeton, 1961), Chap. I.

The strange and suggestive Court struggle in Kentucky is examined in Arndt M. Stickles, *The Critical Court Struggle in Kentucky* (Bloomingdale, 1929); Robert M. McKelroy, *Kentucky in the Nation's History* (New York,

1909); Lewis Collins, *History of Kentucky* (2 vols., rev. ed., Covington, 1878), I; R. G. Swemm (ed.), *Letters on the Condition of Kentucky in 1825* (New York, 1916); Arndt M. Stickles, "Joseph R. Underwood's Fragmentary Journal of the New and Old Court Contest in Kentucky," *Filson Club Historical Quarterly,* XIII (1939); and Philip Lindsley, "A Kentucky Judicial Episode," *Green Bag,* XVI (1904). Its background is well drawn by Paul W. Gates, "Tenants of the Log Cabin," *Mississippi Valley Historical Review,* XLIX (1962), 3–31.

Chapter 8: The Election of 1824

The passing of the congressional caucus may be examined especially in the Gallatin Papers, John W. Taylor Papers, and Van Buren Papers for 1823–24. See also Livermore, *Twilight of Federalism;* M. Ostrogorski, *Democracy and the Organization of Political Parties* (2 vols., New York, 1902), II; Sydnor, *Southern Sectionalism;* and Walters, *Gallatin.*

The constitutional conventions of Massachusetts, *Journal of the Debates and Proceedings . . . begun and holden at Boston, November 15, 1820* (New ed., Boston, 1853), and of New York, *Reports on the Proceedings and Debates of the Convention of 1821 . . .* (Albany, 1821), are particularly interesting for suffrage reform. Chilton Williamson, *American Suffrage from Property to Democracy, 1760–1860* (Princeton, 1961), is a careful study of a most complex subject, pointing out that Americans have been more democratic in practice than institutionally, but needs a tabulation of suffrage qualification changes in the several states. Hitherto, Kirk H. Porter, *A History of Suffrage in the United States* (Chicago, 1918), has been the standard work.

Public land policies for these years can be studied in *American State Papers, Public Lands,* III, and *Finance,* III; in Benjamin A. Hibbard, *A History of the Public Land Policies* (New York, 1939), and in Ernest L. Bogert, *Economic History of American Agriculture* (New York, 1923).

The election of 1824 and its preliminaries can be studied in the already cited biographies of Adams, Buchanan, Calhoun, Clay, Jackson, and Van Buren; it is also treated in detail in Livermore, *Twilight of Federalism,* and Albert R. Newsome, *The Presidential Election of 1824 in North Carolina,* The James Sprunt Studies, XXIII, No. 1 (1939); and mentioned effectively in Klein, *Pennsylvania Politics,* and more casually in Edwin A. Miles, *Jacksonian Democracy in Mississippi,* The James Sprunt Studies XLII (1960). The *Autobiography* of Van Buren and Jabez D. Hammond, *History of Political Parties in the State of New York* (2 vols., New York, 1842), are enlightening when it comes to the important New York election, particularly when studied side by side with the Van Buren and John W. Taylor Papers. Adams, *Memoirs,* VI, and Jackson, *Correspondence,* III, speak for the two real rivals; and, although Adams is silent on the actual "bargain" with Clay—which is judiciously handled in Van Deusen, *Clay,* and Bemis, *John Quincy Adams and the Union,* in particular—he is otherwise confiding to the verge, and beyond, of discretion.

Chapter 9: The Perilous Experiment

J. H. Powell, *Richard Rush, Republican Diplomat* (Philadelphia, 1942), a fine biography, is especially important at this point because Rush's protectionist views, along with his sturdy character, gave him a great influence in Adams' administration. Powell is, of course, friendly to Rush's views; and one needs to commune with *A Letter From The Secretary of the Treasury Enclosing the Annual Report on the State of the Finances* (Washington, 1825) and "Report on the State of the Finances," December 8, 1827, in *American State Papers, Finance,* V, 638, to discover a more downright and less beguiling expression of them.

Brooks Adams' bitter, passionate, eccentric, and eloquent defense of his grandfather in his introduction to Henry Adams, *The Degradation of the Democratic Dogma* (New York, 1919), is also well worth study, but *cave canem.*

For congressional response to Adams' invitation to a feast of internal improvements there are *Statement of Land Grants Made by Congress to Aid Land Office by Order of the Secretary of the Interior* (Washington, 1908), pp. 22–27; E. C. Nelson, "Presidential Influence in the Policy of Internal Improvements," *Iowa Journal of History and Politics,* IV (1906); *Reports of Committees of the House of Representatives,* 21 Cong., 2 sess., No. 77, pp. 36–67; Sydnor, *Southern Sectionalism;* Taylor, *Transportation Revolution;* and Julius Rubin, *Canal or Railroad? Imitation and Innovation in the Response to the Erie Canal in Philadelphia, Baltimore and Boston* (Philadelphia, 1961), which, though more exploratory than conclusive, very forcibly suggests to my mind the numbing influence of intrastate jealousies upon effective congressional action.

Chapter 10: George Canning's Revenge

F. Lee Benns, *The American Struggle for the British West Indies Carrying Trade, 1815–1830,* already cited, is indispensable for this chapter, although it seems possible that even he may not quite have realized the inner clash between the liberal tendencies of Liverpool's government and its angry response to American opposition. Lowell J. Ragatz, *The Fall of the Planter Class in the British Caribbean, 1763–1833* (New York, 1928), is valuable for West Indian influences on British policy. Kaufmann, *British Policy,* is illuminating on the Congress of Panama. J. Fred Rippy, *Rivalry of the United States and Great Britain over Latin America* (Baltimore, 1929), is particularly good for this juncture. For the Cuban side of the argument the best documentary evidence is in Manning, *Diplomatic Correspondence;* but Manning is silent on Panama and here Webster, *Great Britain and the Independence of Latin America,* takes over. Logan, *No-Transfer,* and Manning, *Early Diplomatic Relations Between the United States and Mexico* (Baltimore, 1916), should be consulted; and two exceptionally useful books for Panama are Joseph B. Leckey, *Pan-Americanism: Its Beginnings* (New York, 1926), and Harold A. Bierck, Jr., *Vida Publica de Pedro Gual* (Caracas, 1947).

For Oregon one should look to *American State Papers, Foreign Relations,* VI, and to Frederick Merk, *Albert Gallatin and the Oregon Question* (Cambridge, 1950), which is indispensable for the many implications latent in the phrase "Oregon country" at this time, particularly for the anti-British rather than anti-Russian susceptibilities of Adams, as he contemplated the far Northwest. For Congressional concern in the far Northwest see Charles H. Ambler, "The Oregon Country, 1810–1830: A Chapter in Territorial Expansion," *Mississippi Valley Historical Review,* XXX (1943), 3–24.

The Gallatin-Clay Correspondence in *Senate Docs.,* 22 Cong., 1 sess., III No. 132, is of interest for the aftermath to the American Act of 1823.

(Since President Adams made great play with the Farewell Address in his plea for the Panama Congress, a reading of Felix Gilbert, *To the Farewell Address: Ideas of Early American Foreign Policy* [Princeton, 1961], would be in order, particularly pp. 137–147.)

Chapter 11: Abominations
Chapter 12: The Election of 1828

Dorfman, *Economic Mind,* II, 362–404, gives an extremely helpful account of the flowering of economic thought in this period. Rothbard, *Panic of 1819,* should be consulted for a description of federal and state efforts to cope with the aftermath of the Panic.

For the Georgia controversy see Amanda Johnson, *Georgia as Colony and State* (Atlanta, 1938), p. 209; U. B. Phillips, "Georgia and State Rights," American Historical Association, *Annual Report for 1901* (Washington, 1902), II; Paul Murray, "Economic Sectionalism in Georgia, 1825–1855," *Journal of Southern History,* X (1945); Sydnor, *Development of Southern Sectionalism;* Miles, *Jacksonian Democracy;* and R. S. Cotterill, *The Southern Indians.* The documentation is in *American State Papers, Indian Affairs,* II; U. S. *Senate Docs.,* 57 Cong., 1 sess., No. 452; and H. V. Ames (ed.), *State Documents.*

For the Harrisburg Convention see *Niles' Weekly Register,* XXXII, 388–396; Taussig; Stanwood; Wiltse, *Calhoun: Nationalist,* K. W. Rowe, *Mathew Carey, A Study in American Economic Development* (Baltimore, 1933).

The Tariff of 1828, the "Tariff of Abominations," has been given a very careful and persuasive, though not I think a conclusive, revisionist interpretation in Robert V. Remini, "Martin Van Buren and the Tariff of Abominations," *American Historical Review,* LXIII (1958), 903–917; Remini's contention, of course, being that Van Buren wished the Tariff to succeed.

The reader is particularly referred to Richard Hofstadter's essay on Calhoun in Hofstadter, *The American Political Tradition* (New York, 1948), which refutes Wiltse's position in *Calhoun: Nationalist* that Calhoun was "the supreme champion of minority rights and interests everywhere." Wiltse's discussion of the *Exposition and Protest* is, however, like the rest of his book, extremely able; as is Turner's in *The Rise of the New West.* The *Exposition* itself will be found in Calhoun, *Works,* VI, 1–59.

For the reformist ferment J. R. Commons *et al., History of Labor in the United States,* Foner, *History of the Labor Movement,* and Pesson, "Workingmen's Movements," are excellent for the beginnings of a labor movement in this period. McMaster, *History,* V, Chap. XLIX, shows this historian at his best in a discussion of the state of free education up to 1830; see also F. T. Carlton, *Economic Influences upon Educational Progress in the United States, 1820–1850* (Madison, 1908); Commons *et al., History of Labor,* I, 172 ff.; William O. Bourne, *History of the Public School Society of the City of New York* (New York, 1870). Imprisonment for debt is admirably and succinctly covered in Arthur M. Schlesinger, Jr., *Age of Jackson,* Chap. XI; and for the conditions to which the unfortunate debtor was exposed when in prison, see Prison Discipline Society of Boston, *Fourth Annual Report* (Boston, 1829), *Historical and Chronological Account of the Origin and Progress of the City of New York* (New York, 1829), and Philadelphia *National Gazette,* November 15, 1827. However, E. T. Randall, "Imprisonment for Debt in America: Fact and Fiction," *Mississippi Valley Historical Review,* XXXIX (1952) 89–102, argues that "arrest for debt" would be a more adequate description than "imprisonment" in most cases: but compare with this Richard B. Morris, "Measure of Bondage in the Slave States," *ibid.* XLI (1954) 219–240, for the harsh treatment of white debtors in the slave states.

The Anti-Masonic movement has not been treated in full since Charles McCarthy's *Anti-Masonic Party* in the American Historical Association's *Annual Report for 1902* (Washington, 1903). See also Whitney R. Cross, *The Burned-Over District* (Ithaca, 1950), and David M. Ludlum, *Social Ferment in Vermont, 1790–1850* (New York, 1939), where two able historians illustrate, in agreement no less than in disagreement, the somewhat ambiguous nature of this movement. I think that by far the most useful interpretation of Anti-Masonry's role in this period will be found in Lee Benson, *Concept of Jacksonian Democracy,* already cited.

The election of 1828 has been ably studied in Florence Weston, *The Presidential Election of 1828* (Washington, 1938) and in Robert V. Remini, *The Election of Andrew Jackson* (Philadelphia and New York, 1964); and, from the Federalist point of view, very thoroughly researched in Livermore, *Twilight of Federalism.* A most interesting and suggestive study, in terms of the influence of manhood suffrage, and as an answer to the theory that Jackson's victory was accomplished by a rush to the polls, will be found in Richard P. McCormick, "New Perspectives on Jacksonian Politics," *American Historical Review,* LXV (1960), 288–301. The anti-intellectual element in this election is in Ward, *Andrew Jackson,* already cited. For the civil service at this period, see Paul P. Van Riper, *History of the United States Civil Service* (Evanston, 1958), as to its competence and incorruptibility, and for a most invaluable study of every aspect of administrative history, there is Leonard D. White, *The Jeffersonians* (New York, 1951), and particularly Chapter XXXV, where the civil service under Monroe and Adams is considered as a home for character and talent, but also as somewhat of a self-perpetuating elite.

Index

Adams, Brooks, 235, 243
Adams, Henry, 1
Adams, John Quincy, offered State Department, 25, 27; character, 25–29; and cession of Floridas, 37; as neomercantilist, 37, 158, 181, 211, 244, 265; as continentalist, 58, 66, 161, 166, 181, 243, 252; and line to the Pacific, 56–59, 68; and Southwestern border, 42, 47, 56–57, 60; supports Jackson, 52–53; 54; rebukes Pizarro, 61–62; on Transcontinental Treaty, 68; and Florida land grants, 69; and Missouri, 121, 125–126; and Convention of 1815, 149; on Navigation Act of 1820, 150; and "Elsewhere" Act, 158; and commercial reciprocity, 158, 252; on Latin America, 164–166; and British Empire, 166; and Stratford Canning, 166; anti-British oration, 167; and noncolonization, 167–168, 187; and no-transfer, 169, 186; and Cuba, 169; on neutral rights, 174; and Russian note, 181; rejects Canning's overtures, 181; persuades Monroe, 182; response to Russian note, 185–186; and no-transfer principle, 186, 244; and Monroe Doctrine, 186–187, 189, 191–192; favors Kentucky Old Court party, 210; candidate for Presidency, 214, 218, 224, 225; meeting with Clay, 225; with Webster, 226; elected, 228; offers State Department to Clay, 228; and "bargain and cor-

ruption," 228–230; his First Annual Message, 231–239; Cabinet's dismay, 228–233; and Washington's Potomac System, 235; and Cuba, 244–247; and Congress of Panama, 248–257; and the Farewell Address, 250–252; newspaper battle with Calhoun, 257; and freedom of the seas, 254, 258; his nominal interdict, 264; his Third Annual Message, 267; predicts Jackson's victory, 269; silent on tariffs, 275; on Van Buren, 278; and election of 1828, 289–297; future, 300–301
Albany Regency, 223–224, 274, 293
Alexander I, Tsar, 4, 163
Ambrister, Robert C., 49–50, 62–63
American Colonization Society, 103, 138–139
"American Trade Act" of 1822 (British), and industrialism, 154–155; "Liberal," 156–157; American response to, 157; acceptance necessary, 244
Anderson, Richard C., 248, 249, 253
Anti-Masonic Party, 294
Antislavery societies, 103
Appleton, Nathan, 271
Arator, 100
Arbuthnot, Alexander, 49–50, 62–63
Astor, J. J., 9–10, 77

Bank system in 1819, 86–87
Bank of the United States, First, incorporation and support of, 11
Bank of the United States, Second, incorporation of, 11; and Jefferso-